THE CHRISTIAN WRITERS
MARKET GUIDE
2024

THE CHRISTIAN WRITERS
MARKET GUIDE

2024

Your Comprehensive Resource for Getting Published

STEVE LAUBE

CHRISTIAN
WRITERS
INSTITUTE

THE CHRISTIAN WRITERS MARKET GUIDE 2024

ISBN: 978-162-184-2460 (paperback)
       978-162-184-2477 (ebook)

Cover design by Hannah Linder (*hannahlinderdesigns.com*)
Typesetting by Jamie Foley (*jamiefoley.com*)
Edited by Lin Johnson (*wordprocommunicationservices.com*)

Printed in the United States of America.

Visit The Christian Writers Institute at *www.ChristianWritersInstitute.com*.

E-mail: *admin@christianwritersmarketguide.com*

Disclaimer: The information in this guide is provided by the individuals or companies through online questionnaires and email inquiries, as well as their websites and writers guidelines. The individuals or companies do not pay to be listed in this guide. The entries are not necessarily endorsed by Steve Laube or The Christian Writers Institute. Steve Laube and The Christian Writers Institute make every attempt to verify the accuracy of the information provided. The entries are for information only. Any transaction(s) between a user of the information and the individuals or companies listed is strictly between those parties.

TABLE OF CONTENTS

PART 5: SUPPORT FOR WRITERS 239

FOREWORD

I KNOW WRITERS WHO COLLECT REJECTION LETTERS, hoard them, fill their hard drives with them, even paper their walls with them—believing this proves they are busy, in the game.

Here's a better idea: Avoid rejection letters like radioactive waste. I don't want even one.

And you don't need to ever read another.

Here's how: *Do your homework.* Know what your target market is looking for. Sure, occasionally you'll hear back that your idea didn't ring a bell. But that's not a rejection; that's a business transaction. You did a bit of work, solicited editors' interest, they passed. You move on.

Now, had you written an entire article or even a whole book before determining their interest, you deserved that rejection.

Even if you're new to writing, save yourself fruitless work by trying to get an editor on board with you early. Even if she expresses only speculative interest (e.g., "Happy to give it a look, provided you . . ."), consider what comes after that as your marching orders.

Does she want it longer than you proposed? Shorter? In first person, rather than third? Does she have suggestions for other angles, other people to interview?

To the best of your ability, do everything she suggests. By proving yourself able to work with an editor, you're nearly forcing her to stick with you—even if your writing is light-years from where it will be someday.

By showing that you can take input and you recognize that published work is never a solo performance, but always a duet between writer and editor, you've given yourself the best chance at a sale.

And you've avoided rejection.

That, I assume, is why you've chosen this book. You've come to the right place.

As you immerse yourself in all that's offered here, remember:

Writing takes skill. When you hang out your shingle as a writer, be prepared for unintended slights. People tell me all the time that they have a book in them, if they only had time to write. That would be like my saying

I have a mansion in me, if only I had the time to build it. Writing, and building, take a lot more than time.

Don't think of writing as competition. Anyone who has succeeded was once unknown and unpublished. Rejoice with, and learn from, those ahead of you.

Read everything you can find on the craft. Your goal should be to become a lifelong learner.

Even sacred writing can be edited. Only Scripture is God-breathed. The result of your writing might very well be sacred. But if you regard your word choices sacred, as in untouchable, each word had better be divinely perfect. Or God gets a bad rap. Frankly, writers who make this claim are immediately branded amateurs. An inside joke among editors in inspirational publishing is that God is the worst literary agent ever.

Too few writers do their homework. Pitch writing that makes sense for your target market based on your research, and that research starts right here with this unparalleled resource.

The Christian Writers Market Guide is no cover-to-cover read. Peruse the Contents page, and zero in on your areas of specialty and interest. Then, when you're ready, start shopping your writing.

As inspirational writers, we have a duty to do justice to a worldview that may bend but will never be crushed under the weight of hopelessness. Our burden, our task, our privilege is to represent hope. That doesn't mean Pollyanna stories in which everyone lives happily ever after—at least this side of heaven.

People suffer. Innocents die. But if we believers cannot crack the door to hope, we dare not call ourselves inspirational writers.

Ours is a message of hope, of reconciliation, of forgiveness. True art will communicate that without preaching.

The path is crowded and the passage long, but the reward is worth it.

Welcome to the journey.

— Jerry B. Jenkins
Colorado Springs, Colorado
www.JerryJenkins.com

INTRODUCTION

WRITING IS A SERIOUS BUSINESS. It is also a serious calling. The privilege of having your words influence other people's thinking or inspiring their spirit is a gift from God. A number of publication opportunities for great writing from great authors exist. Traditional methods for publication remain, but the diversity of online opportunities are seemingly endless. In addition, independent-publication options have made it easier to see your byline on a book, on a blog post, or in an online magazine.

Since many Christian bookstores have closed, it may seem like the Christian publishing industry is shrinking; but it is not. It is simply changing. Therefore, you must research more effectively to find the best place for your work. The problem with online search engines is the immense number of results you receive. Then the results depend on that site's search-engine optimization and those who have paid to have their sites show at the top. *The Christian Writers Market Guide* has curated the information for you. Now you can find what is targeted specifically for the Christian market and your areas of interest.

One of the biggest mistakes a writer can make is to ignore the guidelines of an agent, an editor, or a publishing house. In the past, some publications dropped their listings in this guide because writers failed to follow the instructions in it. Editors are looking for writers who understand their periodicals or publishing houses and their unique approaches to the marketplace. This book will help you be such a writer. With a little time and effort, you can meet an editor's expectations, distinguish yourself as a professional, and sell what you write.

If you can, I recommend you attend a writers conference, whether virtual or in person. (We have many listed inside.) It is good to meet new people and become familiar with the best teachers in the industry. If you cannot get to a conference, consider exploring the courses available online at *ChristianWritersInstitute.com*. There are more than 110 to choose from, and you can enjoy them at any time on any device.

If this is the first time you've used this guide, read the "How to Use This Book" section. If you run into an unfamiliar term, look it up in the "Publishing Lingo" section in back and learn the terminology.

Please be aware that the information in this guide is provided by the companies or individuals through online questionnaires and email inquiries, as well as their websites and writers guidelines. The companies or individuals do not pay to be listed in this guide. The entries are not endorsed by me or The Christian Writers Institute. We make every attempt to verify the accuracy of the information provided. The entries are for information only. Any transaction(s) between a user of the information and the individuals or companies listed is strictly between those parties.

May God bless your writing journey. We are on a mission to change the world, word by word. To that end, strive for excellence and make your work compelling and insightful. Great writing is still in demand. But it must be targeted, crafted, critiqued, edited, polished, and proofread until it shines.

My thanks go to Lin Johnson whose invaluable work makes this all possible. She keeps tabs throughout the year on market changes, so every listing is accurate to the best of our information at the time of publication. (Our online version of this guide, *ChristianWritersMarketGuide.com*, is updated regularly during the year.) As the administrator of the online and print editions, she is the genius behind the details. In addition, I would also like to acknowledge my wife, Lisa. Her love, support, and encouragement have been incalculable. We make a great team!

Steve Laube
President
The Christian Writers Institute
and
The Steve Laube Agency
24 W. Camelback Rd. A-635
Phoenix, AZ 85013
www.christianwritersinstitute.com
www.stevelaube.com

To update a listing or to be added to the next edition or online, go to *christianwritersmarketguide.com*. Click on the Get Listed tab, and fill out the form.

For direct-sales questions, email the publisher: *admin@christianwritersinstitute.com.*

For books and courses on the writing craft, visit The Christian Writers Institute: *www.christianwritersinstitute.com.*

HOW TO USE THIS BOOK

THE CHRISTIAN WRITERS MARKET GUIDE 2024 IS DESIGNED to make it easier for you to sell your writing. It will serve you well if you use it as a springboard to become thoroughly familiar with the markets best suited to your writing style and areas of interest and expertise.

As you look through this guide, you may run into words in the listings that you are not familiar with. If so, check "Publishing Lingo" at the back of the book.

GETTING ACQUAINTED WITH THIS BOOK

Start by getting acquainted with the setup of this guide.

Book Publishers

Part 1 lists traditional book publishers and anthology series with information about what they are looking for. Notice that many houses accept manuscripts only from agents or through meeting with their editors at a writers conference. If you need a literary agent, check the agent listings in chapter 17.

Independent Book Publishing

Since independent book publishing is a viable option today, Part 2 provides resources to help you. Chapter 3 lists independent book publishers, many of which provide all the services you need as packages or à la carte options. If you decide to publish on your own, chapters 4 and 5 list design, production, and distribution services. You'll also want to hire a professional editor and proofreader, so see chapter 20 for help in this area.

Periodical Publishers

Part 3 lists periodical—magazine, newspaper, and newsletter—publishers. Chapter 6 will help you find markets by topics (e.g., marriage, evangelism) and types (e.g., how-to, poetry, personal experience). Although these lists are not comprehensive, they provide a shortcut for finding appropriate markets for your ideas.

Cross-referencing may be helpful. For example, if you have an idea for a how-to article on parenting, look at the lists in both the how-to and parenting categories. Also, don't overlook writing on the same topic for different periodicals, such as money management for a general adult magazine, a teen magazine, a women's newsletter, and a magazine for pastors. Each would require a different slant, but you would get more mileage from one idea.

Specialty Markets

In Part 4, "Specialty Markets," you'll find nonbook, nonperiodical markets like daily devotionals and drama. Here you can explore types of writing you may not have thought about but can provide a steady writing income.

Support for Writers

As a writer, you'll need support to keep going. Part 5 provides information for various kinds of support.

One of the best ways to get published today is to meet editors at writers conferences. Check out chapter 18 for a conference or seminar near you or perhaps in a location you'd like to visit. Before deciding which conference to attend, check the websites for who is on faculty, what houses are represented, and what classes are offered that can help you grow your craft and writing business. You may also want to factor in the size of the conference. Don't be afraid to stretch outside your comfort zone.

For ongoing support and feedback on your manuscripts, join a writers group. Chapter 19 lists groups by state and internationally. If you can't find one near you, consider starting one or join an online group.

Since editors and literary agents are looking for polished manuscripts, you may want to hire a professional editor. See chapter 20 for people who offer a variety of editorial services, including coaching.

Whether you publish your book with a royalty house or go the independent route, you'll need to do most, if not all, of the promotion. If you want to hire a specialist with contacts, check out chapter 21, "Publicity and Marketing Services." And if you need accounting or legal help, check out chapter 22.

One way to promote your message and your books is through speaking. If you need help in this area—and most writers do—see chapter 23, "Speaking Services." There you will find organizations and conferences that train speakers and/or connect them with groups looking for speakers.

Since writers who stagnate don't get published, check out chapter 24 for education resources to help you improve your writing style, write different types of manuscripts, and learn the business of writing and publishing. You'll find a variety of free and paid resources, including podcasts and classes.

Entering a writing contest can boost your sales, supplement your writing income, lead to publication, and sometimes give you valuable feedback on your writing. Check out chapter 25 for a list of contests and awards by genre. Many of them are not Christian oriented, but you can enter manuscripts with a Christian worldview.

USING THIS BOOK

Once you get acquainted with this guide, start using it. After you identify potential markets for your ideas and/or manuscripts, read their writers guidelines. If these are available on the website, the URL is included. Otherwise, email or send (with a SASE) for a copy. Also study at least one sample copy of a periodical (information to obtain one is given in most listings) or the book publisher's website to see if your idea truly fits there. Never send a manuscript without doing this market study.

Above all, keep in mind that this guide is only a starting point for your research and change is the one constant in the publishing industry. It is impossible for any market guide to be 100 percent accurate since editors move around, publications and publishing houses close, and new ones open. But this guide is an essential tool for getting published in the Christian market and making an impact on God's Kingdom with your words.

PART 1

TRADITIONAL BOOK PUBLISHERS

1

TRADITIONAL BOOK PUBLISHERS

Before submitting your query letter or book proposal, it's critical that you read and follow a publisher's guidelines exactly. In many cases, the guidelines are available on the website and a direct link is given in the listing. If you do not have a literary agent—and even if you do—check out a publisher thoroughly before signing a contract.

Note: Not all the imprints listed in imprint entries below are in this book. Some may be in other sections.

1517 MEDIA
Augsburg Fortress, Beaming Books, Broadleaf Books, Fortress Press

ABINGDON PRESS
810 12th Ave. S, Nashville, TN 37203 | 615-749-6000
www.abingdonpress.com
Constance Stella, senior acquisitions editor
Susan Salley, editor, resources for small-group study
   Denomination: United Methodist
   Parent company: United Methodist Publishing House
   Mission statement: to provide the best, most effective religious publications available
   Submissions: Publishes 120 titles per year; receives 2,000 submissions annually. First-time authors: fewer than 5%. Submit proposal with sample chapters through the website. Bible: CEB.

Topics and genres: Christian living/spirituality, leadership, theology, academic

Royalty: minimum 7.5%

Guidelines: *www.abingdonpress.com/submissions*

Tip: "We're focusing on material to help pastors and other leaders do their jobs and focusing more squarely on Methodist and other mainline leaders, churches, readers."

ABUNDANCE BOOKS

417 Forest St. #445, Kalamazoo, MI 49048 | 616-648-1795

books@abundance-books.com | abundance-books.com

Jenn Dafoe-Turner, acquisitions

Mission statement: to publish books that inspire people to live life full and free

Submissions: Publishes four titles per year; receives 20 submissions annually. First-time authors: 75%. Length: 90–300 pages. Email proposal with sample chapters through the website. Conference contact a plus. Responds in two to four weeks. Bible: ESV, NLT, NKJV, NASB.

Topics and genres: African-American, Asian, Christian living/spirituality, Hispanic, self-help, Bible studies, children, devotionals; fiction: mystery, romance

Royalty: 7–15%, no advance

Types of books: audiobook, ebook, hardcover, offset paperback, POD

Guidelines: *abundance-books.com/guidelines*

Tip: "All proposals should include a marketing plan that includes current audience reach."

AMBASSADOR INTERNATIONAL

411 University Ridge, Ste. B14, Greenville, SC 29601 | 864-751-4844

www.ambassador-international.com

Katie Cruice Smith, senior editor

Mission statement: to magnify Jesus while promoting His gospel through the written word

Submissions: Publishes 50 titles per year; receives 750 submissions annually. First-time authors: 50%. Length: minimum 144 pages. Submit proposal with sample chapters through the website. Responds in one month. Bible: KJV, NIV, ESV, NKJV, NASB.

Topics and genres: biography, business, Christian living/spirituality,

4

finances, theology, Bible studies, children, devotionals, fiction, teen/YA

Royalty: 15–20% for print, 25% for ebooks; no advance

Types of books: ebook, hardcover, paperback

Guidelines: *ambassador-international.com/get-published/submission-guidelines*

Tip: "We're most open to a book which has a clearly defined market and the author's total commitment to the project. We do well with first-time authors. We have full international coverage. Many of our titles sell globally."

AMERICAN CATHOLIC PRESS

16565 S. State St., South Holland, IL 60473-2025 | 708-331-5485

acp@acpress.org | www.americancatholicpress.org

Rev. Michael Gilligan, executive director

Denomination: Catholic

Submissions: Publishes four titles per year; receives ten submissions annually. Query first by mail. No simultaneous submissions. Responds in two months. Bible: NAS.

Flat fee: $25–100

Topics and genres: liturgy, nonfiction

First print run: 3,000

Tip: "We publish only materials on the Roman Catholic liturgy. No poetry or fiction."

AMG PUBLISHERS

6815 Shallowford Rd., Chattanooga, TN 37421 | 423-894-6060

sales@amgpublishers.com | www.amgpublishers.com

Amanda Jenkins, acquisitions and sales manager

Parent company: AMG International

Mission statement: to meet people's deepest needs, spiritual and physical, while inspiring hope, restoring lives, and transforming communities in Jesus' name

Submissions: Publishes 10 titles per year; receives 300 submissions annually. First-time authors: 50%. Length: minimum 150 pages. Agent not required. Email proposal with sample chapters, or submit through *ChristianBookProposals.com*. Responds in six months. Bible: NASB, ESV, NIV, KJV, CSB.

Topics and genres: Bible characters, Bible study, Christian living/spirituality, self-help, spiritual growth, women's issues, Bible

studies, devotionals
Royalty: starts at 14%, sometimes gives advance
Types of books: ebook, offset paperback, POD
Imprints: AMG (reference, Bible studies, Bibles, devotionals), Living Ink (YA fiction), God and Country Press (military/history devotionals)
Guidelines: *amgpublishers.com/index.php/author-guidelines*
Tip: "Looking for good, biblical content that does not offer a personal or denominational slant."

ANCIENT FAITH PUBLISHING

PO Box 748, Chesterton, IN 46304 | 800-967-7377
khyde@ancientfaith.com | *www.ancientfaith.com/publishing*
Katherine Hyde, editorial director
Jane Meyer, children's project manager; jmeyer@ancientfaith.com
Lynnette Horner, editorial assistant; lhorner@ancientfaith.com
   (submit adult queries to her)

Denomination: Orthodox Christian
Parent company: Antiochian Orthodox Christian Archdiocese of North America
Mission statement: to carry out the Great Commission of Jesus Christ through accessible and excellently crafted publications and creative media that educate, edify, and evangelize, leading to a living experience of God through His Holy Orthodox Church
Submissions: Publishes 12–16 titles per year; receives 100 submissions annually. First-time authors: 50%. Length: 40,000–100,000 words. Query first by email. Responds in two months. Bible: NKJV.
Topics and genres: Christian living/spirituality, prayer, worship, board books, children, fiction, first-chapter, middle-grade fiction, picture books, teen/YA
Royalty: 10–15%, no advance
First print run: 2,000
Guidelines: *www.ancientfaith.com/publishing#af-resources*
Tip: "Read and follow the guidelines. Look through our website to see the kinds of books we publish. Do not submit material that is not intended specifically for an Eastern Orthodox audience."

ANEKO PRESS

PO Box 652, Abbotsford, WI 54405 | 715-223-3013

jeremiah@lspbooks.com | *www.anekopress.com*
Jeremiah Zeiset, president

Parent company: Life Sentence Publishing, Inc.
Mission statement: to publish books for ministry
Submissions: Niche is publishing ministry-related books. Publishes 20 titles per year; receives 50 submissions annually. First-time authors: 20%. Length: 30,000–100,000 words. Submit proposal with complete manuscript through the website. Responds in two weeks. Bible: KJV, ESV, NKJV.
Topics and genres: Christian living/spirituality
Royalty: 30%, no advance
First print run: 1,000–5,000
Types of books: audiobook, ebook, hardcover, offset paperback
Guidelines: *anekopress.com/write-for-us*
Tip: "The majority of our authors are in ministry as missionaries or other similar ministries."

ASHBERRY LANE

13607 Bedford Rd. NE, Cumberland, MD 21502 | 866-245-2211
r.white@whitefire-publishing.com | *AshberryLane.com*
Roseanna White, senior fiction editor

Parent company: WhiteFire Publishing
Mission statement: to publish heartfelt stories of faith
Submissions: Publishes 5–10 titles per year; receives 50 submissions annually. First-time authors: 10%. Length: 60,000–110,000 words. Email proposal with sample chapters. Responds in three months.
Topics and genres: fiction: historical romance, romance, romantic suspense
Royalty: 50% for ebooks, 10% of retail for print; sometimes gives advance of $500–2,000
Type of books: POD
Guidelines: *ashberrylane.com/submissions*
Tip: "Please be familiar with our titles and mission."

ASPIRE PRESS

PO Box 3473, Peabody, MA 01961 | 800-358-3111
LynnettePennings@tyndale.com | *www.hendricksonrose.com/lp/hr-aspire-press*
Lynette Pennings, managing editor

Parent company: Hendrickson Publishing Group/Tyndale House Ministries

Mission statement: to provide counseling for Christian living

Submissions: Only agent, *ChristianBookProposals.com*, or conference contact. Need credentials in helping others.

Topics and genres: Christian living/spirituality, counseling

Tip: Publishes books that are "compassionate in their approach and rich with Scripture," giving "godly insight and counsel for those personally struggling and for believers who have a heart to minister and encourage others."

AUGSBURG FORTRESS

PO Box 1209, Minneapolis, MN 55440-1209

afsubmissions@1517.media | www.augsburgfortress.org

Suzanne Burke, director of development and senior editor

Denomination: Evangelical Lutheran Church in America

Parent company: 1517 Media

Mission statement: to develop engaging resources for Lutheran congregations

Submissions: Email proposal with sample chapters or a query. Responds in 60 days, only if fits publishing needs.

Topics and genres: Bible study, Christian living/spirituality, leadership, worship

Guidelines: *ms.augsburgfortress.org/downloads/Submission%20 Guidelines.pdf*

AVE MARIA PRESS

PO Box 428, Notre Dame, IN 46556 | 800-282-1865, ext. 1

submissions@mail.avemariapress.com | www.avemariapress.com

Heidi Hess Saxton, senior acquisitions editor

Denomination: Catholic

Mission statement: to serve the spiritual and educational needs of individuals, groups, and the Church as a whole

Submissions: Publishes 40 titles per year; receives 350 submissions annually. First-time authors: 30%. Length: 20,000–60,000 words. Email or mail proposal with sample chapters. Responds in three to four weeks. Bible: RSV2CE, NABRE.

Topics and genres: Advent, African-American, Christian living/ spirituality, death and dying, evangelism, faith formation, family, grief, healing, Hispanic, marriage, ministry, parenting, prayer, theology, curriculum, ministry resources, small-group study guides

Royalty: 10%; advance, $1,000

Types of books: ebook, hardcover, offset paperback
Guidelines: *www.avemariapress.com/manuscript-submissions*
Tip: "Our most successful books identify and address a specific felt-need for a potential reader. We are eager to work with authors who have robust platforms and direct connections to their potential readers."

B&H KIDS
200 Powell Pl., Ste. 100, Brentwood, TN 37027-7707 | 615-251-2000
michelle.freeman@lifeway.com | *www.bhpublishinggroup.com/categories/kids*
Michelle Freeman, publisher
Anna Sargeant, associate publisher; anna.sargeant@lifeway.com
> **Denomination:** Southern Baptist
> **Parent company:** B&H Publishing/Lifeway Christian Resources
> **Mission statement:** to help kids develop a lifelong relationship with Jesus and to empower parents and church leaders to guide the spiritual growth of the next generation
> **Submissions:** Publishes 18–24 titles per year; receives hundreds of submissions annually. First-time authors: 10–20%. Length: depends on age group. Agent only. Responds in one to three months. Bible: CSB. Any book for children or teens with a Christian message. Themes include but are not limited to adventure, attributes of God, Bible-story retellings, biblical virtues, church, community, diversity and inclusion, family, relationships, friendships, prayer, emotions, and theology.
> **Topics and genres:** Bible stories, board books, devotionals, fiction, first-chapter, middle grade, picture books, teen/YA
> **Royalty:** 18–22%, gives advance
> **Types of books:** audiobook, board books, ebook, hardcover, offset paperback, picture books
> **Guidelines:** available via email
> **Tip:** "We are a conservative Christian publishing house that publishes Protestant authors. Note that illustrations for children's books are not necessary or suggested."

B&H PUBLISHING GROUP
200 Powell Pl., Ste. 100, Brentwood, TN 37027-7707 | 615-251-2000
www.bhpublishinggroup.com
Matthew Hawkins, senior acquisitions editor
Ashley Gorman, women's publisher
> **Denomination:** Southern Baptist

Parent company: LifeWay Christian Resources

Mission statement: to provide Bible-centered content that impacts hearts and minds, inspiring people in their lifelong relationship with Jesus Christ, because every word matters

Submissions: Publishes 90 titles per year; receives thousands of submissions annually. First-time authors: 10%. Agent only. Responds in two to three months. Bible: CSB.

Topics and genres: Bible study, Christian living/spirituality, church growth, evangelism, leadership, marriage, parenting, theology, women, worship, academic, Bible reference/commentaries, children

Royalty: gives advance

Types of books: ebook, hardcover, offset paperback

Imprints: B&H Publishing (trade books), B&H Kids (children), B&H Academic (textbooks), Holman Bibles

Guidelines: not available

Tip: "Be informed that the market in general is very crowded with the book you might want to write. Do the research before submitting."

BAAL HAMON PUBLISHERS

244 Fifth Ave., Ste. T279, New York, NY 10001 | 646-233-4017

submissions@baalhamon.com | *www.baalhamonpublishers.com*

Temitope Oyetomi, director

Mission statement: to be a global leader in publishing, distinguished by superlative production and distribution and an unwavering commitment to truth and integrity

Submissions: Publishes 30 titles per year; receives 90 submissions annually. First-time authors: 60%. Length: 50,000–70,000 words. Agent not required. Email proposal with sample chapters. Responds in one to two weeks. Bible: ESV.

Topics and genres: African-American, Christian living/spirituality, counseling, health, marriage, parenting, self-help, biography, devotionals; fiction: most genres except fantasy, science fiction, and apocalyptic

Royalty: 60%, sometimes gives advance

First print run: hardcover, 1,000; paperback, 3,000

Types of books: ebook, hardcover, offset paperback, POD

Guidelines: *www.baalhamonpublishers.com/guidelines.html*

Tip: "Include a good analysis of similar books in the market and why yours will be better than most."

BAKER ACADEMIC

6030 E. Fulton Rd., Ada, MI 49301 | 616-676-9185

submissions@bakeracademic.com | *bakeracademic.com*

Robert Hosack, senior acquisitions editor

Anna Moseley Gissing, senior acquisitions editor
Brandy Scritchfield, acquisitions editor

Parent company: Baker Publishing Group

Mission statement: to serve the academy and the church by publishing high-quality works that bring Christian faith to bear on the pursuit of knowledge, wisdom, and human flourishing

Submissions: Publishes 50 titles per year. First-time authors: 10%. Agent preferred, *ChristianBookProposals.com*, conference contact, Writers Edge. Email proposal with sample chapters.

Topics and genres: Bible, Christian education, counseling, evangelism, leadership, ministry, missions, preaching, religion, spiritual formation, theology, worship, academic, professional

Royalty: gives advance

Types of books: ebook, hardcover, paperback

Guidelines: *bakeracademic.com/pages/submit-a-proposal*

Tip: "Baker Academic welcomes book proposals from prospective authors holding relevant academic credentials (which usually means a PhD or similar degree in the field of the proposed book and a teaching position at a recognized institution of higher learning)."

BAKER BOOKS

6030 E. Fulton Rd., Ada, MI 49301 | 616-676-9185

bakerpublishinggroup.com/bakerbooks

Rebekah Guzman, editorial director

Brian Vos, senior acquisitions editor
Stephanie Duncan Smith, acquisitions editor
Patnacia Goodman, acquisitions editor

Parent company: Baker Publishing Group

Mission statement: to build up the body of Christ through books that are relevant, intelligent, and engaging

Submissions: Only agent, *ChristianBookProposals.com*, or conference contact.

Topics and genres: apologetics, Christian living/spirituality, culture, discipleship, leadership, marriage, ministry, parenting, theology

Types of books: ebook, hardcover, offset paperback

Guidelines: *bakerpublishinggroup.com/contact/submission-policy*

BAKER PUBLISHING GROUP

Baker Academic, Baker Books, Bethany House, Brazos Press, Chosen, Revell

BANNER OF TRUTH

PO Box 621, Carlisle, PA 17013 | 717-249-5747
info@banneroftruth.co.uk | *banneroftruth.org*
Ian Thompson

> **Mission statement:** to inform, encourage, strengthen, and equip ordinary Christians, with a particular concern for ministers/pastors and those training for the ministry
>
> **Topics and genres:** biography, Christian living/spirituality, church life, history, ministry, theology, children, commentaries, devotionals
>
> **Types of books:** ebook, hardcover, offset paperback
>
> **Guidelines:** *banneroftruth.org/us/about/contact-us/submit-a-manuscript*
>
> **Tip:** "What makes a Banner book? It must be a book worthy of publication irrespective of its likely commercial success; it must pass theological and doctrinal scrutiny; it must promote practical Christian living; it most likely has enduring application and will be as relevant in 100 years as it is today; it must be well written and carefully edited; it must be well produced."

BARBOUR PUBLISHING, INC.

PO Box 719, Uhrichsville, OH 44683 | 740-922-6045
submissions@barbourbooks.com | *www.barbourbooks.com*
Annie Tipton, senior acquisitions editor
Paul Muckley, senior acquisitions editor, Bible and reference
Rebecca Germany, senior editor and acquisitions, fiction

> **Mission statement:** to inspire the world with the life-changing message of the Bible
>
> **Submissions:** Agent only.
>
> **Topics and genres:** Christian classics, Christian living/spirituality, activities and puzzles, Bible reference/commentaries, Bible stories, children, devotionals, journals, planners, puzzles/quizzes; fiction: Amish, contemporary, historical, romance, suspense/thriller
>
> **Types of books:** offset paperback
>
> **Imprints:** Barbour Books (nonfiction), Barbour Fiction (novels), Barbour Reference, DayMaker (planners), Barbour Young Adult (nonfiction, devotionals), Barbour Kidz (children), Barbour Bibles
>
> **Guidelines:** *www.barbourbooks.com/frequently-asked-questions*

BEAMING BOOKS

510 Marquette Ave., Minneapolis, MN 55403 | 800-960-9705

www.beamingbooks.com

Naomi Krueger, acquisitions editor

Denomination: Evangelical Lutheran Church in America

Parent company: 1517 Media

Submissions: Publishes 24 titles per year; receives 250 submissions annually. First-time authors: 50%. Length: 500 words for picture books. Agent only. Responds in three months. Bible: NIV, CEB.

Topics and genres: board books for ages birth–3, picture books for ages 3–8, activity books for ages 3–8, early-reader and first-chapter books for ages 5–9, nonfiction books for ages 5–9 and 8–12, fiction for ages 8–12, activity books for families, devotionals for children ages 0–12 and families

Royalty: gives advance

Tip: "Look at what we've published before. Read a few of our books."

BETHANY HOUSE PUBLISHERS

7808 Creekridge Cir., Ste. 250, Bloomington, MN 55439 | 952-829-2500

bakerpublishinggroup.com/bethanyhouse

Andy McGuire, editorial director

David Long, nonfiction acquisitions editor

Jeff Braun, nonfiction acquisitions editor

Jennifer Dukes Lee, nonfiction acquisitions editor

Jessica Sharpe, fiction acquisitions editor

Rochelle Gloege, fiction acquisitions editor

Parent company: Baker Publishing Group

Mission statement: to publish high-quality writings that represent historical Christianity and serve the diverse interests and concerns of evangelical readers

Submissions: Publishes 75–85 titles per year. Agent only or conference contact. Bible: NIV.

Topics and genres: Christian living/spirituality, family, prayer, relationships, theology, devotionals; fiction: Amish, biblical, contemporary, fantasy, historical, Regency, romance, romantic suspense

Royalty: gives advance

Types of books: ebook, hardcover, offset paperback

Tip: "The best opportunities for new authors come via literary agencies, conferences, writing communities, and author referrals. Get connected."

BOLD VISION BOOKS

PO Box 2011, Friendswood, TX 77549-2011 | 832-569-4282
boldvisionbooks@gmail.com | *www.boldvisionbooks.com*
Rhonda Rhea, chief acquisitions officer
Kaley Rhea, fiction acquisition editor

Mission statement: to publish compelling, creative, and beautiful books to change the world and further the message of Christ through the written word

Submissions: Publishes 25 titles per year; receives 150 submissions annually. First-time authors: 85%. Length: 50,000–70,000 words. Only agent or conference contact for nonfiction. Fiction query through the website. Responds in three to four months. Bible: any.

Topics and genres: arts, business, Christian living/spirituality, family, parenting, productivity, speaking, teaching, time management, writing, YA; fiction: adventure, contemporary, historical, humor, mystery, romance, teen/YA

Royalty: 25–50%, sometimes gives advance of $1,000–5,000

First print run: 2,000–10,000

Types of books: ebook, hardcover, offset paperback

Imprints: Nuts 'n Bolts (writing, teaching, speaking, management, craft books for arts and business), Optasia Books (pastors)

Guidelines: *www.boldvisionbooks.com/bold-vision-books-publishing*

Tip: "To become a successful writer, learn the craft of writing and attend writers conferences and take courses to understand this industry. Keep your message firmly planted in the Word of God. Know your audience and what they need. Read and follow our guidelines, and send a professional proposal. We want to see timeless truth told in fresh creative language."

BRAZOS PRESS

6030 E. Fulton Rd., Ada, MI 49301 | 616-676-9185
submissions@brazospress.com | *bakerpublishinggroup.com/brazospress*
Katelyn Beaty, editorial director and acquisitions

Parent company: Baker Publishing Group

Mission statement: to draw upon the riches of the Christian story to deepen our understanding of God's world and inspire faithful reflection and engagement

Submissions: Publishes books that creatively draw on the riches of our catholic Christian heritage to deepen our understanding of God's creation and inspire faithful reflection and engagement.

Authors typically hold advanced degrees and have established publishing platforms.

Topics and genres: nonfiction

Guidelines: *bakerpublishinggroup.com/brazospress/submitting-a-proposal*

Tip: "We welcome book proposals from scholars, church leaders, activists, artists, and writers who have something to say and can write with both skill and passion, demonstrating that serious writing can also be lively and compelling."

BRIMSTONE FICTION

1440 W. Taylor St., Ste. 449, Chicago, IL 60607 | 224-339-4159

brimstonefiction@gmail.com | *www.brimstonefiction.com*

Rowena Kuo, CEO and executive editor

Submissions: Publishes 8–12 titles per year; receives 60 submissions annually. First-time authors: 60%. Length: 60,000–100,000 words. Prefers agent or conference contact. Email proposal with sample chapters or complete manuscript. Responds in six to eight weeks. Bible: NIV.

Topics and genres: fiction: adventure, fantasy, historical, romantic suspense, science fiction, speculative, teen/YA, time travel, women's

Royalty: 30% of profits, no advance

Types of books: ebook, POD

Guidelines: *brimstonefiction.com/submission-guidelines*

Tip: "We welcome new and multipublished authors and/or authors with or without agents. If you have a good story, come and meet us at writers conferences or through our website."

BROADLEAF BOOKS

PO Box 1209, Minneapolis, MN 55440-1209 | 800-328-4648

submissions@broadleafbooks.com | *www.broadleafbooks.com*

Valerie Weaver-Zercher, acquisitions editor

Denomination: Evangelical Lutheran Church in America

Parent company: 1517 Media

Mission statement: to inspire transformation in readers and their communities to foster a more open, just, and compassionate world

Topics and genres: Christian living/spirituality, culture, social justice

Guidelines: *www.broadleafbooks.com/info/submissions*

Tip: "Please note that we receive a large volume of proposals. You will receive a response only if we see your proposal as a potential fit for our program."

BROADSTREET PUBLISHING

8646 Eagle Creek Cir., Ste. 210, Savage, MN 55378 | 855-935-2000
proposals@broadstreetpublishing.com | *www.broadstreetpublishing.com*
Tim Payne, editorial director

Submissions: Publishes 100+ titles per year. Agent preferred, or email proposal with sample chapters.

Topics and genres: Bible promises, biography, Christian living/spirituality, biography, children, coloring books, devotionals, fiction, journals

Imprints: Belle City Gifts (journals and planners), Broadstreet Kids (children)

Guidelines: *broadstreetpublishing.com/contact*

CALLA PRESS PUBLISHING, LLC

1495 Timbercreek Dr., Stephenville, TX 76401 | 972-971-8745
callapresspublishing@gmail.com | *www.callapress.com*
Samantha Cabrera, founder

Submissions: Publishes one to three titles per year; receives 350–500 submissions annually. First-time authors: 75%. Length: 35,000–50,000 words. Agent not required. Email proposal with complete manuscript or sample chapters or a query. Responds in six to eight weeks. Bible: ESV.

Topics and genres: Christian living/spirituality, memoir/personal narrative, academic, children, devotionals, poetry, teen/YA; fiction: adventure, historical, romance

Royalty: 20–30%, no advance

First print run: 500–1,000

Types of books: ebook, hardcover, offset paperback, POD

Guidelines: *callapress.com/book-submissions*

Tip: "We are a conservative Christian book publisher. Follow our submission guidelines verbatim, and we add a gold star to your query."

CASCADE BOOKS

199 W. 8th Ave., Ste. 3, Eugene, OR 97401 | 541-344-152
proposal@wipfandstock.com
wipfandstock.com/search-results-grid/?imprint=cascade-books

Parent company: Wipf and Stock

Submissions: Email proposal with sample chapters. Responds in one to two months.

Topics and genres: religion, theology

Types of books: ebook, POD

Guidelines: *wipfandstock.com/submitting-a-proposal*

CASCADIA PUBLISHING HOUSE

126 Klingerman Rd., Telford, PA 18969

editor@CascadiaPublishingHouse.com | *CascadiaPublishingHouse.com*

Michael A. King, publisher and editor

> **Submissions:** Looking for creative, thought-provoking, Anabaptist-related material.
> **Topics and genres:** nonfiction
> **Imprints:** DreamSeeker Books
> **Guidelines:** *www.cascadiapublishinghouse.com/submit.htm*
> **Tip:** "All Cascadia books receive rigorous evaluation and some form of peer or consultant review."

CASTLE QUAY BOOKS

10265 S.E. Banyan Way, Jupiter, FL 33469 | 416-573-3249

larrywillard@rogers.com | *castlequaybooks.com*

Larry Willard, manager of acquisitions

> **Parent company:** Castle Quay Communications, Inc.
> **Mission statement:** to develop and publish high value, quality moral titles, with traditional, family-friendly themes, by both established and new authors, striving to find and promote quality messages that will inform, challenge, inspire and uplift all our readers
> **Submissions:** Publishes 12–14 titles per year; receives 50+ submissions annually. First-time authors: 35%. Length: 180 pages. Agent not required. Email query first, or submit through *ChristianBookProposals.com*. No simultaneous submissions. Responds in four to six weeks. Bible: ESV.
> **Topics and genres:** African-American, business, Christian living/spirituality, culture, family, finances, history, leadership, memoir/personal narrative, politics, self-help, social issues, social justice, teaching, theology, women, academic, art, biography, children, devotionals, gift books, teen/YA; fiction: apocalyptic, historical
> **Royalty:** 12-15% print, 45% ebooks; sometimes gives advance of $1,000–20,000
> **First print run:** 3,000
> **Types of books:** audiobook, ebook, hardcover, offset paperback, POD
> **Guidelines:** *www.castlequaybooks.com/pages/submitting-a-manuscript*
> **Tip:** "Be clear in what is the creative new core to your story."

CATHOLIC BOOK PUBLISHING CORP.

77 W. End Rd., Totowa, NJ 07572 | 973-890-2400

info@catholicbookpublishing.com | *www.catholicbookpublishing.com*
Anthony Buono, editor

Denomination: Catholic
Submissions: Mail query first. No simultaneous submissions. Responds in two to three months.
Topics and genres: Christian living/spirituality, liturgy, prayer
Royalty: negotiable, no advance
Imprint: Resurrection Press (popular nonfiction)
Guidelines: *catholicbookpublishing.com/page/faq#manuscript*

CELEBRATE LIT PUBLISHERS

35459 Stockton St., Beaumont, CA 92223 | 909-520-8603
Celebratelit@celebratelit.com | *www.celebratelitpublishing.com*
Denise Barela, acquisitions editor
Sandra Barela, president

Denomination: Reformed
Mission statement: to encourage readers and change their lives
Submissions: Publishes 20–30 titles per year; receives 100 submissions annually. First-time authors: 80%. Length: 70,000 words. Agent not required. Email proposal with complete manuscript. Responds in eight weeks. Bible: ESV.
Topics and genres: African-American, Asian, Bible study, Hispanic, first-chapter, journals; fiction: all except science fiction
Royalty: 70%, no advance
Guidelines: *www.celebratelitpublishing.com/submit-a-manuscript*
Tip: "Include a solid marketing plan."

CF4K

Geanies House, Fearn, Tain, Ross-shire IV20 1TW, Scotland, UK | 01862-871011
Catherine.Mackenzie@christianfocus.com
www.christianfocus.com/products/category/309/childrens-books
Catherine MacKenzie, children's editor

Parent company: Christian Focus Publications
Mission statement: to help children find out about God and get them enthusiastic about reading the Bible, now and later in their lives
Submissions: Email or mail proposal with sample chapters. Responds in three to six months.
Topics and genres: Christian living/spirituality, Bible stories,

biography, crafts, devotionals, game books, puzzles and activities

Types of books: hardcover, paperback

Guidelines: *www.christianfocus.com/about/childrens-guidelines*

Tip: "Read our website please. Don't send us stuff we don't publish."

CHARISMA HOUSE

600 Rinehart Rd., Lake Mary, FL 32746 | 407-333-0600

Debbie.Marrie@CharismaMedia.com | *www.charismahouse.com*

Debbie Marrie, VP of acquisitions and content development

Denomination: Charismatic/Pentecostal

Parent company: Chrisma Media/Plus Communications, Inc.

Mission statement: to inspire people to encounter the power of the Holy Spirit

Submissions: Publishes 50–60 titles per year; receives 150–200 submissions annually. First-time authors: fewer than 10%. Length: 50,000–60,000 words/224–256 pages. Agent preferred. Email proposal with sample chapters. Responds in one month. Bible: MEV.

Topics and genres: African-American, Christian living/spirituality, end-times prophecy, fitness, health, Hispanic, spiritual warfare

Royalty: 16–25%, sometimes gives advance

Types of books: audiobook, ebook, hardcover, offset paperback, POD

Imprints: Siloam (natural health remedies), FrontLine (current events, end-time prophecy)

Guidelines: available via email

Tip: "Three key areas we evaluate are the concept, the writing quality, and the author's platform."

CHOSEN

7808 Creekridge Cir., Ste. 250, Bloomington, MN 55439 | 952-829-2500

dsluka@chosenbooks.com | *bakerpublishinggroup.com/chosen*

David Sluka, senior acquisitions editor

Kim Bangs, editorial director; kbangs@bakerpublishinggroup.com

Denomination: Charismatic

Parent company: Baker Publishing Group

Mission statement: to publish authors who recognize the gifts and active ministry of the Holy Spirit today

Submissions: Publishes 33 titles per year; receives 200 submissions annually. First-time authors: 45%. Length: 224 pages. Download the query form from the guidelines page, and email it. Responds in four weeks only if interested. Bible: any.

Topics and genres: African-American, Asian, Charismatic, deliverance, dreams, Hispanic, Holy Spirit, prayer, prophecy, revival, spiritual warfare, supernatural

Royalty: varies, sometimes gives advance

Types of books: audiobook, ebook, hardcover, offset paperback, POD

Guidelines: *bakerpublishinggroup.com/chosen/contact/preparing-a-proposal-for-chosen-books*

Tip: "Have a well-established platform on social media, enewsletter, etc."

CHRISM PRESS

13607 Bedford Rd. NE, Cumberland, MD 21502 | 301-876-4876

submissions@chrismpress.com | *www.chrismpress.com*

Karen Ullo, editor

Rhonda Ortiz, editor

Marisa Stokely, editor

William Gonch, editor

Parent company: WhiteFire Publishing

Mission statement: to publish stories informed by Catholic and Orthodox Christianity that may not be able to find a home in either mainstream secular or Christian (evangelical) presses

Submissions: Publishes 6–12 titles per year; receives 50 submissions annually. First-time authors: 25%. Length: 60,000–120,000 words. Email query first. Responds in three months.

Topics and genres: fiction: all, teen/YA

Royalty: 50% for ebooks, 10% for print; sometimes gives advance

Types of books: audiobook, ebook, POD

Guidelines: *www.chrismpress.com/submissions*

Tip: "We are acquiring adult and young-adult fiction that reflects a Catholic or Orthodox Christian worldview and appeals to Catholic and/or Orthodox readers. Please read our submissions guidelines and FAQ."

CHRISTIAN FOCUS PUBLICATIONS

Geanies House, Fearn, Tain, Ross-shire IV20 1TW, Scotland, UK | 01862-871011

submissions@christianfocus.com | *www.christianfocus.com*

Willie MacKenzie, director of publishing

Catherine Mackenzie, children's editor; Catherine.Mackenzie@christianfocus.com

Topics and genres: Christian living/spirituality, theology, academic, biography, children, commentaries

Types of books: hardcover, paperback

Imprints: Christian Focus (popular adult titles), CF4K (children), Mentor (serious readers), Christian Heritage (classic writings from the past)

Guidelines: *www.christianfocus.com/about/adult-guidelines, www. christianfocus.com/about/childrens-guidelines*

Tip: "Read our website please. Don't send us stuff we don't publish."

CHURCH PUBLISHING INCORPORATED

19 E. 34th St., New York, NY 10016 | 800-242-1918

astuart@cpg.org | www.churchpublishing.org

Airié Stuart, publisher

Denomination: Episcopal

Topics and genres: Bible study, biography, Christian living/ spirituality, finances, leadership, prayer, retirement, social justice, theology, worship, academic

Types of books: audiobook, ebook, hardcover, paperback

Guidelines: *www.churchpublishing.org/manuscriptsubmission*

Tip: "CPI's core publishing program is structured around *The Book of Common Prayer; The Hymnal 1982*; and the specialized books and resources used in the liturgy, faith formation, governance, life, and mission of the Episcopal Church."

CKN CHRISTIAN PUBLISHING

submissions@cknchristianpublishing.com | cknchristianpublishing.com

Patience Bramlett, editor

Parent company: Wolfpack Publishing

Mission statement: to publish books that will help readers to rise and develop their understanding of God's Word and to apply it more abundantly to their lives

Submissions: Agent only. Responds in three months.

Topics and genres: fiction: Amish, historical, mystery, romance, science fiction, westerns

Royalty: up to 35%

Types of books: ebook, POD

Guidelines: *cknchristianpublishing.com/christian-manuscript-submissions*

Tip: "We are dedicated to bringing readers wholesome novels that ensure there's something for everyone to read. No sexually explicit scenes, graphically violent descriptions, or streams of profanity."

CLADACH PUBLISHING

PO Box 336144, Greeley, CO 80633 | 970-371-9530
cathyl@cladach.com | *www.cladach.com*
Catherine Lawton, publisher and editor
Christina Slike, assistant editor

Submissions: Publishes three or four titles per year; receives 50 submissions annually. First-time authors: 50%. Length: 120–300 pages. Agent not required. Author referral or conference contact a plus. Responds in three months. Bible: NIV, NRSV.

Topics and genres: Christian living/spirituality, healing, memoir/ personal narrative, nature, relationships, devotionals, memoir, poetry; fiction: frontier, literary

Royalty: 10–20%; advance, $100

Types of books: audiobook, ebook, offset paperback, POD

Imprints: AGATES (poetry)

Guidelines: *cladach.com/authors*

Tip: "We seek creative, marketable book ideas from Christian authors who are credible, in community, and who share our vision to publish books that show God at work in this world and that inspire readers to get involved."

CLC PUBLICATIONS

PO Box 1449, Fort Washington, PA 19034 | 215-542-1242
submissions@clcpublications.com | *www.clcpublications.com*
David Fessenden, editorial coordinator

Parent company: CLC Ministries International

Mission statement: to make evangelical Christian literature available to all nations so that people may come to faith and maturity in the Lord Jesus Christ

Submissions: Publishes 6–12 titles per year; receives 60 submissions annually. First-time authors: 30%. Length: 20,000–80,000 words. Agent preferred. Email proposal with sample chapters. Responds in six to eight weeks. Bible: ESV.

Topics and genres: Christian living/spirituality

Royalty: 12–16%, sometimes gives advance

Types of books: audiobook, ebook, offset paperback

Guidelines: *www.clcpublications.com/about/prospective-authors-submissions*

Tip: "Try to be both succinct and complete in your submission."

COLLEGE PRESS PUBLISHING

1307 W. 20th St., Joplin, MO 64804 | 417-623-6280

collpressjoplin@gmail.com | *www.collegepress.com*

> **Denomination:** Church of Christ
> **Submissions:** Email or mail proposal with sample chapters or a query. Responds in two to three months.
> **Topics and genres:** apologetics, biography, Christian living/spirituality, academic, Bible reference/commentaries, Bible studies
> **Guidelines:** *www.collegepress.com/pages/for-authors*

CONVERGENT BOOKS

1745 Broadway, New York, NY 10019 | 212-366-2724

kbaltzer@penguinrandomhouse.com

www.randomhousebooks.com/imprint/convergent-books

Keren Baltzer, VP, editorial director

> **Parent company:** The Crown Publishing Group/Penguin Random House
> **Mission statement:** to seek out diverse viewpoints and honest conversations that shed light on the defining challenges facing people of faith today; to help readers ask important questions, find paths forward in disagreement, and shape the way faith is expressed in the modern world
> **Submissions:** Publishes 12-16 titles per year; receives 100-150 submissions annually. First-time authors: 10%. Length: 204-300 pages/45,000-65,000 words. Agent only. Responds in a few weeks to two months. Bible: NIV, ESV.
> **Topics and genres:** African-American, Asian, Christian living/spirituality, deconstruction/reconstruction of faith, friendship, Hispanic, marriage, memoir/personal narrative, parenting, self-help, social issues, social justice, wellness, essays
> **Royalty:** 10-15%; advance, $10,000 to high six figures
> **Types of books:** audiobook, ebook, hardcover, offset paperback
> **Guidelines:** not available
> **Tip:** "Have a good agent and a good platform."

CROSSLINK PUBLISHING

1601 Mt. Rushmore Rd., Ste. 3288, Rapid City, SD 57701 | 888-697-4851

publisher@crosslink.org | *www.crosslinkpublishing.com*

Rick Bates, managing editor

> **Parent company:** CrossLink Ministries

Submissions: Publishes 35 titles per year; receives 500 submissions annually. First-time authors: 85%. Length: 12,000–60,000 words. Submit through the website. Responds in one week.

Topics and genres: Christian living/spirituality, Bible studies, children, devotionals, fiction

Royalty: 10% for print, 20% for ebooks; no advance

First print run: 2,000

Imprints: New Harbor Press

Guidelines: *www.crosslinkpublishing.com/submit-a-manuscript*

Tip: "We are particularly interested in providing books that help Christians succeed in their daily walk (inspirational, devotional, small groups, etc.)."

CROSSRIVER MEDIA GROUP

4810 Gene Field Rd. #2, St. Joseph, MO 64506 | 816-752-2171

deb@crossrivermedia.com | *www.crossrivermedia.com*

Debra L. Butterfield, editorial director

Mission statement: to publish high-quality books and materials that help women build a battle-ready faith

Submissions: Publishes four to eight titles per year; receives 60–75 submissions annually. First-time authors: 30–40%. Length: 50,000–80,000 words. Conference contact a plus. Email proposal with sample chapters, or submit it through the website. Responds in 12–16 weeks. Bible: any except NIV.

Topics and genres: Bible study, Christian living/spirituality, family, inspirational, marriage; fiction: biblical, contemporary, historical, mystery, romance

Royalty: 8–12%, no advance

Types of books: ebook, hardcover, POD

Guidelines: *www.crossrivermedia.com/guidelines*

Tip: "Read our website, and follow the proposal guidelines."

CROSSWAY

1300 Crescent St., Wheaton, IL 60187 | 630-682-4300

submissions@crossway.org | *www.crossway.org*

Todd Augustine, director of acquisitions

Parent company: Good News Publishers

Mission statement: to bring men, women, and children to Christ as their Lord and Savior; help individual Christians and the church grow in knowledge and understanding of the Christian life; bear witness to God's truth, beauty, and holiness, and to the Lordship of Christ in every area of life; and glorify our Lord and Savior Jesus Christ in every way

Submissions: Publishes 100 titles per year; receives 700 submissions annually. First-time authors: 1%. Length: 25,000–40,000 words. Agent not required. Email query first, or use the website form. Responds in six weeks but only if interested in receiving a proposal. Bible: ESV.

Topics and genres: Bible study, Christian living/spirituality, contemporary issues, spiritual growth, worldview, academic, Bible reference/commentaries, devotionals

Royalty: varies, gives advance

First print run: varies

Types of books: audiobook, ebook, hardcover, offset paperback

Guidelines: *www.crossway.org/submissions*

Tip: "Be sure to follow our guidelines, and send a well-written query letter."

CSS PUBLISHING COMPANY, INC.

5450 N. Dixie Hwy., Lima, OH 45807-9559 | 419-227-1818

editor@csspub.com | www.csspub.com

David Runk, publisher

Mission statement: to help Protestant pastors and lay leaders share the Good News of Jesus Christ

Submissions: Publishes 20 titles per year; receives 50 submissions annually. First-time authors: 10%. Length: 80–240 pages, depending on subject matter. Email or mail proposal with sample chapters or a query. Responds in six months. Bible: NRSV, NIV, RSV, ESV, TLB.

Topics and genres: Christian education, ministry, preaching, stewardship, worship, Bible studies, church resources, drama, ministry resources, sermons

Royalty: 7–10%, no advance; flat fee of $350–500 for sermon books

Types of books: ebook, POD

Guidelines: *store.csspub.com/page.php?Custom%20Pages=10*

Tip: "Use solid biblical research."

D6 FAMILY MINISTRY (formerly Randall House)

PO Box 17306, Nashville, TN 37217 | 615-361-1221

books@d6family.com | D6family.com

Dr. Danny Conn, director of editorial

Denomination: Free Will Baptist

Mission statement: to build believers through church and home

Submissions: Publishes 10–12 titles per year; receives 50 submissions annually. First-time authors: 50%. Length: 20,000–100,000 words. Agent not required. Conference contact, or email proposal with sample chapters. Responds in three months. Bible: ESV, NASB, NIV, KJV, NKJV.

Topics and genres: discipleship, family, Hispanic, theology, nonfiction

Royalty: 10–20%, sometimes gives advance

Types of books: audiobook, ebook, hardcover, offset paperback, POD

Imprints: D6 Family (family ministry, discipleship), Randall House (Free Will Baptist history and theology), Randall House Academic (academic texts)

Guidelines: *rhpweb.s3.amazonaws.com/Book-Proposal-Guide.pdf*

Tip: "Review the resources promoted on our website."

DAVID C COOK

4050 Lee Vance Dr., Colorado Springs, CO 80918 | 719-536-0100

www.davidccook.org

Michael Covington, VP of publishing and acquisitions for pastors, leaders, and women's

Susan McPherson, acquisitions, women in leadership

Luke McKinnon, acquisitions, apologetics and worldview

Mission statement: to equip the Church with Christ-centered resources for making and teaching disciples

Submissions: Publishes 40 titles per year; receives 1,200 submissions annually. First-time authors: 10%. Length: 45,000–50,000 words. Agent only or conference contact. Responds in one month.

Topics and genres: Christian living/spirituality, discipleship, family, leadership, marriage, men, parenting, women, Bible reference/commentaries, Bible studies, church resources, devotionals, teen/YA

Royalty: 12–22%, advance varies

Types of books: ebook, hardcover, offset paperback, POD

Imprints: Esther Press (women)

Guidelines: *shop.davidccook.org/pages/frequently-asked-questions*

Tip: "We look for significant platform, excellent writing, and relevant content."

DOVE CHRISTIAN PUBLISHERS

PO Box 611, Bladensburg, MD 20710 | 240-342-3293

editorial@dovechristianpublishers.com | *www.dovechristianpublishers.com*

Raenita Wiggins, acquisitions editor

Parent company: Kingdom Christian Enterprises

Mission statement: to entertain, edify, equip, and encourage people through products that glorify and honor Jesus Christ and His Kingdom and to provide new and emerging Christian authors with a forum for their creative and Kingdom-building voices

Submissions: Publishes 10 titles per year; receives 300 submissions annually. First-time authors: 95%. Length: 100–220 pages. Submit proposal with sample chapters through the website. Responds in four to six weeks or not interested. Bible: NIV.

Topics and genres: Christian living/spirituality, church life, discipleship, ministry, prayer, Bible studies, children, devotionals; fiction: fantasy, historical, humor, mystery, romance, science fiction, suspense/thriller

Royalty: 10–25%, no advance

Types of books: ebook, hardcover, POD

Guidelines: *www.dovechristianpublishers.com/publish-with-us*

Tip: "Author should establish a platform and familiarize themselves with book marketing and promotion prior to submission."

EERDMANS BOOKS FOR YOUNG READERS

4035 Park East Ct. SE, Grand Rapids, MI 49546 | 800-253-7521

kmerz@eerdmans.com | *www.eerdmans.com/youngreaders*

Kathleen Merz, editorial director

Courtney Zonnefeld, assistant editor

Parent company: Wm. B. Eerdmans Publishing Co.

Mission statement: to engage young minds with books—books that are honest, wise, and hopeful; books that delight us with their storyline, characters, or good humor; books that inform, inspire, and entertain

Submissions: Publishes 12–18 titles per year; receives 1,500 submissions annually. First-time authors: 5–10%. Length: picture books, 1,000 words; middle-grade books, 15,000–30,000 words. Mail proposal with complete manuscript or sample chapters. Responds in four months only if interested.

Topics and genres: African-American, animals, history, multicultural, nature, social issues, middle grade, picture books, teen/YA

Royalty: gives advance

Types of books: audiobook, ebook, hardcover

Guidelines: *www.eerdmans.com/Pages/Item/2237/EBYR-Guidelines.aspx*

Tip: "We are always looking for well-written picture books and novels for young readers. Make sure that your submission is a unique, well-crafted story; and take a look at our current list of titles to get a sense of whether yours would be a good fit for us."

EERDMANS, WM. B. PUBLISHING CO.

4035 Park East Ct. SE, Grand Rapids, MI 49546 | 800-253-7521
submissions@eerdmans.com | *www.eerdmans.com*
Andrew Knapp, acquisitions editor
Lisa Ann Cockrel, acquisitions editor

Submissions: Publishes 100 titles per year. Email proposal with complete manuscript or sample chapters. Responds in two months.

Topics and genres: biography, Christian living/spirituality, contemporary issues, ethics, history, ministry, theology, academic, Bible reference/commentaries

Royalty: sometimes gives advance

Imprints: Eerdmans Books for Young Readers (children and teens)

Guidelines: *www.eerdmans.com/Pages/Item/2068/Submission-Guidelines.aspx*

Tip: "Review submission guidelines carefully and check recent catalogs for suitability. Target readerships range from academic to semipopular. We are publishing a growing number of books in Christian life, spirituality, and ministry."

ELK LAKE PUBLISHING, INC.

35 Dogwood Dr., Plymouth, MA 02360-3166 | 508-746-1734
Deb@ElkLakePublishingInc.com | *ElkLakePublishingInc.com*
Deb Haggerty, publisher and editor in chief

Mission statement: to captivate our readers and carry them to places of escape, encouragement, education, and entertainment—to broaden their horizons and urge them to new heights

Submissions: Publishes 70–100 titles per year; receives 350 submissions annually. First-time authors: 60%. Length: fiction, 80,000–90,000 words/300 pages; speculative fiction, 80,000–130,000 words; nonfiction, 40,000–60,000 words. Agent preferred; conference contact a plus. Submit proposal with sample chapters by email or through the website. Responds in two weeks or less. Bible: NASB, NLT.

Topics and genres: Bible study, Christian living/spirituality, middle grade, YA; fiction: contemporary, juvenile, mystery, speculative, suspense, women's

Royalty: 40%, no advance

Types of books: audiobook, ebook, hardcover, POD

Guidelines: *tinyurl.com/2s3zyuyb*

Tip: Submit "letter perfect proposals, well-edited manuscripts."

EMANATE BOOKS

PO Box 141000, Nashville, TN 37214-1000 | 615-889-9000

Janene.MacIvor@harpercollins.com | *www.thomasnelson.com/emanatebooks*

Janene MacIvor, senior editor

Parent company: Thomas Nelson Publishers/HarperCollins Christian Publishing

Mission statement: to reflect the work of the Holy Spirit, feed His church, and help a new generation hear from God and grow in their spiritual journeys

Topics and genres: Charismatic, Christian classics

Types of books: audiobook, ebook, hardcover, offset paperback

ENCLAVE PUBLISHING

24 W. Camelback Rd. A-635, Phoenix, AZ 85013

acquisitions@enclavepublishing.com | *www.enclavepublishing.com*

Steve Laube, publisher and acquisitions editor

Parent company: Oasis Family Media

Mission statement: to publish out-of-this-world stories that are informed by a coherent theology

Submissions: Publishes 12–18 titles per year; receives 200 submissions annually. First-time authors: 20–30%. Length: 80,000–140,000 words. Author referral, conference contact, or proposal with sample chapters through the website. Responds in 60–90 days.

Topics and genres: fiction: allegory, fantasy, science fiction, speculative, supernatural, YA

Royalty: industry standard, no advance

First print run: 2,000–5,000

Types of books: audiobook, ebook, hardcover, offset paperback

Imprints: Enclave Escape (YA)

Guidelines: *www.enclavepublishing.com/guidelines*

Tip: "Keep word count above 80,000 words and below 140,000. Too often we are sent books that are either far too short or extremely long."

END GAME PRESS

PO Box 206, Nesbit, MS 38651 | 901-590-6584

submissions@endgamepress.com | *www.endgamepress.com*

Hope Bolinger, managing and acquisitions editor

Michelle Medlock Adams, children's acquisitions

Edwina Perkins, executive editor and acquisitions, Harambee Press

Mission statement: to leverage all of its resources to make the greatest positive impact possible by holding a high standard for the books it publishes in both design and quality, while also making the experience a good one for each of the authors in the End Game Press family

Submissions: Publishes 20 titles per year; receives 300 submissions annually. First-time authors: 25%. Length: depends on the genre. Agent only. Responds in two to three months. Bible: any.

Topics and genres: Christian living/spirituality, faith, marriage, parenting, prayer, fiction

Royalty: 20–25%, gives advance

Types of books: audiobook, ebook, hardcover, paperback

Imprints: Wren and Bear Books (children and YA), Harambee Press (ethnic/BIPOC), Generation Hope (chapter books, middle grade, and YA)

Guidelines: *www.endgamepress.com/submissions*

Tip: Also publishes general-market books.

EXEGETICA PUBLISHING

312 Greenwich #112, Lee's Summit, MO 64082 | 816-269-8505
editor@exegeticapublishing.com | *www.exegeticapublishing.com*

Mission statement: to encourage Christians and non-Christians alike to engage with the Bible, to understand the world around them, and to "taste and see that the Lord is good," as Psalm 34:8 exhorts

Submissions: Publishes 10 titles per year; receives 30 submissions annually. First-time authors: 10%. Length: 200–300 pages. Email proposal with sample chapters. Responds in two to four weeks. Bible: NASB, NKJV, ESV.

Topics and genres: Bible, Christian living/spirituality, theology, academic

Royalty: 10%, no advance

Types of books: ebook, offset paperback

Imprints: Grace Acres Press (trade nonfiction)

Guidelines: *exegeticapublishing.com/submit-a-proposal*

Tip: "Follow submission guidelines with solid biblical resources."

EXPANSE BOOKS

15 Lucky Ln., Morrilton, AR 72110 | 501-289-9319
scriveningspress@gmail.com | *expansebooks.pub*
Linda Fulkerson, owner and acquisitions editor
Erin R. Howard, managing editor; expansebooks@gmail.com

Parent company: Scrivenings Press, LLC

Mission statement: to spread God's word through our writing

Submissions: Publishes three titles per year; receives 100 submissions annually. First-time authors: 30%. Length: 60,000–90,000 words. Agent not required. Conference contact a plus. Submit proposal with sample chapters by email or through the website. Responds in four to six weeks. Bible: any.

Topics and genres: fiction: YA, dystopian, fairy tales, fantasy, magical realism, speculative, time travel

Royalty: 12% print, 50% ebook, 40% pages read in Kindle Unlimited; no advance

Types of books: ebook, hardcover, POD

Guidelines: *expansebooks.pub/submissions*

Tip: "We are a small publishing house, and we try to keep a family feel among our staff and authors. We encourage all our authors to encourage one another and cross-promote their books."

FAITHWORDS

1 Franklin Park, 6100 Tower Cir., Ste. 210, Franklin, TN 37067 | 615-221-0996

www.faithwords.com

Beth Adams, acquisitions editor

Sean McGowan, editor and acquisitions

India Hunter, associate editor and acquisitions

Submissions: Agent only.

Parent company: Hachette Book Group

Topics and genres: African-American, apologetics, Bible study, Christian living/spirituality, culture, Hispanic, marriage, memoir/personal narrative, parenting, social issues, theology

Royalty: minimum 10%, gives advance

Types of books: ebook, hardcover, offset paperback

Tip: "Have a clear, well-written proposal and a solid platform."

FIRST STEPS PUBLISHING

PO Box 571, Gleneden Beach, OR 97388 | 541-961-7641

publish@firststepspublishing.com | *www.FirstStepsPublishing.com*

RJ McRoberts, submissions editor

Submissions: Publishes three to five titles per year; receives 30 submissions annually. First-time authors: 90%. Length: 50,000–80,000 words. Submit query first via the website form. Responds in 8–12 weeks, although reply is not guaranteed.

Topics and genres: fiction: fantasy, historical, mystery, science fiction, suspense/thriller

Royalty: 15–30%, no advance

Types of books: audiobook, ebook, hardcover, POD

Imprints: White Parrot Press (children), WestWind Press (middle grade and YA)

Guidelines: *www.firststepspublishing.com/get-published*

Tip: "Initial response is based on your query letter, so ensure that it is enticing and well-written. We only accept unpublished, professionally edited manuscripts. Overuse of gratuitous language will not be accepted."

FLYAWAY BOOKS

100 Witherspoon St., Louisville, KY 40202-1396

submissions@flyawaybooks.com | *www.flyawaybooks.com*

Jessica Miller Kelley, senior acquisitions editor

Denomination: Presbyterian

Parent company: Westminster John Knox Press/Presbyterian Publishing Corporation

Submissions: Email proposal with complete manuscript. Responds in six weeks or not interested.

Topics and genres: picture books

Types of books: hardcover, paperback, picture books

Guidelines: *www.flyawaybooks.com/submissions*

Tip: "Flyaway Books embraces diversity, inclusivity, compassion, care for each other, and care for our world. Many of our books explore social justice and other contemporary issues. Some retell familiar religious stories in new ways, while others carry universal themes appealing to those with any, or no, religious background."

FOCUS ON THE FAMILY

8605 Explorer Dr., Colorado Springs, CO 80995 | 719-531-5181

www.focusonthefamily.com

Larry Weeden, editor in chief

Submissions: Only agent, *ChristianBookProposals.com,* or Writer's Edge. Books are published by Tyndale House Publishers.

Topics and genres: family, marriage, parenting, children

Types of books: ebook, hardcover, offset paperback

Imprints: Focus Fiction

Tip: "We're looking for proposals that exhibit great content and good writing, hopefully combined with a strong author platform. And we're always looking for good children's books."

FORTRESS PRESS

PO Box 1209, Minneapolis, MN 55440-1209

hemmerr@fortresspress.com | *www.fortresspress.com*

Ryan Hemmer, editor-in-chief

Yvonne D. Hawkins, acquisitions editor, ministry; hawkinsy@fortresspress.com
Laura Gifford, acquisitions editor, ministry; giffordl@fortresspress.com
Bethany Dickerson, associate acquisitions editor, theology, culture, literature, religious history, and biblical studies; dickersonb@fortresspress.com
Daniel José Camacho, acquisitions editor; camachod@fortresspress.com

Denomination: Evangelical Lutheran Church in America
Parent company: 1517 Media
Topics and genres: Bible study, Christian living/spirituality, counseling, culture, ethics, history, leadership, ministry, philosophy, social justice, theology, academic, Bible reference/commentaries
Types of books: hardcover, offset paperback
Guidelines: *www.fortresspress.com/info/submissions*

FORWARD MOVEMENT

412 Sycamore St., Cincinnati, OH 45202-4110 | 800-543-1813

editorial@forwardmovement.org | *www.forwardmovement.org*

Richelle Thompson, managing editor

Denomination: Episcopal
Mission statement: to offer resources that strengthen and support discipleship and evangelism
Submissions: Email proposal with sample chapters. Responds in four to six weeks.
Topics and genres: Bible study, discipleship, evangelism, leadership, prayer, nonfiction
Types of books: ebook, offset paperback
Guidelines: *www.forwardmovement.org/Pages/About/Writers-Guidelines.aspx*
Tip: "While many of our resources are targeted for an Episcopal/Anglican audience, we also offer some materials for a broader reach."

THE FOUNDRY PUBLISHING

PO Box 419527, Kansas City, MO 64141 | 800-877-0700

RMcFarland@thefoundrypublishing.com | *www.thefoundrypublishing.com*

René McFarland, submissions editor

Bonnie Perry, editorial director

Denomination: Nazarene, Wesleyan

Mission statement: to empower people with life-changing ways to engage in the mission of God

Submissions: Length: 45,000–60,000 words. Email proposal with sample chapters. Responds in eight weeks.

Topics and genres: Christian living/spirituality, ministry

Guidelines: *www.thefoundrypublishing.com/book-manuscript-submission-faqs.html*

Tip: "Because we are a denominational publisher of holiness literature, our books reflect an evangelical Wesleyan stance in accord with the Church of the Nazarene. We seek practical as well as serious treatments of issues of faith consistent with the Wesleyan tradition."

FOUR CRAFTSMEN PUBLISHING

PO Box U, Lakeside, AZ 85929-0585 | 928-367-2076

info@fourcraftsmen.com | *www.fourcraftsmen.com*

CeCelia Jackson, editor in chief

Mission statement: to publish truth that works for Christian readers

Submissions: Publishes four to six titles per year. First-time authors: 100%. Length: 40,000–80,000 words. Email or mail proposal with complete manuscript or sample chapters. Responds in two weeks. Bible: NASB, NKJV, TLB, TEV.

Topics and genres: Bible study, Christian living/spirituality, finances, spiritual warfare, testimony

Royalty: 10% gross, 50–60% ebook; no advance

First print run: 500

Types of books: ebook, hardcover, offset paperback, POD

Guidelines: *fourcraftsmen.com/additional-info*

Tip: "Original work, not compilation of source quotes. Necessary quotes correctly attributed and permissions provided."

FRANCISCAN MEDIA

28 W. Liberty St., Cincinnati, OH 45202 | 513-241-5615

proposal@FranciscanMedia.org | *www.FranciscanMedia.org*

Christopher Heffron, editorial director

Denomination: Catholic

Submissions: Publishes 20–30 titles per year. Email proposal with sample chapters. Responds in six to eight weeks. Bible: NRSV. Seeks manuscripts that inform and inspire adult Catholics, other Christians, and all who are seeking to better understand and live their faith. Goal is to help people "Live in love. Grow in faith."

Topics and genres: Christian living/spirituality, spiritual growth, fiction

Royalty: 10–14%; advance, $1,000–3,000

Guidelines: *www.franciscanmedia.org/writers-guidelines*

Tip: "Special consideration will be given to book proposals that show how the book relates to one or more of the teachings of St. Francis or the Franciscan charism."

GENERATION HOPE

PO Box 206, Nesbit, MS 38651 | 901-590-6584

submissions@endgamepress.com | *www.endgamepress.com/generation-hope*

Hope Bolinger, imprint editor

Parent company: End Game Press

Mission statement: to grow young writers, between the ages of 10 to 24, in their craft, encourage entrepreneurial pursuits, and publish their work to reach readers in their generation in a unique way

Submissions: First-time authors: 100%. Submit proposal with complete manuscript. Responds in two to three months. Bible: any.

Topics and genres: fiction: first-chapter, middle grade, teen/YA

Types of books: ebook, paperback

Guidelines: *www.endgamepress.com/submissions*

Tip: "We are looking for clean manuscripts that are safe for readers in the age group of the book, books that aren't afraid to tackle some harder issues, while still being filled with hope."

THE GOOD BOOK COMPANY

1805 Sardis Rd. N, Ste. 102, Charlotte, NC 28270 | 866-244-2165

submissions@thegoodbook.com | *www.thegoodbook.com*

Brian Thomasson, VP of editorial

Mission statement: to promote, encourage, and equip people to serve our Lord and Master Jesus Christ

Submissions: Email or mail proposal with sample chapters.

Topics and genres: Bible study, Christian living/spirituality, evangelism, children, devotionals, teen/YA

Types of books: ebook, paperback

Guidelines: *www.thegoodbook.com/authors*

Tip: "Our aim with all our resources is to get people directly interacting with the Bible. So we expect our authors to facilitate that process, rather than just commenting on their own view of what the Bible says. A primary question we ask of any resource submitted to us is: Does it handle the Bible well (i.e., taking note of the context of each passage), and is it helping people understand its message?"

GRACE ACRES PRESS

PO Box 22, Larkspur, CO 80118 | 303-681-9995

Anne@graceacrespress.com | *www.GraceAcresPress.com*

Anne R. Fenske, publisher

Parent company: Exegetica Publishing

Mission statement: to grow your faith one page at a time

Submissions: Publishes six titles per year; receives 20 submissions annually. First-time authors: 75%. Length: 100–300 pages. Email or mail query first. Responds in one month. Bible: NKJV, NIV.

Topics and genres: Bible study, biography, discipleship, evangelism, missions

Royalty: 10–15%, no advance

First print run: 500–2,000

Types of books: ebook, hardcover, offset paperback, POD

Guidelines: available via email.

Tip: "Explain your contribution as a copartner in marketing your book."

GRACE PUBLISHING

PO Box 1233, Broken Arrow, OK 74013-1233 | 918-346-7960

editorial@grace-publishing.com | *www.grace-publishing.com*

Terri Kalfas, publisher

Parent company: The Jomaga Group, LLC

Mission statement: to develop and distribute biblically based resources that challenge, encourage, teach, equip, and entertain Christians young and old in their personal journeys

Submissions: Publishes four to eight titles per year; receives 50 submissions annually. First-time authors: 50%. Length: 50,000 words. Agent not required. Conference contact, or email proposal with sample chapters. Responds in six months. Bible: any.

Topics and genres: Christian living/spirituality, anthologies, Bible studies, devotionals

Royalty: varies, no advance
Types of books: offset paperback, POD
Guidelines: *grace-publishing.com/manuscript-submission*
Tip: "Make sure your submission is something that makes people want to read the Bible for themselves in addition to reading books and studies about the Word."

GUIDEPOSTS BOOKS

110 William St., Ste. 901, New York, NY 10038 | 212-251-8100
bookeditors@guideposts.org | *www.guideposts.org*
Carolyn Mandarano, content team leader; cmandarano@guideposts.org
Jane Haertel, fiction editor; jhaertel@guideposts.org
Tarice Gray, acquisitions, devotionals; TGray@guideposts.org

Parent company: Guideposts, Inc.
Submissions: Publishes 20–30 titles per year. Agent only.
Topics and genres: Christian living/spirituality, memoir/personal narrative, devotionals; fiction: contemporary, women's
Tip: "For new Guideposts writers, devotionals require an audition by sending in three sample devotions. We select only a few new writers each year. Contributors write on a work-for-hire basis. Guideposts holds the copyright. For more information or to submit devotional auditions, please email Carolyn Mandarano."

HARAMBEE PRESS

PO Box 206, Nesbit, MS 38651 | 901-590-6584
submissions@endgamepress.com | *www.endgamepress.com/harambee-press*
Edwina Perkins, acquisitions editor

Parent company: End Game Press
Mission statement: to raise up the ethnic voice; and to give a place for BIPOC authors to communicate, through publication, with each other and the world
Submissions: Agent not required. Email proposal with sample chapters. Responds in two to three months. Bible: any.
Topics and genres: fiction, nonfiction, African American
Types of books: ebook, paperback
Guidelines: *www.endgamepress.com/submissions*
Tip: "We are looking for writers who want to express the diversity of their culture and writers who have stories or life lessons, whether through fiction or nonfiction. Authors should carry a message of hope and redemption."

HARBOURLIGHT BOOKS

PO Box 1738, Aztec, NM 87410

customer@harbourlightbooks.com | *www.pelicanbookgroup.com*

Nicola Martinez, editor-in-chief

Parent company: Pelican Book Group

Mission statement: to publish quality books that reflect the salvation and love offered by Jesus Christ

Submissions: Length: 25,000–80,000 words. Submit proposal with sample chapter through the website. Responds in three to four months. Bible: NIV, NAB.

Topics and genres: fiction: adventure, crime, family saga, mystery, suspense, westerns, women's

Royalty: 40% on download, 7% on print; sometimes gives advance

Types of books: audiobook, ebook, hardcover, offset paperback, POD

Guidelines: *tinyurl.com/22zruzzw*

HARPERCHRISTIAN RESOURCES

501 Nelson Pl., Nashville, TN 37214

harperchristianresources.com

Parent company: HarperCollins Christian Publishing

Mission statement: to equip people to understand the Scriptures, cultivate spiritual growth, and live an inspired faith with Bible study and video resources from today's most trusted voices

Topics and genres: Bible studies, ministry programs, small-group study guides

Types of books: offset paperback, video

HARPERCOLLINS CHRISTIAN PUBLISHING

HarperChristian Resourses

WestBow Press

Thomas Nelson: Emanate Books, Nelson Books, Thomas Nelson Fiction, Thomas Nelson Gift, Tommy Nelson, W Publishing Group, Grupo Nelson

Zondervan: Zonderkidz, Zondervan Academic, Zondervan Books, Zondervan Fiction, Zondervan Gift, Zondervan Reflective, Editorial Vida

HARPERONE

353 Sacramento St. #500, San Francisco, CA 94111-3653 | 415-477-4400

Anna.Paustenbach@harpercollins.com | *harperone.com*

Anna Paustenbach, executive editor

Parent company: HarperCollins Publishing
Mission statement: to publish books for the world we want to live in
Submissions: Publishes 75 titles per year; receives 10,000 submissions annually. First-time authors: 5%. Length: 160–256 pages. Agent only. Responds in three months.
Topics and genres: Christian living/spirituality
Royalty: 7.5–15%, gives advance
Types of books: ebook, hardcover, offset paperback
Imprint: Shelf-Seekers (millennials)

HARVEST HOUSE PUBLISHERS

PO Box 41210, Eugene, OR 97404-0322 | 800-547-8979

harvesthousepublishers.com

Audrey Greeson, acquisitions editor, nonfiction

Ruth Samsel, acquisitions editor, gifts

Kyle Hatfield, acquisitions editor, children and family

Emma Saisslin, acquisitions editor, nonfiction

Mission statement: to glorify God by providing high-quality books and products that affirm biblical values, help people grow spiritually strong, and proclaim Jesus Christ as the answer to every human need
Topics and genres: Christian living/spirituality, family, relationships, Bible reference/commentaries, Bible studies, children, fiction, gift books
Types of books: board books, ebook, hardcover, paperback
Imprints: Harvest Kids (children)

HENDRICKSON PUBLISHERS

PO Box 3473, Peabody, MA 01961-3473 | 800-358-3111

hannahterenzoni@tyndale.com | www.hendricksonrose.com

Hannah Terenzoni, publisher

Patricia Anders, editorial director

Parent company: Tyndale House Ministries
Mission statement: to meet the publication needs of the religious studies academic community worldwide and to produce thoughtful books for thoughtful Christians
Submissions: Publishes 16 titles per year; receives 50–100 submissions annually. First-time authors: 40%. Length: trade, 75-000–100,000 words; academic, 100,000–200,000 words. Only agent, *ChristianBookProposals.com*, or conference contact. Responds in two to three months.

Topics and genres: archaeology, church history, culture, marriage, ministry, parenting, theology, academic, Bible reference/commentaries, biblical studies, language studies

Royalty: 12–14%, gives advance

First print run: varies

Types of books: audiobook, ebook, hardcover, offset paperback

Imprints: Hendrickson Publishers (trade books), Hendrickson Academic (academic), Rose Publishing (Bible reference for everyone), RoseKidz (children), Aspire Press (counseling), Hendrickson Bibles (Bibles)

Guidelines: available via email

Tip: "Please be sure to look at our website to see what kind of books we publish."

INTERVARSITY PRESS

430 Plaza Dr., Westmont, IL 60559 | 630-734-4000

mail@ivpress.com | ivpress.com

Al Hsu, associate editorial director, trade and acquisitions
Ethan McCarthy, editorial assistant and acquisitions
Jon Boyd, editorial director, IVP Academic
Elissa Schauer, executive editor and IVP Kids editor
Cindy Bunch, VP of editorial and trade editorial director

Parent company: InterVarsity Christian Fellowship

Mission statement: to publish thoughtful Christian books that shape both the lives of readers and the cultures they inhabit, speaking boldly into important cultural moments, providing timeless tools for spiritual growth, and equipping Christians for a vibrant life of faith

Submissions: Publishes 100 titles per year; receives 800 submissions annually. First-time authors: 20%. Length: 30,000–100,000 words. Only agent or conference contact. Responds in three months. Bible: NIV.

Topics and genres: African-American, Asian, Bible study, Christian living/spirituality, church leadership, church life, counseling, culture, Hispanic, justice, ministry, psychology, spiritual formation, theology, academic, Bible reference/commentaries, Bible studies, children

Royalty: 14–18%, sometimes gives advance

Types of books: audiobook, ebook, hardcover, offset paperback, POD

Imprints: IVP Academic (undergraduate and graduate students, professors, scholars), IVP Formatio (spiritual formation), IVP Praxis (church leadership), IVP Kids (children)

Guidelines: available via email

Tip: "We accept submissions only from agents or from authors who have had direct contact with an editor."

INVITE RESOURCES

5700 W. Plano Pkwy., Ste. 1600, Plano, TX 75093 | 214-291-8094

lwagner@inviteresources.com | *www.inviteresources.com*

Lori Wagner, content editor

> **Denomination:** Wesleyan/Arminian
>
> **Parent company:** St. Andrew Methodist Church, Plano, Texas
>
> **Mission statement:** to share the promise of Christ's New Creation
>
> **Submissions:** Publishes 22–26 titles per year; receives 40 submissions annually. First-time authors: 30%. Length: 20,000–50,000 words. Agent not required. Email proposal with complete manuscript or sample chapters. Responds in two to four weeks. Bible: no preference.
>
> **Topics and genres:** Bible study, Christian living/spirituality, theology, academic, devotionals
>
> **Royalty:** 8–15%, no advance
>
> **Types of books:** ebook, hardcover, offset paperback, POD
>
> **Imprints:** Invite Press (trade books), Invite Academic (focus on the academy)
>
> **Guidelines:** *www.inviteresources.com/editorial-standards*
>
> **Tip:** "We are about accessible ideas, presented in an engaging and relatable fashion. This is not to say we want fluff; in fact, we desire books with academic rigor and theological reasoning, but without the difficult writing. We are not interested in boring books. We want our books to be approachable and helpful resources that speak to today's issues."

IRON STREAM MEDIA

100 Missionary Ridge, Birmingham, AL 35242 | 888-811-9934

submissions@ironstreammedia.com | *www.ironstreammedia.com*

Dr. John Herring, publisher

> **Submissions:** Publishes 20–25 titles per year; receives 150 submissions annually. First-time authors: 30%. Length: 50,000–90,000 words. Only agent or conference contact. Responds in three months. Bible: NASB.

Topics and genres: Christian living/spirituality, family, leadership, memoir/personal narrative, parenting, relationships, women, Bible studies, devotionals; fiction: romance, romantic suspense, speculative, suspense, westerns

Royalty: escalating, gives advance

Types of books: audiobook, ebook, offset paperback, POD

Imprints: Iron Stream (nonfiction), Iron Stream Fiction (novels), Iron Stream Kids (board and picture books, Bible storybooks), Brookstone Publishing Group (independent publishing), Life Bible Study (digital Bible study curriculum direct to churches)

Guidelines: *www.ironstreammedia.com/submission-process*

Tip: "Focus on hook, comps, and marketing sections in book proposal. Also, provide a great list of influencers."

JOURNEYFORTH

1430 Wade Hampton Blvd., Greenville, SC 29609 | 864-546-4600
journeyforth@bjupress.com | *www.bjupress.com/books/journeyforth*
Charlotte Bradley, acquisitions editor

Parent company: BJU Press

Mission statement: to provide well-written, biblically sound resources for readers of varying reading abilities and interests— books with a Christian worldview and excellent in every facet of their presentation

Submissions: Publishes two to five titles per year; receives 100–150 submissions annually. First-time authors: 45%. Length: ages 6–8, 8,000–10,000 words; ages 9–12, 30,000–40,000 words; ages 12 and up, 40,000–60,000 words. Email or mail proposal with sample chapters. Responds in four to six months. Bible: KJV, NKJV, ESV, NASB.

Topics and genres: Bible study, Christian living/spirituality, youth fiction, Bible studies, first-chapter, middle grade, teen/YA

Royalty: 10–15%, sometimes gives advance

Types of books: ebook, offset paperback

Guidelines: *www.bjupress.com/books/freelance.php*

Tip: "We use in-house authors for short stories, picture books, rhyming text, and poetry. Our market is not open to stories that include profanity or minced oaths, magic or witchcraft, time travel, and characters who engage in unscriptural activities without a biblical consequence."

JUDSON PRESS

1075 First Ave., King of Prussia, PA 19406 | 800-458-3766
acquisitions@judsonpress.com | *www.judsonpress.com*
Rachael Lawrence, senior editor

Denomination: American Baptist
Parent company: American Baptist Home Mission Societies
Mission statement: to produce Christ-centered leadership resources for the transformation of individuals, congregations, communities, and cultures
Submissions: Publishes 12 titles per year; receives 300 submissions annually. First-time authors: 25%. Length: 128–244 pages. Email or mail proposal with sample chapters or a query. Responds in three to six months. Bible: NRSV.
Topics and genres: African-American, Asian, Christian education, Christian living/spirituality, discipleship, Hispanic, history, ministry, church resources, devotionals, ministry resources
Royalty: 10–15%, sometimes gives advance
First print run: 2,500
Types of books: ebook, offset paperback, POD
Guidelines: *www.judsonpress.com/Pages/Info/For-Authors.aspx*
Tip: "Most open to practical books that are unique and compelling, for a clearly defined niche audience. Theologically and socially we are a moderate publisher. And we like to see a detailed marketing plan from an author committed to partnering with us."

KREGEL PUBLICATIONS

2450 Oak Industrial Dr. NE, Grand Rapids, MI 49505 | 616-451-4775
KPacquisitions@kregel.com | *www.kregel.com*
Lindsay Danielson, editorial coordinator
Janyre Tromp, acquisitions editor, fiction, women's
Robert Hand, academic director

Mission statement: to develop and distribute—with integrity and excellence—trusted, biblically based resources that lead individuals to know and serve Jesus Christ
Submissions: Only agent, *ChristianBookProposals.com*, Writers Edge, or conference contact.
Topics and genres: Bible study, biography, Christian living/ spirituality, church life, contemporary issues, discipleship, family, marriage, ministry, parenting, theology, women, Bible reference/ commentaries, Bible studies, children, devotionals, teen/YA;

fiction: historical, romance, romantic suspense, teen/YA

Guidelines: *www.kregel.com/contact-us/submissions-policy*

LEAFWOOD PUBLISHERS

1694 Campus Ct., ACU Box 29138, Abilene, TX 79699 | 325-674-2720

jason.fikes@acu.edu | www.leafwoodpublishers.com

Jason Fikes, director

Denomination: Church of Christ

Parent company: Abilene Christian University

Mission statement: to inspire fresh and deeper conversations about faith and life one book at a time

Submissions: Publishes 20 titles per year; receives 200 submissions annually. First-time authors: 40%. Length: 50,000 words. Agent preferred, submit to *ChristianBookProposals.com*, or send proposal with sample chapters through the website. Responds in at least six months. Bible: NIV.

Topics and genres: Bible studies, Christian living/spirituality, ministry, spiritual formation, spiritual growth, theology, women's interests

Royalty: negotiated based on experience, advance negotiated based on experience

First print run: 1,500

Types of books: ebook, hardcover, offset paperback

Guidelines: *store.acupressbooks.com/pages/author-resources*

Tip: "We enhance diverse and innovative authors (neurotypicals and those who are more atypical, age, gender, race, Christian tradition). Our audience is university based (Christian higher education) and laypeople. Fresh conversations require innovation, creativity, love, courage, humility, gentleness, hospitality, freedom, and grace. We talk a lot about being practical. Practical means 'Will this book inspire fresh and deep conversations about faith and life?'"

LEXHAM PRESS

1313 Commercial St., Bellingham, WA 98225

thains@lexhampress.com | www.lexhampress.com

Todd Hains, associate publisher for acquisitions

Parent company: FaithLife Corporation, makers of Logos Bible Software

Mission statement: to increase biblical literacy, thoughtful Christian reflection, and faithful action around the world by publishing a range of Bible study materials, scholarly works, and pastoral resources

Submissions: Submit proposal with sample chapters through the website.

Responds in eight weeks or not interested. Publishes innovative resources for Logos Bible Software.

Topics and genres: Bible study, ministry, theology, academic, Bible reference/commentaries, children

Types of books: ebook, hardcover, paperback

Imprints: Kirkdale Press (trade books)

Guidelines: *www.lexhampress.com/manuscript-submission*

LIGHTHOUSE PUBLISHING

754 Roxholly Walk, Buford, CA 30518 | 770-709-2268

info@lighthousechristianpublishing.com | *lighthousechristianpublishing.com*

Andy Overett, president

Parent company: Lighthouse eMedia and eMusic

Mission statement: to provide high-quality original works at the least possible prices

Submissions: Publishes 30 titles per year; receives 200 submissions annually. First-time authors: 80%. Length: fiction, 300–320 pages. Email proposal with complete manuscript. Responds in four to six weeks. Bible: NASB.

Topics and genres: African-American, Hispanic, all topics fiction and nonfiction

Royalty: 50%, no advance

Types of books: audiobook, ebook, POD

Guidelines: *lighthouseebooks.com/custom.html*

Tip: Looking for unique stories.

LIGUORI PUBLICATIONS

1 Liguori Dr., Liguori, MO 63057-9999 | 800-325-9521

manuscript_submission@liguori.org | *www.liguori.org*

Denomination: Catholic

Mission statement: to be the leading provider of Roman Catholic publications for every stage of faith and life in an ever-changing world

Submissions: No simultaneous submissions. Submit proposal with sample chapters. Responds in 8–12 weeks.

Topics and genres: sacraments, saints, Bible studies, biography, devotionals

LITURGICAL PRESS

PO Box 7500, Collegeville, MN 56321-7500

submissions@litpress.org | www.litpress.org

Denomination: Catholic

Mission statement: to cultivate and amplify texts and voices that deepen the faith and knowledge of a richly diverse Church

Submissions: Submit proposal with sample chapters or complete manuscript through the website. Responds in six weeks.

Topics and genres: Bible, liturgy, prayer, theology

Guidelines: *www.litpress.org/Authors/submit_manuscript*

LOVE INSPIRED

195 Broadway, 24th floor, New York, NY 10007 | 212-207-7900

www.LoveInspired.com

Tina James, executive editor, Love Inspired Suspense

Melissa Endlich, senior editor, Love Inspired

Emily Rodmell, editor

Shana Asaro, editor

Parent company: Harlequin/HarperCollins Publishers

Mission statement: to uplift and inspire through stories

Submissions: Publishes 144 titles per year; receives 500–1,000 submissions annually. First-time authors: 15%. Length: 55,000 words. Agent not required. Submit complete manuscript through the website. Responds in three months. Bible: KJV.

Topics and genres: fiction: romance, romantic suspense

Royalty: on retail, gives advance

Types of books: mass-market paperback

Imprints: Love Inspired (contemporary romance), Love Inspired Suspense (contemporary romantic suspense)

Guidelines: *harlequin.submittable.com/submit*

Tip: "We're looking for compelling stories with engaging characters, a sustained conflict, and an emotionally satisfying romance."

LOVE2READLOVE2WRITE PUBLISHING, LLC

PO Box 103, Camby, IN 46113 | 317-550-9755

editor@love2readlove2writepublishing.com | www.love2readlove2writepublishing.com

Michele Israel Harper, acquisitions editor

Mission statement: to publish compelling stories masterfully told, all in the fantasy or science fiction genres and their many subgenres

Submissions: Publishes four to six titles per year; receives 200+ submissions annually. First-time authors: 40%. Length: 60,000–120,000 words. Agent preferred or conference contact. Email proposal with sample chapters. Responds in two to three months. Bible: NKJV.

Topics and genres: fiction: alternative history, fantasy, horror, legends and myths, paranormal, science fiction, space opera, speculative, steampunk, superhero, supernatural, time travel

Royalty: 25–50%, advance $50

Types of books: ebook, hardcover, POD

Guidelines: available on website.

Guidelines: *love2readlove2writepublishing.com/submissions*

Tip: "We publish clean or Christian speculative fiction, and we prefer to work with professional authors who will partner with us to get their books in front of as many readers as possible, as well as who wish to build a long-lasting and sustainable career. Please only submit well-edited manuscripts and proposals. We would love to diversify our titles with underrepresented ethnic authors."

LOYOLA PRESS

8770 W. Bryn Mawr Ave., Chicago, IL 60631-3515 | 773-281-1818
submissions@loyolapress.com | *www.loyolapress.com*
Gary Jansen, executive editor, acquisitions

Denomination: Catholic

Mission statement: to create books and multimedia products that facilitate transformative experiences of God so that people of all ages can lead holy and purposeful lives with and for others

Submissions: Publishes 20 titles per year; receives 500 submissions annually. Length: 25,000–75,000 words/150–300 pages. Email or mail query. Responds in four to six weeks. Bible: NRSV (Catholic Edition).

Topics and genres: Catholicism, Christian living/spirituality

Royalty: gives advance

Types of books: paperback

Guidelines: *www.loyolapress.com/general/submissions*

Tip: "Looking for books and authors that help make Catholic faith relevant and offer practical tools for the well-lived spiritual life."

MOODY PUBLISHERS

820 N. LaSalle Blvd., Chicago, IL 60610 | 800-678-8812
submissions@moody.edu | *www.moodypublishers.com*

Trillia Newbell, acquisitions director

Judy Dunagan, acquisitions editor, women and Bible study

John Hinkley, acquisitions editor, marriage, family, parenting, workplace, church

Catherine Strode Parks, acquisitions editor

Parent company: Moody Bible Institute

Mission statement: to resource the church's work of discipling all people

Submissions: Publishes 50 titles per year; receives thousands of submissions annually. First-time authors: 20%. Length: depends on genre. Agent preferred, conference contact, or proposal with sample chapters. Responds in six to eight weeks. "Most open to books that (1) have a great idea at the core, (2) are executed well, and (3) can demonstrate an audience clamoring for the content."

Topics and genres: Christian living/spirituality, counseling, leadership, women, Bible studies, devotionals, middle grade

Royalty: gives advance

Types of books: audiobook, ebook, hardcover, offset paperback

Guidelines: *www.moodypublishers.com/About/faq/submitting-proposals*

Tip: "Please review our website to see the latest books to help determine what we are looking for."

MOUNTAIN BROOK FIRE

submissions@fire.mountainbrookink.com | fire.mountainbrookink.com

Alyssa Roat, managing editor

Parent company: Mountain Brook Ink

Mission statement: to publish quality worldbuilding, spellbinding plots, and high-stakes adventures with a whole lot of heart for middle grade, young adult, and adult audiences

Submissions: Length: middle grade, 50,000–65,000 words; YA, 75,000–100,000 words; adult, 80,000–120,000 words. Conference contact only. Responds in two months. Bible: KJV, NKJV, NIV.

Topics and genres: fiction: middle grade, YA, fantasy, science fiction, speculative, steampunk, superhero, supernatural

Royalty: 30–40%, gives advance of $25

Types of books: audiobook, ebook, POD

Guidelines: *fire.mountainbrookink.com/submission-guidelines*

Tip: "Manuscripts need not be explicitly 'Christian'; we are equally happy with general market. However, we're looking for fiction that is clean. Books having a Christian worldview without having a faith thread will work as well."

MOUNTAIN BROOK INK

submissions@mountainbrookink.com | *www.mountainbrookink.com*

Miralee Ferrell, publisher and lead acquisitions editor

Mission statement: to publish fiction you can believe in that embodies restoration and/or renewal

Submissions: Publishes 12 titles per year; receives 50+ submissions annually. First-time authors: 75%. Length: minimum 75,000 words. Email proposal with sample chapters or a query. Responds in two months. Bible: KJV, NKJV, NIV.

Topics and genres: fiction: biblical, contemporary, historical, mystery, romance, romantic suspense, suspense/thriller, women's

Royalty: 30–40%, gives advance of $25

Types of books: audiobook, ebook, POD

Imprints: Mountain Brook Fire (speculative fiction)

Guidelines: *mountainbrookink.com/submission-guidelines-for-inquiries*

Tip: "Send the best work you've done, preferably that's been edited so it shines."

MT ZION RIDGE PRESS

295 Gum Springs Rd. NW, Georgetown, TN 37336 | 423-458-4256

mtzionridgepress@gmail.com | *mtzionridgepress.com*

Tamera Lynn Kraft, managing editor

Mission statement: to publish Christian fiction off the beaten path and Christian nonfiction for those who want to go deeper in their faith

Submissions: Publishes 12–15 titles per year; receives 30 submissions annually. First-time authors: 70%. Length: 60,000–100,000 words. Agent not required. Conference contact, or email query first. Responds in two to three months. Bible: NIV, NKJV, ESV, NLT, KJV.

Topics and genres: Christian living/spirituality, Bible studies, children, devotionals; fiction: fantasy, historical, mystery, romance, romantic suspense, science fiction, speculative, suspense/thriller, teen/YA, westerns, women's

Royalty: 30%, no advance

Types of books: audiobook, ebook, offset paperback, POD

Guidelines: *www.mtzionridgepress.com/about*

Tip: "Submit stellar writing."

MY HEALTHY CHURCH

1445 N. Boonville Ave., Springfield, MO 65802 | 417-831-8000

newproducts@myhealthychurch.com | *www.myhealthychurch.com*

Denomination: Assemblies of God

Parent company: Gospel Publishing House

Mission statement: to equip believers and church leaders who seek a healthy, Spirit-empowered life

Submissions: Agent only. Responds in two to three months.

Topics and genres: Christian living/spirituality, church leadership, discipleship, leadership, ministry, academic, Bible studies, church resources

Types of books: ebook, hardcover, paperback

Guidelines: *myhealthychurch.com/store/startcat.cfm?cat=tWRITGUID*

Tip: "The content of all our books and resources must be compatible with the beliefs and purposes of the Assemblies of God."

NAVPRESS

3820 N. 30th St., Colorado Springs, CO 80904

inquiries@navpress.com | *www.navpress.com*

Caitlyn Carlson, acquisitions editor

Deborah Gonzalez, associate acquisitions and developmental editor

Parent company: The Navigators

Mission statement: to support readers as they know Christ, make Him known, and help others do the same

Submissions: Publishes 20 titles per year; receives 1,000 submissions annually. First-time authors: 40%. Length: 40,000 words. Agent only. Responds in two months.

Topics and genres: Christian living/spirituality, discipleship, leadership, practical theology, prayer, spiritual growth, women, Bible studies

Royalty: 16–22%, gives advance

Guidelines: *www.navpress.com/faq*

Tip: "Proposals with strong discipleship elements are preferred. Authors should have a ministry platform that supports their discipleship elements. NavPress does not accept unsolicited manuscripts."

NELSON BOOKS

PO Box 141000, Nashville, TN 37214-1000 | 615-889-9000

www.thomasnelson.com/nelsonbooks

Janet Hill Talbert, senior acquisitions editor

Jennifer Smith, acquisitions and VP of marketing

Parent company: Thomas Nelson Publishers/HarperCollins

Christian Publishing

Mission statement: to publish biblically informed books from a Christian perspective that enhance the spiritual and personal growth of our readers

Submissions: Agent only.

Topics and genres: biography, business, Christian living/spirituality, leadership, spiritual growth, devotionals

Types of books: audiobook, ebook, hardcover, offset paperback

Guidelines: not available

NEW GROWTH PRESS

PO Box 4485, Greensboro, NC 27404 | 336-378-7775

submissions@newgrowthpress.com | www.newgrowthpress.com

Rush Witt, acquisitions editor and manager

Mission statement: to reach every church and home with gospel-centered resources that point to Jesus and help every person grow closer to Christ

Submissions: Email proposal with sample chapters. Responds in six weeks or not interested.

Topics and genres: Christian living/spirituality, counseling, family, parenting, relationships, Bible studies, children, devotionals, fiction, teen/YA

Types of books: audiobook, ebook, paperback

Guidelines: *newgrowthpress.com/manuscript-submissions*

Tip: "Manuscript submissions must follow the downloadable, standard New Growth Press template."

NEW LIFE PUBLISHING HOUSE

1041 N.E. 208th St., Miami, FL 33179 | 305-742-4602

admin@newlifepublishinghouse.life | newlifepublishinghouse.life

Tassyane Assis, publisher

Mission statement: to do more than publish books, to help authors build their legacies

Submissions: First-time authors: 100%. Length: 30,000–50,000 words. Email or mail proposal with sample chapters, or use the website form. No agents. Conference contact a plus. Responds in two to four weeks. Offers writing coaching for new writers who do not know how to get started. Also publishes general-market books that add value to readers as long as they do not contradict the Bible in any way.

Topics and genres: Christian living/spirituality, family, finances, marriage, parenting, psychology, self-help, devotionals
Royalty: 70%, no advance
Types of books: audiobook, ebook, hardcover, offset paperback, POD
Guidelines: available via email
Tip: "Writing a book and getting it published with the right people is more than about the money. It's about the legacy you are leaving behind."

NORTHWESTERN PUBLISHING HOUSE

N16W23379 Stone Ridge Dr., Waukesha, WI 53188-1108 | 800-662-6022
submissions@nph.wels.net | online.nph.net
John Braun

Denomination: Wisconsin Evangelical Lutheran Synod
Mission statement: to deliver biblically sound, Christ-centered resources within the Wisconsin Evangelical Lutheran Synod and beyond
Submissions: Email or mail proposal with sample chapters.
Topics and genres: family, history, theology, Bible reference/ commentaries, devotionals
Types of books: hardcover, paperback
Guidelines: *online.nph.net/manuscript-submission*
Tip: "We are always looking for new and exciting Bible-based materials to publish!"

OLIVIA KIMBRELL PRESS

PO Box 470, Fort Knox, KY 40121-0470 | 859-577-1071
admin@oliviakimbrellpress.com | myokpress.com
Gregg Bridgeman, editor-in-chief

Submissions: Specializes in true-to-life, meaningful Christian fiction and nonfiction titles intended to uplift the heart and engage the mind. Primary focus on "Roman Road" small-group guides or reader's guides to accompany nonfiction and fiction.
Topics and genres: Christian living/spirituality, family, health, social issues, devotionals; fiction: biblical, contemporary, fantasy, historical romance, military, mystery, romance, romantic suspense, science fiction, speculative, suspense
Types of books: ebook, paperback
Imprints: CAVË (historical fiction around the time of Christ), Sign of the Whale (biblical and speculative fiction), House of Bread (nutrition)

Guidelines: *myokpress.com/editorial-standards/submission-guidelines*
Tip: "Must meet our stated editorial standards. Follow our submission guidelines. Fiction series preferred over standalone titles. Complete manuscripts only."

OUR DAILY BREAD PUBLISHING

3000 Kraft Ave. SE, Grand Rapids, MI 49507 | 616-974-2210
Katara.patton@odb.org | ourdailybreadpublishing.org
Katara Patton, senior editor

Parent company: Our Daily Bread Ministries
Mission statement: to feed the soul with the Word of God
Submissions: Publishes 24–36 titles per year; receives 100 submissions annually. First-time authors: fewer than 10%. Length: approximately 192 pages. Agent preferred or conference contact. Responds in three months. Bible: NIV, NLT, ESV.
Topics and genres: African-American, Asian, Bible study, Christian living/spirituality, contemporary issues, Hispanic, men, pop reference, prayer, social issues, women, Bible studies, children, devotionals
Royalty: 12–18%, no advance
First print run: 3,000–50,000
Types of books: audiobook, board books, ebook, hardcover, offset paperback
Imprints: VOICES Collection (primarily African Americans)
Guidelines: not available
Tip: "We look for strong Bible-based content with practical application for everyday living."

OUR SUNDAY VISITOR, INC.

200 Noll Plaza, Huntington, IN 46750-4303 | 260-356-8400
www.osv.com
Scott Richert, publisher

Denomination: Catholic
Mission statement: to help Catholics fulfill their calling to discipleship, strengthen their relationship with Christ, deepen their commitment to the Church, and contribute to its growth and vitality in the world
Submissions: Publishes 30–40 titles per year; receives 500 submissions annually. First-time authors: 10%. No simultaneous submissions. Query first through the website. Responds in 8–10

weeks. Actively seeking submissions for children: board books for infants and toddlers, picture books for younger readers (ages 3-6), short chapter books for middle-grade readers (ages 7-10), and works of interest to tweens and young teens.

Topics and genres: apologetics, biography, Christian living/spirituality, church life, culture, evangelism, family, history, marriage, ministry, parenting, prayer, children, devotionals, prayer guides

Royalty: 10-12%; advance, $1,500

Types of books: board books, ebook, hardcover, paperback, picture books

Imprints: OSV Kids (children and teens)

Guidelines: *osv.submittable.com/submit*

Tip: "All books published must relate to the Catholic Church; unique books aimed at our audience. Give as much background information as possible on author qualification, why the topic was chosen, and unique aspects of the project. Follow our guidelines. We are expanding our religious-education product line and programs."

P&R PUBLISHING

1102 Marble Hill Rd., Phillipsburg, NJ 08865 | 908-454-0505
submissions@prpbooks.com | *www.prpbooks.com*
David Almack, acquisitions director
Amanda Martin, editorial director
Melissa Craig, children's editor

Denomination: Reformed

Mission statement: to serve Christ and His church by producing clear, engaging, fresh, and insightful applications of Reformed theology to life

Submissions: Publishes 40 titles per year; receives 200 submissions annually. First-time authors: 10-15%. Length: 40,000-50,000 words. Email proposal with sample chapters through the website. Responds in three months. Bible: ESV.

Topics and genres: Christian living/spirituality, counseling, parenting, prayer, theology, women, academic, children, devotionals

Royalty: 14-16%, sometimes gives advance

First print run: 3,000-5,000

Types of books: audiobook, ebook, hardcover, offset paperback

Guidelines: *www.prpbooks.com/manuscript-submissions*

Tip: "We are looking for authors with a Reformed theological conviction, and we utilize the Westminster Confession of Faith as a guideline."

PACIFIC PRESS

PO Box 5353, Nampa, ID 83653-5353 | 208-465-2500

booksubmissions@pacificpress.com | *www.pacificpress.com*

Scott Cady, acquisitions editor

Denomination: Seventh-day Adventist

Parent company: Seventh-day Adventist Church

Mission statement: to provide readers with a wide variety of books that connect them with God and help them develop a relationship with Him; provide information about God, His character, and His ways; and encourage and uplift them in the struggles of life

Submissions: Publishes 35–40 titles per year; receives 500 submissions annually. First-time authors: 5%. Length: 40,000–90,000 words/128–320 pages. Email query first. Responds in one to three weeks.

Topics and genres: Bible study, biography, Christian living/ spirituality, contemporary issues, health, history, marriage, memoir/personal narrative, parenting, prayer, theology, children; fiction: end times, historical

Royalty: 12–16%; advance, $1,500

Types of books: ebook, hardcover, paperback, picture books

Guidelines: *www.pacificpress.com/authors___artists/books*

Tip: "Most open to spirituality, inspirational, and Christian living. Our website has the most up-to-date information, including samples of recent publications. For more information, see *www. adventistbookcenter.com*. Do not send full manuscript unless we request it after reviewing your proposal."

PARACLETE PRESS

PO Box 1568, Orleans, MA 02653-1568 | 508-255-4685

submissions@paracletepress.com | *www.paracletepress.com*

Lillian Miao, director

Denomination: Catholic, Protestant

Submissions: Publishes 40 titles per year. Agent only or author with Paraclete relationship. Responds in one month.

Topics and genres: Advent/Christmas picture books, Christian living/spirituality, grief, Lent/Easter picture books, prayer, children; fiction: contemporary, fantasy, horror, science fiction

Imprint: Raven (fiction)

Guidelines: *www.paracletepress.com/pages/submission-guidelines*

PARAKLESIS PRESS

113 Winn Ct., Waleska, GA 30183 | 404-274-8615
submissions@paraklesispress.com | *ParaklesisPress.com*
Sally Apokedak, editor

Mission statement: to delight children with fun language; smart, humble, comical, relatable characters; charming illustrations; and exciting plots, all while also giving these young minds plenty of food for thought

Submissions: Publishes four titles per year; receives 75 submissions annually. First-time authors: 50%. Length: 32–400 pages. Email proposal with complete manuscript. Responds in three months. Bible: ESV.

Topics and genres: children: picture books, contemporary, fantasy, mystery

Royalty: 10–50%, gives advance

Types of books: POD hardcover and paperback

Guidelines: *paraklesispress.com/submit-to-us*

Tip: "Write something interesting and entertaining that doesn't need a ton of editing and that is not offensive to Christians and you'll have a good chance of getting published here."

PARSONS PUBLISHING HOUSE, LLC

PO Box 410063, Melbourne, FL 32941 | 850-867-3061
info@parsonspublishinghouse.com | *www.parsonspublishinghouse.com*
Diane Parsons, owner and senior editor

Mission statement: to allow authors' voices to be heard as they lift up the name of Jesus Christ

Submissions: Publishes four to six titles per year; receives 20 submissions annually. First-time authors: 35%. Length: 40,000 words. Submit by email. No agents. Responds in three to four weeks. Bible: NKJV, ESV.

Topics and genres: Christian living/spirituality, spiritual growth

Royalty: 10%, no advance

Types of books: ebook, hardcover, offset paperback, POD

Guidelines: available via email

Tip: "Use scriptural teachings that point to the good news of the Gospel of Christ (uplifting/positive)."

PAULINE BOOKS & MEDIA

50 Saint Paul's Ave., Boston, MA 02130-3491 | 617-522-8911
editorial@paulinemedia.com | *pauline.org/PBMPublishing*

Denomination: Catholic

Parent company: Daughters of St. Paul

Mission statement: to help people know and love God and live their relationship with God in their everyday lives

Submissions: Publishes 20 titles per year; receives 300+ submissions annually. First-time authors: 10%. Length: 10,000–60,000 words. Email or mail proposal with sample chapters. Responds in six to eight weeks. Bible: NRSV.

Topics and genres: Christian living/spirituality, evangelism, family, prayer, spiritual formation, theology, activities and puzzles, board books, children, first-chapter, middle grade, picture books, prayer guides, teen/YA; fiction: teen/YA

Royalty: 5–10%, gives advance

Types of books: ebook, paperback

Imprints: Pauline Kids, Pauline TEEN

Guidelines: *tinyurl.com/mr2e8zny*

PAULIST PRESS

997 Macarthur Blvd., Mahwah, NJ 07430-9990

submissions@paulistpress.com | *www.paulistpress.com*

Donna Crilly, senior academic editor

Denomination: Catholic

Mission statement: to publish quality materials that bring the good news of the Gospel to Catholics and people of other religious traditions; support dialogue and welcome good scholarship and religious wisdom from all sources across denominational boundaries; foster religious values and wholeness in society, especially through materials promoting healing, reconciliation, and personal growth

Submissions: Email or mail proposal with sample chapters. Responds in six to eight weeks.

Topics and genres: academic, children, nonfiction

Types of books: ebook, paperback

Guidelines: *www.paulistpress.com/Pages/Center/auth_res_0.aspx*

PELICAN BOOK GROUP

Harbourlight Books, Prism Book Group, Pure Amore, Watershed Books, White Rose Publishing

PRAYERSHOP PUBLISHING

PO Box 10667, Terre Haute, IN 47802 | 812-238-5504

jon@prayershop.org | prayershop.org
Jonathan Graf, publisher

Parent company: Harvest Prayer Ministries, Church Prayer Leaders Network

Mission statement: to encourage and equip individuals and local-church prayer leaders to grow prayer in their spheres of influence

Submissions: Publishes six to eight titles per year; receives 15-25 submissions annually. First-time authors: 25%. Length: 80-144 pages. Email or mail proposal with complete manuscript or sample chapters. Responds in six to ten weeks. Bible: NIV. "We are looking for prayer topics that would move believers from just praying for their own needs to prayer that is focused on growing God's Kingdom."

Topics and genres: prayer, revival, devotionals, prayer guides

Royalty: 10-15%, no advance

First print run: 1,000-5,000

Types of books: ebook, offset paperback

Guidelines: not available

Tip: "Currently looking for book manuscripts, booklets, and materials that can be formatted into training kits. We are mostly interested in products that will in some way enhance the prayer life of a local church."

PRISM BOOK GROUP

PO Box 1738, Aztec, NM 87410
customer@prismbookgroup.com | www.prismbookgroup.com
Jacqueline Hopper, acquisitions editor; jhopper@prismbookgroup.com
Paula Mowery, acquisitions editor; pmowery@prismbookgroup.com

Parent company: Pelican Book Group

Mission statement: to publish quality books that reflect the salvation and love offered by Jesus Christ

Submissions: Length: 25,000-80,000 words. Submit proposal with sample chapters through the website. Responds in three to four months. Bible: NIV, NAB.

Topics and genres: fiction: contemporary, fantasy, historical, mystery, romance, romantic suspense, science fiction, suspense/thriller, teen/YA

Royalty: 40% download, 7% print; sometimes gives advance

Types of books: ebook, POD

Imprints: Prism Lux (Christian), Prism CW (clean and wholesome)

Guidelines: *pelicanbookgroup.com/ec/index.php?main_page=page&id=76*
Tip: "Our books offer clean and compelling reads for the discerning reader. We will not publish graphic language or content and look for well-written, emotionally charged stories, intense plots, and captivating characters."

PURE AMORE

PO Box 1738, Aztec, NM 87410

customer@pelicanbookgroup.com | *pelicanbookgroup.com*

Nicola Martinez, editor-in-chief

Parent company: Pelican Book Group
Mission statement: to publish quality books that reflect the salvation and love offered by Jesus Christ
Submissions: Length: 40,000–45,000 words. Submit proposal with sample chapters through the website. Responds in one to four months. Only contemporary Christian romance. Pure Amore romances are sweet in tone and in conflict. These stories are the emotionally driven tales of youthful Christians between the ages of 21 and 33 who are striving to live their faith in a world where Christ-centered choices may not fully be understood.
Topics and genres: fiction: romance
Royalty: 40% download, 7% print; sometimes gives advance
Types of books: ebook, POD
Guidelines: *pelicanbookgroup.com/ec/index.php?main_page=page&id=69*
Tip: "Pure Amore romances emphasize the beauty in chastity, so physical interactions, such as kissing or hugging, should focus on the characters' emotions, rather than heightened sexual desire; and scenes of physical intimacy should be integral to the plot and/or emotional development of the character or relationship."

RESOURCE PUBLICATIONS

199 W. 8th Ave., Ste. 3, Eugene, OR 97401 | 541-344-1528

proposal@wipfandstock.com

wipfandstock.com/search-results/?imprint=resource-publications

Parent company: Wipf and Stock
Submissions: Email proposal with sample chapters. Responds in one to two months.
Topics and genres: biography, fiction, poetry, sermons
Types of books: ebook, POD
Guidelines: *wipfandstock.com/submitting-a-proposal*

RESURRECTION PRESS

77 West End Rd., Totowa, NJ 07572 | 973-890-2400

info@catholicbookpublishing.com | *www.catholicbookpublishing.com*

Anthony Buono, editor

Denomination: Catholic

Parent company: Catholic Book Publishing Corp.

Submissions: Mail proposal with sample chapters. Responds in four to six weeks.

Topics and genres: Christian living/spirituality, healing, ministry, prayer

Royalty: negotiable, no advance

Guidelines: *www.catholicbookpublishing.com/page/faq#manuscript*

REVELL

6030 E. Fulton Rd., Ada, MI 49301 | 616-676-9185

bakerpublishinggroup.com/revell

Andrea Doering, editorial director

Kelsey Bowen, senior acquisitions editor

Rachel McRae, acquisitions editor

Grace Cho, nonfiction acquisitions editor

Parent company: Baker Publishing Group

Mission statement: to publish practical books that will help bring the Christian faith to everyday life

Submissions: Only agent, *ChristianBookProposals.com,* or conference contact.

Topics and genres: apologetics, Bible study, biography, Christian living/spirituality, church life, culture, family, marriage, memoir/personal narrative, children, fiction, teen/YA

Types of books: ebook, hardcover, mass-market paperback, offset paperback

ROSE PUBLISHING

PO Box 3473, Peabody, MA 01961 | 800-358-3111

lpennings@tyndale.com | *www.hendricksonrose.com*

Lynette Pennings, managing editor

Parent company: Hendrickson Publishing Group/Tyndale House Ministries

Mission statement: to make the Bible and its teachings easy to understand

Topics and genres: Bible reference, pamphlets, wall charts

Types of books: hardcover, paperback

ROSEKIDZ

PO Box 3473, Peabody, MA 01961 | 800-358-3111

kmcgraw@tyndale.com | www.hendricksonrose.com

Karen McGraw, senior acquisitions editor

Parent company: Hendrickson Publishing Group/Tyndale House Ministries

Mission statement: to help kids grow closer to God in a hands-on way

Submissions: Email manuscript.

Topics and genres: activities and puzzles, children, crafts, devotionals, fiction

Types of books: board books, hardcover, offset paperback, PDF download

SALEM BOOKS

300 New Jersey Ave. NW, Ste. 500, Washington, DC 20001

www.regnery.com/custom/salem-books

Kathyrn Riggs, senior acquisitions editor

Parent company: Regnery Publishing/Salem Media Group

Mission statement: to help people grow in their faith and find comfort, encouragement, practical advice, and timeless wisdom in compelling books by trusted authors

Submissions: Agent only.

Topics and genres: apologetics, Christian living/spirituality, culture, end-times prophecy, family, leadership, memoir/personal narrative, men, spiritual formation, spiritual growth, women, women's issues, worldview, biography, devotionals, memoir

Types of books: ebook, paperback

Tip: Especially interested in books by female and minority authors.

SCEPTER PUBLISHERS

PO Box 360694, Strongsville, OH 44136 | 212-354-0670

info@scepterpublishers.org | www.scepterpublishers.org

Nathan Davis, editor

Denomination: Catholic

Mission statement: to help people find God in ordinary life and realize sanctity in work, family life, and everyday activities

Submissions: Publishes 8–18 titles per year. Query through the website.

Topics and genres: Christian living/spirituality

Types of books: ebook, paperback

Guidelines: *scepterpublishers.org/pages/publishing-services*

SCRIVENINGS PRESS

15 Lucky Ln., Morrilton, AR 72110 | 501-289-9319
scriveningspress@gmail.com | *scriveningspress.com*
Linda Fulkerson, owner and acquisitions editor

Mission statement: to spread God's word through our writing

Submissions: Publishes 36 titles per year; receives 100 submissions annually. First-time authors: 30%. Length: 55,000–100,000 words. Agent not required. Conference contact a plus. Email proposal with complete manuscript or sample chapters through the website. Responds in four to six weeks. Bible: any.

Topics and genres: writing craft, devotionals; fiction: novella collections, historical, mystery, romance, romantic suspense, women's

Royalty: 12% print, 50% ebook, 40% pages read in Kindle Unlimited; no advance

Types of books: ebook, hardcover, POD

Imprints: Scrivenings Press (general fiction), Expanse Books (speculative fiction), ScrivKids (upper middle grade/YA), Ideas to Books (writing craft), ScrivInspire (niche devotionals)

Guidelines: *scriveningspress.com/submissions*

Tip: "We are a small publishing house, and we try to keep a family feel among our staff and authors. We encourage all our authors to encourage one another and to cross-promote books from other authors within our company."

SCRIVKIDS

15 Lucky Ln., Morrilton, AR 72110 | 501-289-9319
scriveningspress@gmail.com | *scrivkids.com*
Linda Fulkerson, owner and acquisitions editor

Parent company: Scrivenings Press, LLC

Mission statement: to spread God's word through our writing

Submissions: Publishes two or three titles per year; receives 100 submissions annually. First-time authors: 30%. Length: 30,000–50,000 words. Agent not required. Conference contact a plus. Email proposal with sample chapters through the website. Responds in four to six weeks. Bible: any.

Topics and genres: fiction: middle grade

Royalty: 12% print, 50% ebook, 40% pages read in Kindle Unlimited; no advance

Types of books: ebook, hardcover, POD

Guidelines: *scriveningspress.com/submissions*

Tip: "We are a small publishing house, and we try to keep a family feel among our staff and authors. We encourage all our authors to encourage one another and to cross-promote books from other authors within our company."

SMYTH & HELWYS BOOKS

6316 Peake Rd., Macon, GA 31210-3960 | 478-757-0564

proposal@helwys.com | *www.helwys.com*

Leslie Andres, editor

Mission statement: to contribute to the life and ministry of the church and provide a bridge between the church and the academy

Submissions: Email or mail proposal with sample chapters. Responds in several weeks.

Topics and genres: Bible study, Christian living/spirituality, leadership, ministry

Types of books: ebook, hardcover, paperback

Guidelines: *www.helwys.com/submit-a-manuscript*

THOMAS NELSON FICTION

PO Box 141000, Nashville, TN 37214-1000 | 615-889-9000

www.thomasnelson.com/fiction

Laura Wheeler, acquisitions editor

Parent company: Thomas Nelson Publishers/HarperCollins Christian Publishing

Mission statement: to inspire the world by meeting the needs of people with content that promotes biblical principles and honors Jesus Christ

Submissions: Agent only.

Topics and genres: fiction: historical, humor, mystery, romance, suspense/thriller

Types of books: audiobook, ebook, offset paperback

Guidelines: not available

Tip: "What we are looking for: great writers who are passionate about their stories, a willingness to work hard and engage with readers—coupled with a true love of readers—a unique angle on or a unique connection to their story matter, a great attitude."

THOMAS NELSON GIFT

PO Box 141000, Nashville, TN 37214-1000 | 615-889-9000

www.thomasnelson.com/gift

Adria Haley, senior acquisitions editor

Parent company: Thomas Nelson Publishers/HarperCollins Christian Publishing

Mission statement: to inspire the world by meeting the needs of people with content that promotes biblical principles and honors Jesus Christ

Submissions: Agent only.

Topics and genres: devotionals, gift books

Types of books: ebook, hardcover, offset paperback

Guidelines: not available

Tip: "A gift book is designed to be shared. It's a beautiful keepsake that makes an ideal gift, a way to mark a special occasion or holiday, a message of the heart; and it usually satisfies a strong felt need. Featuring two or four-color interiors, sometimes photography or illustrations, and beautiful covers complete with special effects like foil, fabric, gilding, and padding, gift books are as much an experience as a collection of words to be read."

THOMAS NELSON PUBLISHERS

Emanate Books, Grupo Nelson, Nelson Books, Thomas Nelson Fiction, Thomas Nelson Gift, Tommy Nelson, W Publishing, WestBow Press

TOMMY NELSON

PO Box 141000, Nashville, TN 37214-1000 | 615-889-9000

www.tommynelson.com

Mackenzie Howard, associate publisher

Parent company: Thomas Nelson Publishers/HarperCollins Christian Publishing

Mission statement: to expand children's imaginations and nurture their faith while pointing them to a personal relationship with God

Submissions: Only agent or conference contact.

Topics and genres: Bible storybooks, board books, devotionals, first-chapter, middle grade, picture books

Types of books: board books, hardcover, offset paperback, picture books

THE TRINITY FOUNDATION

PO Box 68, Unicoi, TN 37692 | 423-743-0199

tjtrinityfound@aol.com | *www.trinityfoundation.org*

Thomas W. Juodaitis, president

Mission statement: to promote the Christian religion

Submissions: Publishes two or three titles per year; receives five submissions annually. First-time authors: 5%. Length: 100-200 pages. Email or mail proposal with sample chapters. Responds in two weeks. Bible: KJV, NKJV.

Topics and genres: philosophy, theology

Royalty: flat fee only, $1,500-2,000; no advance

First print run: 1,000-1,500

Types of books: ebook, offset paperback

Guidelines: not available

Tip: "Follow content on website."

TULIP PUBLISHING

PO Box 3150, Lansvale, NSW 2166, Australia | +61 2 9055 2195

submissions@tulippublishing.com.au | *tulippublishing.com.au*

Brett Lee-Price, general manager

Denomination: Reformed

Mission statement: to equip the Church with resources that will help stretch and grow readers in their spiritual formulation, development, and knowledge

Submissions: Publishes four titles per year; receives 20 submissions annually. First-time authors: 40%. Length: 250-350 pages. Email proposal with sample chapters through the website. Responds in two to three months. Bible: ESV.

Topics and genres: Christian living/spirituality, theology

Royalty: 30-40%, no advance

First print run: 1,000

Types of books: ebook, hardcover, offset paperback

Guidelines: *tulippublishing.com.au/about/submissions*

Tip: "Be concise and succinct in your proposal; have your manuscript read and proofed by others, like family or friends, before submission."

TULPEN PUBLISHING

11043 Depew St., Westminster, CO 80020 | 303-438-7276

TulpenPublishing.com

Sandi Rog, acquisitions editor

Mission statement: to provide Christian stories that take readers beyond what they can find on the bookshelves

Submissions: Length: novellas, 15,000–55,000 words; novels, 60,000–80,000 words; historical novels, 65,000–110,000 words. Email query first.

Topics and genres: devotionals, self-help, chapter books; fiction: contemporary, fantasy, historical, science fiction, teen/YA

Royalty: 10% print, 50% ebook

Types of books: ebook, paperback

Guidelines: *www.tulpenpublishing.com/submission-guidelines.html*

Tip: "All stories must have a Christian worldview or a moral worldview pleasing to our heavenly Father. Please, no preaching and no conversion scenes, *unless* baptism by immersion for the forgiveness of sins is used (Acts 2:38). Don't use miracles and/ or mysticism to resolve conflicts or to 'fix' a difficult plot. Miracles may be used only in biblical fiction. No profanity please. By the end of the story, the main character should have experienced spiritual and/or character growth."

TYNDALE HOUSE PUBLISHERS

351 Executive Dr., Carol Stream, IL 60188 | 630-668-8300

www.tyndale.com

Kara Leonino, acquisitions manager, nonfiction

Elizabeth Jackson, acquisitions editor, fiction

Jillian Schlossberg, senior acquisitions editor, nonfiction

Jan Stob, associate publisher, fiction and acquisitions

Mission statement: to help readers discover the life-giving truths of God's Word

Submissions: Publishes 100+ titles per year. First-time authors: 5%. Length: fiction, 75,000–100,000. Only agent, author referral, or conference contact. Responds in three to six months. Bible: NLT.

Topics and genres: biography, Christian living/spirituality, counseling, family, finances, leadership, marriage, memoir/ personal narrative, parenting, children, devotionals, teen/YA; fiction: biblical, contemporary, historical, mystery, romance, suspense/thriller

Types of books: audiobook, ebook, hardcover, offset paperback

Imprints: Tyndale Kids (children), Wander (YA), Tyndale Español (Spanish), Tyndale Refresh (health and wellness), Tyndale Elevate (Christian worldview topics and apologetics), Tyndale Momentum (nonfiction), Hendrickson Publishers (nonfiction), Rose Publishing (Bible study helps)

TYNDALE KIDS

351 Executive Dr., Carol Stream, IL 60188 | 630-668-8300
kidsandwandersubmissions@tyndale.com | www.tyndale.com/kids
Talia Messina, acquisitions editor

Parent company: Tyndale House Publishers
Mission statement: to bring kids and families closer to God through publishing books with excellent content, creative formats, and outstanding design
Submissions: Publishes 10–15 titles per year; receives 300–400 submissions annually. First-time authors: 5%. Length: varies according to the age group. Only agent or conference contact. Responds in two to three months. Bible: NLT.
Topics and genres: Bible stories, board books, devotionals, fiction, first-chapter, middle grade, picture books, teen/YA
Royalty: 10–24%; gives advance according to platform, previous sales history, and uniqueness of proposal
Types of books: audiobook, ebook, hardcover, offset paperback, POD
Imprints: Wander (YA fiction and nonfiction)
Guidelines: not available
Tip: "Looking for a solid, well-written proposal; strong platform; excellent writing."

UPPER ROOM BOOKS

1908 Grand Ave., Nashville, TN 37212 | 800-972-0433
proposals@upperroom.org | upperroombooks.com
Michael S. Stephens, editorial director

Denomination: United Methodist
Parent company: The Upper Room
Mission statement: to encourage prayer and daily disciplines that help people create daily life with God
Submissions: Publishes 12 titles per year; receives 50 submissions annually. First-time authors: 50%. Length: 112–248 pages. Mail proposal with sample chapters. Responds only if interested. Bible: NRSV.
Topics and genres: Christian living/spirituality, culture, healing, leadership, Lent, relationships, spiritual formation, stewardship, church resources, devotionals, worship resources
Royalty: 10–15%, sometimes gives advance
Types of books: audiobook, ebook, hardcover, offset paperback, POD
Imprints: Fresh Air Books (spiritually curious people interested in

the relevance of faith in our culture), Discipleship Resources (leadership and stewardship resources)

Guidelines: *upperroombooks.com/submissions*

Tip: "Upper Room Books encourage the use of inclusive language in reference to God and humanity."

W PUBLISHING

PO Box 141000, Nashville, TN 37214-1000 | 615-889-9000

www.thomasnelson.com/wpublishing

Kyle Olund, senior acquisitions editor

Lisa-Jo Baker, acquisitions editor

Parent company: Thomas Nelson Publishers/HarperCollins Christian Publishing

Submissions: Agent only.

Topics and genres: Christian living, memoir/personal narrative

Types of books: audiobook, ebook, hardcover, offset paperback

Guidelines: not available

Tip: "W prides itself on the ability to provide authors a nurturing, faith-friendly, boutique style publishing experience."

WARNER CHRISTIAN RESOURCES

2902 Enterprise Dr., Anderson, IN 46013 | 765-644-7721

editors@warnerpress.org | *www.warnerpress.org*

Julie Campbell, product and acquisitions editor

Denomination: Church of God

Mission statement: to equip the church, to advance the Kingdom, and to give hope to future generations

Submissions: Publishes three to five titles per year; receives 50+ submissions annually. First-time authors: 50%. Email complete manuscript. Responds in six to eight weeks. Bible: KJV, NIV, ESV, NKJV.

Topics and genres: Bible studies, small group resources, small-group study guides

Royalty: based on the author and type of book, sometimes gives advance

Types of books: ebook, offset paperback

Guidelines: *www.warnerpress.org/submission-guidelines*

Tip: "Do your research, and visit our website to view what we already produce."

WATERBROOK & MULTNOMAH

10807 New Allegiance Dr. #500, Colorado Springs, CO 80921 | 719-590-4999

info@waterbrookmultnomah.com | www.waterbrookmultnomah.com

Jamie Lapeyrolerie, acquisitions editor

Sara Rubio, executive editor, children's

Bunmi Ishola, children's editor

Drew Dixon, executive editor

Parent company: The Crown Publishing Group/Penguin Random House

Submissions: Publishes 60 titles per year; receives 300 submissions annually. First-time authors: 15%. Length: 208–400 pages. Agent only. Responds in one to two months.

Topics and genres: Christian living/spirituality, home and lifestyle, memoir/personal narrative, relationships, spiritual growth, Bible studies, children, devotionals; fiction: Amish, historical, romantic suspense

Royalty: gives advance

Types of books: audiobook, ebook, hardcover, offset paperback, POD

Imprints: Ink & Willow (gifts)

Tip: "We recommend working with an agent whose clientele aligns with your strengths as a writer."

WATERSHED BOOKS

PO Box 1738, Aztec, NM 87410

customer@pelicanbookgroup.com | www.pelicanbookgroup.com

Nicola Martinez, editor-in-chief

Parent company: Pelican Book Group

Mission statement: to publish quality books that reflect the salvation and love offered by Jesus Christ

Submissions: Length: 25,000–65,000 words. Submit proposal with sample chapters through the website. Responds in three to four months. Bible: NIV, NAB. Interested in series ideas.

Topics and genres: fiction: teen/YA, adventure, coming-of-age, crime, mystery, romance, science fiction, supernatural, suspense, westerns

Royalty: 40% on download, 7% on print; sometimes gives advance

Types of books: POD

Guidelines: *pelicanbookgroup.com/ec/index.php?main_page=page&id=60*

Tip: "We want to see something other than dystopian."

WESTMINSTER JOHN KNOX PRESS

100 Witherspoon St., Louisville, KY 40202-1396

submissions@wjkbooks.com | www.wjkbooks.com
David Dobson, publisher and acquisitions
Jessica Miller Kelley, editor, Flyaway Books

Denomination: Presbyterian
Parent company: Presbyterian Publishing Corporation
Submissions: Publishes 60 titles per year. Email proposal with sample chapters. Responds in two to three months.
Topics and genres: Bible study, culture, ethics, ministry, theology, worship, academic
Types of books: hardcover, offset paperback
Imprints: Flyaway Books (children), Geneva Press (Presbyterian Church USA)
Guidelines: *www.wjkbooks.com/Pages/Item/1345/Author-Relations.aspx*

WHITAKER HOUSE

1030 Hunt Valley Cir., New Kensington, PA 15068 | 724-334-7000
www.whitakerhouse.com
Amy Bartlett, acquisition editor
Christine Whitaker, publisher and fiction acquisitions

Denomination: Charismatic/Pentecostal
Parent company: Whitaker Corporation
Mission statement: to advance God's Kingdom by publishing biblically focused authors who proclaim the power of the gospel and minister to the spiritual needs of people around the world
Submissions: Publishes 75–100 titles per year; receives 200 submissions annually. First-time authors: 30%. Length: 50,000–80,000 words. Only takes proposals if requested by a specific Whitaker House representative or sent by a recognized source. Responds in one to six months. Bible: KJV.
Topics and genres: African-American, Asian, Charismatic, Christian living/spirituality, Hispanic, children, devotionals, fiction
Royalty: 15–18%, sometimes gives advance
Types of books: audiobook, board books, ebook, hardcover, offset and POD paperback
Imprint: Whitaker Playhouse (parents of young children)
Guidelines: *tinyurl.com/43sstw9s*
Tip: "Follow the questions and suggestions on our submission guidelines."

WHITE ROSE PUBLISHING

PO Box 1738, Aztec, NM 87410
customer@pelicanbookgroup.com | www.pelicanbookgroup.com

Nicola Martinez, editor-in-chief

Parent company: Pelican Book Group

Mission statement: to publish quality books that reflect the salvation and love offered by Jesus Christ

Submissions: Length: short stories, 10,000–20,000 words; novelettes, 20,000–35,000 words; novellas, 35,000–60,000 words; novels, 60,000–80,000 words. Submit proposal with sample chapters through the website. Responds in three to four months. Bible: NIV, NAB.

Topics and genres: fiction: romance

Royalty: 40% on download, 7% on print; sometimes gives advance

Types of books: ebook, POD

Guidelines: *pelicanbookgroup.com/ec/index.php?main_page=page&id=58*

Tip: "The setting for White Rose books can be contemporary, historical, or futuristic. They can be straight romances or include other factors, such as mystery, suspense, or supernatural elements, etc.; however, an element of faith must be present in all White Rose stories—without becoming overbearing or preachy. Please specify in your proposal if your story includes elements beyond simple romance."

WHITECROWN PUBLISHING

13607 Bedford Rd. NE, Cumberland, MD 21502 | 866-245-2211

marisa@whitecrownpublishing.com | *www.whitecrownpublishing.com*

Marisa Stokley, editorial director

Janelle Leonard, managing editor; janelle@whitecrownpublishing.com

Parent company: WhiteFire Publishing Group

Mission statement: to meld faith and royal fiction in romantic tales that will appeal to teens and adults and encourage them to embrace being daughters of the King

Submissions: Publishes 6–12 titles per year; receives 100 submissions annually. First-time authors: 25%. Length: 60,000–110,000 words. Agent not required. Email proposal with sample chapters. Responds in three months. Bible: KJV for historicals.

Topics and genres: fiction: royal romance, royalty

Royalty: print, 10% on retail; ebooks, 50% on net; sometimes gives advance that depends on sales history

Types of books: audiobook, ebook, hardcover, offset paperback, POD

Guidelines: *whitecrownpublishing.com/submissions*

Tip: "We're looking for stories that include royalty as one of the primary elements, which appeal to lovers of 'princess stories' but also offer depth and faith."

WHITEFIRE PUBLISHING

13607 Bedford Rd. NE, Cumberland, MD 21502 | 866-245-2211
r.white@whitefire-publishing.com | *www.whitefire-publishing.com*
Roseanna White, managing editor

Mission statement: to publish books that shine the Light of God into the darkness and embrace the motto of "Where Spirit Meets the Page"

Submissions: Publishes 24 titles per year; receives 200 submissions annually. First-time authors: 20%. Length: 60,000–100,000 words. Email query first. Responds in three months. Bible: KJV for historicals.

Topics and genres: nonfiction: all topics; fiction: contemporary, general, historical, romance, suspense, women's

Royalty: 50% on ebooks, 10% on print; advance, $1,500–2,000

Types of books: audiobook, ebook, POD

Imprints: WhiteSpark (young readers), Ashberry Lane (romance), WhiteFire (nonfiction and fiction), Chrism Press (Catholic and Orthodox fiction)

Guidelines: *whitefire-publishing.com/submissions*

Tip: "Familiarize yourself with our titles and mission."

WHITESPARK PUBLISHING

13607 Bedford Rd. NE, Cumberland, MD 21502 | 866-245-2211
r.white@whitefire-publishing.com | *www.whitefire-publishing.com*
Roseanna White, managing editor

Parent company: WhiteFire Publishing

Mission statement: to engender a love of reading in kids with faith-based books

Submissions: Publishes 5–10 titles per year; receives 100 submissions annually. First-time authors: 10%. Email query first. Responds in three months.

Topics and genres: all topics, middle grade, picture books, YA

Royalty: 50% on ebooks, 10% on print; advance, $200–1,000

Types of books: audiobook, ebook, picture books, POD

Guidelines: *whitespark-publishing.com/submissions*

Tip: "Come with fresh ideas on how to reach the young readership."

WILD HEART BOOKS

14250 Hwy. 55 W, Blacksburg, SC 29702 | 704-363-0360
submissions@mistymbeller.com | *wildheartbooks.org*
Denise Weimer, acquisitions and editorial liaison

Misty M. Beller, managing editor; misty@wildheartbooks.org

Parent company: Misty M. Beller Books, Inc.

Mission statement: to provide the kind of exciting historical stories readers love, complete with heroes to make them swoon, strong heroines, and inspirational messages to encourage their faith

Submissions: Publishes 30 titles per year; receives 50 submissions annually. First-time authors: 20%. Length: 55,000–80,000 words. Agent not required; conference contact a plus. Email proposal with complete manuscript or sample chapters. Responds in one week. Bible: KJV.

Topics and genres: fiction: historical romance

Royalty: 35–45%, no advance

Types of books: audiobook, ebook, hardcover, large print, POD

Guidelines: *www.wildheartbooks.org/submissions.html*

Tip: "We prefer series instead of standalones."

WILLIAM CAREY PUBLISHING

10 W. Dry Creek Cir., Littleton, CO 80120 | 720-372-7036

submissions@WCLBooks.com | *www.missionbooks.org*

Vivian Doub, publishing manager

Parent company: Frontier Ventures

Mission statement: to edify, equip, and empower disciples of Jesus to make disciples of Jesus and prompt breakthrough among unreached peoples

Submissions: Email query first. Responds in three to six months.

Topics and genres: biography, ethnography, missions, academic

Types of books: ebook, paperback

Guidelines: *missionbooks.org/pages/submission-guidelines*

Tip: "We want our books to sound like the intelligent conversation you have with friends over dinner. You may site statistics and research (like you might reference an article in a reputable source), but you are sharing it in the context of a story that makes the research matter to real people doing Kingdom work."

WINGED PUBLICATIONS

PO Box 8047, Surprise, AZ 85374 | 623-910-4279

cynthiahickey@outlook.com | *www.wingedpublications.com*

Cynthia Hickey, CEO/president

Gina Welborn, acquisitions editor

Christina Rich, acquisitions editor

Patty Smith Hall, acquisitions editor

Submissions: Publishes 50 titles per year. First-time authors: 25%. Length: minimum 20,000 words. Conference contact a plus. Email proposal with sample chapters. Responds in two weeks. Bible: NIV.

Topics and genres: self-help, devotionals, humor; fiction: dystopian, fantasy, historical romance, mystery, romance, romantic suspense, science fiction, suspense/thriller, teen/YA, women's

Royalty: 60%, no advance

Types of books: ebook, POD

Imprints: Soaring Beyond (nonfiction), Aisling Books (fantasy, dystopian, science fiction), Jurnee Books (young adult, middle grade), Gordian Books (mystery, suspense, thriller), Forget Me Not Romances (contemporary and historical romances), Take Me Away Books (noninspirational)

Guidelines: *wingedpublications.com/what-were-looking-for*

Tip: "Send the cleanest proposal you can."

WIPF AND STOCK PUBLISHERS

199 W. 8th Ave., Ste. 3, Eugene, OR 97401-2960 | 541-344-1528

rodney@wipfandstock.com | *www.wipfandstock.com*

Rodney Clapp, editor

Submissions: Publishes 500+ titles per year in all imprints. Email proposal with sample chapters. Responds in two months.

Topics and genres: Bible, church history, ethics, history, ministry, philosophy, theology, academic

Types of books: ebook, offset paperback

Imprints: Resource Publications (leaders, pastors, educators), Cascade Books (academic)

Guidelines: *wipfandstock.com/submitting-a-proposal*

Tip: "It is your responsibility to submit a manuscript that has been fully copyedited by a professional copy editor."

WORDCRAFTS PRESS

912 E. Lincoln, Tullahoma, TN 37388 | 615-397-8376

mike@wordcrafts.net | *wordcrafts.net*

Mike Parker, publisher

Paula K. Parker, acquisitions editor; paula@wordcrafts.net
Kristen Ownby, acquisitions editor; kristen@wordcrafts.net
Shanda Perkins, acquisitions editor; shanda@wordcrafts.net

Parent company: WordCrafts, LLC

Mission statement: to tell stories that help us make sense of the world

Submissions: Publishes 24–36 titles per year; receives 300 submissions annually. First-time authors: 50%. Length: fewer than 100,000 words. Agent not required. Conference contact a plus. Query first through the website. Responds in four weeks. Bible: any.

Topics and genres: Bible study, Christian living/spirituality, memoir/personal narrative; fiction: biblical, historical

Royalty: 70% of income, no advance

Types of books: audiobook, ebook, hardcover, POD

Tip: "Send us your best work."

WORTHY KIDS

6100 Tower Cir., Ste. 210, Franklin, TN 37067 | 615-221-0996

www.hachettebookgroup.com/imprint/worthykids

Melinda Rathjen, senior editor

Parent company: Worthy Publishing/Hachette Book Group

Mission statement: to create books that are much more than just words and pictures—they're an opportunity for a moment of joy between a child and his or her loved one

Submissions: Publishes 30–35 titles per year; receives 200 submissions annually. First-time authors: fewer than 10%. Length: maximum 200 words for board books, 600 words for picture books. Agent only. Responds in one month. Bible: NLT.

Topics and genres: holidays, board books, children, fiction, first-chapter, middle-grade, nonfiction, picture books

Royalty: varies, sometimes gives advance

First print run: 10,000

Types of books: audiobook, board books, ebook, hardcover, offset paperback, picture books

Guidelines: available via email

Tip: "Carefully study the types of books our house has published; and submit proposals that show an understanding of the marketplace, include recent competitive titles, and identify what sets your book apart."

WORTHY PUBLISHING

6100 Tower Cir., Ste. 210, Franklin, TN 37067 | 615-932-7600

www.worthypublishing.com

Beth Adams, editorial director

Sean McGowan, editor and acquisitions

Ryan Peterson, senior editor and acquisitions

India Hunter, associate editor and acquisitions

Parent company: Hachette Book Group

Mission statement: to publish books that combine faith, creativity, and culture while establishing the next generation of voices who believe that living faith can transform the world

Submissions: Publishes 36 titles per year. Agent only.

Topics and genres: biography, Christian living/spirituality, contemporary issues, culture, leadership, marriage, parenting, relationships, social justice, spiritual growth, devotionals, fiction, gift books

Types of books: audiobook, ebook, hardcover, paperback

Imprints: Worthy Books (broad spectrum of genres), Worthy Kids (children), Ellie Claire (gifts)

YWAM PUBLISHING

PO Box 55787, Seattle, WA 98155 | 800-922-2143

books@ywampublishing.com | *www.ywampublishing.com*

Tom Bragg, publisher

Parent company: Youth With A Mission

Mission statement: to encourage Christians to make a difference in a needy world

Submissions: Email proposal with sample chapters. Responds only if interested.

Topics and genres: Christian living/spirituality, evangelism, family, leadership, missions, prayer, relationships, Bible studies, biography, devotionals

Types of books: audiobook, ebook, paperback

Guidelines: *www.ywampublishing.com/topic.aspx?name=submission*

ZONDERKIDZ

3900 Sparks Dr. SE, Grand Rapids, MI 49512 | 616-698-6900

ZonderkidzSubmissions@harpercollins.com | *www.zonderkidz.com*

Katherine Easter, senior acquisitions editor

Parent company: Zondervan/HarperCollins Christian Publishing

Mission statement: to inspire young lives through imaginative, innovative, and educational resources that represent a Christian worldview and build up God's children and teens

Submissions: Agent only.

Topics and genres: Bibles, children, fiction, nonfiction, teen/YA

Types of books: board books, ebook, hardcover, offset paperback, picture books

Guidelines: not available.

Tip: "We are seeking fresh fiction and nonfiction for children ages 0–18. We look for engaging picture books and board books, timeless storybook Bibles, faith-centric fiction from established authors, and nonfiction from key voices in the Christian sphere."

ZONDERVAN

Editorial Vida, Zonderkidz, Zondervan Academic, Zondervan Books, Zondervan Fiction, Zondervan Gift, Zondervan Reflective, WestBow Press

ZONDERVAN ACADEMIC

3900 Sparks Dr. SE, Grand Rapids, MI 49512 | 616-698-6900

submissions@zondervan.com | *www.zondervanacademic.com*

Katya Covrett, VP and publisher

Parent company: Zondervan/HarperCollins Christian Publishing

Mission statement: to reflect the breadth and diversity—both theological and global—within evangelical scholarship while maintaining our commitment to the heart of orthodox Christianity

Submissions: Email query. Responds in six weeks or not interested. Bible: NIV.

Topics and genres: academic, Bible reference/commentaries

Types of books: ebook, hardcover, offset paperback

Guidelines: *zondervanacademic.com/publishing-with-us*

ZONDERVAN BOOKS

PO Box 141000, Nashville, TN 37214 | 615-889-9000

www.zondervan.com

Paul Pastor, senior acquisitions editor

Carolyn McCready, executive editor and trade acquisitions

Kyle Rohane, acquisitions editor

Parent company: Zondervan/HarperCollins Christian Publishing

Submissions: Publishes 120 titles per year. Agent only. Bible: NIV.

Topics and genres: biography, Christian living/spirituality, church life, contemporary issues, family, finances, marriage, ministry

Types of books: audiobook, ebook, hardcover, offset paperback

ZONDERVAN FICTION

PO Box 141000, Nashville, TN 37214 | 615-889-9000

www.zondervan.com/fiction

Becky Monds, editorial director

Kimberly Carlton, acquisitions editor

Laura Wheeler, acquisitions editor

> **Parent company:** Zondervan/HarperCollins Christian Publishing
>
> **Submissions:** Agent only. Bible: NIV.
>
> **Topics and genres:** fiction: Amish, contemporary, historical, mystery, romance, suspense/thriller
>
> **Types of books:** ebook, offset paperback
>
> **Tip:** We are looking for "great writers who are passionate about their stories, a willingness to work hard and engage with readers—coupled with a true love of readers, a unique angle on or a unique connection to their story matter, a great attitude."

ZONDERVAN REFLECTIVE

3900 Sparks Dr. SE, Grand Rapids, MI 49512 | 616-698-6900

submissions@zondervan.com | www.zondervan.com/zondervanreflective

Ryan Pazdur, VP and publisher

> **Parent company:** Zondervan/HarperCollins Christian Publishing
>
> **Mission statement:** to provide guidance and inspiration for effective leadership in business and ministry
>
> **Submissions:** Email query. Responds in six weeks or not interested. Bible: NIV.
>
> **Topics and genres:** contemporary issues, culture, leadership, ministry
>
> **Types of books:** ebook, hardcover, offset paperback
>
> **Guidelines:** *www.harpercollinschristian.com/authors/manuscript-information*
>
> **Tip:** "The authors are expected to have demonstrable expertise on the subject being addressed."

2

BOOK ANTHOLOGY SERIES

CHICKEN SOUP FOR THE SOUL

PO Box 700, Cos Cob, CT 06807-0700

www.chickensoup.com

Amy Newmark, publisher and editor-in-chief

> **Parent company:** Chicken Soup for the Soul Publishing, LLC
>
> **Purpose statement:** to share happiness, inspiration, and hope
>
> **Submissions:** Submit the complete manuscript only through the website form. If no response by 60 days before the book's on-sale date, not interested. Accepts 101 manuscripts per book. Accepts submissions from children and teens.
>
> **Types of manuscripts:** personal experience, poetry, theme-related
>
> **Topics/upcoming books:** *www.chickensoup.com/story-submissions/ possible-book-topics*
>
> **Length:** 1,200 words maximum
>
> **Rights:** nonexclusive
>
> **Payment:** $250 plus ten copies of the book, one month after publication
>
> **Guidelines:** *www.chickensoup.com/story-submissions/story-guidelines*
>
> **Tip:** "We love poems that tell a story. A Chicken Soup for the Soul poem does the same job as a story. The reader goes away having learned your story, just through poetry instead of prose. We do not publish poems that do not tell a story. We also do not publish poems that seem overly focused on rhyming and read more like greeting cards."

DIVINE MOMENTS

PO Box 1233, Broken Arrow, OK 74013-1233 | 918-346-7960

terri@grace-publishing.com | grace-publishing.com

Terri Kalfas, compiler and editor

> **Parent company:** Grace Publishing

Purpose statement: to show the possibility of changing someone's life, heart, or mind

Submissions: Email complete manuscript as attachment. Response depends on the book. Accepts 150–200 manuscripts per year.

Types of manuscripts: personal experience, poetry, theme-related

Topics/upcoming books: *Lost Moments, Questionable Moments, Favorite Moments, Divine Detours, Unexpected Kindness, Patriotic Moments, Hopeful Moments, Christmas*

Length: 500–2,000 words

Rights: first, one time, reprint

Payment: copy of book; royalties are donated to Samaritan's Purse

Guidelines: *grace-publishing.com/manuscript-submission/divine-moments-guidelines*

Tip: "Make sure the content of the manuscript reflects the message of the title."

LIFE REPURPOSED

michelle@faithcreativitylife.com | www.faithcreativitylife.com

Michelle Rayburn, publisher and editor-in-chief

Parent company: Faith Creativity Life Books

Purpose statement: to help readers find hope in the trashy stuff of life

Submissions: Submit complete manuscript only through the website form. Responds in two weeks to two months. Accepts 60–100 manuscripts per year. Bible: NLT.

Types of manuscripts: devotion, fiction, humor, personal experience, poetry, theme-related

Topics/upcoming books: *Christmas, Empty Nest, Whiskers and Wags, Resilience*

Length: 300–1800 words

Rights: first, reprint with info on where and when previously published

Payment: copies of book

Guidelines: *www.faithcreativitylife.com*

Tip: "Pieces should be encouraging and uplifting, inspiring readers by showing how the writer found hope through their own struggle. They should be faith-based but not preachy. Writers should show vulnerability and authenticity as well as creativity. Humor is a plus!"

SHORT AND SWEET

PO Box 1233, Broken Arrow, OK 74013-1233 | 918-346-7960

susan@susankingedits.com | grace-publishing.com

Susan King, compiler and editor

Parent company: Grace Publishing

Purpose statement: to show readers and writers that good storytelling doesn't have to use big, long words

Submissions: Email complete manuscript as attachment. Response depends on the book. Accepts 150–200 manuscripts per year.

Types of manuscripts: personal experience, poetry, theme-related

Topics/upcoming books: *What Patriotism Means to Me, Mishaps and Misadventures, Memorable Mutts, The Feline in the Family, Facing Fears*

Length: 250–1,000 words

Rights: first, one time, reprint

Payment: copy of book; royalties are donated to World Christian Broadcasting

Guidelines: *grace-publishing.com/manuscript-submission/short-sweet-anthology-guidelines*

Tip: "Articles must convey the message of the title."

PART 2

INDEPENDENT BOOK PUBLISHING

3

INDEPENDENT BOOK PUBLISHERS

PUBLISHING A BOOK YOURSELF NO LONGER CARRIES THE STIGMA self-publishing has had in the past—if you do it right. Even some well-published writers are now hybrid authors, with independently published books alongside their royalty books. Others have built their readerships with traditional publishers, then moved to independent publishing where it is possible to make more money per sale.

Independent book publishers require the author to pay for part of the publishing costs or to buy a certain number of books. They call themselves by a variety of names, such as book packager, cooperative publisher, self-publisher, hybrid publisher, custom publisher, subsidy publisher, or simply someone who helps authors get their books printed. Services vary from including different levels of editing and proofreading to printing your manuscript as is.

Whenever you pay for any part of the production of your book, you are entering into a nontraditional relationship. Some independent publishers also offer a form of royalty publishing, so be sure you understand the contract they give you before signing it.

Some independent publishers will publish any book, as long as the author is willing to pay for it. Others are as selective about what they publish as a royalty publisher is. Some independent publishers will do as much promotion as a royalty publisher—for a fee. Others do none at all.

If you are unsuccessful in placing your book with a royalty publisher but feel strongly about seeing it published, an independent publisher can make printing your book easier and often less expensive than doing it yourself. POD, as opposed to a print run of 1,000 books or more, could save you upfront money, although the price per copy is higher. Having your manuscript produced only as an ebook is also a less-expensive option.

Entries in this chapter are for information only, not an endorsement of publishers. For every complaint about a publisher, several other authors may sing the praises of it. Before you sign with any company, get more than one bid to determine whether the terms you are offered are competitive.

A legitimate independent publisher will provide a list of former clients as references. Also buy a couple of the publisher's previous books to check the quality of the work: covers, bindings, typesetting, etc. See if the books currently are available through any of the major online retailers.

Get answers before committing yourself. You may also want someone in the book-publishing industry to review your contract before you sign it. Some experts listed in the "Editorial Services" chapter review contracts.

If you decide not to use an independent publisher but do the work yourself, at least hire an editor, proofreader, cover designer, and interior typesetter-designer. The "Editorial Services" and "Design and Production Services" chapters will help you locate professionals with skills in these areas, as well as printing companies. Plus the "Distribution Services" and "Publicity and Marketing Services" chapters can help you solve one of the biggest problems of independent publishing: getting your books to readers.

AMPELOS PRESS

951 Anders Rd., Lansdale, PA 19446 | 267-436-2503
mbagnull@aol.com | *writehisanswer.com/ampelospress*
Marlene Bagnull, publisher

> **Types:** ebooks, POD
> **Services:** copyediting, design, manuscript evaluation, proofreading, substantive editing
> **Production time:** six months
> **Books per year:** two
> **Tip:** "Especially interested in issues fiction and nonfiction, as well as books about missions and the needs of children. Author pays a one-time fee, maintains all rights, and receives 100% royalty from Amazon KDP."

BELIEVERS BOOK SERVICES

2329 Farragut Ave., Colorado Springs, CO 80907 | 719-641-7862
dave@believersbookservices.com | *believersbookservices.com*
Dave Sheets, owner

> **Types:** ebooks, gift books, hardcover, paperback, picture books, POD
> **Services:** à la carte options, author websites, copyediting, design, distribution, manuscript evaluation, packages of services,

proofreading, substantive editing

Production time: three months

Books per year: 45–50

Tip: "Start thinking about strategy for publishing, marketing, and launching as soon as possible in the process. This strategy process will help produce a stronger book."

BK ROYSTON PUBLISHING

303 E. Court Ave. #4321, Jeffersonville, IN 47131 | 502-594-2143

bkroystonpublishing@gmail.com | *www.bkroystonpublishing.com*

Julia A. Royston, CEO

Types: audiobooks, ebooks, hardcover, offset paperback, picture books

Services: à la carte options, author websites, copyediting, design, manuscript evaluation, marketing, online bookstore, packages of services, promotional materials, proofreading

Production time: two to three months

Books per year: 50

Tip: "Prior to submission for review, please at least spell-check."

BOOKBABY

7905 N. Crescent Blvd., Pennsauken, NJ 08110 | 877-961-6878

info@bookbaby.com | *www.bookbaby.com*

Types: comic book, ebooks, gift books, hardcover, offset paperback, picture books, POD

Services: copyediting, design, distribution, manuscript evaluation, online bookstore, proofreading, social-media ads, substantive editing

Production time: varies

Tip: Has ebook and printed-book distribution network for self-published authors around the globe.

BRIDGE LOGOS, INC.

17750 N.W. 115th Ave., Bldg. 200, Ste. 220, Alachua, FL 32615 | 386-462-2525

swooldridge@bridgelogos.com | *www.bridgelogos.com*

Peggy Hildebrand, acquisitions editor

Types: ebooks, hardcover, paperback

Services: copyediting, design, distribution, proofreading, substantive editing

Production time: 12–18 months
Books per year: 40
Also does: royalty contracts
Tip: Traditional house that requires new Bridge Logos authors and authors with no established marketing platform to purchase 1,000–3,000 books. "Looking for well-written, timely books that are aimed at the needs of people and that glorify God. Have a great message, a well-written manuscript, and a specific plan and willingness to market your book. Looking for previously published authors with an active ministry who are experts on their subject."

BROWN CHRISTIAN PRESS

16250 Knoll Trail Dr., Ste. 205, Dallas, TX 75248 | 972-381-0009
publishing@brownbooks.com | *www.brownbooks.com/brown-christian-press*

Types: audiobooks, ebooks, gift books, hardcover, paperback
Services: copyediting, design, distribution, ghostwriting, indexing, marketing, proofreading, substantive editing
Production time: six months
Tip: "We are a relationship publisher and work with our authors from beginning to end in the journey of publishing."

CALLED WRITERS CHRISTIAN PUBLISHING

1900 Rice Mine Rd. N. 401, Tuscaloosa, AL 35406 | 205-872-4509
shannon@calledwriters.com | *CalledWriters.com*
Shannon McKinney, relationship builder

Types: offset paperback, POD
Services: à la carte options, copyediting, design, manuscript evaluation, marketing, packages of services, proofreading, substantive editing
Production time: six months
Books per year: two
Also does: royalty contracts
Tip: "God will open the right doors for you at the right time. Don't give up."

CHRISTIAN FAITH PUBLISHING

832 Park Ave., Meadville, PA 16335 | 800-955-3794
Chris@christianfaithpublishing.com | *www.Christianfaithpublishing.com*
Chris Rutherford, president

Types: ebooks, hardcover, offset paperback, POD
Services: à la carte options, copyediting, design, distribution,

indexing, manuscript evaluation, marketing, packages of services, promotional materials

Production time: eight to ten months

Books per year: 1,200

Also does: royalty contracts

Tip: "Be mindful of the fact that it is quite challenging to publish a book and have commercial success."

CLM PUBLISHING

PO Box 1217, Grand Cayman, Cayman Islands KY-11108 | 345-926-2507

production@clmpublishing.com | www.clmpublishing.com

Types: ebooks, gift books, hardcover, offset paperback, picture books, POD

Services: author websites, copyediting, design, distribution, indexing, manuscript evaluation, marketing, online bookstore, promotional materials, proofreading, substantive editing

Production time: three to six months

Books per year: eight

Tip: "Be willing to do some marketing."

CLOVERCROFT PUBLISHING GROUP

307 Verde Meadow Dr., Franklin, TN 37067 | 615-538-8557

shane@clovercroftpublishing.com | clovercroftpublishing.com

Shane Crabtree, COO

Types: audiobooks, ebooks, gift books, hardcover, offset paperback, picture books, POD

Services: à la carte options, author websites, coaching, copyediting, design, distribution, indexing, manuscript evaluation, marketing, online bookstore, packages of services, promotional materials, proofreading, substantive editing, international rights, book coaching, ghostwriting

Production time: four to six months

Books per year: 25

Also does: royalty contracts, international rights

Tip: "Start planning your marketing early!"

COLE STREET PRESS

1602 Cole St,, Enumclaw, WA 98022 | 360-226-3488

micah@redemption-press.com | www.colestreetpress.com

Micah Juntunen, director of acquisitions

> **Types:** audiobooks, ebooks, gift books, hardcover, offset paperback, picture books, POD
>
> **Services:** à la carte options, author websites, copyediting, design, distribution, indexing, manuscript evaluation, marketing, packages of services, proofreading, substantive editing
>
> **Production time:** six months
>
> **Books per year:** 50+
>
> **Tip:** "Cole Street Press is a DIY imprint of Redemption Press that takes the author from manuscript to distribution. We cater to a variety of genres, including fiction, nonfiction, and children's books, as well as the unique needs of coaches and business owners. We are here to help you share your message with the world."

COLEMAN JONES PRESS

info@colemanjonespress.com | *colemanjonespress.com*

Tracee and Ross Jones, owners

> **Types:** audiobooks, curriculum, ebooks, hardcover, picture books, POD
>
> **Services:** author websites, design, distribution, marketing, packages of services, promotional materials
>
> **Production time:** three to six months
>
> **Tip:** "Write for the sake of getting the gospel out, not for the money. When choosing a cover or illustrator, make sure your design looks like something that is in major retail stores."

COVENANT BOOKS

11661 Hwy. 707, Murrells Inlet, SC 29576 | 843-507-8373

contact@covenantbooks.com | *www.covenantbooks.com*

Denice Hunter, president

> **Types:** ebooks, hardcover, offset paperback, POD
>
> **Services:** à la carte options, copyediting, design, distribution, marketing, online bookstore, packages of services
>
> **Production time:** six months
>
> **Also does:** royalty contracts
>
> **Tip:** "Publishing a book can be a fun and enlightening process. Take your time, and choose a publisher you feel comfortable with."

CREATIVE ENTERPRISES STUDIO

1507 Shirley Way, Ste. A, Bedford, TX 76022-6737 | 817-312-7393

AcreativeShop@aol.com | *CreativeEnterprisesStudio.com*

Mary Hollingsworth, publisher

> **Types:** audiobooks, ebooks, gift books, hardcover, offset paperback, picture books, POD
>
> **Services:** author websites, book trailer, coaching, copyediting, design, ghostwriting, marketing, proofreading, substantive editing, warehousing
>
> **Production time:** seven months, depending on type and length of book
>
> **Books per year:** varies
>
> **Tip:** "Contact us by email to set a phone conference to discuss your work before proceeding otherwise."

CREDO HOUSE PUBLISHERS

2200 Boyd Ct. NE, Grand Rapids, MI 49525-6714

publish@credocommunications.net | *www.credohousepublishers.com*

Timothy J. Beals, publisher

> **Types:** offset paperback
>
> **Services:** à la carte options, author websites, copyediting, design, distribution, indexing, manuscript evaluation, marketing, online bookstore, packages of services, promotional materials, proofreading, substantive editing
>
> **Production time:** three months
>
> **Books per year:** 30
>
> **Tip:** "Come prepared. Be persistent. Get published."

DEEP RIVER BOOKS, LLC

PO Box 310, Sisters, OR 97759 | 541-549-1139

andy@deepriverbooks.com | *www.deepriverbooks.com*

Andy Carmichael, publisher

> **Types:** audiobooks, ebooks, hardcover, offset paperback, POD
>
> **Services:** copyediting, design, distribution, manuscript evaluation, marketing, online bookstore, packages of services, promotional materials, substantive editing
>
> **Production time:** 9–14 months
>
> **Books per year:** 30–35
>
> **Also does:** royalty contracts
>
> **Tip:** "Check our website on how we work with authors before you submit."

DEEPER REVELATION BOOKS

PO Box 4260, Cleveland, TN 37320-4260 | 423-478-2843
pastormikeshreve@gmail.com | *www.deeperrevelationbooks.org*
Mike Shreve, founder and president

Types: ebooks, hardcover, offset paperback, POD
Services: à la carte options, author websites, coaching, copyediting, design, distribution, ghostwriting, manuscript evaluation, online bookstore, promotional materials, proofreading, substantive editing, transcribing
Production time: three to six months
Books per year: 35
Tip: Imprints: Deeper Revelation Books (nonfiction), Pure Heart Publications (fiction), Children of Promise (children), Pivotal Publications (success and social issues), Prism Graphics (graphics). "The root of the word *authority* is the word *author*. When you become a published author in a certain subject area, you become a more reputable authority in the eyes of those you can influence."

DESCENDANT PUBLISHING

PO Box 29, Byron Center, MI 49315 | 616-290-7829
contact@descendantpublishing.com | *www.descendantpublishing.com*
Troy Hooker, managing editor

Types: audiobooks, curriculum, ebooks, POD
Services: coaching, copyediting, design, distribution, marketing, online bookstore, packages of services, proofreading
Also does: royalty publishing
Tip: "We can walk you through the process one step at a time, helping you to bring your story to market at a fraction of the cost."

DESTINY IMAGE PUBLISHERS

167 Walnut Bottom Rd., Shippensburg, PA 17257 | 717-532-3040
manuscripts@norimediagroup.com | *norimediagroup.com/pages/publish-with-us*

Types: ebooks, paperback
Services: copyediting, design, manuscript evaluation, marketing, proofreading, substantive editing
Production time: 12 months
Tip: Traditional publisher that requires prepurchase of 500 to 3,000 copies. "Focuses on Spirit-empowered themes: supernatural God encounters, healing/deliverance, prophecy and prophetic ministry,

gifts of the Holy Spirit, prayer and intercession, the presence and glory of God, and dreams/dream interpretation."

EABOOKS PUBLISHING

5840 Red Bug Lake Rd., Winter Springs, FL 32708 | 407-712-3431
Cheri@eabookspublishing.com | *www.eabookspublishing.com*
Cheri Cowell, founder and publisher

Types: audiobooks, ebooks, gift books, hardcover, POD
Services: à la carte options, author websites, copyediting, design, distribution, indexing, manuscript evaluation, marketing, packages of services, promotional materials, proofreading, substantive editing
Production time: six months
Books per year: 50
Also does: royalty contracts
Tip: "Contact for a free consultation to see if we can partner with you to make your publishing dreams come true."

EBOOK CONVERSION AND LISTING SERVICES

PO Box 57, Glenwood, MD 21738 | 443-280-5077
sales@taegais.com | *ebooklistingservices.com*
Amy Deardon, CEO

Types: audiobooks, ebooks, POD
Services: à la carte options, design, distribution, marketing, packages of services, promotional materials
Production time: one to three months
Books per year: 20
Tip: "We empower independent authors to become successful. Unlike most other independent publishers, we set you up so you are the publisher, rather than publishing through the independent company. You can create your own publishing company name and logo, and we help you with that. You remain fully in charge of all decisions, rights, and profits from start to forever. Once your book is published, you can buy as few or as many books as you want at the lowest printer's price (a 200-page book costs less than $3.50); and books are delivered in a week or two through Amazon. We also have additional packages that can list your book with the Library of Congress and help you rank higher on Amazon's search engines so readers can actually find your book and buy it. We provide you with ownership of your book and work with you to make that succeed."

ELECTRIC MOON PUBLISHING, LLC

PO Box 466, Stromsburg, NE 68666 | 402-366-2033

laree@emoonpublishing.com | www.emoonpublishing.com

Laree Lindburg, owner

> **Types:** audiobooks, ebooks, gift books, hardcover, offset paperback, picture books, POD
>
> **Services:** à la carte options, author websites, copyediting, design, distribution, indexing, manuscript evaluation, promotional materials, proofreading, substantive editing
>
> **Production time:** nine months
>
> **Books per year:** 8–12
>
> **Tip:** "Feel free to ask questions of the services and publishing models offered. We are here to help and would enjoy an initial conversation with you."

FAIRWAY PRESS

5450 N. Dixie Hwy., Lima, OH 45807-9559 | 419-227-1818

david@csspub.com | www.fairwaypress.com

David Runk, president

> **Types:** ebooks, hardcover, offset paperback, POD
>
> **Services:** à la carte options, copyediting, design, manuscript evaluation, proofreading
>
> **Production time:** 6–12 months
>
> **Books per year:** 10–15
>
> **Tip:** "No derogatory racist content. Christian content preferred."

FAITH BOOKS & MORE

PO Box 1024, Athens, OH 45701 | 678-232-6156

publishing@faithbooksandmore.com | www.faithbooksandmore.com

Nicole Antoinette Smith, owner

> **Types:** hardcover, offset paperback, POD
>
> **Services:** copyediting, design, manuscript evaluation, proofreading
>
> **Production time:** three months
>
> **Books per year:** five
>
> **Tip:** "Write, rewrite, write, and rewrite again until you're 100% satisfied with your manuscript."

FIESTA PUBLISHING

PO Box 44984, Phoenix, AZ 85064 | 602-795-5868

julie@fiestapublishing.com | www.fiestapublishing.com

Julie Castro, owner

Types: ebooks, hardcover, offset paperback, POD

Services: à la carte options, copyediting, distribution, marketing, promotional materials, proofreading, substantive editing

Production time: four to six months

Books per year: five to seven

Tip: "Be willing to listen to an established publisher and act accordingly. There is a difference between a book and a great book! Look for publisher integrity and their purpose for having the publishing company."

FUSION HYBRID PUBLISHING

PO Box 206, Nesbit, MS 38651 | 901-590-6584

victoria@endgamepress.com | www.endgamepress.com/fusion

Alice, acquisitions editor

Types: audiobooks, ebooks, gospel tracts, hardcover, offset paperback, picture books, POD

Services: à la carte options, copyediting, design, distribution, indexing, manuscript evaluation, marketing, online bookstore, packages of services, promotional materials, proofreading, substantive editing

Production time: 6–12 months

Books per year: three to four

Tip: "Fusion is a great option for those who are excited to get to market faster than traditional houses and have a great audience already."

GOODWILL MEDIA SERVICES CORP.

105 Macclamrock Ct., Cary, NC 27518 | 347-247-2106

goodwillmediaservices.sofia@gmail.com | goodwillmediaservices.com

Sofia Delgado, author relations consultant

Types: audiobooks, ebooks, gift books, hardcover, offset paperback, picture books, POD

Services: à la carte options, author websites, coaching, copyediting, design, distribution, indexing, manuscript evaluation, marketing, online bookstore, packages of services, promotional materials, proofreading, substantive editing

Production time: three months

Books per year: 25+

Tip: "Don't settle for limitations. Break free from the constraints of traditional publishing and experience the freedom of self-publishing. With our support, you can chart your own course as a Christian author."

THE GRACE CHAPTER

244 Fifth Ave., Ste. T279, New York, NY 10001 | 646-233-4017
publishers@gracechapter.com | *www.gracechapter.com*
Temitope Oyetomi, director

Types: ebooks, hardcover, offset paperback, POD
Services: à la carte options, author websites, copyediting, design, distribution, indexing, manuscript evaluation, marketing, online bookstore, packages of services, proofreading, substantive editing
Production time: three to eight weeks
Books per year: 30
Also does: royalty contracts
Tip: "We prefer you tell us your budget for what you need to do, and we'll see what services we can tailor to the budget. This way, you can achieve your goals no matter your budget."

HARRISON HOUSE

167 Walnut Bottom Rd., Shippensburg, PA 17257 | 717-532-3040
manuscripts@norimediagroup.com | *norimediagroup.com/pages/publish-with-us*

Types: ebooks, paperback
Services: copyediting, design, manuscript evaluation, marketing, proofreading, substantive editing
Production time: 12 months
Also does: royalty contracts
Tip: Traditional publisher that requires prepurchase of 500 to 3,000 copies.

HONEYCOMB HOUSE PUBLISHING

315 3rd St., New Cumberland, PA 17070 | 215-767-9600
dave@fessendens.net | *www.davefessenden.com/honeycomb-house-publishing-llc*
David Fessenden, publisher

Types: POD
Services: à la carte options, author websites, copyediting, design, distribution, manuscript evaluation, marketing, packages of services, promotional materials, proofreading, substantive editing
Production time: three to six months

Books per year: one or two

Tip: "Prepare a book proposal even if you plan to self-publish/subsidy publish."

IMMORTALISE

PO Box 656, Noarlunga Centre, SA 5168 Australia

toastercide@gmail.com | *www.immortalise.com.au*

Ben Morton, editor

Types: ebooks, hardcover, offset paperback, picture books

Services: à la carte options, copyediting, design, manuscript evaluation, online bookstore, proofreading, substantive editing

Production time: varies

Tip: "All our services are optional and there is no cost for enquiries. We will publish any book so long as the content is not likely to get anyone sued."

INSCRIPT BOOKS

PO Box 611, Bladensburg, MD 20710 | 240-342-3293

inscript@dovechristianpublishers.com | *www.inscriptpublishing.com*

Allison Kelsey, editorial director

Types: ebooks, hardcover, POD

Services: à la carte options, copyediting, design, distribution, indexing, marketing, packages of services, proofreading, substantive editing

Production time: three to five months

Books per year: eight

Also does: royalty contracts

Tip: "Detailed information about approaching us with your book and an application form is contained on our website. We do not accept postal mail or email submissions."

LAKE DRIVE BOOKS

6757 Cascade Rd. SE #162, Grand Rapids, MI 49546 | 616-737-1480

david.morris@lakedrivebooks.com | *lakedrivebooks.com*

David Morris, publisher

Types: audiobooks, ebooks, hardcover, offset paperback, POD

Services: distribution, marketing

Production time: one year

Books per year: eight

Tip: "See our website to understand our publishing and if you would be a fit. Submissions must be in book-proposal form. There's a template on the About section of the site."

MORGAN JAMES PUBLISHING

5 Penn Plaza, 23rd Floor, New York City, NY 10001 | 516-900-5711
terry@morganjamespublishing.com | *www.morganjamespublishing.com*
W. Terry Whalin, acquisition editor

> **Types:** audiobooks, ebooks, offset paperback, picture books, POD
> **Services:** design, distribution, manuscript evaluation, marketing, online bookstore, proofreading
> **Production time:** 10–12 weeks, bookstore distribution in 9–10 months
> **Books per year:** 180–200, 25–30 in the faith division
> **Also does:** royalty contracts with 20–25% royalties and small advance
> **Tip:** "Beginning our 20th year in publishing. General-market publisher with a Christian division. Our books have been on *The New York Times* bestseller list over 28 times and on the *USA Today* and *Wall Street Journal* bestseller lists over 100 times (broad distribution to over 1,800 online and brick and mortar bookstores). Author is required to purchase 2,000 books at print cost plus $3 over the lifetime of the agreement. Our author support team also builds a webpage for each new author to give away the ebook (free); we send those emails to the author (to build their email list), and the free ebooks count against the book purchase requirement and drive print book sales. Email proposal with sample chapters or full manuscript. Only 30% of authors have literary agents."

NORDSKOG PUBLISHING

2716 Sailor Ave., Ventura, CA 93001 | 805-642-2070
jerry@nordskogpublishing.com | *nordskogpublishing.com*
Michelle Shelfer, managing editor

> **Types:** hardcover, paperback
> **Services:** copyediting, design, marketing
> **Tip:** "Looking for the best in sound theological and applied Christian-faith books, both nonfiction and fiction."

PRAIRIE FALLS BOOKS EDITING & DESIGN SERVICES

4810 Gene Field Rd. #2, St. Joseph, MO 64506 | 816-752-2171
deb@crossrivermedia.com | *prairiefallsbooks.com*
Debra L. Butterfield, managing editor

Types: ebooks, hardcover, offset paperback, POD
Services: à la carte options, copyediting, design, packages of services, proofreading, substantive editing
Production time: one to two months
Books per year: 15–20
Tip: "Review our website first and then schedule a consultation."

REDEMPTION PRESS

1602 Cole St., Enumclaw, WA 98022 | 360-226-3488
micah@redemption-press.com | www.redemption-press.com
Micah Juntunen, director of acquisitions

Types: audiobooks, ebooks, gift books, hardcover, offset paperback, picture books, POD
Services: à la carte options, author websites, copyediting, design, distribution, indexing, manuscript evaluation, marketing, online bookstore, promotional materials, proofreading, substantive editing
Production time: 6–18 months
Books per year: 100+
Tip: "Redemption Press is known for our commitment to sustaining the finest standards of editing and publishing in the Christian publishing industry. As an established collaborative custom publishing house, we offer both the individualized care of a small press and the comprehensive resources of a traditional house. At our core, we are dedicated to fulfilling our mission of amplifying the message of Christian authors with excellence.

"With our specialized services, we strive to maintain the utmost purity and integrity of your message while simultaneously ensuring its reach extends to the widest possible audience. We take great joy in delivering books that not only enrich and inspire readers but also demonstrate the care, passion, and commitment put into each step of the production process. You can place your trust in Redemption Press, the premier publisher specializing in transforming stories into powerful and inspiring messages of unwavering faith, boundless hope, and ultimate redemption."

SALVATION PUBLISHER AND MARKETING GROUP

PO Box 40860, Santa Barbara, CA 93140 | 805-252-9822
opalmaedailey@aol.com
Opal Mae Dailey, editor

Types: ebooks, hardcover, offset paperback
Services: copyediting, design, manuscript evaluation, proofreading, substantive editing
Production time: six to nine months
Books per year: five to seven
Tip: "Turning taped messages into book form for pastors is a specialty of ours. We do not accept any manuscript we would be ashamed to put our name on."

SERMON TO BOOK

424 W. Bakerview Rd., Ste. 105 #215, Bellingham, WA 98226 | 360-223-1877

info@sermontobook.com | www.sermontobook.com

Caleb Breakey, lead book director

Types: audiobooks, ebooks, offset paperback, POD
Services: author websites, copyediting, design, distribution, indexing, manuscript evaluation, marketing, online bookstore, packages of services, promotional materials, proofreading, substantive editing
Production time: seven to nine months
Books per year: 60
Tip: "Check out our materials on our website."

SOUTHERN WOMEN PUBLISHING

lamoniquemac@icloud.com | www.southernwomenpublishing.com

LaMonique Mac, publisher

Types: ebooks, hardcover, POD
Services: copyediting, illustrations, marketing, online bookstore, packages of services, proofreading, substantive editing
Tip: "All submissions must adhere to our statement of faith."

SPRINKLE PUBLISHING

1675 Lucia Ln., Mansfield, OH 44907-2778 | 419-709-1435

Dr.Sprinkle@wsministries.ws | www.wsministries.ws

Dr. Wanda J. Sprinkle, CEO & editor

Types: ebooks, hardcover, offset paperback
Services: à la carte options, copyediting, design, manuscript evaluation, online bookstore, packages of services, proofreading, substantive editing
Production time: seven months
Books per year: five

Also does: royalty contracts

Tip: "Pray for confirmation from the Holy Spirit that Sprinkle Publishing can be your publisher." Requires authors to order a minumum of 100 copies, which is included in the publishing cost.

STONE OAK PUBLISHING

PO Box 2011, Friendswood, TX 77549 | 832-569-4282

stoneoakpublishing@gmail.com | *stoneoakpublishing.com*

Karen Porter, acquisitions

Types: ebooks, hardcover, offset paperback, POD

Services: à la carte options, copyediting, design, distribution, indexing, manuscript evaluation, marketing, packages of services, promotional materials, proofreading, substantive editing

Production time: six to eight months

Books per year: 10

Also does: royalty contracts

Tip: "Send us a well-thought-out email detailing the information about your book."

TEACH SERVICES, INC.

11 Quartermaster Cir., Fort Oglethorpe, GA 30742-3886 | 800-367-1844

T.Hullquist@TEACHServices.com | *www.teachservices.com*

Timothy Hullquist, author advisor

Types: ebooks, gift books, hardcover, offset paperback, picture books, POD

Services: à la carte options, author websites, copyediting, design, distribution, indexing, manuscript evaluation, marketing, online bookstore, packages of services, promotional materials, proofreading, substantive editing

Production time: one to four months

Also does: royalty contracts

Tip: "We specialize in marketing our titles to Seventh-day Adventists."

TMP BOOKS

3 Central Plaza, Ste. 307, Rome, GA 30161

info@tmpbooks.com | *www.TMPbooks.com*

Tracy Ruckman, publisher

Types: audiobooks, ebooks, hardcover, picture books, POD

Services: à la carte options, author websites, coaching, copyediting, design, manuscript evaluation, marketing, packages of services, promotional materials, proofreading, substantive editing

Production time: six to nine months

Books per year: five to ten

Tip: "We work with each author individually, customizing our services to meet their needs. We've published beautiful books that started with notes on scraps of paper, from handwritten pages of legal pads, and even from fragments of an idea. We believe everyone has a story worth telling; our job is to get it to the publishable state, professionally and affordably. Check our website for client reviews."

TRAIL MEDIA

PO Box 1285, Orange, CA 92856

admin@ChisholmTrailMedia.com | *www.chisholmtrailmedia.com*

Christine "CJ" Simpson, publishing director

Types: ebooks, gift books, picture books, POD

Services: à la carte options, copyediting, manuscript evaluation, marketing, packages of services, promotional materials, proofreading, substantive editing

Production time: negotiable

Tip: "Our goal is to help new authors publish their work by coordinating the services needed with experts in the field and publishing in a co-op fashion under the Trail Media imprint, so 100% of the revenue generated goes to ministry of the authors. In many cases, we find scholarships and grants to help missionaries and those in the persecuted church. Trail Media is a ministry of modified tentmaking models."

TRILOGY CHRISTIAN PUBLISHING

PO Box A, Santa Ana, CA 92711 | 855-214-2665

www.trilogy.tv

Bryan Norris, director of publications

Types: ebooks, hardcover, POD

Services: copyediting, design, illustrations, marketing, online bookstore

Also does: royalty contracts

Tip: "The Trinity Broadcasting Family of Networks is blazing a trail worldwide, with fresh, innovative programs that entertain, inspire, and change lives. In addition to the 8,000 cable and satellite affiliates that reach over 100 million homes across America and every inhabited continent, the TBN Family of Networks will continue to aggressively expand their reach as they deliver content across all social media and digital platforms. As part of your book release TBN will use its social media platforms such as Facebook (1.4 million followers), Twitter (133,700 followers) and Instagram (913,000 followers) to promote it. From there, all of the social media strength of Trilogy Christian Publishing will be deployed."

VIDE PRESS

videpress.com

Tom Frieling, publisher

> **Types:** ebooks, paperback
> **Services:** copyediting, design, distribution, marketing, proofreading
> **Tip:** "We are always searching for new voices, articulate Christian writers who have the courage to confront the issues challenging today's culture and our faith."

WARNER HOUSE PRESS

1325 Lane Switch Rd., Albertville, AL 35951 | 256-660-0232

robert@warner.house | *warner.house*

Robert Warner, managing editor

> **Types:** ebooks, hardcover, offset paperback, picture books
> **Services:** à la carte options, author websites, copyediting, distribution, manuscript evaluation, online bookstore, proofreading, substantive editing
> **Production time:** three months
> **Books per year:** eight
> **Also does:** royalty contracts
> **Tip:** "Everyone has a story in them! No matter what stage of writing you're at, we can help."

THE WELL PUBLISHERS

PMB #533, 520 Butternut Dr., Ste. B, Holland, MI 49424 | 616-212-0151

kbruins77@gmail.com | *thewellpublishers.com*

Sandy Gould, project coordinator

> **Types:** ebooks, gift books, hardcover, offset paperback, picture books
> **Services:** à la carte options, copyediting, design, distribution, ghostwriting, indexing, manuscript evaluation, marketing, packages of services, promotional materials, proofreading, substantive

editing

Production time: three months

Books per year: 10

Also does: royalty contracts

Tip: "Have your manuscript as ready as possible."

WESTBOW PRESS

1663 Liberty Dr., Bloomington, IN 47403 | 844-714-3454

www.westbowpress.com

Types: audiobooks, ebooks, gift books, hardcover, offset paperback, POD

Services: book trailer, copyediting, design, distribution, illustrations, indexing, manuscript evaluation, marketing, packages of services, Spanish translation, substantive editing

Tip: Independent publishing division of Thomas Nelson and Zondervan.

WORD ALIVE PRESS

119 De Baets St., Winnipeg, MB R2J 3R9, Canada | 866-967-3782

jen@wordalivepress.ca | *www.wordalivepress.ca*

Jen Jandavs-Hedlin, publishing consultant

Types: audiobooks, ebooks, gift books, hardcover, offset paperback, picture books, POD

Services: à la carte options, copyediting, design, distribution, indexing, manuscript evaluation, marketing, online bookstore, packages of services, promotional materials

Production time: three to six months

Books per year: 100

Also does: royalty contracts

Tip: "Start with a manuscript evaluation from a reputable editor or publisher. They will help you to identify and address any big-picture trouble spots prior to investing in copyediting or publishing."

XULON PRESS

555 Winderley Pl., Ste. 225, Maitland, FL 32751 | 407-339-4217

www.xulonpress.com

Donald Newman, executive director of publishing

Types: ebooks, hardcover, offset paperback, POD

Services: à la carte options, book trailer, copyediting, design, ghostwriting, illustrations, manuscript evaluation, marketing, online bookstore, packages of services, promotional materials, substantive editing

Production time: three to six months

YOUR BACKYARD

2867 Jefferson St., Marianna, FL 32448 | 615-613-5040

ybymedia@gmail.com | yourbackyard.us

shELAH, publisher

Types: ebooks, hardcover, offset paperback, picture books, POD

Services: à la carte options, author websites, coaching, design, distribution, indexing, manuscript evaluation, packages of services, proofreading, substantive editing

Production time: 3–12 months

Books per year: three

Tip: "Study to shew [show] thyself approved unto God, a workman that needeth not to be ashamed, rightly dividing the word of truth" (2 Timothy 2:15).

Note: See "Editorial Services" and "Publicity and Marketing Services" for help with these needs.

DESIGN AND PRODUCTION SERVICES

4

1DOLLARSCAN

2470 Winchester Blvd., Ste. A, Campbell, CA 95008 | 669-212-0185
contact@1dollarscan.com | 1dollarscan.com

Contact: email

Services: document scanning, file conversion

Charges: custom, flat fee

Credentials/experience: "1DollarScan is the most affordable scanning/digitizing service in the world. Through innovative technology solutions and the best practices, we are able to create the lowest priced and most affordable service with the best quality in the business."

829 DESIGN | LINNÉ GARRETT

8749 Cortina Cir., Roseville, CA 95678-2940 | 408-410-8072
linne@829design.com | www.829design.com

Contact: email, phone, website form

Services: book-cover design, book-interior design, branding design, ebook conversion, graphic design, illustrations, marketing design, typesetting, website design

Charges: custom, flat fee, hourly rate

Credentials/experience: "For over two decades, our unwavering commitment to delivering exceptional creative design services has left a lasting impact on brands, ambitious startups, small businesses, and private clients around the globe. While custom book design remains one of our cherished specialties, our portfolio encompasses a wide spectrum of offerings. From brand strategy and identity design to publication design, user-centric digital experiences with bespoke web development, and comprehensive digital marketing services encompassing SEO and Google ads—we deliver it all. Print design and brand collateral marketing are also part of our diverse expertise."

BACK·DOOR DESIGN

backdoordesign99@gmail.com | backdoordesign99.wixsite.com/info

Contact: email, website form

Services: book-cover design, book-interior design, ebook conversion, illustrations, typesetting

Charges: custom, flat fee

Credentials/experience: "At back • door DESIGN, our mission is to create high-quality book designs at DIY prices. We are all about book design, from front cover to back cover and everything in between. Adobe Certified Associate in Print & Digital Publication Using Adobe InDesign."

BBS PUBLISHING AND COMMUNICATIONS, LLC | PAMELA GOSSIAUX

734-846-0112

pam@pamelagossiaux.com | BestsellingBookShepherd.com

Contact: email

Services: book trailer, book-cover design, book-interior design, e-book conversion, newsletter design, printing, website design

Charges: custom, flat fee, hourly rate

Credentials/experience: "Let me turn your fiction or nonfiction manuscript into a bestseller! Experienced book shepherd can help you with design, publication, distribution, and more. I've coached and promoted authors to Amazon, *USA Today* and *Wall Street Journal* bestsellers. Degrees in Creative Writing & English Language and Literature from University of Michigan. International bestselling author."

BELIEVERS BOOK SERVICES | DAVE SHEETS

2329 Farragut Ave., Colorado Springs, CO 80907 | 719-641-7862

dave@believersbookservices.com | www.believersbookservices.com

Contact: email

Services: book-cover design, book-interior design, ebook conversion, illustrations, printing, typesetting, website design

Charges: custom

Credentials/experience: "Our team has decades of experience in traditional publishing (Tyndale, Multnomah, Harvest House,

NavPress), book wholesaling (STL Distribution), book distribution (Advocate Distribution Solutions), book printing (Bethany Press, Snowfall Press), book retailing (Glen Eyrie Bookstore), and independent publishing (Believers Press, BelieversBookServices). We know how to help our clients achieve their goals while maintaining control over their own book project. We have helped hundreds of authors successfully publish, both in the United States and around the world."

BETHANY PRESS INTERNATIONAL
6820 W. 115th St., Bloomington, MN 55438 | 888-717-7400
info@bethanypress.com | *www.bethanypress.com*

Contact: email, website form
Services: printing
Charges: flat fee
Credentials/experience: Printer for the majority of Christian publishing houses since 1997. "We partner with authors, ministries, and publishers to create, produce, and distribute millions of life-changing Christian books each year. We invest our proceeds in training and sending missionaries through Bethany International."

BLUE LEAF BOOK SCANNING | DON O'DANIEL
618 Crowsnest Dr., Ballwin, MN 63021 | 314-606-9322
blue.leaf.it@gmail.com | *www.blueleaf-book-scanning.com*

Contact: email, website form
Services: audiobook, document scanning, ebook conversion
Charges: flat fee
Credentials/experience: "We have been providing low-cost scanning services since 2008."

BREADBOX CREATIVE | ERYN LYNUM
1437 N. Denver Ave. #167, Loveland, CO 80538 | 970-308-3654
eryn@breadboxcreative.com | *www.breadboxcreative.com/creators*

Contact: website form
Services: website design
Charges: flat fee
Credentials/experience: "At Breadbox Creative, we have more than twenty years of experience in web design. The owner, Eryn Lynum, is an author herself and marries her passion for writing with her passion for web design to come alongside writers and speakers

and help them further spread the messages God has laid on their hearts. Breadbox Creative works with businesses, writers, and speakers by creating professional WordPress websites, as well as assisting with SEO and social-media platforms."

BREE ROSE CREATIVE | BREE BYLE

MI | 616-425-8816
breerosecreative@gmail.com | *www.BreeRoseCreative.com*

Contact: email
Services: book-branding photography and marketing design, book-interior design, illustrations, typesetting, website design
Charges: custom, flat fee
Credentials/experience: "I started my own business after working in Christian book publishing and retail for 10 years (Baker Book House, Baker Publishing Group). During that time my photography was published in *Publishers Weekly,* and I was the graphic designer for Breathe Christian Writers Conference (two years). I now work freelance with publishing houses, bookstores, conferences, and independent authors by offering a variety of design services to the word world."

BRENDA WILBEE

4631 Quinn Ct. #202, Bellingham, WA 98226 | 360-389-6895
Brenda@BrendaWilbee.com | *www.BrendaWilbee.com*

Contact: website form
Services: book-cover design, illustrations, promotional materials, typesetting
Charges: flat fee
Credentials/experience: "My clients have included Habitat for Humanity, Windstar Cruise Lines, Whatcom Community College, Edirol, Lions Club International, and other organizations. I currently specialize in cover design and spin-off marketing products like bookmarks and flyers."

BRIAN WHITE DESIGN | BRIAN WHITE

Lawrence, KS | 785-841-5500
brianwhite.design

Contact: phone, website form
Services: book-cover design, graphic design, illustrations, logo design, website design
Charges: flat fee, hourly rate

Credentials/experience: Twenty years in the design/web design/ branding industry.

BROOKSTONE CREATIVE GROUP | JOHN HERRING

100 Missionary Ridge, Birmingham, AL 35242 | 302-514-7899
www.brookstonecreativegroup.com

Contact: phone
Services: book-cover design, book-interior design, logo design, printing, promotional materials, website design
Charges: flat fee
Credentials/experience: "Brookstone Creative Group is changing the landscape for how writers, authors, speakers, pastors, musicians, and other creatives navigate the ever-changing landscape of platform development. Through true and tested solutions, training, and community-building, Brookstone Creative Group guides their clients in the who, where, when, and how to inspirational success."

BUTTERFIELD EDITORIAL SERVICES | DEBRA L. BUTTERFIELD

4810 Gene Field Rd., Saint Joseph, MO 64506 | 816-752-2171
deb@debralbutterfield.com | themotivationaleditor.com

Contact: email
Services: book-cover design, book-interior design, ebook conversion
Charges: flat fee
Credentials/experience: "Over six years of experience."

CELEBRATION WEB DESIGN | BRUCE SHANK

PO Box 471068, Kissimmee, FL 34747 | 877-313-7593
info@celebrationwebdesign.com | CelebrationWebDesign.com

Contact: email, phone, website form
Services: website design
Charges: custom
Credentials/experience: "Celebration Web Design develops handcrafted websites, branding packages, and marketing solutions. Since 2002, our expert staff has been helping individuals and organizations enhance their online presence. Celebration Web Design's team is enthusiastic with focused analysts, developers, and designers who have a passion for technology and online marketing solutions. We consider it a privilege to serve God by helping individuals and organizations with their website and online marketing needs."

CREATIVE CORNERSTONES | CAYLAH COFFEEN and GALADRIEL COFFEEN

Huntsville, AL | 318-553-1625

creativecornerstones@gmail.com | *creativecornerstones.com/pre-release-materials*

Contact: email, website form

Services: audiobook, book trailer, book-cover design, book-interior design, ebook conversion, illustrations, typesetting, website design

Charges: custom

Credentials/experience: "Creative Cornerstones is a team of creatives who can make your book stand out from the crowd. We can create all your designs in one place: book exterior, interior, and visual marketing. Galadriel is an artist with over 10 years of experience. She can bring your vision to life, creating a sharp, hyperrealistic digital cover, character illustrations, maps, and even audiobooks. She specializes in fantasy and sci-fi art and can make the inside of a book pop as much as the outside. Caylah is a designer with experience creating WordPress websites, book trailers, and illustrations for social media and has worked as a content creator for Monster Ivy Publishing and Eschler Editing. We'll create a plan for each design step with our knowledge of the industry, so you can focus on what you love: writing."

DESERT RAIN EDITING | GLENIECE LYTLE

PO Box 8163, Hualapai, AZ 86412 | 928-715-7125

desert.rain.editing@gmail.com | *desertrainediting.com*

Contact: email, website form

Services: book-interior design, ebook conversion, typesetting

Charges: flat fee, page rate

Credentials/experience: "I began the typesetting journey a few years ago when one of my editing clients was dissatisfied with her final printed book from a vanity publisher. I learned quickly and discovered how much I enjoy interior book design. Now, I look forward to taking my editing clients' final manuscripts and creating clean, elegant, and readable print-ready PDFs and EPUB ebook files that look as polished and professional as they read."

DESIGN CORPS | JOHN WOLLINKA

1370 Carlson Dr., Colorado Springs, CO 80910 | 719-260-0500

general@designcorps.us | *designcorps.us*

Contact: email, phone, website form

Services: book-cover design, book-interior design, ebook conversion, illustrations, typesetting

Charges: flat fee

Credentials/experience: "Design Corps has been serving the Christian community for over 20 years. Our publishing clients have ranged from big publishers (such as Zondervan and Moody Publishers) to self-publishers. We have a love for the word that we bring with extensive experience in design to covers, interiors, page composition, illustration, and production (printed books and ebooks)."

THE DESIGN IN YOUR MIND | MARY C. FINDLEY

Tulsa, OK | 918-805-0669

mjmcfindley@gmail.com | *findleyfamilyvideopublications.com/the-design-in-your-mind*

Contact: email

Services: book-cover design, book-interior design

Charges: flat fee

Credentials/experience: "More than ten years video and graphic design experience, book covers, formatting, and trailers."

DIGGYPOD | KEVIN OSWORTH

301 Industrial Dr., Tecumseh, MI 49286 | 877-944-7844

kosworth@diggypod.com | *www.diggypod.com*

Contact: phone, website form

Services: book-cover design, printing

Charges: custom

Credentials/experience: "DiggyPOD has been printing books since 2001. All facets of the book printing take place in our facility."

EAH CREATIVE | EMILIE HANEY

PO Box 69, Taylorsville, IN 47280 | 661-904-9409

emilie.eahcreative@gmail.com | *www.eahcreative.com*

Contact: email

Services: book-cover design, book-interior design

Charges: custom, flat fee

Credentials/experience: "Emilie works with small and large traditional publishers, as well as independent authors to create vibrant and marketable covers and graphics. Over the last six years, her covers have been finalists for awards and allowed her opportunities to speak about cover design and other aspects of graphic design specifically for authors. She approaches each new project with the desire to make the best and most marketable cover that will be at home on the digital or physical shelf."

EDENBROOKE PRODUCTIONS | MARTY KEITH

615-415-1942

johnmartinkeith@hotmail.com | *www.edenbrookemusic.com/booktrailers*

    Contact: email, phone, website form

    Services: book trailer

    Charges: flat fee

    Credentials/experience: "Edenbrooke Productions believes your story deserves a unique soundtrack. We've produced music for everyone from CBS Television to Discovery Channel, and now we want to give your story the star treatment."

ERIN ULRICH CREATIVE | ERIN ULRICH

PO Box 80282, Simpsonville, SC 29680

hello@erinulrichcreative.com | *erinulrichcreative.com*

    Contact: website form

    Services: website design

    Charges: flat fee

    Credentials/experience: "In today's world, your website matters more than ever. You need an online space designed to help you reach your goals. Sometimes that's easier said than done. We're here to listen to what you hope to achieve and develop a website strategy that gets results. We have been designing and building WordPress sites for over 13 years. Our clients include writers, small-business owners, nonprofits, and more. Whether you're starting from scratch or ready to take your web presence to the next level, we want to partner with you to see your vision become a reality."

FISTBUMP MEDIA, LLC | DAN KING

115 E. 4th Ave., Ste. 212, Mount Dora, FL 32757 | 941-681-8015

dan@fistbumpmedia.com | *fistbumpmedia.com*

    Contact: email

    Services: book-cover design, book-interior design, ebook conversion, website design

    Charges: flat fee, hourly rate, page rate

    Credentials/experience: "With our roots in building an online presence as a blogger-author and growing authentic social-media community, we are a digital marketing (and managed WordPress hosting) agency which knows how to grow a brand online from the ground up. We're WordPress specialists, and our goal is to help you manage the technical side of being online."

THE FOREWORD COLLECTIVE | MOLLY HODGIN

1726 Charity Dr., Brentwood, TN 37027 | 615-497-4322
info@theforewordcollective.com | *www.theforewordcollective.com*

> **Contact:** email, phone, website form
> **Services:** book-cover design
> **Charges:** flat fee, hourly rate
> **Credentials/experience:** "The Foreword Collective was founded by Molly Hodgin, a publishing professional with two decades of experience. Most recently, she served as the Associate Publisher for the Specialty Division of HarperCollins Christian Publishing, working to acquire and create gift books, children's books, and new media products with authors and brands."

HANNAH LINDER DESIGNS | HANNAH LINDER

hannah@hannahlinderdesigns.com | *www.hannahlinderdesigns.com*

> **Contact:** email, website form
> **Services:** book-cover design, book-interior design
> **Charges:** custom, flat fee
> **Credentials/experience:** "Hannah Linder Designs specializes in professional book-cover design with affordable prices. Having designed for both traditional publishing houses and individual authors, including *New York Times*-, *USA Today*-, national-, and international-bestsellers, Hannah understands the importance of an attractive book cover and the trends of today's industry. Also, Hannah is a *magna cum laude* Graphic Design Associates Degree graduate and an award-winning book-cover designer."

HEADSHOTS OF CHICAGO | JIM MUELLER

66 Grove Ct. #1155, Elgin, IL 60120 | 847-220-4239
jim@headshotsofchicago.com | *headshotsofchicago.com*

> **Contact:** email, phone
> **Services:** PR photo
> **Charges:** flat fee
> **Credentials/experience:** "I am an award-winning photographer with 20+ years of experience with a concentration on people. Over the years I've photographed a diverse range of faces—a wide array of backgrounds, emotions, and aspirations—with the goal of delighting my clients with best-in-class service and excellent images."

INKSNATCHER | SALLY HANAN

429 S. Avenue C, Elgin, TX 78621 | 512-265-6403
bookhelp@inksnatcher.com | *inksnatcher.com*

> **Contact:** email, website form
> **Services:** book trailer, book-cover design, book-interior design, ebook conversion, typesetting, website design
> **Charges:** custom
> **Credentials/experience:** "Sally Hanan, an author herself, started Inksnatcher in 2008 with just editing services. Today, Inksnatcher provides self-publishing authors with every service they need to produce and publish with excellence. Inksnatcher is an approved service provider with the Alliance of Independent Authors, the Christian Editor Connection, and Reedsy."

JENNIFER EDWARDS COMMUNICATIONS | JENNIFER EDWARDS

2839 Sleeping Bear Rd., Montrose, CO 81401 | 916-768-4207
mail.jennifer.edwards@gmail.com | *jedwardsediting.net*

> **Contact:** email
> **Services:** production management for self-publishing
> **Charges:** flat fee
> **Credentials/experience:** "I manage the production of printed/ digital books and consult with self-publishing authors through the publishing process. Includes working with cover and interior designers and illustrators to produce hardcovers, paperbacks, and ebooks. I have six years of experience working wih Amazon KDP and Ingram Spark to self-publish books."

JENNIFER WESTBROOK

14030 Connecticut Ave. #6813, Silver Spring, MD 20916
support@jenwestwriting.com | *www.jenwestwriting.com/web-design*

> **Contact:** email
> **Services:** website design
> **Charges:** custom, flat fee
> **Credentials/experience:** "I build Wix websites that pack a punch, complete with all the must-haves you need to keep thriving online. As a copywriter and web designer with over eight years of experience, I create the right mix of words, design, and behind-the-scenes systems to make everything work together seamlessly so you can get next-level results."

JESSICA LINN EVANS, LLC | JESSICA LINN EVANS

736 E 8th St., Moscow, ID 83843 | 208-882-5530
jessicaevans915@gmail.com | *jessicalinnevans.com*

Contact: email
Services: book-cover design, illustrations
Charges: custom, flat fee
Credentials/experience: "Jessica Linn Evans is an author-illustrator. Her illustrations are rendered with traditional media, including watercolor, graphite, and ink. With her books, she wants to reinforce wonder for creation, inspire adventure and invention, and encourage loyalty and friendship with the lovely."

KELLIE BOOK DESIGN | KELLIE PARSONS

Unit 1, 23 Apara Way, Nollamara, WA 6061, Australia | 0412 591 687
kellie@kelliemaree.com | *www.kelliemaree.com*

Contact: website form
Services: book-cover design, book-interior design, ebook conversion, typesetting
Charges: flat fee
Credentials/experience: "Book designer for over six years, graphic designer for over ten years. Experience with various software, including Vellum for ebook conversion. Primarily working with self-publishers."

LAUNCH MISSION CREATIVE | TRAVIS D. PETERSON

travis@launchmissions.com | *www.launchmissioncreative.com*

Contact: website form
Services: Amazon A+ content, book-cover design, book-interior design, Kickstarter graphics, printing, typesetting
Charges: custom
Credentials/experience: "Not only am I an award-winning Christian children's author myself, but also an award-winning print designer with over a decade of experience both in-house for a couple of internationally recognized ministries and as a freelancer. I hold a degree in Computer Graphics Technology from Purdue University."

MARTIN PUBLISHING SERVICES | MELINDA MARTIN

Palestine, TX | 903-948-4893
martinpublishingservices@gmail.com | *melindamartin.me*

Contact: email, phone

Services: book-cover design, book-interior design, ebook conversion, typesetting

Charges: flat fee

Credentials/experience: "More than five years of working with clients' manuscripts to achieve a design that is best for their platforms."

MISSION AND MEDIA | MICHELLE RAYBURN

11510 County Highway M, New Auburn, WI 54757
info@missionandmedia.com | *missionandmedia.com*

Contact: email, website form

Services: book-cover design, book-interior design, ebook conversion, typesetting

Charges: flat fee, hourly rate, free consultation

Credentials/experience: "Michelle works with indie and self-published authors to design a quality book cover and interior. She also coaches those who want to create their own imprint with full control of their own publishing process. Her area of specialty is with Amazon KDP. Michelle has more than 20 years of experience on the writing and editing side of publishing. Portfolio and additional information are available on the website."

MOUNTAIN CREEK BOOKS | KARA STARCHER

PO Box 93, Chloe, WV 25235 | 330-705-3399
mtncreekbooks@gmail.com | *mountaincreekbooks.com*

Contact: website form

Services: book-cover design, book-interior design, ebook conversion, typesetting

Charges: custom, flat fee

Credentials/experience: "BA in publishing, Columbia Scholastic Press Association medalist, West Virginia Press Association winner."

PAGE & PIXEL PUBLICATIONS | SUSAN MOORE

La Crosse, WI
pageandpixelpublications@gmail.com | *pageandpixelpublications.com*

Contact: email

Services: book trailer, book-cover design, book-interior design, ebook conversion, typesetting

Charges: hourly rate

Credentials/experience: "Are you preparing to self-publish? I can format your manuscript to give it that professional look within the parameters of your publishing house. The design would include the entire interior of your book. A digital, print-ready PDF of your book's completed interior layout is provided. I can convert your manuscript into the digital format that is readable on devices like Kindle, Nook, tablets, phones, computers, and notebooks, as well as generic brand e-readers. Working from your original document in Microsoft Word, InDesign, PDF, or other format, I will provide you with a digital file that you can upload to Amazon, Barnes and Noble, or other suppliers. Your finished product will feature a navigable table of contents and hyperlinked footnotes, as well as any graphic images that you choose to include."

PRAIRIE FALLS BOOKS | DEBRA L. BUTTERFIELD and TAMARA CLYMER
St. Joseph, MO
deb@prairiefallbooks.com | prairiefallsbooks.com

> **Contact:** website form
> **Services:** book-cover design, book-interior design, ebook conversion, website design
> **Charges:** flat fee
> **Credentials/experience:** "Our professional designers have a wide variety of experience in book design, interior layout, catalogs, and magazines in both freelance and traditional publishing."

PROFESSIONAL PUBLISHING SERVICES | CHRISTY CALLAHAN
912-388-1898
professionalpublishingservices@gmail.com | professionalpublishingservicesus.weebly.com

> **Contact:** website form
> **Services:** book-cover design, book-interior design, ebook conversion, typesetting
> **Charges:** custom
> **Credentials/experience:** "Christy graduated Phi Beta Kappa from Carnegie Mellon University, where she first learned how to use Adobe software. While she earned her MA in Intercultural Studies from Fuller Seminary, she edited sound files for distance-learning classes for the Media Center and designed ads as Women's Concerns Committee chairperson. Christy is an Adobe Certified Associate in Print & Digital Publication Using Adobe InDesign, leveraging her expertise as an editor and proofreader and extensive

knowledge of *Chicago* style to create professional-looking book covers and interior layouts."

REDEMPTION PRESS | ATHENA DEAN HOLTZ

1602 Cole St., Enumclaw, WA 98022 | 360-226-3488
athena@redemption-press.com | *www.redemption-press.com*

Contact: website form
Services: website design, audiobook
Charges: flat fee
Credentials/experience: "Our website partner helps authors create well-branded and effective websites with email marketing integration, including a compelling lead magnet. Our audiobook services offer both author- and professional-narrated books with full distribution. We don't list all our services on our website."

RICK STEELE EDITORIAL SERVICES | RICK STEELE

26 Dean Rd., Ringgold, GA 30736 | 706-937-8121
rsteelecam@gmail.com | *steeleeditorialservices.myportfolio.com*

Contact: website form
Services: book-interior design, ebook conversion, typesetting
Charges: flat fee
Credentials/experience: "Working for smaller Christian publishing houses has required me to wear many hats. Through the years, I have gained ample experience using page-layout software. I have the skills to take your edited manuscript to printed-page format with a professional, attractive page layout. If you are wanting to publish your manuscript with Amazon's Kindle or similar platform, I can help prepare your manuscript file for publication and assist with file submission steps."

ROSEANNA WHITE DESIGNS | ROSEANNA WHITE

roseannamwhite@gmail.com | *www.RoseannaWhiteDesigns.com*

Contact: email, website form
Services: book-cover design, book-interior design, ebook conversion, illustrations, typesetting
Charges: custom, flat fee, hourly rate
Credentials/experience: "Roseanna has been designing and typesetting books for nearly ten years, combining her keen eye and artistic skills with her insider knowledge of the industry. As an author herself, she knows how important it is for the appearance of a book to match the words and strives to bring your story to

life at a single glance. She has worked for publishing houses and independently for some of Christian fiction's top authors."

SCOTT LA COUNTE

Anaheim, CA | 714-404-7182
Roboscott@gmail.com | *scottdouglas.org/coaching*

Contact: website form
Services: book-cover design, ebook conversion
Charges: flat fee
Credentials/experience: "I've worked in publishing for over 20 years (both in traditional publishing and self-publishing). Over those years, I have helped indie publishers sell over 2,000,000 books."

STORYWRAP.CA | LYSA

Saskatchewan, Canada
designer@storywrap.ca | *storywrap.ca*

Contact: email, website form
Services: advertising, book-cover design, book-interior design, graphics
Charges: custom, flat fee
Credentials/experience: "Storywrap.ca is a team of graphic designers with several years of experience. We are committed to offering quality design services at an affordable price for authors. We invite potential clients to browse our website; and if our design style is what you're looking for, get in touch with us to discuss your needs."

SUZANNE FYHRIE PARROTT

PO Box 571, Gleneden Beach, OR 97388
author@suzannefyhrieparrott.com | *www.SuzanneFyhrieParrott.com*

Contact: website form
Services: book-cover design, book-interior design, ebook conversion, illustrations, typesetting
Charges: custom, flat fee
Credentials/experience: "With over 40 years of experience in graphic design, illustration, and advertising, Suzanne Parrott's design services include logos, book-cover design, book layout and formatting, ebook formatting and design. She prioritizes each client's specific needs, ensuring they receive the utmost attention and tailored solutions. Additionally, Parrott guides authors throughout the entire publication process, leveraging POD

publishing sources like Ingram Spark and Amazon KDP. Her dedication to delivering high-quality work has been recognized through several awards for design excellence."

TLC BOOK DESIGN | TAMARA DEVER
Austin, TX
tamara@tlcgraphics.com | *www.TLCBookDesign.com*
   Contact: website form
   Services: book-cover design, book-interior design, ebook conversion, printing, typesetting
   Charges: custom, flat fee
   Credentials/experience: "We are a small, Christ-loving group of professionals; and we are honored to share this ministry with authors worldwide. Whether you need complete production or just design, we're here to build your book and coach you through the process. Serving the publishing industry for over 30 years, our books have garnered more than 280 awards; and we'd love to add you to the TLC family of authors and publishers!"

TWO WORDS PUBLISHING | CLATON BUTCHER
3213 W. Main St. #166, Rapid City, SD 57702
cbutcher@twowordspublishing.com | *www.twowordspublishing.com*
   Contact: email
   Services: audiobook
   Charges: hourly rate
   Credentials/experience: "We have had the privilege of publishing and producing audiobooks with various Christian publishers, both large and small, such as Baker Publishing Group, Tyndale House, Charisma House, Crossway, Harvest House, Barbour Publishing, 10ofThose, Cruciform, and many others. Our projects have extended beyond publishers to include talented individual authors like Robin Lee Hatcher, Joel C. Rosenberg, and Elizabeth Camden. With a wide selection of Christian narrators, we are able to bring a personal touch to every project we undertake, all to expand the reach of the Gospel and strengthen the Church."

VIVID GRAPHICS | LARRY VAN HOOSE
221 S. Main St., Ste. 200, Galax, VA 24333 | 276-233-0276
info@vivid-graphics.com | *www.vivid-graphics.com*
   Contact: email, phone, website form
   Services: book-cover design, book-interior design, ebook conversion,

graphic design, website design

Charges: custom, flat fee, hourly rate

Credentials/experience: "Larry Van Hoose is the creative director for Vivid Graphics and has over 20 years of experience in design, writing, photography, and marketing."

WRITER'S TABLET AGENCY | TERRI WHITEMORE

4371 Roswell Rd. #315, Marietta, GA 30062 | 770-648-4101

twhitemore@writerstablet.org | www.Writerstablet.org

Contact: email, website form

Services: book-cover design, book-interior design, ebook conversion, illustrations, typesetting

Charges: flat fee

Credentials/experience: "Becoming a published author requires a lot more than a knack for writing and a great story. Partnering with the Writer's Tablet Agency will put you on the fast-track to seeing your name in print. Learn how to navigate the complex world of publishing alongside passionate published authors with years of experience. From polishing your final manuscript to launching your book, Writer's Tablet simplifies the Road to Publication."

YO PRODUCTIONS, LLC | YOLANDA SANDERS

7185 E. Main St., Unit 1543, Reynoldsburg, OH 43068 | 614-452-4920

info_4u@yoproductions.net | www.yoproductions.net

Contact: email, phone, website form

Services: book-cover design, book-interior design, ebook conversion, typesetting

Charges: custom, flat fee, hourly rate

Credentials/experience: "Yo Productions, LLC is a publishing consultant that helps authors get their work from paper to print. The company is owned by author and scholar, Yolonda Tonette Sanders, PhD., and provides clients with book-cover designs and formatting for digital and print works."

Note: See "Editorial Services" and "Publicity and Marketing Services" for help with these needs.

5

DISTRIBUTION SERVICES

AMAZON SELLER CENTRAL

sell.amazon.com

Amazon has two selling plans: individual for 99¢ per book and professional for $39.99 per month. Both plans have other selling fees as well. You can manage inventory, update pricing, communicate with buyers, contact support, and add new products all from the Seller Central website.

BCH FULFILLMENT & DISTRIBUTION

33 Oakland Ave., Harrison, NY 10528 | 914-835-0015

bookch@aol.com | www.bookch.com/home.taf

Provides exclusive fulfillment and distribution services, including relationships with wholesalers and bookstores, warehousing your books, taking orders from wholesalers and bookstores, fulfilling those orders, billing and collecting monies, processing returns, and getting your books into Ingram if you qualify. Fees vary, depending on the services.

MIDPOINT TRADE BOOKS

27 W. 20th St., Ste. 1102, New York, NY 10011 | 212-727-0190

eric@midpointtrade.com | www.midpointtrade.com

A full-service book distribution division of Independent Publishers Group. Provides warehousing, fulfillment, and catalog inclusion under Covenant Media Resources, an extension of sales and distribution services specifically tailored to meet the needs of the Christian marketplace. In addition to reaching the traditional CBA market, it has access to a wide range of general bookstores and wholesalers that successfully sell Christian and other likeminded titles.

PATHWAY BOOK SERVICE

34 Production Ave., Keene, NH 03431 | 800-345-6665

pbs@pathwaybook.com | www.pathwaybook.com

Provides warehousing, order fulfillment, and trade distribution. It is a longtime distributor to Ingram and Baker & Taylor, the vendors of choice for most bookstores. Pathway uploads new-title spreadsheets to Ingram and Baker & Taylor, as well as to *Amazon.com*, Barnes & Noble, and Books-A-Million on a weekly basis. Distribution outside of North America is available through Gazelle Book Services in the United Kingdom. Also provides the option of having Pathway add titles to its Amazon Advantage account, which is at a lower discount and often a lower shipping cost per book than individual accounts.

PUBLISHERS STORING AND SHIPPING
660 S. Mansfield, Ypsilanti, MI 48197 | 734-487-9720
pssc.com

Provides warehousing, call center, order fulfillment, and returns for single-title self-publishers to large publishing houses. Has a second facility at 46 Development Rd., Fitchburg, MA 01420; 978-345-2121.

PART 3

PERIODICAL PUBLISHERS

6

TOPICS AND TYPES

This chapter is not an exhaustive list of types of manuscripts and topics periodical editors are looking for, but it is a starting place for some of the more popular ones. For instance, almost all periodicals take manuscripts in categories like Christian living, so they are not listed here. Plus writers guidelines tend to outline general areas, not every specific type and topic an editor will buy.

CONTEMPORARY ISSUES

Anglican Journal
The Baptist Bulletin
Canadian Mennonite
Caring Magazine
Catholic Sentinel
Celebrate Life Magazine
The Christian Century
Christianity Today
Columbia
The Covenant Companion
Faith Today
Influence
Light
Ministry
Mutuality
Now What?
Our Sunday Visitor
St. Anthony Messenger
The War Cry

DEVOTIONS

Brio
Eternal Ink
Focus on the Family Clubhouse
Gather
Gems of Truth
Inspire a Fire
Mature Living
ParentLife
Power for Living
Words for the Way

ESSAYS

America
The Canadian Lutheran
The Christian Century
Commonweal
Ekstasis
Faith Today
Image
Ink & Quill Quarterly

Love Is Moving
The Lutheran Witness
Our Sunday Visitor
Poets & Writers Magazine
U.S. Catholic
The Writer
The Writer's Chronicle
Writer's Digest

EVANGELISM

Baptist Standard
Blue Ridge Christian News
Christian Herald
Evangelical Missions Quarterly
Faith on Every Corner
Just Between Us
Mature Living
Net Results
Outreach
The War Cry

FAMILY

The Baptist Bulletin
Baptist Standard
Boundless
Brio
Caring Magazine
Columbia
Creative Inspirations
Faith & Friends
Focus on the Family
Focus on the Family Clubhouse
Focus on the Family Clubhouse Jr.
Gems of Truth
Guideposts
HomeLife
Influence
Inspire a Fire

Joyful Living Magazine
Light
Mature Living
Ministry
The Mother's Heart
ParentLife
St. Anthony Messenger

FICTION

See Short Story.

FILLERS

Angels on Earth
Bible Advocate
Blue Ridge Christian News
Christian Herald
Eternal Ink
Focus on the Family Clubhouse
Focus on the Family Clubhouse Jr.
Guideposts
LIVE
The Mother's Heart
StarLight Magazine
Words for the Way
yOur Backyard

HOW-TO

Baptist Standard
Blue Ridge Christian News
Cadet Quest
Canada Lutheran
Celebrate Life Magazine
Christian Herald
Christian Standard
Evangelical Missions Quarterly
Faith Today
Focus on the Family

Focus on the Family Clubhouse
HomeLife
Influence
InSite
The Journal of Adventist Education
Joyful Living Magazine
Just Between Us
Leading Hearts
Light
LIVE
The Lutheran Witness
Mature Living
Ministry
The Mother's Heart
Mutuality
Net Results
Outreach
ParentLife
Parish Liturgy
Poets & Writers Magazine
Prayer Connect
Teachers of Vision
Words for the Way
The Writer
Writer's Digest
WritersWeekly.com
Writing Corner
yOur Backyard

INTERVIEWS

The Arlington Catholic Herald
The Baptist Bulletin
Baptist Standard
Brio
byFaith
Cadet Quest
Canada Lutheran
Celebrate Life Magazine
Charisma

The Christian Century
Christian Herald
The Christian Journal
Christianity Today
Columbia
The Covenant Companion
DTS Magazine
Evangelical Missions Quarterly
Faith & Friends
Faith Today
Focus on the Family
Focus on the Family Clubhouse
Focus on the Family Clubhouse Jr.
Friends Journal
Guide
Image
Influence
InSite
Joyful Living Magazine
Leading Hearts
The Lutheran Witness
Nature Friend
Our Sunday Visitor
Outreach
Peer
Poets & Writers Magazine
Power for Living
Presbyterians Today
Relevant
Sports Spectrum
St. Anthony Messenger
testimony/Enrich
Today's Christian Living
U.S. Catholic
The War Cry
The Writer
The Writer's Chronicle
Writer's Digest

LEADERSHIP/MINISTRY

The Baptist Bulletin
Baptist Standard
Evangelical Missions Quarterly
Holiness Today
Influence
InSite
Inspire a Fire
Just Between Us
Love Is Moving
Mature Living
Ministry
Outreach
testimony/Enrich

MARRIAGE

The Baptist Bulletin
Boundless
Faith & Friends
Focus on the Family
Gems of Truth
HomeLife
Joyful Living Magazine
Mature Living
St. Anthony Messenger

NEWSPAPERS

Anglican Journal
The Arlington Catholic Herald
Blue Ridge Christian News
Christian Courier
Christian Herald
Christian News Northwest
Good News
The Messianic Times
Our Sunday Visitor

PARENTING

The Baptist Bulletin
Columbia
Faith on Every Corner
Focus on the Family
HomeLife
Just Between Us
Light
Mature Living
The Mother's Heart
Parenting Teens
ParentLife

PERSONAL EXPERIENCE

Angels on Earth
Anglican Journal
The Baptist Bulletin
Bible Advocate
Blue Ridge Christian News
The Breakthrough Intercessor
Café
Canada Lutheran
Canadian Mennonite
Celebrate Life Magazine
Commonweal
The Covenant Companion
Creation Illustrated
CT Pastors
DTS Magazine
Ekstasis
Eternal Ink
Faith & Friends
Faith on Every Corner
Friends Journal
Gather
Gems of Truth
Guide
Guideposts

Highway News
Holiness Today
Inspire a Fire
The Journal of Adventist Education
Joyful Living Magazine
Just Between Us
Leading Hearts
LEAVES
LIVE
The Lutheran Witness
Mature Living
The Mother's Heart
Mutuality
Now What?
Power for Living
Standard
Teachers of Vision
testimony/Enrich
Today's Christian Living
The War Cry
Words for the Way
yOur Backyard

POETRY
America
Bible Advocate
The Christian Century
Christian Courier
Commonweal
Creative Inspirations
Ekstasis
Eternal Ink
Faith on Every Corner
Focus on the Family Clubhouse Jr.
Friends Journal
Gems of Truth
Image
Ink & Quill Quarterly

Inspire a Fire
LEAVES
LIVE
Love Is Moving
The Lutheran Witness
Power for Living
Sharing
Sojourners
StarLight Magazine
Teachers of Vision
Time Of Singing
U.S. Catholic
Words for the Way
yOur Backyard

PROFILES
See Interviews.

REVIEWS
Anglican Journal
Baptist Standard
byFaith
Caring Magazine
Celebrate Life Magazine
Charisma
The Christian Century
Christian Courier
Christian Herald
The Christian Journal
Christianity Today
Evangelical Missions Quarterly
Faith & Friends
Faith on Every Corner
Faith Today
HeartBeat
The Journal of Adventist Education
Leading Hearts
LEAVES

Light
Love Is Moving
The Messianic Times
Ministry
The Mother's Heart
Mutuality
Net Results
Sojourners
Time Of Singing
U.S. Catholic
Words for the Way
The Writer

SHORT STORIES
Beginner's Friend
Blue Ridge Christian News
Brio
Cadet Quest
Creation Illustrated
Explorers
Faith on Every Corner
Focus on the Family Clubhouse
Focus on the Family Clubhouse Jr.
Gems of Truth
Image
LIVE
Mature Living
Nature Friend

St. Anthony Messenger
Sharing
StarLight Magazine
Teachers of Vision
yOur Backyard
Youth Compass

SUNDAY SCHOOL TAKE-HOME PAPERS
Beginner's Friend
Explorers
Gems of Truth
Guide
LIVE
Our Little Friend
Power for Living
Primary Treasure
Standard
Youth Compass

THEOLOGY
byFaith
The Canadian Lutheran
Faith & Friends
Mature Living
Ministry
Presbyterians Today

7

ADULT MARKETS

AMERICA

106 W. 56th St., New York, NY 10019-3803 | 212-581-4640

www.americamagazine.org

Sam Sawyer, S.J., editor in chief

Denomination: Catholic

Parent company: America Media, Jesuit Conference of the United States and Canada

Type: monthly digital and print magazine; circulation: 46,000

Audience: primarily Catholic, two-thirds laypeople, college educated

Purpose: to provide a smart Catholic take on faith and culture

Submissions: Submit complete manuscript or query letter through the website. Unsolicited freelance: 100%. Responds in two weeks.

Types of manuscripts: articles, essays, poetry

Length: articles and essays, 800–2,000 words; poetry, 40 lines maximum

Topics: Christian living/spirituality, culture, trends

Rights: electronic, first

Payment: on acceptance, competitive rates

Guidelines: *americamedia.submittable.com/submit*

Tip: "We are known across the Catholic world for our unique brand of excellent, relevant, and accessible coverage. From theology and spirituality to politics, international relations, arts and letters, and the economy and social justice, our coverage spans the globe."

ANGELS ON EARTH

110 William St., Ste. 901, New York, NY 10038 | 212-251-8100

www.shopguideposts.org/angels-on-earth-magazine.html

Colleen Hughes, editor-in-chief

Parent company: Guideposts

Type: bimonthly digital and print magazine; circulation: 550,000

Audience: general

Purpose: to tell true stories of heavenly angels and earthly ones who find themselves on a mission of comfort, kindness, or reassurance

Submissions: Submit complete manuscript through the website at *guideposts.org/tell-us-your-story*. Unsolicited freelance: 90%. Responds in two months or not interested.

Types of manuscripts: fillers, personal experience, recipes

Length: 1,500 words maximum

Topics: angels

Rights: all

Payment: on publication, $25-500

Kill fee: 20%

Manuscripts accepted per year: 40-60

Guidelines: *www.guideposts.org/writers-guidelines*

Sample: 7"x10" SASE with four stamps

Tip: "We are not limited to stories about heavenly angels. We also accept stories about human beings doing heavenly duties."

ANGLICAN JOURNAL

80 Hayden St., Toronto, ON M4Y 3G2, Canada | 416-924-9199

editor@national.anglican.ca | *www.anglicanjournal.com*

Tali Folkins, editor

Denomination: Anglican

Parent company: Anglican Church of Canada

Type: monthly digital and print newspaper; circulation: 123,000; advertising accepted

Audience: denomination

Purpose: to share compelling news and features about the Anglican Church of Canada and the Anglican communion and religion in general

Submissions: Email query letter as attachment. Query first. Responds in two weeks.

Types of manuscripts: news, personal experience, reviews

Length: 500-1,000 words

Topics: Christian living/spirituality, denomination, events, issues

Rights: first

Payment: on acceptance, $75-100

Seasonal submissions: two months in advance

Preferred Bible version: NRSV

Guidelines: *www.anglicanjournal.com/about-us/writers-guidelines*

Sample: on the website

Tip: "Stories should be of interest to a national audience. They are usually about a national event or a local issue that reflects the larger picture."

THE ARLINGTON CATHOLIC HERALD

200 N. Glebe Rd., Ste. 600, Arlington, VA 22203 | 703-841-2590

editorial@catholicherald.com | www.catholicherald.com

Ann M. Augherton, managing editor

Denomination: Catholic

Parent company: Arlington, Virginia, Diocese

Type: weekly digital and print newspaper; circulation: 70,000 advertising accepted

Audience: denomination

Purpose: to support the Church's mission to evangelize by providing news from a Catholic perspective

Submissions: Email query letter.

Types of manuscripts: feature articles, news, profiles

Sample: on the website

THE BAPTIST BULLETIN

244 S. Randall Rd. #1188, Elgin, IL 60123 | 888-588-1600

submissions@BaptistBulletin.org | baptistbulletin.org

Melissa Meyer, managing editor

Denomination: Baptist

Parent company: Regular Baptist Ministries

Type: monthly digital and print magazine; circulation: 5,300

Audience: Baptist church members

Purpose: to provide a "kitchen table" where church members gather to discuss important topics

Submissions: Email complete manuscript as attachment.

Types of manuscripts: personal experience, profiles, teaching

Length: 800–2,000 words

Topics: Christian living, denomination, discipleship, family, marriage, ministry, parenting

Rights: all

Preferred Bible version: NKJV

Guidelines: *baptistbulletin.org/write-for-us*

Tip: "The magazine is your gateway to articles addressing current issues from a Baptist perspective, inspiring stories about people who serve in unique ways, and exciting coverage of what's happening in Regular Baptist Ministries."

BAPTIST STANDARD

PO Box 941309, Plano, TX 75094 | 214-630-4571
kencamp@baptiststandard.com | *www.baptiststandard.com*
Ken Camp, managing editor, news, features, book reviews
Eric Black, editor, opinion articles, sermons; eric.black@baptiststandard.com

Denomination: Baptist
Parent company: Baptist Standard Publishing
Type: quarterly website
Audience: denomination
Purpose: to connect God's story and God's people through information, inspiration, and challenge
Submissions: Email complete manuscript as attachment.
Types of manuscripts: how-to, profiles
Length: articles, 750–1,000 words; book reviews, 250–500 words
Topics: evangelism, family, leadership, ministry, missions, Texas Baptist history
Guidelines: *www.baptiststandard.com/submissions*
Tip: "When we consider something for publication, we ask: Does a news story or opinion piece inform, inspire or challenge people to live like Jesus? If so, it passes the most general test for consideration. Does a news story involve Baptists, in general? If so, we consider it. Does a story involve or have importance to Baptists in Texas? If so, we consider it. Does it involve the Baptist General Convention of Texas and Texas Baptists? An almost automatic yes."

BIBLE ADVOCATE

PO Box 33677, Denver, CO 80233
bibleadvocate@cog7.org | *baonline.org*
Sherri Langton, associate editor

Denomination: Church of God (Seventh Day)
Type: bimonthly digital and print magazine; circulation: 13,000
Audience: denomination, general
Purpose: to advocate the Bible and represent the Church of God (Seventh Day)
Submissions: Email complete manuscript. Unsolicited freelance: 25–30%. Responds in four to ten weeks.
Types of manuscripts: fillers, personal experience, poetry, teaching, testimonies

Length: 600–1,300 words

Topics: Christian living/spirituality, theme-related

Rights: electronic, first, onetime, reprint (with info on where/when previously published)

Payment: on publication; articles, $25–65; poems and fillers, $20

Manuscripts accepted per year: 10–20

Preferred Bible version: NIV, NKJV

Theme list: available on website

Guidelines: *baonline.org/write-for-us*

Sample: 9"x12" envelope with three stamps

Tip: "Please read past issues of the magazine before you submit and become familiar with our style. No snail mail submissions or PDFs. No Christmas or Easter manuscripts."

BLUE RIDGE CHRISTIAN NEWS

152 Summit Ave., Spruce Pine, NC 28777 | 828-765-6800

cathy@brcnews.com | *blueridgechristiannews.com*

Cathy Pritchard, editor

Parent company: The Ninevah Productions, Inc.

Type: monthly digital and print newspaper; circulation: 12,000; advertising accepted

Audience: people seeking to know more about God

Purpose: to share the good news of Jesus and other positive, uplifting, and good news from around the world

Submissions: Email only. Unsolicited freelance: 10%. Responds in one week.

Types of manuscripts: columns, fillers, how-to, personal experience, short stories

Length: 1,000 words

Topics: Christian living/spirituality, evangelism

Rights: all, electronic, first, reprint (with info on where/when previously published)

Payment: none

Manuscripts accepted per year: 100

Seasonal submissions: one month in advance

Preferred Bible version: KJV, NKJV, NASB

Guidelines: not available

Sample: $3, email request

Tip: "Looking for positive, uplifting, good news."

THE BREAKTHROUGH INTERCESSOR

PO Box 121, Lincoln, VA 20160-0121 | 540-338-4131
breakthrough@intercessors.org | www.intercessors.org
Claudette Ammons, managing editor

Parent company: Breakthrough
Type: quarterly digital and print magazine; circulation: 4,000
Audience: adults interested in growing their prayer lives
Purpose: to encourage people to pray and equip them to do so more effectively
Submissions: Email or mail complete manuscript.
Types of manuscripts: personal experience, teaching
Length: 600–1,000 words
Topics: prayer
Rights: electronic, first, onetime
Payment: none
Guidelines: *www.intercessors.org/media/downloads/Guidelines%20 &%20PermissionForm.pdf*
Sample: on the website

byFAITH

1700 N. Brown Rd., Ste. 105, Lawrenceville, GA 30043 | 678-825-1005
editor@byfaithonlineonline.wpengine.com | byfaithonline.com
Richard Doster, editor

Denomination: Presbyterian
Type: quarterly digital and print magazine, advertising accepted
Audience: denomination
Purpose: to provide news of the Presbyterian Church in America, to equip readers to become a more active part of God's redemptive plan for the world, and to help them respond biblically and intelligently to the questions our culture is asking
Submissions: Submit complete manuscript by email.
Types of manuscripts: news, profiles, reviews, teaching
Length: 500–3,000 words
Topics: Christian living/spirituality, culture, denomination, theology
Guidelines: *byfaithonline.com/about*
Tip: "Theologically, the writers are Reformed and believe the faith is practical and applicable to every part of life. Most of our writers (though not all) come from the PCA."

CAFÉ

8765 W. Higgins Rd., Chicago, IL 60631 | 800-638-3522

cafe@elca.org | www.boldcafe.org

Elizabeth McBride, editor

Denomination: Lutheran

Parent company: Women of the Evangelical Lutheran Church in America

Type: monthly website

Audience: Lutheran women ages 18–35+

Purpose: to share stories written by bold, young women who write about faith, relationships, advocacy, and more

Submissions: Email query letter with clips. Simultaneous submissions accepted. Responds only if interested.

Types of manuscripts: personal experience

Length: 700–1,000 words

Topics: theme-related

Rights: first, onetime, reprint (with info on where/when previously published)

Payment: $20 per 100 published words, excluding biblical text

Seasonal submissions: seven months

Preferred Bible version: NRSV

Guidelines: *www.boldcafe.org/add-voice-boldcafe*

Sample: see the website

Tip: "We ask particular established authors to write on specific themes far in advance of publication. We publish very few articles that originated as unsolicited manuscripts or queries. Those we do accept are most likely to be accepted from Christian women (though we accept queries from men) that include stories about women or reflections that especially speak to young adult women."

CANADA LUTHERAN

400-185 Carlton St., Winnipeg, MB R3C 3J1, Canada | 888-786-6707

editor@elcic.ca | canadalutheran.ca

Kenn Ward, editor

Rachel Genge, British Columbia Synod, csynodeditor@gmail.com

Richard Janzen, Synod of Alberta and the Territories, cleditor.richard@gmail.com

Anno Bell, Saskatchewan Synod, clsaskeditor@gmail.com

Rev. R. David Lowe, Manitoba/Northwestern Ontario Synod, mnoeditor@gmail.com

Liz Zehr, Eastern Synod, ezehr@elcic.ca

Denomination: Lutheran

Parent company: Evangelical Lutheran Church in Canada
Type: monthly print magazine; circulation: 14,000
Audience: denomination
Purpose: to engage the Evangelical Lutheran Church in Canada in a dynamic dialogue in which information, inspiration, and ideas are shared in a thoughtful and stimulating way
Submissions: Email only.
Types of manuscripts: documentary, how-to, personal experience, profiles
Length: 700–1,200 words
Topics: Christian living/spirituality, denomination, seasonal
Rights: onetime
Tip: "As much as is possible, the content of the magazine is chosen from the work of Canadian writers. The content strives to reflect the Evangelical Lutheran Church in Canada in the context of our Canadian society."

THE CANADIAN LUTHERAN

3074 Portage Ave., Winnipeg, MB R3K 0Y2, Canada | 800-588-4226
editor@lutheranchurch.ca | *www.canadianlutheran.ca*
Matthew Block, editor
Michelle Heumann, regional news
  Denomination: Lutheran
  Parent company: Lutheran Church–Canada
  Type: bimonthly digital and print magazine; circulation: print, 12,000; digital, 10,000 hits
  Audience: denomination
  Purpose: to inspire, motivate, and inform
  Submissions: Email complete manuscript.
  Types of manuscripts: essays, news, teaching
  Topics: culture, denomination, theology
  Rights: first
  Payment: none
  Guidelines: *www.canadianlutheran.ca/editors-and-submissions*
  Sample: *issuu.com/thecanadianlutheran*
  Tip: "All feature articles with doctrinal content must go through doctrinal review to ensure fidelity to the Scriptures. As a result, authors may occasionally be asked to rewrite some sections of their article before publication."

CANADIAN MENNONITE

490 Dutton Dr., Waterloo, ON N2L 6H7, Canada | 519-884-3810
submit@canadianmennonite.org | *www.canadianmennonite.org*
Will Braun, editor

Denomination: Mennonite
Parent company: Canadian Mennonite Publishing Service
Type: biweekly digital and print magazine; circulation: 9,000;
advertising accepted
Audience: denomination
Purpose: to educate, inform, inspire and foster dialogue on issues
facing Mennonites in Canada
Submissions: Email query letter as attachment or in body of message.
Gives assignments to known writers. Accepts simultaneous
submissions. Unsolicited freelance: 10%. Responds in one day.
Also accepts submissions from children and teens.
Types of manuscripts: opinion, personal experience
Length: 750 words
Topics: social issues, theme-related
Rights: first, reprint (with info on where/when previously published)
Payment: on publication, 12¢/word
Manuscripts accepted per year: few; publish primarily the writing
of correspondents and related organizations
Seasonal submissions: three months
Preferred Bible version: none
Theme list: available on website
Guidelines: *canadianmennonite.org/submissions*
Sample: on the website
Tip: "Our content is focused on the Mennonite experience in Canada.
We do not usually take submissions from USA. If the writer is
in Canada and has a suggestion for a topic of known interest to
Mennonites, we'd like to hear about it."

CARING MAGAZINE

30840 Hawthorne Blvd., Rancho Palos Verde, CA 90275 | 562-491-8343
karen.gleason@usw.salvationarmy.org | *caringmagazine.org*
Karen Gleason, senior editor
Hillary Jackson, managing editor, hillary.jackson@usw.salvationarmy.org

Denomination: The Salvation Army
Parent company: The Salvation Army Western Territory
Type: weekly digital newsletter; circulation: 18,000

Audience: denomination in the territory

Purpose: to provide tools for building well-being in the life and soul of readers' neighbors and family while featuring real-life change happening in communities across the US through The Salvation Army

Submissions: Query only.

Types of manuscripts: articles, reviews

Topics: denomination

Sample: *issuu.com/newfrontierpublications*

Tip: "Shares information from across The Salvation Army world, reports that analyze effective programs to identify the unique features and trends for what works, tips to help local congregations better engage in the issues of today, and influential voices on relevant (and sometimes controversial) matters."

CELEBRATE LIFE MAGAZINE

PO Box 6170, Falmouth, VA 22403 | 540-659-4171

clmag@all.org | *www.clmagazine.org*

Susan Ciancio, editor

Denomination: Catholic

Parent company: American Life League

Type: quarterly digital and print magazine; circulation: 7,500; advertising accepted

Audience: pro-life

Purpose: to inspire, encourage, and educate pro-life activists

Submissions: Email complete manuscript as attachment, or mail it. Unsolicited freelance: 25%. Responds in one to two months.

Types of manuscripts: how-to, interviews, personal experience, reviews, teaching

Length: 800–1,800 words

Topics: ethics, issues; see list of possible topics in the guidelines

Rights: first

Payment: on publication, 10–25¢/word

Kill fee: sometimes

Manuscripts accepted per year: six

Seasonal submissions: six months ahead

Preferred Bible version: *Jerusalem Bible*

Guidelines: *www.clmagazine.org/submission-guidelines*

Sample: email for copy

Tip: "Current-events articles, holiday articles, and articles with appropriate photos or artwork get top priority in our processing procedure."

CHARISMA

600 Rinehart Rd., Lake Mary, FL 32746 | 407-333-0600
robert.caggiano@charismamedia.com | *www.charismamag.com*
Robert Caggiano, managing editor

Denomination: Charismatic/Pentecostal
Parent company: Charisma Media
Type: monthly digital and print magazine; circulation: 207,000;
advertising accepted
Audience: passionate, Spirit-filled Christians
Purpose: to empower believers for life in the Spirit
Submissions: Email query letter. Unsolicited freelance: 20%.
Responds in two to three months.
Types of manuscripts: feature articles, interviews, profiles, reviews
Length: 700–2,600
Topics: Christian living/spirituality, Christmas, Easter, prayer,
prophecy, seasonal, spiritual warfare
Rights: all
Payment: on publication
Seasonal submissions: five months in advance
Preferred Bible version: MEV
Guidelines: *charismamag.com/about/write-for-us*
Sample: on the website
Tip: "Please take time to read—even study—at least one or two of
our recent issues before submitting a query. Sometimes people
submit their writing without ever having read or understood our
magazine or its readers, and sometimes people will have read our
magazine years ago and think it's the same as it has always been,
but magazines undergo many changes through the years."

THE CHRISTIAN CENTURY

104 S. Michigan Ave., Ste. 1100, Chicago, IL 60603-5901 | 312-263-7510
submissions@christiancentury.org | *www.christiancentury.org*
Steve Thorngate, managing editor
Jill Peláez Baumgaertner, poetry; poetry@christiancentury.org

Type: monthly print magazine; advertising accepted
Audience: ecumenical, mainline ministers, educators, and church
leaders
Purpose: to explore what it means to believe and live out the
Christian faith in our time
Submissions: Email query letter. Unsolicited freelance: 90%.

Responds in four to six weeks.

Types of manuscripts: essays, humor, interviews, opinion, poetry, reviews

Length: articles, 1,500–3,000 words; poetry, to 20 lines

Topics: culture, issues, justice

Rights: all, reprint (with info on where/when previously published)

Payment: on publication; articles, $100–300; poems, $50; reviews, to $75

Manuscripts accepted per year: 150

Seasonal submissions: four months in advance

Preferred Bible version: NRSV

Guidelines: *www.christiancentury.org/submission-guidelines*

Sample: *www.christiancentury.org/magazine*

Tip: "Keep in mind our audience of sophisticated readers, eager for analysis and critical perspective that goes beyond the obvious. We are open to all topics if written with appropriate style for our readers."

CHRISTIAN COURIER

PO Box 124, Wainfleet, ON L0S 1V0, Canada | 800-275-9185

editor@christiancourier.ca | *www.christiancourier.ca*

Angela Reitsma Bick, editor-in-chief

Marlene Bergsma, features; features@christiancourier.ca
Adele Gallogly, reviews; reviews@christiancourier.ca
Maaike Vandermeer, poetry; maaike@christiancourier.ca

Denomination: Christian Reformed

Type: biweekly digital and print newspaper; circulation: 2,500; advertising accepted

Audience: general

Purpose: to connect Christians with a network of culturally savvy partners in faith for the purpose of inspiring all to participate in God's renewing work with His creation

Submissions: Email complete manuscript or query letter. Simultaneous accepted. Responds in one to two weeks, only if accepted.

Types of manuscripts: columns, feature articles, news, opinion, poetry, reviews

Length: articles, 700–1,200 words; reviews, 750 words

Rights: onetime, reprint (with info on where/when previously published)

Payment: on publication; articles, $50–70; reviews, $30–70; poetry, $45; reprints, none; all CAD

Seasonal submissions: three months in advance

Preferred Bible version: NIV

Guidelines: *www.christiancourier.ca/write-for-us*

Sample: *www.christiancourier.ca/past-issues*

Tip: "Suggest an aspect of the theme which you believe you could cover well, have insight into, could treat humorously, etc. Show that you think clearly, write clearly, and have something to say that we should want to read. Have a strong biblical worldview and avoid moralism and sentimentality."

CHRISTIAN HERALD

PO Box 68526, Brampton, ON L6R 0J8, Canada | 905-874-1731

info@christianherald.ca | *christianherald.ca*

Fazal Karim, Jr., editor-in-chief

Type: monthly digital and print newspaper; circulation: 21,000; advertising accepted

Audience: Christians living in the Greater Toronto Area

Purpose: to keep the Christian community in the greater Toronto area informed and aware of news and events of interest

Submissions: Email query as attachment. To get an assignment, contact editor by email indicating experience, areas of interest. Unsolicited freelance: 10%. Responds in 30 days.

Types of manuscripts: columns, event coverage, fillers, how-to, interviews, news, profiles, reviews, sidebars

Length: 350–600 words

Topics: business, education, evangelism, travel

Rights: all, first, onetime, reprint (with info on where/when previously published)

Payment: on publication, 10¢/word

Kill fee: sometimes

Manuscripts accepted per year: six

Seasonal submissions: three months

Preferred Bible version: no paraphrases

Theme list: available on website

Guidelines: *www.christianherald.ca/writing-guidelines.html*

Sample: on the website

Tip: "'Resource Reviews' and 'Seven Question Interviews' are the easiest ways to get started."

THE CHRISTIAN JOURNAL

1032 W. Main, Medford, OR 97501 | 541-773-4004

info@thechristianjournal.org | *thechristianjournal.org*

Chad McComas, editor

Parent company: Set Free Christian Fellowship

Type: monthly digital and print magazine; circulation: 1,200; advertising accepted

Audience: both Christians and non-Christians

Purpose: to provide inspiration and encouragement for the body of Christ in the Rogue Valley, Oregon

Submissions: Email complete manuscript or query letter. Responds in two weeks.

Types of manuscripts: children's stories, feature articles, profiles, reviews, testimonies

Length: 300–500 words, average around 400

Topics: Christian living/spirituality, theme-related

Rights: onetime

Payment: none

Seasonal submissions: one month in advance

Preferred Bible version: NIV

Theme list: available on website

Guidelines: *thechristianjournal.org/writers-information/guidelines-for-writers*

Sample: on the website

Tip: "*The Christian Journal* solicits articles of encouragement and hope. These articles need to be uplifting and point to a God of grace, love, and acceptance. Each article needs to inspire the reader to reconnect with God and his faith."

CHRISTIAN NEWS NORTHWEST

710 E. Foothills Dr., Ste. 103C, Newberg, OR 97132 | 503-537-9220

tim@pacificcitysun.com | *cnnw.com*

Tim Hirsch, editor and publisher

Parent company: Salt Media, LLC

Type: monthly digital and print newspaper; circulation: 10,000; advertising accepted

Audience: evangelical Christian community in western and central Oregon and southwest Washington

Purpose: to encourage and inform the evangelical Christian community in our part of the Pacific Northwest

Submissions: Email only.

Types of manuscripts: news, opinion

Preferred Bible version: NIV

Sample: on the website

CHRISTIAN STANDARD
16965 Pine Ln., Ste. 202, Parker, CO 80134 | 800-543-1353
cs@christianstandardmedia.com | *www.christianstandard.com*
Jim Nieman, managing editor

Denomination: Christian Churches, Churches of Christ
Parent company: Christian Standard Media
Type: bimonthly digital and print magazine
Audience: paid and volunteer leaders
Purpose: to leverage the power of our unity and to resource Christian churches to fulfill Christ's commission
Submissions: Query first. Unsolicited freelance: 5%; 95% assigned. Responds in one to three months.
Types of manuscripts: Communion meditations for website, how-to
Length: maximum 1,800 words, prefers 500–1,200 words
Topics: theme-related
Rights: first, reprint (with info on where/when previously published)
Payment: on acceptance, $50–250
Kill fee: sometimes
Manuscripts accepted per year: 15
Seasonal submissions: six to eight months
Preferred Bible version: NIV
Theme list: available on website
Guidelines: *christianstandard.com/writersguidelines*
Tip: "Writers with journalism backgrounds who are interested in covering stories, conducting interviews, and writing news articles are invited to contact us about becoming a freelance general assignment reporter. These reporters may develop their own leads or they may write on assignment by editors; they should be available to write news stories on relatively short notice. If you are interested in being considered, please email us at *cs@ christianstandardmedia.com* and include your journalism education and experience as well as several published clips."

CHRISTIANITY TODAY
465 Gundersen Dr., Carol Stream, IL 60188-2498 | 630-260-6200
editor@christianitytoday.com | *www.christianitytoday.com*
Andy Olsen, managing editor
Matt Reynolds, books editor; mreynolds@christianitytoday.com

Parent company: Christianity Today International
Type: monthly digital and print magazine; circulation: 100,000, 3.5

million page views/month; advertising accepted

Audience: Christian leaders throughout North America

Purpose: to equip Christians to renew their minds, serve the church, and create culture to the glory of God

Submissions: Query through the website. Unsolicited freelance: few. If no response in three weeks, assume not interested.

Types of manuscripts: feature articles, interviews, opinion, profiles, reviews

Length: 300–1,800 words

Topics: Christian living/spirituality, culture, issues

Rights: electronic, first

Payment: on acceptance, varies

Preferred Bible version: NIV

Guidelines: *help.christianitytoday.com/hc/en-us/articles/360047411253-How-do-I-write-for-CT-*

Sample: articles are on the website

Tip: "We are most interested in stories of Christians living out their faith in unique ways that impact the world for the better and communicate truth in a way that is deep, nuanced, and challenging."

COLUMBIA

1 Columbus Plaza, New Haven, CT 06510-3326 | 203-752-4398
columbia@kofc.org | *www.kofc.org/en/news-room/columbia/index.html*
Alton J. Pelowski, editor

Denomination: Catholic

Parent company: Knights of Columbus

Type: monthly digital and print magazine; circulation: 1.7 million

Audience: general Catholic family

Submissions: Email or mail query letter.

Types of manuscripts: feature articles, profiles

Length: 700–1,500 words

Topics: current events, family, finances, health, issues, parenting, trends

Rights: first

Payment: on acceptance, varies

Seasonal submissions: six months in advance

Guidelines: *www.kofc.org/en/news-room/columbia/guidelines.html*

Sample: link on the website

COMMONWEAL

475 Riverside Dr., Rm. 405, New York, NY 10115 | 212-662-4200
editors@commonwealmagazine.org | *www.commonwealmagazine.org*

Dominic Preziosi, editor

Denomination: Catholic

Type: monthly digital and print magazine; circulation: 20,000; advertising accepted

Audience: liberal Catholics

Purpose: to provide a forum about faith, public affairs, and the arts, centered on belief in the common good

Submissions: Submit complete manuscript through the website, or query via email. Responds in six to eight weeks. Articles fall into three categories: "Short Takes," running from 1,000–2,000 words, are brief, "newsy" and reportorial, giving facts, information, and some interpretation behind the "headlines of the day." Feature articles, running from 2,500–5,000 words, are more reflective and detailed, bringing new information or a different point of view to a subject, raising questions, and/or proposing solutions to the dilemmas facing the world, nation, church, or individual. "Last Word" columns, running from 750–1,500 words, are more personal reflections on some aspect of the human condition: spiritual, individual, political, or social.

Types of manuscripts: essays, news, opinion, poetry

Length: 750–5,000 words

Topics: literature and the arts, public affairs

Rights: all

Payment: on publication, amount varies

Manuscripts accepted per year: 30 poems

Guidelines: *commonweal.submittable.com/submit*

Sample: request by email

Tip: "Articles should be written for a general but well-educated audience. While religious articles are always topical, we are less interested in devotional and 'churchy' pieces than in articles which examine the links between 'worldly' concerns and religious beliefs."

THE COVENANT COMPANION

8303 W. Higgins Rd., Chicago, IL 60631 | 773-907-3328

Cathy.NormanPeterson@covchurch.org | *covchurch.org/stories-news*

Cathy Norman Peterson, editorial director

Denomination: Evangelical Covenant

Parent company: The Evangelical Covenant Church

Type: biannual print magazine; circulation: 5,000

Audience: denomination

Purpose: to connect Covenanters to one another and to challenge and inspire them in their faith

Submissions: Email or mail.
Types of manuscripts: news, personal experience, profiles
Length: 1,200–1,800 words
Topics: Christian living/spirituality, church, church outreach, denomination, issues, justice
Rights: onetime
Payment: two months after publication, $35–100
Tip: "We are interested in what is happening in local churches, conferences, and other Covenant institutions and associations, as well as reports from missionaries and other staff serving around the world. Human interest stories are also welcome."

CREATION ILLUSTRATED

PO Box 141103, Spokane Valley, WA 99214 | 530-269-1424
ci@creationillustrated.com | *creationillustrated.com*
Jennifer Ish, associate editor

Parent company: Creation Illustrated Ministries, Inc.
Type: quarterly digital and print magazine; circulation: 15,000; advertising accepted
Audience: families, homeschoolers
Purpose: to help one get away to nature and reconnect to the knowledge, power, and beauty found in God's creation
Submissions: Email query letter with clips as attachment or in body of message. Unsolicited freelance: 75%+. Responds in four weeks.
Types of manuscripts: articles, personal experience, short stories, travel
Length: 700–1,500
Topics: nature
Rights: first, reprint (with info on where/when previously published)
Payment: 30 days past publication, $75–100
Kill fee: sometimes
Manuscripts accepted per year: 32
Seasonal submissions: two to three months
Preferred Bible version: KJV, NKJV, NASB, ESV
Guidelines: *www.creationillustrated.com/writer-and-photo-guidelines*
Sample: *www.creationillustrated.com/free-digital-copy*
Tip: "Send a good query (helps us avoid repeating a subject recently covered) that is focused on one of the key features. Make sure it can be illustrated with stunning photographs, as each story is beautifully illustrated with many full-colored photos. Looking especially for articles about creatures, nature up close, children's stories that have nature and character-building lessons, and gardening."

CREATIVE INSPIRATIONS

PO Box 19051, Kalamazoo, MI 49009 | 269-348-5712

creativeinspirations01@gmail.com | *creativeinspirationspp.blogspot.com*

MJ Reynolds, publisher and editor

Type: bimonthly digital magazine

Audience: poets and people who appreciate poetry

Purpose: to publish inspirational poetry

Submissions: Email as attachment or in body of message, or mail it. Unsolicited freelance: 100%. Responds in one to two weeks. Also accepts submissions from teens.

Types of manuscripts: poetry

Topics: Christian living/spirituality, family, nature

Rights: onetime

Payment: none

Manuscripts accepted per year: varies

Preferred Bible version: NIV

Guidelines: by email

Sample: request by email

Tip: "Follow the submission guidelines."

CT PASTORS

465 Gundersen Dr., Carol Stream, IL 60188 | 630-260-6200

www.christianitytoday.com/pastors

Parent company: Christianity Today International

Type: semi-annual digital and print magazine

Audience: working pastors, including laypeople who serve in pastoral roles

Purpose: to provide wisdom and tools for working pastors

Submissions: Query via email. Unsolicited freelance: only a few.

Types of manuscripts: personal experience

Topics: pastoral/preaching

Preferred Bible version: NIV

Guidelines: *www.christianitytoday.com/pastors/help/about-us/writers-guidelines.html*

Sample: articles on website

Tip: "We're looking for pieces that provide wisdom and tools for working pastors. A published article describes real experiences in powerful prose, painting vivid scenes that pastors can identify with. Tell the story of what happened and what you learned. Offer insight on the practical issues: the conflicts, temptations, mistakes, and successes."

DTS MAGAZINE

3909 Swiss Ave., Dallas, TX 75204 | 800-387-9673

magazine@dts.edu | *voice.dts.edu/article*

Neil Coulter, editor

Parent company: Dallas Theological Seminary (DTS)

Type: quarterly digital and print magazine; circulation: 15,000

Audience: evangelical laypeople, students, alumni, donors, and friends

Purpose: to apply biblical truth to life as a ministry to friends of Dallas Theological Seminary

Submissions: Email query letter.

Types of manuscripts: personal experience, profiles, teaching

Length: 1,500–2,000 words

Topics: Christian living/spirituality

Rights: first, reprint

Payment: $300, $100 for reprints, $50–100 for web articles

Seasonal submissions: six months in advance

Guidelines: *voice.dts.edu/magazine/editorial-policies*

Sample: *voice.dts.edu/magazine*

Tip: "*DTS Magazine* is a ministry of Dallas Theological Seminary. We prefer articles written by our alumni, faculty, students, staff, board members, donors and their families."

EKSTASIS

465 Gundersen Dr., Carol Stream, IL 60188 | 416-912-7454

editor@ekstasismagazine.com | *www.ekstasismagazine.com*

Conor Sweetman, senior editor

Parent company: Christianity Today International

Type: monthly digital magazine + annual print, digital newsletter; circulation: 10,000; advertising accepted

Audience: intellectuals and creatives

Purpose: to revive the Christian imagination

Submissions: Email as attachment. Simultaneous accepted. Unsolicited freelance: 30%. Responds in two months.

Types of manuscripts: essays, poetry

Length: 1,500–3,000 words

Topics: arts, faith, literature

Rights: first

Payment: on publication, $75

Kill fee: sometimes

Manuscripts accepted per year: 50

Theme list: available on website
Guidelines: *www.ekstasismagazine.com/submit*
Sample: buy on website
Tip: "Connect with us if you would like to submit your work. We want to hear from readers, writers, artists, and thinkers. We publish essays that combine personal narrative with literary, theological, and artistic history. We publish poetry that speaks to the wide breadth of the Christ-infused core of everyday experience; all forms welcome."

ETERNAL INK

4706 Fantasy Ln., Alton, IL 62002 | 618-466-7860
sonsong@charter.net
Mary-Ellen Grisham, editor

Type: bimonthly e-zine; circulation: 450
Audience: general
Purpose: to inspire, edify, and enlighten
Submissions: Email manuscript in body of message. Unsolicited freelance: 5–10%. Responds in two weeks.
Types of manuscripts: devotions, fillers, humor, personal experience, poetry
Length: 400–600 words
Topics: Christian living/spirituality, seasonal
Rights: onetime, reprint
Payment: none
Manuscripts accepted per year: 200
Seasonal submissions: two months
Preferred Bible version: NIV
Guidelines: by email
Sample: by email
Tip: Looking for "scriptural studies, verses or passages, clearly focused and easy to understand."

EVANGELICAL MISSIONS QUARTERLY

PO Box 398, Wheaton, IL 60187 | 678-392-4577
EMQ-Editor@MissioNexus.org | *missionexus.org/emq*
Heather Pubols, editorial director
David Dunaetz, book review editor

Parent company: Missio Nexus
Type: quarterly digital journal

Audience: missionaries, mission agency executives, mission professors, missionary candidates, students, mission pastors, mission-minded church leaders, mission supporters, and agency board members

Purpose: to increase the effectiveness of the evangelical missionary enterprise

Submissions: Email complete manuscript as attachment or through the website.

Types of manuscripts: how-to, profiles, reviews

Length: 2,000–3,000 words

Topics: church planting, culture, discipleship, evangelism, leadership, missions, trends

Rights: first

Guidelines: *missionexus.org/emq/submit-an-article-to-emq*

Tip: "We are not a scholarly journal written for academics, but desire material that is academically respectable, reflecting careful thought and practical application to missions professionals, and especially working missionaries. We like to see problems not only diagnosed, but solved either by way of illustration or suggestion."

FAITH & FRIENDS

The Salvation Army, 2 Overlea Blvd., Toronto, ON M4H 1P4, Canada | 416-422-6226

faithandfriends@salvationarmy.ca | *salvationist.ca/editorial/faith-and-friends*

Ken Ramstead, editor

Denomination: The Salvation Army

Type: bimonthly digital and print magazine; circulation: 14,600

Audience: general

Purpose: to show Jesus Christ at work in the lives of real people and to provide spiritual resources for those who are new to the Christian faith

Submissions: Email as attachment.

Types of manuscripts: personal experience, profiles, reviews, testimonies

Length: 600–900 words

Topics: Christian living/spirituality, family, marriage, theology

Rights: first, reprint

Payment: none

Preferred Bible version: TNIV

Guidelines: *salvationist.ca/files/salvationarmy/Magazines/Writers_Guidelines_2023/Writers_Guidelines_-_Faith_Friends_2023-08_.pdf*

Sample: on the website

Tip: "Looking for stories about people whose lives have been changed through an encounter with Jesus: conversion, miracles, healing, faith in the midst of crisis, forgiveness, reconciliation, answered prayers, and more. Profiles of people who have found hope and healing through their ministries, including prisoners, hospital patients, nursing-home residents, single parents in distress, addicts, the unemployed, or homeless."

FAITH ON EVERY CORNER

159 Hudson Cajah Mountain Rd., Hudson, NC 28638 | 828-305-8571

team@faithoneverycorner.com | *www.faithoneverycorner.com/magazine*

Craig Ruhl, managing editor

Karen Ruhl, publisher and editor in chief

Parent company: Faith On Every Corner, LLC

Type: monthly digital magazine; circulation: 2,500

Audience: families, seekers

Purpose: to inspire, educate, and show how everyday people are making a difference in their communities through acts of faith and service

Submissions: Email as attachment. Simultaneous accepted. Unsolicited freelance: 85%. Responds in one week. Also accepts submissions from teens.

Types of manuscripts: columns, personal experience, poetry, reviews, short stories, testimonies

Length: 250–1,000 words

Topics: Christian living/spirituality, evangelism, humor, parenting

Rights: first

Payment: none

Manuscripts accepted per year: 400

Seasonal submissions: one to two months

Preferred Bible version: KJV, NKJV, ESV, NIV, NLT, NASB, CSB

Theme list: on the website

Guidelines: *www.faithoneverycorner.com/submission-guidelines.html*

Sample: on the website

Tip: "Feel free to pitch ideas for articles, stories or other content by email."

FAITH TODAY

10 Huntingdale Blvd., Scarborough, ON M1W 2S5, Canada | 866-302-3362

editor@faithtoday.ca | *www.faithtoday.ca*

Bill Fledderus, senior editor

Karen Stiller, senior editor

Parent company: The Evangelical Fellowship of Canada

Type: bimonthly digital and print magazine; circulation: 20,000, 9,500 online; advertising accepted

Audience: Canadian evangelicals

Purpose: to connect, equip, and inform Canada's four million evangelical Christians from Anglican and Baptist to Pentecostal and The Salvation Army

Submissions: Email query letter with clips. Unsolicited freelance: 10%. Responds in one week.

Types of manuscripts: essays, feature articles, how-to, news, profiles, reviews

Length: 350–1,800 words

Topics: church, issues, trends

Rights: electronic, first, onetime, reprint (with info on where/when previously published)

Payment: on acceptance, 30–40¢ CAD/word

Kill fee: sometimes

Manuscripts accepted per year: 100

Seasonal submissions: four months

Guidelines: *www.faithtoday.ca/writers*

Sample: *www.faithtoday.ca/digital*

Tip: "What is the Canadian angle? How does your approach include diverse Canadian voices from different churches, regions, generations, etc.?"

FOCUS ON THE FAMILY

8605 Explorer Dr., Colorado Springs, CO 80920 | 800-232-6459

FocusMagSubmissions@family.com | *www.focusonthefamily.com/magazine*

Andrea Gutierrez, managing editor

Parent company: Focus on the Family

Type: bimonthly print magazine; circulation: 240,000

Audience: married parents with children in the home

Purpose: to support couples in their marriage and parents when training their children

Submissions: Email complete manuscript as attachment or in body of message. Unsolicited freelance: 20%. Responds in two to eight weeks. Also buys articles on parenting and marriage for online. Length: 800–1,500 words. Email to *Rhonda.Robinson@fotf.org*.

Types of manuscripts: how-to, profiles, teaching

Length: 400–800 words

Topics: marriage, parenting

Rights: first
Payment: on acceptance; 25¢/word, $50 for short articles
Kill fee: always
Manuscripts accepted per year: 100
Seasonal submissions: nine months
Preferred Bible version: ESV
Guidelines: *www.focusonthefamily.com/magazine/call-for-submissions*
Sample: articles are on the website; for free subscription, email
   HELP@focusonthefamily.com
Tip: "Start with 'Hacks & Facts' for parenting, extended family,
   grandparenting, and adult kids. Find any calls for submissions on
   our site, and follow the directions for that specific article."

FRIENDS JOURNAL

1501 Cherry St., Philadelphia, PA 19102 | 215-563-8629
martink@friendsjournal.org | www.friendsjournal.org
Martin Kelly, senior editor

Denomination: Religious Society of Friends
Type: monthly digital and print magazine
Audience: denomination
Purpose: to communicate Quaker experience in order to connect and
   deepen spiritual lives
Submissions: Email through the website. Departments, around 1,500
   words or fewer: "Celebration," "Earthcare," "Faith and Practice,"
   "First-day School," "Friends in Business," "History," "Humor,"
   "Life in the Meeting," "Lives of Friends," "Pastoral Care," "Q&A,"
   "Reflection," "Religious Education," "Remembrance," Service,"
   "Witness."
Types of manuscripts: personal experience, poetry, profiles, teaching,
   testimonies
Length: 1,200–2,500 words
Topics: theme-related
Rights: first
Payment: none
Manuscripts accepted per year: poems, 22–33
Theme list: available on website
Guidelines: *www.friendsjournal.org/submissions*
Sample: articles are on the website

GATHER

8765 W. Higgins Rd., Chicago, IL 60631 | 844-409-0576

gather@elca.org | *www.gathermagazine.org*

Elizabeth Hunter, editor

Denomination: Lutheran

Parent company: Women of the Evangelical Lutheran Church in America

Type: monthly digital and print magazine

Audience: Lutheran women

Purpose: to help readers grow in faith and engage in ministry and action

Submissions: Email query with clips as attachment. Simultaneous accepted. Responds only if interested.

Types of manuscripts: personal experience

Topics: theme-related

Rights: first, onetime, reprint (with info on where/when previously published)

Payment: on publication

Seasonal submissions: seven months

Guidelines: *www.gathermagazine.org/write-for-gather*

Sample: article samples are on the website

Tip: "Please know that most of what we publish is assigned—we ask particular established authors to write on specific themes far in advance of publication. We publish very few articles that originated as unsolicited manuscripts or queries."

GEMS OF TRUTH

PO Box 4060, Overland Park, KS 66204 | 913-432-0331

sseditor@heraldandbanner.com | *www.heraldandbanner.com*

Arlene McGehee, Sunday school editor

Denomination: Church of God (Holiness)

Parent company: Herald and Banner Press

Type: weekly Sunday school take-home paper; circulation: 4,750

Audience: denomination

Purpose: to build character values without being preachy

Submissions: Mail or email as attachment or in body of message. Unsolicited freelance: 50%. Responds in nine months.

Types of manuscripts: biography, personal experience, poetry, short stories

Length: 1,000–2,000 words

Topics: Christian living/spirituality, family, marriage, prayer

Rights: first, reprint

Payment: on publication; prose, .0005¢/word; poetry, 25¢/line; reprints, 50%
Manuscripts accepted per year: varies
Seasonal submissions: six months in advance
Preferred Bible version: KJV
Guidelines: by email
Sample: 9"x12" SASE with $3.50 postage
Tip: Looking for seasonal stories.

GOOD NEWS

PO Box 670368, Coral Springs, FL 33067 | 954-564-5378
ShellyP@goodnewsfl.org | www.goodnewsfl.org
Shelly Pond, editor

Parent company: Good News Media Group, LLC
Type: monthly digital and print newspaper; circulation: 80,000 print, 30,000 digital; advertising accepted
Audience: Dade, Broward, and Palm Beach, Florida areas
Submissions: Email query letter with clips.
Types of manuscripts: articles
Length: 500–800 words
Payment: 10¢/word
Sample: on the website

GUIDEPOSTS

110 William St., Ste. 901, New York, NY 10038 | 212-251-8100
emiller@guideposts.org | guideposts.org/guideposts-magazine
Evan Miller, senior editor

Parent company: Guideposts
Type: bimonthly digital and print magazine
Audience: general
Purpose: to inspire people to believe that all things are possible with faith, hope, and prayer; to encourage, inform, entertain, and tell true stories of personal change; to affirm the positive, unite rather than divide, and meet people where they are on their spiritual journeys
Submissions: Submit complete manuscript through the website at *guideposts.org/tell-us-your-story*. Unsolicited freelance: 40%. Responds in two months or not interested. Short anecdotes similar to full-length articles for departments: "Someone Cares," stories of kindness and caring, *sc@guideposts.com*; "Mysterious Ways,"

"Family Room," "What Prayer Can Do." Also takes inspiring quotes for "The Up Side," *upside@guideposts.com*.

Types of manuscripts: personal experience
Length: articles, 1,500 words; department anecdotes, 50–250 words
Rights: all
Payment: on acceptance, $100–500
Kill fee: 20% but not to first-time freelancers
Manuscripts accepted per year: 40–60
Guidelines: *www.guideposts.org/writers-guidelines*
Tip: "*Guideposts* magazine stories are about personal change. Narrators face challenges in their lives that they resolve through leaning on faith and God. The challenge can cover everything from relationships to life transitions—such as caregiving, divorce, retirement, or job loss—to life-threatening events. Our true stories deliver hope and inspiration with a clear spiritual point that readers can apply to everyday difficulties in their own lives. We want to be a source of spiritual well-being for our readers."

HEARTBEAT

PO Box 9, Hatfield, AR 71945 | 870-389-6196
heartbeat@cmausa.org | *cmausa.org/Resources/Heartbeat*
Misty Bradley, editor

Parent company: Christian Motorcyclists Association
Type: monthly digital and print magazine; circulation: 18,000
Audience: motorcyclists
Purpose: to inspire leaders and members to be the most organized, advanced, equipped, financially stable organization, full of integrity in the motorcycling industry and the Kingdom of God
Submissions: Email complete manuscript.
Types of manuscripts: articles, reviews
Topics: motorcycling
Payment: none

HIGHWAY NEWS

1525 River Rd., Marietta, PA 17547 | 717-426-9977
editor@transportforchrist.org | *tfcglobal.org/highway-news/current-issue*
Ron Fraser, executive editor

Parent company: TFC Global
Type: monthly digital and print magazine; circulation: 18,000–20,000
Audience: truck drivers and their families

Purpose: to lead truck drivers, as well as the trucking community, to Jesus Christ and help them grow in their faith

Submissions: Email complete manuscript. Unsolicited freelance: 10–20%.

Types of manuscripts: news, personal experience

Length: 800–1,000 words

Topics: trucking life

Rights: first, reprint

Payment: none

Seasonal submissions: six months in advance

Preferred Bible version: ESV

Guidelines: by email

Sample: download from the website

Tip: "Articles submitted for publication do not have to be religious in nature; however, they should not conflict with or oppose guidelines and principles presented in the Bible."

HOLINESS TODAY

17001 Prairie Star Pkwy., Lenexa, KS 66220 | 913-577-0500

holinesstoday@nazarene.org | *www.holinesstoday.org*

Nate Gilmore, content editor

Denomination: Nazarene

Parent company: Church of the Nazarene

Type: bimonthly digital and print magazine; circulation: 8,000; advertising accepted

Audience: denomination

Purpose: to keep readers connected with the Nazarene experience and provide tools for everyday faith

Submissions: Email complete manuscript as attachment. Unsolicited freelance: 30%. Also takes submissions from children and teens.

Types of manuscripts: columns, personal experience

Length: 700–1,100 words

Topics: denomination, ministry, teaching

Rights: first, reprint (with info on where/when previously published)

Payment: on publication, $135

Kill fee: yes

Manuscripts accepted per year: six to eight

Preferred Bible version: NIV

Theme list: available via email

Guidelines: by email

Tip: "We are always interested in hearing from Nazarene pastors, lay leaders, and experts in their fields. We are a Nazarene publication that wants our articles to be relevant and applicable to real-life scenarios and the world we live in."

HOMELIFE

200 Powell Pl., Ste. 100, Brentwood, TN 37027 | 615-251-2196
homelife@lifeway.com | *www.lifeway.com/en/product-family/homelife-magazine*
David Bennett, managing editor

Denomination: Southern Baptist
Parent company: LifeWay Christian Resources
Type: monthly print magazine; circulation: 250,000
Audience: parents
Purpose: to address all things faith, family, and life
Submissions: Email complete manuscript as attachment. Gives assignments. Unsolicited freelance: 10%. Responds in several weeks.
Types of manuscripts: columns, how-to, narrative
Length: 1,500–7,500 words
Topics: faith, living on mission, marriage, parenting
Rights: first
Payment: on publication, $100–400
Manuscripts accepted per year: 20
Seasonal submissions: four months in advance
Preferred Bible version: CSB
Guidelines: by email
Sample: on the website
Tip: "Include full bio, church name, and denomination with submission."

IMAGE

3307 Third Ave. W, Seattle, WA 98119 | 206-281-2988
jkasmith@imagejournal.org | *imagejournal.org*
James K.A. Smith, editor-in-chief
Lauren F. Winner, creative nonfiction editor, nonfiction; lwinner@imagejournal.org
Nick Ripatrazone, culture editor, media essays and reviews;
  nripatrazone@imagejournal.org

Type: quarterly print journal
Audience: people interested in art and literature
Purpose: to demonstrate the continued vitality and diversity of contemporary art and literature that engage with the religious traditions of Western culture

Submissions: Submit complete manuscript through the website, or email query letter. Simultaneous accepted. Responds in five months.
Types of manuscripts: essays, interviews, poetry, short stories
Length: 3,000–6,000 words
Topics: literature and the arts
Rights: first
Payment: $25/published page, $3/line for poetry
Guidelines: *imagejournal.submittable.com/submit*
Tip: "All the work we publish reflects what we see as a sustained engagement with one of the western faiths—Judaism, Christianity, or Islam. That engagement can include unease, grappling, or ambivalence as well as orthodoxy; the approach can be indirect or allusive, but for a piece to be a fit for *Image*, some connection to faith must be there."

INFLUENCE

1445 N. Boonville Ave., Springfield, MO 65802 | 417-862-2781
editor@influencemagazine.com | *influencemagazine.com*
Christina Quick, lead editor

Denomination: Assemblies of God
Parent company: The General Council of the Assemblies of God
Type: quarterly digital and print magazine; circulation: 33,000
Audience: pastors and other leaders
Purpose: to provide a Christ-centered, Spirit-empowered perspective that propels people to engage their faith—as individuals, in community, and with the global Church
Submissions: Email complete manuscript or query letter.
Types of manuscripts: how-to, profiles, teaching
Length: 700–1,000 words
Topics: ethics, family, leadership, ministry, worship
Rights: first
Guidelines: *influencemagazine.com/submission-guidelines*
Sample: *influencemagazine.com/en/issues*
Tip: "We'd love to hear more about your background in leadership and how that might connect to your pitch. Links to sites, social-media profiles, or other writing samples are encouraged. Reprints or excerpts are considered on a case-by-case basis, but original content is preferred."

INSITE

PO Box 62189, Colorado Springs, CO 80962-2189 | 719-260-9400

editor@ccca.org | *www.ccca.org/ccca/Publications.asp*

Parent company: Christian Camp and Conference Association
Type: bimonthly digital and print magazine; circulation: 5,800
Audience: camp and conference-center leaders
Purpose: to maximize ministry for member camps and conference centers
Submissions: Email query letter. Unsolicited freelance: 1–2%. Responds in one week.
Types of manuscripts: how-to, interviews, profiles, sidebars
Length: 1,000–1,500 words
Topics: business, camping ministry, discipleship, facilities, leadership, legal, relationships
Rights: all
Payment: on publication, $300
Kill fee: sometimes
Seasonal submissions: six months ahead
Preferred Bible version: NIV
Theme list: available on website
Guidelines: *www.ccca.org/ccca/Publications.asp*
Sample: via email
Tip: "All articles must be applicable to camps and conference centers."

INSPIRE A FIRE

dianaflegal@gmail.com | *inspireafire.com*

Diana Flegal, senior editor

Eddie Jones, executive editor, WritersCoach.us@gmail.com

Parent company: Christian Devotions Ministry
Type: daily website; circulation: 38,000
Audience: Christians looking for encouragement and inspiration
Purpose: to deliver life-giving articles that inspire hope, convey God's truth, and accompany believers on their spiritual journeys
Submissions: Unsolicited freelance: 40%. Responds in one week.
Types of manuscripts: personal experience, poetry
Length: 1,500 words
Topics: Christian living, culture, family, relationships
Rights: first, reprint if retitled and reworded 25%
Payment: none
Theme list: available on website

Guidelines: *inspireafire.com/submissions-guidelines*
Sample: on the website
Tip: "*Inspire a Fire* is looking for committed writers familiar with WordPress, or willing to learn, to post a monthly article in accordance with submission guidelines. If you would like to become a monthly contributor, email Diana or Eddie to schedule a phone call or Zoom interview."

THE JOURNAL OF ADVENTIST EDUCATION

12501 Old Columbia Pike, Silver Spring, MD 20904-6600 | 301-680-5069
mcgarrellf@gc.adventist.org | *www.journalofadventisteducation.org*
Faith-Ann McGarrell, editor

Denomination: Seventh-day Adventist
Parent company: General Conference of Seventh-day Adventists
Type: quarterly digital journal; circulation: 10,000–16,000; advertising accepted
Audience: educators and administrators
Purpose: to aid professional teachers and educational administrators worldwide, kindergarten to higher education
Submissions: Submit complete manuscript through the website. Unsolicited freelance: 10%. Responds in four to six weeks.
Types of manuscripts: how-to, personal experience, reviews, sidebars
Length: 1,500–4,000 words; book reviews, 900–1,500
Topics: Christian education
Rights: first, reprint (with info on where/when previously published)
Payment: on publication, amount varies
Manuscripts accepted per year: 32
Seasonal submissions: six months in advance
Preferred Bible version: NIV
Guidelines: *www.journalofadventisteducation.org/author-guidelines*
Sample: download from the website
Tip: "JAE accepts invited and freelance submissions from educators, educational administrators, and individuals working in education. Authors must be familiar with Adventist Christian education—its philosophy, structure, and historical foundations."

JOYFUL LIVING MAGAZINE

PO Box 311, Palo Cedro, CA 97073 | 530-227-9330
joyfullivingmagazineredding@gmail.com | *joyfullivingmagazine.com*

Cathy Jansen, editor in chief

Type: quarterly digital magazine; advertising accepted

Audience: general

Purpose: to share encouragement and hope, to help readers grow spiritually and emotionally, and to help them in their everyday lives with practical issues

Submissions: Email complete manuscript as attachment.

Types of manuscripts: how-to, personal experience, profiles, recipes

Length: 200–700 words

Topics: aging, Christian living/spirituality, depression, family, finances, health, marriage, singleness, work

Payment: none

Guidelines: *www.joyfullivingmagazine.com/writers-info*

Sample: *www.joyfullivingmagazine.com/issues*

Tip: "Articles need to be uplifting and encouraging for singles, seniors, young people, and families. Each article needs to inspire the reader to grow spiritually, emotionally, and help them in their everyday lives with very practical issues."

JUST BETWEEN US

777 S. Barker Rd., Brookfield, WI 53045 | 262-786-6478

submissions@justbetweenus.org | *www.justbetweenus.org*

Shelly Esser, executive editor

Parent company: Elmbrook Church

Type: quarterly print magazine; circulation: 10,000

Audience: women

Purpose: to encourage and equip women for a life of faith and service

Submissions: Email complete manuscript as attachment. Responds in six to eight weeks or not interested.

Types of manuscripts: how-to, personal experience, testimonies

Length: articles, 1,000–1,200 words; testimonies, 450 words

Topics: Christian living/spirituality, evangelism, faith, finances, friendship, ministry, parenting, prayer, relationships, spiritual warfare

Payment: none

Preferred Bible version: NIV

Guidelines: *justbetweenus.org/magazine/writers-guidelines*

Sample: *justbetweenus.org/magazine-sample-issue*

Tip: "Articles should be personal in tone, full of real-life anecdotes as well as quotes/advice from noted Christian professionals, and be biblically based. Articles need to be practical and have a distinct

Christian and serving perspective throughout."

LEADING HEARTS

PO Box 6421, Longmont, CO 80501 | 303-835-8473

amber@leadinghearts.com | leadinghearts.com

Amber Weigland-Buckley, editor

> **Parent company:** Right to the Heart Ministries
> **Type:** bimonthly digital magazine; circulation: 10,000; advertising accepted
> **Audience:** women leaders
> **Purpose:** to encourage Christian women who lead hearts at home, work, community and church
> **Submissions:** Assignment only. To audition for an assignment, email an article of 1,200 words maximum and a short résumé. Gives preferred consideration to members of AWSA. Unsolicited freelance: none; 50-60% assigned.
> **Types of manuscripts:** how-to, personal experience, profiles, reviews
> **Length:** articles, 800 words maximum; columns, 250–500 words
> **Topics:** theme-related
> **Rights:** first, reprint
> **Payment:** none
> **Preferred Bible version:** NIV
> **Theme list:** not available
> **Guidelines:** *leadinghearts.com/writers-guidelines*
> **Sample:** download from the website

LEAVES

PO Box 87, Dearborn, MI 48121-0087 | 313-561-2330

editor.leaves@marianhill.us | www.marianhill.us/leaves.html

Rev. Thomas Heier , editor-in-chief

> **Denomination:** Catholic
> **Parent company:** Marianhill Mission Society
> **Type:** bimonthly print magazine; circulation: 10,000
> **Audience:** Catholics, primarily in the Detroit, Michigan, area
> **Purpose:** to promote devotion to God and testimony of His blessings
> **Submissions:** Email or mail complete manuscript.
> **Types of manuscripts:** personal experience, poetry, reviews, testimonies
> **Length:** 250 words
> **Topics:** Christian living/spirituality, prayer

Rights: first, reprint
Payment: none
Manuscripts accepted per year: 40
Preferred Bible version: RSV Catholic edition
Sample: articles are on the website
Tip: Greatest need is for personal testimonies.

LIGHT

901 Commerce St., Ste. 550, Nashville, TN 37203 | 615-244-2495
nicolet@erlc.com | *erlc.com/resource-library/light-magazine-issues*
Lindsay Nicolet, managing editor

Denomination: Southern Baptist
Parent company: The Ethics and Religious Liberty Commission
Type: biannual digital and print journal; circulation: 8,000; advertising accepted
Audience: church and ministry leaders
Purpose: to bear witness to the gospel by speaking to congregations and consciences with a thoroughly Christian moral witness
Submissions: Email complete manuscript as attachment. Unsolicited freelance: 10%. Responds in one week.
Types of manuscripts: columns, how-to, news, reviews
Length: 1,500 words
Topics: culture, ethics, family, justice, parenting, politics
Rights: all
Payment: depends on article and writer
Manuscripts accepted per year: 10
Preferred Bible version: CSB
Guidelines: not available
Sample: email request
Tip: "Looking for articles tied to current events and focus on local church ministry."

LIVE

1445 N. Boonville Ave., Springfield, MO 65802-1894 | 417-862-2781
rl-live@gph.org | *myhealthychurch.com*
Wade Quick, editor

Denomination: Assemblies of God
Parent company: Gospel Publishing House
Type: weekly Sunday school take-home paper; circulation: 40,000
Audience: denomination

Purpose: to encourage Christians in living for God through stories that apply biblical principles to everyday problems

Submissions: Email as attachment. Unsolicited freelance: 100%. Responds in six weeks.

Types of manuscripts: fillers, how-to, personal experience, poetry, short stories

Length: articles, 200–1,200 words; poetry, 12–25 lines

Topics: Christian living/spirituality

Rights: first, reprint

Payment: on acceptance; 10¢/word for first rights, 7¢/word for reprint, $35-60 for poetry

Seasonal submissions: 18 months

Preferred Bible version: NLT

Guidelines: *myhealthychurch.com/store/startcat.cfm?cat=tWRITGUID*

Tip: "Stories should be encouraging, challenging, and/or humorous. Even problem-centered stories should be upbeat. Stories should not be preachy, critical, or moralizing. They should not present pat, trite, or simplistic answers to problems. No Bible fiction or sci-fi. Make sure the stories have a strong Christian element, are written well, have strong takeaways, but do not preach."

THE LUTHERAN WITNESS

1333 S. Kirkwood Rd., St. Louis, MO 63122-7226 | 800-248-1930

lutheran.witness@lcms.org | *witness.lcms.org*

Roy S. Askins, managing editor

Denomination: Lutheran

Parent company: The Lutheran Church Missouri Synod

Type: monthly print magazine; circulation: 120,000

Audience: denomination

Purpose: to interpret the contemporary world from a Lutheran perspective

Submissions: Submit complete manuscript through the website, or query via email.

Types of manuscripts: Bible studies, essays, how-to, humor, personal experience, poetry, profiles, teaching

Length: 500, 1,000, or 1,500 words

Topics: theme-related

Rights: electronic, first

Payment: on acceptance, amount based on both article length and complexity and author's credentials

Preferred Bible version: ESV

Theme list: available on website

Guidelines: *witness.lcms.org/contribute*

Sample: articles on the website

Tip: "Because of the magazine's long lead time, and because many features are planned at least six months in advance of the publication date, your story should have a long-term perspective that keeps it relevant several months from the time you submit it."

MATURE LIVING

200 Powell Pl., Ste. 100, Brentwood, TN 37027-7707 | 615-251-2000

matureliving@lifeway.com

www.lifeway.com/en/product-family/mature-living-magazine

Debbie Dickerson, managing editor

Denomination: Southern Baptist

Parent company: LifeWay Christian Resources

Type: monthly print magazine

Audience: ages 55 and older

Purpose: to equip mature adults as they live a legacy of leadership, stewardship, and discipleship

Submissions: Assignment only. Email for possible assignment. However, open for "Kicks and Grins," fun stories of your grandkids, 25–125 words; challenging biblical word search puzzles; and crossword puzzles.

Types of manuscripts: devotions, how-to, personal experience, puzzles, recipes, short stories, teaching

Topics: caregiving, evangelism, marriage, parenting, relationships, theology

Preferred Bible version: CSB

Guidelines: by email

Sample: on the website

THE MESSENGER

440 Main St., Steinbach, MB R5G 1Z5, Canada | 204-326-6401

messenger@emconference.ca | *emcmessenger.ca*

Rebecca Roman, editor

Denomination: Mennonite

Parent company: Evangelical Mennonite Conference

Type: bimonthly digital and print magazine; circulation: 2,700

Audience: members and adherents of churches within the Evangelical Mennonite Conference

Purpose: to inform concerning events and activities of the denomination, instruct in godliness and victorious living, and inspire to earnestly contend for the faith

Submissions: Email query letter. Unsolicited freelance: 50%. Responds in two weeks.

Types of manuscripts: feature articles

Length: 800–1,500 words

Topics: wide variety

Rights: first

Payment: on publication, $100–150

Kill fee: half payment

Manuscripts accepted per year: few, mostly assigned

Seasonal submissions: six months in advance

Preferred Bible version: NIV

Guidelines: *emcmessenger.ca/submission-guidelines*

Sample: *issuu.com/emcmessenger*

Tip: "Always query first. A lead article involves a mixture of teaching, interpretation, and opinion. Effective writers 'inform, instruct, and inspire.' They display an informed opinion, a balance in approach, a Christ-centered focus, and concern for the well-being of the Church. The writer is expected to observe and comment on conference trends and issues as deemed fit. The purpose of a lead article is not to create controversy, but to motivate thought and action."

THE MESSIANIC TIMES

50 Alberta Dr., Amhurst, NY 14226 | 866-612-7770

editor@messianictimes.com | *www.messianictimes.com*

Kayla Levy, editorial coordinator

Denomination: Messianic

Parent company: Times of the Messiah Ministries

Type: bimonthly digital and print newspaper; advertising accepted

Audience: Messianic community and Christians interested in Jewish roots of their faith

Purpose: to provide accurate, authoritative, and current information to unite the international Messianic Jewish community, teach Christians the Jewish roots of their faith, and proclaim that Yeshua is the Jewish Messiah

Submissions: Email query letter.

Types of manuscripts: news, opinion, reviews, teaching

Sample: on the website

MINISTRY

12501 Old Columbia Pike, Silver Spring, MD 20904 | 301-680-6518
ministrymagazine@gc.adventist.org | *www.ministrymagazine.org*
Pavel Goia, editor

> **Denomination:** Seventh-day Adventist
> **Type:** monthly digital and print magazine; circulation: 18,000+
> **Audience:** pastors, church leaders, church elders
> **Purpose:** to deepen spiritual life, develop intellectual strength, and
> increase pastoral and evangelistic effectiveness of all ministers in the
> context of the three angels' messages of Revelation 14:6-12
> **Submissions:** Email complete manuscript as attachment.
> **Types of manuscripts:** Bible studies, how-to, reviews, teaching
> **Length:** articles, 1,500–2,000 words; reviews, 600 words maximum
> **Topics:** family, issues, ministry, pastoral/preaching, relationships, theology
> **Rights:** all
> **Payment:** on acceptance, determined on amount of research done and
> other work needed to prepare manuscript
> **Guidelines:** *www.ministrymagazine.org/about/article-submission*
> **Sample:** articles are on the website
> **Tip:** "Because *Ministry*'s readership includes individuals from all over
> the world, you will want to use words, illustrations, and concepts that
> will be understood by readers in various parts of the world. Avoid
> illustrations that are understood in one country but may be confusing
> in others."

THE MOTHER'S HEART

PO Box 275, Tobaccoville, NC 27050 | 336-775-8519
KymAWright@gmail.com | *www.the-mothers-heart.com*
Kym A. Wright, publisher and editor

> **Parent company:** alWright! Publishing
> **Type:** bimonthly digital magazine; circulation: 100,000
> **Audience:** moms at home, homeschoolers, large families, homesteaders,
> DIYers
> **Purpose:** to serve and encourage mothers in the many facets of staying
> at home and raising a family
> **Submissions:** Email query letter as attachment or in body of message.
> Email to get an assignment. Simultaneous accepted. Unsolicited
> freelance: 20%. Responds in two months.
> **Types of manuscripts:** columns, fillers, how-to, personal experience,
> reviews

Length: 750–1,000 and 1,250–1,750 words
Topics: adoption story, Christian living/spirituality, DYI, family, fostering, gardening, homeschooling, hospitality, organization, parenting, special needs, time management
Rights: electronic, first
Payment: on publication, $10–75 or 1/8-page ad
Manuscripts accepted per year: 30
Seasonal submissions: six months in advance
Preferred Bible version: any
Guidelines: *tmhmag.com/Writers%20Guidelines%202016-2019.pdf*
Sample: *tmhmag.com/subscribe.htm*
Tip: "Break in with an adoption story, homeschool, gardening, parenting, DIY."

MUTUALITY

122 W. Franklin Ave., Ste. 218, Minneapolis, MN 55404 | 612-872-6898
mutuality@cbeinternational.org
www.cbeinternational.org/primary_page/mutuality-blogmagazine
Carrie Silveira, editor

Parent company: Christians for Biblical Equality
Type: quarterly print magazine + weekly blog; circulation: 400, monthly hits 40,000
Audience: Christian leaders, women in ministry, seminary and university students, and laity interested in gender, the Bible, and issues of justice
Purpose: to provide inspiration, encouragement, and information on topics related to a biblical view of mutuality between men and women in the home, church, and world
Submissions: Email complete manuscript or query as attachment. Responds in one month or more.
Types of manuscripts: how-to, personal experience, reviews
Length: articles, 800–1,800 words; reviews, 500–800 words
Topics: theme-related
Rights: first
Payment: print, $40 gift card; digital, $20 gift card; plus subscription for both
Preferred Bible version: NIV
Theme list: available on website
Guidelines: *www.cbeinternational.org/content/write-mutuality*
Sample: *www.cbeinternational.org/content/mutuality-sample-issue*

NET RESULTS

308 West Blvd. N, Columbia, MO 65203 | 888-470-2456
billtb@netresults.org | netresults.org
Bill Tenny-Brittian, managing editor

Parent company: The Effective Church Group, LLC
Type: bimonthly digital magazine; circulation: 500; advertising accepted
Audience: clergy, church leaders
Purpose: to offer church leaders tested, real-world, how-to articles for church growth
Submissions: Email query as attachment. Simultaneous accepted. Unsolicited freelance: 50%. Responds in two days. Also accepts submissions from teens.
Types of manuscripts: how-to, reviews
Length: 1,750 words
Topics: church growth, evangelism, theme-related
Rights: reprint
Payment: subscription
Manuscripts accepted per year: 50
Seasonal submissions: four months in advance
Preferred Bible version: NIV
Theme list: available on website
Guidelines: *netresults.org/writers*
Sample: email request
Tip: "All our articles have four things in common: (1) written by practitioners—not theoreticians or academics, (2) relevant to the church today, (3) practical in the church today, and (4) are written with a how-to slant."

NOW WHAT?

PO Box 33677, Denver, CO 80233
nowwhat@cog7.org | nowwhat.cog7.org
Sherri Langton, associate editor

Denomination: Church of God (Seventh Day)
Type: monthly digital magazine
Audience: seekers
Purpose: to address the felt needs of the unchurched
Submissions: Email complete manuscript. Unsolicited freelance: 100%. Responds in four to ten weeks.
Types of manuscripts: personal experience

Length: 1,000–1,500 words
Topics: issues, salvation
Rights: electronic, first, reprint (with info on where/when previously published)
Payment: on publication, $25–65
Manuscripts accepted per year: 10–12
Preferred Bible version: NIV
Guidelines: *nowwhat.cog7.org/send_us_your_story*
Sample: on the website
Tip: "Avoid unnecessary jargon or technical terms. No Christmas or Easter pieces or fiction. Think how you can explain your faith, or how you overcame a problem, to a non-Christian. Use storytelling techniques, like dialogue, scenes, etc., with the conflict clearly stated."

OUR SUNDAY VISITOR

200 Noll Plaza, Huntington, IN 46750 | 260-356-8400
oursunvis@osv.com | www.oursundayvisitor.com
Gretchen R. Crowe, editor-in-chief

Denomination: Catholic
Type: weekly digital and print newspaper
Audience: denomination
Purpose: to examine the news, culture, and trends of the day from a faithful and sound Catholic perspective—to see the world through the eyes of faith
Submissions: Send complete manuscript or query letter through the website. Responds in four to six weeks.
Types of manuscripts: essays, interviews, news, profiles
Length: 500–1,350 words
Topics: denomination, issues
Payment: on acceptance
Preferred Bible version: RSV
Guidelines: *osv.submittable.com/submit*
Tip: "Especially interested in writers able to do news analysis (with a minimum of three sources) or news features."

OUTREACH

5550 Tech Center, Colorado Springs, CO 80919 | 800-991-6011, x3208
tellus@outreachmagazine.com | www.outreachmagazine.com
James P. Long, editor

Type: bimonthly print magazine; circulation: 31,000

Audience: pastors and church leadership, as well as laypeople who are passionate about outreach

Purpose: to further the Kingdom of God by empowering Christian churches to reach their communities for Jesus Christ

Submissions: Email or mail query letter with clips. Cover letter required with manuscript. Responds in two months.

Types of manuscripts: how-to, profiles

Length: 200–2,500 words

Topics: church outreach, evangelism, ministry, small groups

Rights: first, reprint (with info on where/when previously published)

Payment: $700–1,000 for feature articles

Seasonal submissions: six months in advance

Guidelines: *www.outreachmagazine.com/magazine/3160-writers-guidelines.html*

Tip: "While most articles are assigned, we do accept queries and manuscripts on speculation. Please don't query us until you've studied at least one issue of *Outreach*. If you're interested in writing on assignment, submit a cover letter, published writing samples, résumé, and a list of topics you specialize in or are interested in covering. We keep these on file and do not respond to all writing queries or return writing samples."

PARENTLIFE

200 Powell Pl., Ste. 100, Brentwood, TN 37027-7707 | 615-251-2196
parentlife@lifeway.com
www.lifeway.com/en/product-family/parentlife-magazine
Nancy Cornwell, content editor

Denomination: Southern Baptist

Parent company: LifeWay Christian Resources

Type: monthly print magazine

Audience: parents of children from birth to preteen

Purpose: to encourage and equip parents with biblical solutions that will transform families

Submissions: Email complete manuscript or query letter. Responds in six to twelve months.

Types of manuscripts: devotions, how-to, sidebars, teaching

Length: 500–1,500 words

Topics: discipline, education, parenting, spiritual growth

Preferred Bible version: CSB

Guidelines: by email

Sample: order from the website

Tip: "Serves as a springboard for parents who may feel exasperated or overwhelmed with information by offering a biblical approach to raising healthy, productive children. Offers practical ideas and information for individual parents and couples."

PARISH LITURGY

16565 S. State St., South Holland, IL 60473 | 708-331-5485
acp@acpress.org | www.americancatholicpress.org/parLit.html
Rev. Michael Gilligan, executive director

Denomination: Catholic
Parent company: American Catholic Press
Type: quarterly print magazine; circulation: 1,500
Audience: parish priests, music directors, liturgy planners
Purpose: to provide material for each Sunday: themes, comments, petitions, and music suggestions
Submissions: Mail complete manuscript. Unsolicited freelance: 50%. Responds in two months.
Types of manuscripts: how-to, teaching
Length: 300 words
Topics: liturgy, music
Rights: all
Payment: on publication, variable
Kill fee: yes
Guidelines: not available
Sample: 9"x12" envelope with $2 postage
Tip: "We use articles on the liturgy only—period. Send us well-informed articles on the liturgy."

POWER FOR LIVING

4050 Lee Vance Dr., Colorado Springs, CO 80918 | 719-536-0100
Powerforliving@davidccook.com | davidccook.org
Karen Bouchard, managing editor

Parent company: David C Cook
Type: weekly Sunday school take-home paper
Audience: general, ages 50 and older
Purpose: to connect God's truth to real life
Submissions: Email complete manuscript.
Types of manuscripts: columns, devotions, interviews, personal experience, poetry
Length: features, 1,200–1,500 words; poems, 20 lines or fewer;

179

columns, 750 words; devotions, 400 words

Topics: Christian living, holidays

Rights: first, onetime, reprint

Payment: on acceptance; $375 for articles, $50 for poems, $150 for columns, $100 for devotions

Manuscripts accepted per year: feature articles, 20; poems, 6-12; columns, 5-8; devotions, rare

Seasonal submissions: 12-18 months in advance

Preferred Bible version: NIV, KJV

Guidelines: *davidccook.org/submissions-and-writer-guidelines*

Sample: buy from website

Tip: "Looking for inspiring stories and articles about famous and ordinary people whose experiences and insights show the power of Christ at work in their lives."

PRAYER CONNECT

PO Box 10667, Terre Haute, IN 47801 | 812-238-5504

prayerconnectmag@aol.com | *prayerleader.com/magazine*

Carol Madison, editor

Parent company: Church Prayer Leaders Network

Type: quarterly digital and print magazine; circulation: 2,000; advertising accepted

Audience: pastors and local-church prayer leaders

Purpose: to encourage and equip you in all aspects of prayer, but with the ultimate goal of developing our readers to be intercessors who pray for their friends and families, churches, communities, and the world effectively and with passion

Submissions: Mail or email complete manuscript as attachment. If mailing a manuscript, send it with an SASE to *PrayerConnect* submissions, 9300 College View Rd. #227, Bloomington, MN 55437. Unsolicited freelance: 15%. Responds in two to three weeks. Usually gives assignments only to regular writers.

Types of manuscripts: columns, how-to, news, prayer guides, short ideas

Length: 250-1,500 words

Topics: prayer, revival

Rights: first, reprint (with info on where/when previously published)

Payment: on publication; 10¢/word after editing, 5¢/word for reprints

Kill fee: sometimes

Manuscripts accepted per year: 30-40

Preferred Bible version: NIV
Guidelines: *www.prayerleader.com/about-us/write-for-us*
Sample: *www.prayerleader.com/free-issue-pdfs*
Tip: "Short ideas, prayer tips, are the easiest way to break in at *Prayer Connect*."

PRESBYTERIANS TODAY

100 Witherspoon St., Louisville, KY 40202-1396 | 800-728-7228
editor@pcusa.org | www.presbyterianmission.org/ministries/today
DeEtte Decker, editor

Denomination: Presbyterian
Parent company: Presbyterian Mission Agency of the Presbyterian Church (U.S.A.)
Type: bimonthly digital and print magazine; circulation: 50,000
Audience: denomination
Purpose: to explore practical issues of faith and life, tell stories of Presbyterians who are living their faith, and cover a wide range of church news and activities
Submissions: Email query letter. Unsolicited freelance: 25%. Responds in 60 days.
Types of manuscripts: feature articles, profiles
Length: 1,500 words maximum
Topics: Bible study, church, denomination, Presbyterians, theology
Rights: all
Payment: on acceptance, $75–300
Seasonal submissions: three months in advance
Preferred Bible version: NRSV
Guidelines: click on Writer's Guidelines
Sample: click on Digital Edition

RELEVANT

55 W. Church St., Ste. 211, Orlando, FL 32801 | 407-660-1411
submissions@relevantmediagroup.com | relevantmagazine.com
Emily Brown, managing editor

Type: bimonthly digital magazine + annual print; hits: five million
Audience: general, ages 20s and 30s
Purpose: to challenge people to go further in their spiritual journeys; live selflessly and intentionally; care about positively impacting the world around them; and find the unexpected places God is speaking in life, music, and culture

Submissions: Email query letter or complete manuscript as attachment. Responds in one to two weeks or not interested.
Types of manuscripts: interviews, opinion, teaching
Length: 750–1,000 words
Topics: Christian living/spirituality, culture, faith, justice
Payment: none
Guidelines: *relevantmagazine.com/write*
Sample: on the website

SHARING: A JOURNAL OF CHRISTIAN HEALING

PO Box 780909, San Antonio, TX 78278-0909 | 877-992-5222
sharing@OSLToday.org | *osltoday.org/sharing-magazine*
Jamie Ferger, editor

Parent company: International Order of St. Luke the Physician
Type: bimonthly digital and print magazine; circulation: 3,000
Audience: membership
Purpose: to empower God's people throughout the world with Jesus' healing ministry
Submissions: Email as attachment. Unsolicited freelance: 80%. Responds in one week.
Types of manuscripts: poetry, short stories
Length: 800–1,500 words
Topics: healing
Rights: all
Payment: none
Manuscripts accepted per year: 40–50
Theme list: available via email
Guidelines: by email
Sample: by email

SOJOURNERS

400 C St. NE, Washington, DC 20002 | 202-328-8842
queries@sojo.net | *sojo.net/magazine/current*
Julie Polter, editor
Review editor, reviews@sojo.net
Poetry editor, poetry@sojo.net

Type: bimonthly digital and print magazine; circulation: 19,000
Audience: community influencers
Purpose: to explore the intersections of faith, politics, and culture; uncover in depth the hidden injustices in the world around us;

and tell the stories of hope that keep us grounded, inspired, and moving forward

Submissions: Email query letter in body of message. Responds in six to eight weeks.

Types of manuscripts: feature articles, poetry, reviews

Length: articles, 1,800–2,000 words; poetry, 25 lines maximum

Topics: Christian living/spirituality, culture, faith, justice, politics

Rights: all

Payment: on publication, $50 per poem

Guidelines: *sojo.net/magazine/write*

Sample: buy from website

SPORTS SPECTRUM

640 Plaza Dr., Ste. 110, Highlands Ranch, CO 80129 | 866-821-2971

jon@sportsspectrum.com | *sportsspectrum.com/magazine*

Jon Ackerman, managing editor

Parent company: Pro Athletes Outreach

Type: quarterly digital and print magazine; circulation: 4,000; advertising accepted

Audience: sports fans

Purpose: to share stories of sports persons displaying an athletic lifestyle pleasing to God

Submissions: Email query letter with clips as attachment. Gives assignments. Simultaneous accepted. Unsolicited freelance: 10%. Responds in one week.

Types of manuscripts: feature articles, interviews, profiles

Length: 1,500–2,000 words

Topics: sports

Rights: all

Payment: on acceptance, 15¢/word

Manuscripts accepted per year: two or three

Seasonal submissions: two to three months

Preferred Bible version: NIV

Guidelines: not available

Sample: call the office

Tip: "Come with a story idea and plan for executing it."

ST. ANTHONY MESSENGER

28 W. Liberty St., Cincinnati, OH 45202-6498 | 513-241-5615

MagazineEditors@Franciscanmedia.org

www.FranciscanMedia.org/st-anthony-messenger

Christopher Heffron, editorial director

Denomination: Catholic

Parent company: Franciscan Media

Type: monthly print magazine

Audience: family-oriented, majority are women ages 40-70

Purpose: to offer readers inspiration from the heart of Catholicism—
the Gospels and the experience of God's people

Submissions: Email query letter. Responds in eight weeks.

Types of manuscripts: profiles, short stories, teaching

Length: 2,000–2,500 words

Topics: church, education, family, issues, marriage, sacraments,
spiritual growth

Rights: first

Payment: on acceptance, 20¢/published word

Manuscripts accepted per year: short stories, 12

Seasonal submissions: one year in advance

Preferred Bible version: NAB

Guidelines: *www.franciscanmedia.org/writers-guidelines*

Sample: articles are on website

STANDARD

PO Box 843336, Kansas City, MO 4184-3336 | 816-931-1900

standard.foundry@gmail.com

www.thefoundrypublishing.com/curriculum/adult.html

Jeanette Gardner Littleton, editor

Denomination: Nazarene

Parent company: The Foundry Publishing

Type: weekly Sunday school take-home paper; circulation: 40,000

Audience: denomination

Purpose: to encourage and inspire our audience and to reinforce
curriculum

Submissions: Email only. Primarily assignment; to get one, send clips
of personal-experience articles.

Types of manuscripts: personal experience

Length: 400 and 800–900 words

Topics: theme-related

Rights: all, first, reprint

Payment: on acceptance, $35 and $50

Manuscripts accepted per year: 104

Seasonal submissions: one year

Preferred Bible version: NIV

Theme list: available via email

Guidelines: by email

Sample: email request

Tip: "Writers should know basics of Wesleyan-Arminian theological perspective. Write to the theme list; please indicate which theme you're proposing it for. Nonfiction cannot be preachy. Put full contact information in the body of the manuscript, not only in the email. It helps to know if you're Nazarene or another Wesleyan/holiness denomination."

TEACHERS OF VISION

PO Box 981, Yorba Linda, CA 92885 | 714-719-0812

dmolnar@christianeducators.org | *christianeducators.org/tov*

Dawn Molnar, managing editor

Lara Busold, assistant editorial manager

Parent company: Christian Educators

Type: triannual digital and print magazine; circulation: 13,500; advertising accepted

Audience: educators in public schools

Purpose: to provide biblically principled resources that encourage, equip, and empower Christian educators

Submissions: Email as attachment. Responds in three weeks. Also accepts submissions from children and teens.

Types of manuscripts: columns, how-to, personal experience, poetry, short stories, sidebars, trends

Length: 600–1,400 words

Topics: teaching

Rights: first, reprint

Payment: on publication, $100–200

Manuscripts accepted per year: 30

Seasonal submissions: six months

Guidelines: *christianeducators.org/tov-write-for-us*

Sample: link on the website

Tip: "Most of our authors write for us because they have a passion for encouraging Christian educators. The stipend is not large enough to motivate. Sometimes authors have the opportunity to push their own book as part of their feature."

TESTIMONY/ENRICH

2450 Milltower Ct., Mississauga, ON L5N 5Z6, Canada | 905-542-7400

testimony@paoc.org | *testimony.paoc.org*
Stacey McKenzie, editor

Denomination: Pentecostal
Parent company: Pentecostal Assemblies of Canada
Type: quarterly digital and print magazine; circulation: 2,200
Audience: general and leaders
Purpose: to celebrate what God is doing in and through the Fellowship, while offering encouragement to believers by providing a window into the struggles that everyday Christians often encounter
Submissions: Email query letter. Responds in six to eight weeks.
Types of manuscripts: interviews, personal experience, sidebars
Length: 800–1,000 words
Topics: Christian living/spirituality, denomination, discipleship, leadership
Rights: first
Seasonal submissions: four months in advance
Preferred Bible version: NIV
Guidelines: *testimony.paoc.org/submit*
Guidelines: on website
Tip: "Our readership is 98% Canadian. We prefer Canadian writers or at least writers who understand that Canadians are not Americans in long underwear. We also give preference to members of this denomination, since this is related to issues concerning our fellowship."

TIME OF SINGING: A Journal of Christian Poetry

PO Box 5276, Conneaut Lake, PA 16316 | 814-439-0914
timesing@zoominternet.net | *www.timeofsinging.com*
Lora Zill, editor

Parent company: Wind & Water Press
Type: quarterly print journal; circulation: 200
Audience: those who love language and its expression through the art and craft of poetry
Purpose: to provide poets and readers a platform for thought-provoking and reflective work
Submissions: Mail or email complete manuscript as attachment or in body of message. Unsolicited freelance: 95%. Responds in three months. Also accepts submissions from teens. Book reviews of *Time Of Singing* poets are assigned; inquire for an assignment.
Types of manuscripts: poetry, reviews
Length: 40 lines maximum

Rights: first, onetime, reprint (with info on where/when previously published)

Payment: none

Manuscripts accepted per year: 150

Seasonal submissions: six months in advance

Preferred Bible version: any

Guidelines: *www.timeofsinging.com*

Sample: $5 each, including postage (checks, money orders payable to Wind & Water Press)

Tip: "I want poems that aren't afraid to take chances or think outside the theological box. Challenge my assumptions about faith, living the Christian life, and loving God. I prefer poems that don't try to provide answers but fearlessly wrestle with the questions. Trust your reader to 'get it.' It's really best to pick up a back issue to analyze to see what I like. I don't publish greeting-card style poetry or sermons that rhyme. I love fresh rhyme, free verse, and beg for forms."

TODAY'S CHRISTIAN LIVING

PO Box 5000, Iola, WI 54945 | 715-445-5000

michellea@jpmediallc.com | *www.todayschristianliving.org*

Michelle Adserias, editor

Parent company: JP Media, LLC

Type: bimonthly digital and print magazine; circulation: 17,000; advertising accepted

Audience: general, over 30 years old

Purpose: to encourage, educate, and equip believers through inspirational stories about God at work in the everyday lives of His people

Submissions: Mail or email complete manuscript as attachment. Simultaneous accepted. Unsolicited freelance: 25%. Responds in two months.

Types of manuscripts: humor, personal experience, testimonies

Length: 700–1,500 words

Topics: Christian living/spirituality

Rights: all

Payment: within 60 days of publication; $75–159, $25 for short humorous anecdotes

Kill fee: yes

Manuscripts accepted per year: 20

Seasonal submissions: six months

Preferred Bible version: none

Guidelines: *todayschristianliving.org/writers-guidelines*
Guidelines: on website
Sample: *todayschristianliving.org/free-digital-issue-with-newsletter-signup*
Tip: "The three areas open to freelance writers are our 'Turning Point' and 'Grace Notes' columns and personal testimony articles (can be someone else's testimony). Please see our writer's guidelines for details."

U.S. CATHOLIC

205 W. Monroe St., Chicago, IL 60606 | 312-544-8169
submissions@uscatholic.org | *www.uscatholic.org*
Emily Sanna, managing editor

Denomination: Catholic
Parent company: Claretian Missionaries
Type: monthly digital and print magazine
Audience: denomination
Purpose: to explore the wisdom of the Catholic faith tradition and apply that faith to the challenges of 21st-century life
Submissions: Email complete manuscript. Responds in six to eight weeks.
Types of manuscripts: essays, feature articles, opinion, poetry, profiles
Length: articles, 800–3,500 words; reviews, 315 words
Topics: denomination
Payment: $75–500
Seasonal submissions: six months in advance
Guidelines: *uscatholic.org/writers-guide*
Tip: "*U.S. Catholic* does not consider submissions that have simultaneously been sent to any other publication or that have appeared elsewhere in any form, either in print or online. This includes articles published on personal blogs or excerpts from books, published or unpublished."

THE WAR CRY

615 Slaters Ln., Alexandria, VA 22314 | 703-684-5500
www.thewarcry.org
Lt. Colonel Lesa Davis, editor-in-chief

Denomination: The Salvation Army
Parent company: The Salvation Army
Type: monthly digital and print magazine; circulation: 165,000; advertising accepted
Audience: denomination and general public
Purpose: to represent the mission of The Salvation Army to proclaim

the Gospel of Jesus Christ and serve human need in His name without discrimination

Submissions: Submit through the website. Unsolicited freelance: 50%. Responds in three to four weeks. Simultaneous accepted.

Types of manuscripts: personal experience, profiles

Length: articles, 800–1,250 words; news items and sidebars, 100–400 words

Topics: Christian living/spirituality, culture, discipleship, evangelism, issues, The Salvation Army, trends

Rights: first

Payment: on acceptance; 35¢/word, 15¢/word for reprints

Kill fee: sometimes

Manuscripts accepted per year: 40

Seasonal submissions: six months in advance

Preferred Bible version: NLT

Theme list: available on website

Guidelines: *www.thewarcry.org/submission-guidelines*

Sample: on the website

Tip: "Some association/connection/explication of The Salvation Army is helpful when possible."

YOUR BACKYARD

2867 Jefferson St., Marianna, FL 32448 | 615-613-5040

shELAH911@gmail.com | *yourbackyard.us/your-backyard-magazine*

shELAH, editor

Parent company: Your Backyard Media

Type: bimonthly digital and print magazine; circulation: 500; advertising accepted

Audience: general

Purpose: to encourage writers, artists, musicians, photographers, and brothers and sisters in Jesus Christ

Submissions: Mail or email complete manuscript in body of message. Simultaneous accepted. Unsolicited freelance: 33%. Responds in one month. Also accepts submissions from teens and children.

Types of manuscripts: columns, fillers, how-to, personal experience, poetry, short stories, sidebars

Length: 1,500 words maximum

Topics: arts, inspirational, music

Rights: electronic, first, onetime, reprint (with info on where/when previously published)

Payment: none

Kill fee: none
Manuscripts accepted per year: 25
Seasonal submissions: four months
Preferred Bible version: KJV, open to others
Sample: on the website
Tip: Write about your personal "reason for the hope that is within you." Also looking for original songs, photos, and artwork.

8

TEEN/YOUNG ADULT MARKETS

BOUNDLESS

8605 Explorer Dr., Colorado Springs, CO 80920 | 719-531-3400
editor@boundless.org | *www.boundless.org*
Lisa Anderson, director

> **Parent company:** Focus on the Family
> **Type:** website
> **Audience:** single young adults in 20s and 30s
> **Purpose:** to help Christian young adults grow up, own their faith, date with purpose, and prepare for marriage and family
> **Submissions:** Email query letter with clips for articles, complete manuscript for blog post. Responds only if interested.
> **Types of manuscripts:** articles, blog posts
> **Length:** articles, 1,200–1,800 words; blog posts, 500–800 words
> **Topics:** adulthood, Christian living/spirituality, relationships
> **Rights:** all
> **Hits per month:** 300,000
> **Preferred Bible version:** ESV
> **Guidelines:** *www.boundless.org/write-for-us*
> **Sample:** see the website
> **Tip:** "We don't typically publish unsolicited articles, but we are always open to considering new writers. If you think you've got what it takes to have your work published on *Boundless,* please feel free to send us a sample or two of your writing, a link to your blog, and a proposal of what you're interested in writing about."

THE BRINK

See entry in "Daily Devotional Booklets and Websites."

BRIO

8605 Explorer Dr., Colorado Springs, CO 80920 | 719-531-3400
submissions@briomagazine.com | *focusonthefamily.com/parenting/brio-magazine*
Laura Pottkotter, managing editor

Parent company: Focus on the Family
Type: bimonthly print magazine
Audience: teen girls
Purpose: to provide inspiring stories, fashion insights, fun profiles, and practical tips, all from a biblical worldview
Submissions: Only accepts complete manuscript; email as attachment or mail.
Types of manuscripts: articles, profiles, short stories, devotions
Length: 200–1,400 words
Topics: entertainment, prayer, relationships, seasonal, social media, fashion, health and beauty, culture and faith
Rights: first
Payment: minimum 30¢ per word on acceptance
Guidelines: *media.focusonthefamily.com/brio/pdf/brio-writers-guidelines-2019.pdf*
Sample: on the website
Tip: "We are looking for unique and interesting nonfiction articles, especially stories about real-life teen girls. Every article should have a Christian emphasis, though it shouldn't be preachy or overbearing. The topics, concepts, and vocabulary should be appropriate for our teen audience."

CADET QUEST

See entry in "Children's Markets."

CAFÉ

See entry in "Adult Markets."

CREATION ILLUSTRATED

See entry in "Adult Markets."

GUIDE

See entry in "Children's Markets."

INSPIRE A FIRE

See entry in "Adult Markets."

LOVE IS MOVING

10 Huntingdale Blvd., Scarborough, ON M1W 2S5, Canada | 905-479-5885

ilana@loveismoving.ca | www.loveismoving.ca

Ilana Reimer, editor

Parent company: The Evangelical Fellowship of Canada

Type: digital and triannual print magazine, circulation 10,000

Audience: Canadian young adults

Purpose: to reflect a biblical concept of love and challenge readers to live out their faith with passion for Jesus and compassion for others

Submissions: Email complete manuscript or query letter. Unsolicited freelance: 20%. Responds in two to four days.

Types of manuscripts: essays, feature articles, opinion, poetry, reviews

Length: features, essays, 1,000–1,200 words; short opinion, news, reviews, 300–800 words

Topics: Christian living/spirituality, church, culture, ministry

Rights: first, reprint (with info on where/when previously published)

Payment: 15–20¢/word, $50 for poetry

Manuscripts accepted per year: 100

Seasonal submissions: three months in advance

Preferred Bible version: NIV

Theme lists: available on website

Guidelines: *loveismoving.ca/about/submit*

Sample: *www.faithtoday.ca/Subscribe-LIM*

Tip: "We're looking for smart, thoughtful writers who are wrestling with timely topics in the Canadian Church and broader culture through the lens of their faith. Demonstrate your knowledge on the topic you're pitching and don't be afraid to show your enthusiasm!"

NATURE FRIEND

See entry in "Children's Markets."

PEER

615 Sisters Ln., Alexandria, VA 22314 | 703-684-5500

peer@usn.salvationarmy.org | peermag.org

Lt. Colonel Lesa Davis, editor-in-chief

Denomination: The Salvation Army

Type: monthly digital and print magazine

Audience: ages 16–22

Purpose: to ignite a faith conversation that will deepen biblical perspective, faith, and holy living by addressing topics related to faith, community, and culture

Submissions: Only accepts complete manuscript through the website. Responds in one week. Accepts submissions from teens.

Types of manuscripts: articles, profiles, testimonies

Length: 300–800 words

Topics: Christian living/spirituality, culture, current events

Rights: first, onetime

Payment: 35¢/word, 15¢/word for reprints

Preferred Bible version: NLT

Guidelines: *peermag.org/contribute*

Tip: "We are *always* welcoming new submissions from young writers. Do you love to write? Do you consider yourself an expert on a topic that would interest 16- to 22-year-olds? *Peer* is a national publication, and you can most certainly add the experience of writing for us on your résumé!"

TAKE 5 PLUS

See entry in "Daily Devotional Booklets and Websites."

UNLOCKED

See entry in "Daily Devotional Booklets and Websites."

YOUTH COMPASS

PO Box 4060, Overland Park, KS 66204 | 913-432-0331

sseditor@heraldandbanner.com | *heraldandbanner.com/product/youth-compass*

Arlene McGehee, Sunday school editor

Denomination: Church of God

Parent company: Herald and Banner Press

Type: weekly Sunday school take-home paper

Audience: teens

Purpose: to apply Christian principles on a junior high and high school level

Submissions: Email or mail. Responds in nine months.

Types of manuscripts: biography, short stories

Length: 800–1,500 words

Rights: first, reprint (with info on where/when previously published)

Payment: .005¢/word, .0025¢/word for reprints; on publication

Manuscripts accepted per year: varies

Seasonal submissions: six months in advance

Preferred Bible version: KJV

Writers guidelines: by email

Sample: 9" x 12" SASE with $3.50 postage

Tip: Looking for seasonal stories.

9

CHILDREN'S MARKETS

BEGINNER'S FRIEND

PO Box 4060, Overland Park, KS 66204 | 913-432-0331

sseditor@heraldandbanner.com | heraldandbanner.com/product/youth-compass

Arlene McGehee, Sunday school editor

Denomination: Church of God

Parent company: Herald and Banner Press

Type: weekly Sunday school take-home paper, circulation 575

Audience: ages 2–5

Purpose: to apply biblical truths to daily life in an understandable way

Submissions: Email manuscript as attachment or in body of message, or mail it. Unsolicited freelance: 33%. Responds in one year.

Types of manuscripts: short stories

Length: 500–800 words

Topics: Christian life

Rights: first, reprint (with info on where/when previously published)

Payment: .005¢/word, .0025¢/word for reprints; on publication

Manuscripts accepted per year: ten

Seasonal submissions: six months

Preferred Bible version: KJV

Guidelines: by email

Sample: 9"x12" SASE with $3.50 postage

Tip: Needs seasonal manuscripts most.

CADET QUEST

4695 44th St. SE, Ste. B-130, Kentwood, MI 49512 | 616-241-5616

submissions@CalvinistCadets.org | www.calvinistcadets.org/cadet-quest-magazine

Steve Bootsma, editor

Parent company: Calvinist Cadet Corps

Type: bimonthly print magazine, circulation 5,700

Audience: boys ages 9–14

Purpose: to help boys grow more Christlike in all areas of life

Submissions: Email complete manuscript in body of message, or mail it. Unsolicited freelance: 5–10%. Responds by four months before publication date. Accepts submissions from children and teens.

Types of manuscripts: cartoons, how-to, profiles, projects, puzzles, short stories

Length: fiction, 1,000–1,300 words; nonfiction, 1,500 words maximum

Topics: camping, Christian athletes, nature, sports, theme-related

Rights: all, first, reprint

Payment: articles, minimum 5¢/word; puzzles, varies; cartoons, $5-15

Manuscripts accepted per year: 20

Preferred Bible version: NIV

Theme Lists: available on website

Guidelines: download from *www.calvinistcadets.org/cadet-quest-magazine*

Sample: download from website

Tip: "Looking for fun fiction, without being preachy, for preteen boys. It needs to have some action, and don't be cliché with a Jesus-always-wins type of ending."

CREATION ILLUSTRATED

See entry in "Adult Markets."

DEVOKIDS

See entry in "Daily Devotional Booklets and Websites."

EXPLORERS

PO Box 4060, Overland Park, KS 66204 | 913-432-0331

sseditor@heraldandbanner.com | *heraldandbanner.com/product/explorers*

Arlene McGehee, Sunday school editor

Denomination: Church of God

Parent company: Herald and Banner Press

Type: weekly Sunday school take-home paper

Audience: grades 1-6

Purpose: to apply biblical truths to daily life in an understandable way

Submissions: Email manuscript as attachment or in body of message, or mail it. Responds in nine months. Accepts serial stories.

Types of manuscripts: biography, puzzles, short stories
Length: 500–1,500 words
Rights: first, reprint (with info on where/when previously published)
Payment: .005¢/word, .0025¢/word for reprints; on publication
Manuscripts accepted per year: varies
Seasonal submissions: six months
Preferred Bible version: KJV
Guidelines: by email
Sample: 9"x12" SASE with $3.50 postage
Tip: Looking for seasonal stories.

FOCUS ON THE FAMILY CLUBHOUSE

8605 Explorer Dr., Colorado Springs, CO 80920 | 719-531-3400
orearsx@fotf.org | focusonthefamily.com/clubhouse-magazine
Stephen O'Rear, senior associate editor

Parent company: Focus on the Family
Type: monthly print magazine, circulation 90,000+
Audience: ages 8–12
Purpose: to inspire, entertain, and teach Christian values to children
Submissions: Only mail manuscript. Unsolicited freelance: 15%. Responds in three months. Accepts submissions from children and teens.
Types of manuscripts: activities, crafts, how-to, interviews, personality features of kids, quizzes, short stories, recipes, devotions
Length: fiction, 1,800–2,000 words; nonfiction, 400–500 or 800–1,000
Topics: apologetics, archaeology, Christian life
Rights: first
Payment: 15–25¢ per word on acceptance
Kill fee: sometimes
Manuscripts accepted per year: 80
Seasonal submissions: eight months in advance
Preferred Bible version: HCSB
Guidelines: *focusonthefamily.com/clubhouse-magazine/about/ submission-guidelines*
Sample: $4.99 at *store.focusonthefamily.com/clubhouse-magazine-single-issue*
Tip: "We are always looking for unique and interesting nonfiction stories and articles, especially stories about real-life kids. Every article should have a Christian angle, though it shouldn't be overbearing. The concepts and vocabulary should be appropriate for our audiences' ages."

FOCUS ON THE FAMILY CLUBHOUSE JR.

8605 Explorer Dr., Colorado Springs, CO 80920 | 719-531-3400

Rachel.Pfeiffer@fotf.org | focusonthefamily.com/clubhouse-jr-magazine

Rachel Pfeiffer, senior associate editor

Parent company: Focus on the Family

Type: monthly print magazine, circulation 50,000

Audience: ages 3–7

Purpose: to inspire, entertain, and teach Christian values to children

Submissions: Only accepts complete manuscript by mail. Unsolicited freelance: 15%. Responds in three months. Accepts submissions from children and teens.

Types of manuscripts: activities, Bible stories retold, crafts, rebus stories, recipes, short stories, poetry

Length: fiction, 800–1,000 words; rebus stories, 200 words; nonfiction, 250–400 words

Topics: animals, Bible stories, Christian life, nature, science

Rights: first

Payment: 15–25¢ per word on acceptance

Manuscripts accepted per year: 50

Seasonal submissions: eight months in advance

Preferred Bible version: NIrV

Guidelines: *www.focusonthefamily.com/clubhouse-jr-magazine/about/submission-guidelines*

Sample: $4.99 at *store.focusonthefamily.com/clubhouse-magazine-single-issue*

Tip: "Read the magazine to learn our style and reading level. Aim at early and beginning readers. Rebus and Bible stories are a great way to break in."

GUIDE

PO Box 5353, Nampa, ID 83653-5353

guide.magazine@pacificpress.com | www.guidemagazine.org

Randy Fishell, editor

Denomination: Seventh-day Adventist

Parent company: Pacific Press Publishing Association

Type: weekly Sunday school take-home paper, circulation 26,000

Audience: ages 10–14

Purpose: to show readers, through stories that illustrate Bible truth, how to walk with God now and forever

Submissions: Email query letter; mail or submit complete manuscript through the website. Unsolicited freelance: 75%; 20% assigned. Responds in four to six weeks. Accepts submissions from teens.

Types of manuscripts: biography, humor, personal experience, profiles, quizzes

Length: 450–850 words

Topics: adventure, Christian living, missions, nature

Rights: first, reprint (with info on where/when previously published)

Payment: 7–10¢ per word, $25–40 for games and puzzles; on acceptance

Seasonal submissions: eight months in advance

Preferred Bible version: NKJV

Guidelines: *www.guidemagazine.org/writers-guidelines*

Tip: "Use your best short-story techniques (dialogue, scenes, a sense of plot) to tell a true story starring a kid ages 10–14. Bring out a clear spiritual/biblical message. We publish multipart true stories regularly, two to twelve parts. All topics indicated need to be addressed within the context of a true story."

KEYS FOR KIDS

See entry in "Daily Devotional Booklets and Websites."

NATURE FRIEND

4253 Woodcock Ln., Dayton, VA 22821 | 540-867-0764

editor@naturefriendmagazine.com | *www.naturefriendmagazine.com*

Kevin Shank, editor

Parent company: Dogwood Ridge Outdoors

Type: monthly print magazine, circulation 10,000

Audience: ages 6–14, 80% are ages 8–12

Purpose: to increase awareness of God and appreciation for God's works and gifts, to teach accountability toward God's works, and to teach natural truths and facts

Submissions: Email complete manuscript as attachment. Accepts simultaneous submissions. Unsolicited freelance: 55%. Accepts submissions from children and teens.

Types of manuscripts: articles, crafts, experiments, photo features, profiles, projects, short stories

Length: 500–1,000 words

Topics: animals, astronomy, first aid, flowers, gardening, marine life, nature, photography, science, weather

Rights: all, first, reprint

Payment: all rights, 10¢/edited word; first rights, 8¢/edited word; reprints, 5¢/edited word; on publication

Manuscripts accepted per year: 40–50
Seasonal submissions: four months in advance
Preferred Bible version: KJV only
Guidelines: *naturefriendmagazine.com/contributors/tips-for-getting-published*
Sample: *naturefriendmagazine.com/sample-issues*
Tip: "While talking animals can be interesting and teach worthwhile lessons, we have chosen to not use them in *Nature Friend*. Excluded are puzzle-type submissions, such as 'Who Am I?'"

OUR LITTLE FRIEND

PO Box 5353, Nampa, ID 83653
anita.seymour@pacificpress.com | *primarytreasure.com*
Anita Seymour, managing editor

Denomination: Seventh-day Adventist
Parent company: Pacific Press Publishing Association
Type: weekly Sunday school take-home paper, circulation 16,000
Audience: ages 1–5
Purpose: to teach about Jesus and the Christian life
Submissions: Only accepts complete manuscript; email as attachment. Responds in one month.
Types of manuscripts: true stories
Length: one to two double-spaced pages
Topics: Christian living, God's love, holidays, nature
Rights: electronic, onetime
Payment: $25–50 on acceptance
Manuscripts accepted per year: 52
Seasonal submissions: eight to nine months in advance
Preferred Bible version: ICB, NIrV
Theme lists: available via mail with SASE
Guidelines: *www.primarytreasure.com/for-writers*
Tip: "Stories that are humorous, yet teach a spiritual lesson, rate high in this office because they rate high with kids."

PRIMARY TREASURE

PO Box 5353, Nampa, ID 83653
anita.seymour@pacificpress.com | *www.primarytreasure.com*
Anita Seymour, managing editor

Denomination: Seventh-day Adventist
Parent company: Pacific Press Publishing Association

Type: weekly Sunday school take-home paper, circulation 14,000

Audience: ages 6–9

Purpose: to teach children about the love of God and the Christian life through true stories

Submissions: Email complete manuscript as attachment. Unsolicited freelance: 80%. Responds in one month.

Types of manuscripts: true stories

Length: four to five double-spaced pages

Topics: Christian living/spirituality, holidays, nature

Rights: electronic, onetime

Payment: $25–50 on acceptance

Manuscripts accepted per year: 104

Seasonal submissions: eight months in advance

Theme lists: available via mail with SASE

Guidelines: *www.primarytreasure.com/for-writers*

Tip: "We look for stories that avoid stereotypical roles for men and women. More than half of today's mothers work outside the home. Stories should reflect that some of the time. A more traditional lifestyle setting is OK too. We also want more stories with Dad as the adult character. We get plenty with Mom."

STARLIGHT MAGAZINE

704 W. Madison St., La Grange, KY 40031 | 704-578-0848

editor@starlightmagazine.com | *www.starlightmagazine.com*

Jean Hall, editor

Type: quarterly digital magazine with monthly bonus material, circulation 400

Audience: ages 5–10

Purpose: to shine God's truth through children's literature

Submissions: Email complete manuscript as attachment. Accepts simultaneous submissions. Unsolicited freelance: 90%. Responds in one month. To get an assignment, email the editor.

Types of manuscripts: Bible stories retold, biography, fillers, poetry, short stories

Length: ages 5–7, 500 words; ages 8–10, 800 words

Topics: Christian life, love of reading, science

Rights: first

Payment: none

Manuscripts accepted per year: 100

Seasonal submissions: three months

10

WRITERS MARKETS

INK & QUILL QUARTERLY
1053 E. 1400 N, Milford, IN 46542 | 574-658-3960
wishesandjoy@gmail.com
Amy Schlabach, prose editor
Arielle C. Walters, poetry

Denomination: Anabaptist
Type: quarterly print magazine, circulation 400, advertising accepted
Audience: Anabaptist poets and writers, but not exclusively
Purpose: to give inspiration to beginning and experienced writers alike
Submissions: Email complete manuscript with cover letter as attachment, or mail it. Unsolicited freelance: 10%. Responds in one month.
Types of manuscripts: articles, essays, poetry, writing exercises
Length: 600–800 words
Topics: poetry appreciation, writing
Rights: first, reprint (with info on where/when previously published)
Payment: articles, $30; poetry, 50¢/line; on acceptance
Manuscripts accepted per year: 80
Seasonal submissions: three months in advance
Preferred Bible version: KJV
Guidelines: by email or mail with SASE
Sample: Write or email *mjhofstetter@hotmail.com* and request a sample copy. Back issues are $5 each.
Tip: "We put a special emphasis on poetry, especially traditional verse forms with rhyme and meter. We currently need high-quality poetry of all kinds (nature, Christian living, devotional, personal, narrative, and the kinds of poems poets write for fun)."

INKSPIRATIONS ONLINE
See entry in "Daily Devotional Booklets and Websites."

POETS & WRITERS MAGAZINE

90 Broad St., Ste. 2100, New York, NY 10004-2272 | 212-226-3586

editor@pw.org | *www.pw.org*

Emma Komlos-Hrobsky, senior editor

Parent company: Poets & Writers, Inc.

Type: bimonthly print magazine, circulation 100,000, advertising accepted

Audience: writers of poetry, fiction, and creative nonfiction

Purpose: to provide practical guidance for getting published and pursuing writing careers

Submissions: Email query letter with clips, or mail it. Responds in four to six weeks.

Types of manuscripts: essays, how-to, interviews, news, profiles

Length: 500–3,000 words

Topic: writing

Rights: all, reprint

Payment: $150–500, when scheduled for production

Seasonal submissions: four months in advance

Guidelines: *www.pw.org/about-us/submission_guidelines*

Sample: sold at large bookstores and online

Tip: Most open to "News & Trends," "The Literary Life," and "The Practical Writer."

WORDS FOR THE WAY

5042 E. Cherry Hills Blvd., Springfield, MO 65809 | 417-832-8409

ozarksACW@yahoo.com | *www.ozarksacw.org*

Renee Vajko-Srch, managing editor

Jeanetta Chrystie, acquisitions editor

Parent company: Ozarks Chapter of American Christian Writers

Type: monthly digital newsletter; circulation 55 print, 150 digital; advertising accepted

Audience: writers at all levels

Purpose: to encourage and educate Christians to follow their call to write and learn to write well

Submissions: Email complete manuscript or query letter. Unsolicited freelance: 95%. Responds in three weeks. Accepts submissions from teens.

Types of manuscripts: columns, fillers, how-to, personal experience, poetry, reviews, sidebars

Length: features, 600–900 words; general writing how-to, 400–600 words; sidebars, 200-400 words; reviews, 200–400 words; devotions,

250–500 words; poetry, 12–40 lines
Topic: writing
Rights: electronic, first, onetime, reprint (with info on where/when previously published)
Payment: none
Manuscripts accepted per year: 45
Seasonal submissions: two months in advance
Preferred Bible version: any
Guidelines: *www.OzarksACW.org/guidelines.php*
Sample: request by email
Tip: "We want content that speaks to our Christian writers by teaching and encouraging them. Specific current needs: how to write in a specific genre (your choice), how to grow spiritually through writing, how to organize a book, how to handle taxes as a freelancer. Also, we need devotions for the website that encourage, inspire, and teach (not preach) Christians to follow their calling to write."

THE WRITER

Editorial, Madavor Media, 35 Braintree Hill Office Park, Ste. 101, Braintree, MA 02184 | 617-209-4339
tweditorial@madavor.com | *www.writermag.com*
T.J. Murphy, editor
   Type: monthly digital and print magazine, circulation 30,000, advertising accepted
   Audience: writers at all levels
   Purpose: to expand and support the work of professional and aspiring writers with a straightforward presentation of industry information, writing instruction, and professional and personal motivation
   Submissions: Email query letter. Accepts simultaneous submissions. Unsolicited freelance: 80%. If no response in two weeks, probably not interested.
   Types of manuscripts: articles, essays, how-to, interviews, reviews, sidebars
   Length: 300–4,000 words
   Topic: writing
   Rights: first
   Payment: by type and department, on acceptance
   Theme lists: available on website
   Guidelines: *www.writermag.com/the-magazine/submission-guidelines*
   Sample: sold at large bookstores
   Tip: "Personal essays must provide takeaway advice and benefits for

writers. Include plenty of how-to, advice, and tips on techniques. Be specific. All topics must relate to writing."

THE WRITER'S CHRONICLE

5700 Rivertech Ct., Ste. 225, Riverdale Park, MD 20737-1250 | 240-696-7700

chronicle@awpwriter.org | *www.awpwriter.org/magazine_media/writers_ chronicle_overview*

Supriya Bhatnagar, editor

Parent company: The Association of Writers & Writing Programs

Type: quarterly digital magazine, advertising accepted

Audience: serious writers, writing students and teachers

Purpose: to provide diverse insights into the art of writing that are accessible, pragmatic, and idealistic for serious writers; articles are used as tcaching tools

Submissions: Email query; submit complete manuscript through the website. Accepts simultaneous submissions. Unsolicited freelance: 90%. Responds in three months.

Types of manuscripts: essays, interviews, news, sidebars

Length: 5,000 words maximum

Topic: writing

Rights: electronic, first

Payment: $18 per 100 words on publication

Guidelines: *www.awpwriter.org/magazine_media/submission_guidelines*

Tip: The magazine is published four times during the academic year. Submit only from February 1 through July 15. Also buys blog posts year round for *The Writer's Notebook,* 1,000–2,000 words, $100 per post.

WRITER'S DIGEST

4665 Malsbary Rd., Blue Ash, OH 45242

wdsubmissions@aimmedia.com | *www.writersdigest.com*

Amy Jones, editor-in-chief

Parent company: Active Interest Media

Type: bimonthly digital and print magazine, circulation 60,000, advertising accepted

Audience: aspiring and professional writers

Purpose: to celebrate the writing life and what it means to be a writer in today's publishing environment

Submissions: Email query letter in body of message. Unsolicited freelance: 20%, 60% assigned. Responds in two to four months.

Types of manuscripts: essays, how-to, humor, profiles, sidebars

Length: 300–2,500 words
Topic: writing
Rights: electronic, first
Payment: 30-50¢ per word on acceptance
Kill fee: 25%
Seasonal submissions: eight months in advance
Theme lists: available on website
Guidelines: *www.writersdigest.com/resources/submission-guidelines*
Sample: available at newsstands and through *www.writersdigestshop.com*
Tip: "Although we welcome the work of new writers, we believe the established writer can better instruct our readers. Please include your publishing credentials related to your topic with your submission."

WRITERSWEEKLY.COM

12441 N. Main St. #38, Trenton, GA 30752 | 305-768-0261
brian@booklocker.com | *writersweekly.com*
Brian Whiddon, managing editor

Parent company: BookLocker.com
Type: weekly digital newsletter, circulation 100,000
Audience: freelance writers
Purpose: to help freelance writers find writing opportunities and improve their business
Submissions: Only accepts query letter. Unsolicited freelance: 30%. Responds in one to two weeks.
Types of manuscripts: feature articles, how-to
Length: 600 words
Topics: marketing, writing
Rights: first, reprint
Payment: $60 on acceptance
Manuscripts accepted per year: 100–200
Theme lists: available on website
Guidelines: *writersweekly.com/writersweekly-com-writers-guidelines*
Sample: on the website
Tip: "Understand that we are not a publication about writing but earning income through writing. Proofread your query letter; spelling, capitalization, and punctuation errors leap out at us and tell us what we can expect from you as a writer. *Sell* us your idea; don't just say, "I want to write about . . . .""

WRITING CORNER

contests@writingcorner.com | *writingcorner.com*

Type: website

Audience: writers at all levels

Purpose: to provide concrete, useful advice from those who have been in the trenches and made a successful journey with their writing

Submissions: Email complete manuscript or query letter. Responds in two days.

Types of manuscripts: how-to

Length: 600–900 words

Topic: writing

Rights: onetime, reprint

Payment: none

Guidelines: *writingcorner.com/submission-guidelines*

Sample: on the website

Tip: "Our site visitors are from all areas of writing, so keep that audience in mind when writing for us."

PART 4

SPECIALTY MARKETS

11

DAILY DEVOTIONAL BOOKLETS AND WEBSITES

Note that many of these markets assign all manuscripts. If there is no information listed on getting an assignment, request a sample copy and writers guidelines if they are not on the website. Then write two or three sample devotions to fit that particular format, and send them to the editor with a request for an assignment.

THE BRINK

114 Bush Rd., Nashville, TN 37217 | 800-877-7030

thebrink@randallhouse.com | d6family.com/d6curriculum/adult

David Jones, senior editor

Denomination: Free Will Baptist
Parent company: D6 Family Ministry
Audience: young adults
Type: print
Frequency: bimonthly
Submissions: Devotions are by assignment only to coordinate with the curriculum. Length: 200 words. Rights: all. Bible: ESV. Email for information on getting an assignment. For articles, email query with 100–200-word excerpt if available. Length: 1,000–1,500 words. Does not respond unless interested. Rights: first, reprint, onetime.
Guidelines: by email

Payment: varies

Tip: "We do not accept freelance devotions, but we do accept freelance articles on topics of faith, culture, young adult life, etc."

CHRIST IN OUR HOME

PO Box 1209, Minneapolis, MN 55440-1209 | 800-328-4648

afsubmissions@1517.media | *www.augsburgfortress.org*

Denomination: Evangelical Lutheran Church in America
Parent company: Augsburg-Fortress/1517 Media
Audience: adults
Type: print; also email, audio
Frequency: quarterly
Submissions: Assignments only. Submit sample devotions as explained in the guidelines. Length: 1190 characters, including spaces, maximum. Rights: all. Bible: NRSV.
Guidelines: download from *ms.augsburgfortress.org/downloads/Submission%20Guidelines.pdf?redirected=true*
Tip: "*Christ in Our Home* is read by people in many nations, so avoid thinking only in terms of those who live in the U.S."

CHRISTIAN DEVOTIONS

Kingsport, TN 37663 | 423-384-4821

martin@christiandevotions.us | *www.ChristianDevotions.us*

Martin Wiles, managing editor

Cindy Sproles, executive editor

Parent company: Christian Devotions Ministries
Audience: adults, teens
Type: website
Frequency: daily
Submissions: Accepts freelance submissions. Email as attached Word document. Length: 400 words. Rights: onetime. Bible: any.
Guidelines: *www.christiandevotions.us/writeforus*
Payment: none
Tip: "Follow our guidelines."

DEVOKIDS

Kingsport, TN | 423-384-4821

WritersCoach.us@gmail.com | *devokids.com*

Eddie Jones, managing editor

Parent company: Christian Devotions Ministries

Audience: children

Type: website

Frequency: weekly

Submissions: Takes freelance submissions. Length: 250 words. Email as an attached Word document. Rights: onetime. Bible: NIV.

Also accepts: submissions from children

Guidelines: *devokids.com/write-for-us*

Payment: none

Tip: "We need kid-friendly posts related to crafts, puzzles, coloring pages, games, fun activities, art, and photography. Share an easy and fun recipe for children."

DEVOTIONS

See *The Quiet Hour*.

FORWARD DAY BY DAY

412 Sycamore St., Cincinnati, OH 45202-4110 | 800-543-1813

editorial@forwardmovement.org | *www.forwardmovement.org*

Richelle Thompson, managing editor

Denomination: Episcopal

Parent company: Foreward Movement

Audience: adults

Type: print; also website, email, podcast

Frequency: quarterly

Submissions: Devotions are written on assignment. To get an assignment, send three sample meditations based on three of the following Bible verses: Psalm 139:21; Mark 8:31; Acts 4:12; Revelation 1:10. Responds in six weeks. Authors complete an entire month's worth of devotions. Length: 220 words, including Scripture.

Guidelines: *www.forwardmovement.org/Pages/About/Writers-Guidelines.aspx*

Payment: $300 for a month of devotions

Tip: "*Forward Day by Day* is not the place to score points on controversial topics. Occasionally, when the Scripture passage pertains to it, an author chooses to say something about such a topic. If you write about a hot-button issue, do so with humility and make certain your comment shows respect for persons who hold a different view."

FRUIT OF THE VINE

211 N. Meridian St., Ste. 101, Newberg, OR 97132 | 503-538-9775

fv@barclaypress.com | *www.barclaypress.com*
Cleta Crisman, editor

Denomination: Quaker
Parent company: Barclay Press
Audience: adults
Type: print, also website
Frequency: quarterly
Submissions: Accepts freelance submissions, one week at a time. Length: 250 words. Rights: onetime. Bible: NIV.
Guidelines: *tinyurl.com/y8vwx5gj*
Payment: subscription
Tip: "Writers should be Friends (Quaker) or familiar with the Friends denomination."

INKSPIRATIONS ONLINE

PO Box 3847, Mooresville, NC 28117
tina@inkspirationsonline.com | *inkspirationsonline.com*
Tina Yeager, publisher

Audience: writers
Type: website
Frequency: weekly
Submissions: Accepts freelance submissions. Length: 400 words. Rights: reprint, onetime, electronic. Bible: any.
Guidelines: *inkspirationsonline.com/submission-guidelines*
Payment: none
Tip: "Be sure the devotion centers on writing or a writer's life. Please read published content and submission guidelines."

INSPIRE A FIRE

dianaflegal@gmail.com | *inspireafire.com*
Diana Flegal, senior editor

Parent company: Christian Devotions Ministry
Audience: adults, teens
Type: website
Frequency: daily
Submissions: Assignment only. Looking for advanced, long-term writers whose work needs little to no editing and who would be willing to make a monthly contribution commitment. *Inspire a Fire* is an author-maintained website. Interested writers must be familiar with WordPress (or be willing to learn), so they can post

their articles under the appropriate category in a timely manner each month. Length: 1500 words.

Guidelines: *inspireafire.com/submissions-guidelines*
Payment: none

KEYS FOR KIDS DEVOTIONAL

2060 43rd St. SE, Grand Rapids, MI 49508 | 888-224-2324
editorial@keysforkids.org | *www.keysforkids.org*
Courtney Lasater, editor

> **Parent company:** Keys for Kids Ministries
> **Audience:** children
> **Type:** print; also website, phone app
> **Frequency:** quarterly
> **Submissions:** Takes only freelance submissions. Rights: all. Length: 375 words, including short fiction story. Buys 30–40 per year. Seasonal four to five months ahead. Bible: NKJV.
> **Guidelines:** *keysforkids.org/writersguidelines*
> **Payment:** $30 on acceptance
> **Tip:** "Include illustration in devotional story that uses a real-world object/situation to help kids understand a spiritual truth. Download free PDFs of past issues for sample stories at *www.keysforkids.org/pdf*."

LIGHT FROM THE WORD

PO Box 50434, Indianapolis, IN 46250-0434 | 317-774-7900
submissions@wesleyan.org | *www.wesleyan.org/communication/dailydevo*
Susan LeBaron, publishing services director

> **Denomination:** Wesleyan
> **Parent company:** Wesleyan Publishing House
> **Audience:** adults
> **Type:** print, also website
> **Frequency:** quarterly
> **Submissions:** Must be affiliated with The Wesleyan Church. Email three sample devotions to fit the format and request an assignment. Write "Devotion Samples" in the subject line. Length: 200–240 words. Rights: all. Bible: NIV.
> **Guidelines:** *www.wesleyan.org/wph/writers-guidelines*
> **Payment:** $200 for seven devotions
> **Tip:** "Writing must lead readers to discover a biblical truth and *apply* that truth to their lives."

LIVING FAITH

PO Box 292824, Kettering, OH 45429 | 800-246-7390
info@livingfaith.com | *livingfaith.com*

Denomination: Catholic
Parent company: Bayard, Inc.
Audience: adults
Type: print
Frequency: quarterly
Submissions: Assignments only; email one or two samples and credentials to request an assignment. Bible: NAB.
Tip: "*Living Faith* provides daily reflections based on a Scripture passage from the daily mass. With readings for daily mass listed at the bottom of each devotion, this booklet helps Catholics pray and meditate in spirit with the seasons of the church year."

LIVING FAITH KIDS

PO Box 292824, Kettering, OH 45429 | 800-246-7390
editor@livingfaithkids.com | *www.livingfaith.com/kids*
Connie Clark, editor

Denomination: Catholic
Parent company: Bayard, Inc.
Audience: children
Type: print
Frequency: quarterly
Submissions: Assignments only; email samples and credentials to request an assignment.
Tip: "*Living Faith Kids* features daily devotions based on the daily Scripture readings from the Catholic mass. Each quarterly issue helps children 8–12 develop the habit of daily prayer and build their relationship with Jesus and the church."

LOVE LINES FROM GOD

128 Leyland Ct., Greenwood, SC 29649 | 864-554-3204
mandmwiles@gmail.com | *lovelinesfromgod.blogspot.com*
Martin Wiles, managing editor

Audience: adults
Type: website
Frequency: daily
Submissions: Accepts freelance submissions. Length: 400 words. Rights: first. Bible: NIV.

Guidelines: *lovelinesfromgod.blogspot.com/p/write-for-us_3.html*
Payment: none
Tip: "We are looking for devotions that encourage, not preach. Following the submission guidelines will result in a better chance of having the submission accepted."

THE QUIET HOUR and DEVOTIONS

4050 Lee Vance Dr., Colorado Springs, CO 80919
thequiethour@davidccook.com | davidccook.org
Scott Stewart, editor

Parent company: David C Cook
Audience: adults
Type: print
Frequency: quarterly
Submissions: *Devotions* and *The Quiet Hour* jointly publish new devotionals. By assignment only. Must have North American postal address for contract and payment. Length: 200 words. Rights: all. Bible: NIV, KJV.
Guidelines: *tinyurl.com/yc5pes8m*
Payment: $170 for seven
Tip: "Submit spec devotional on a key verse you select in a Scripture passage of your choice. Begin with anecdotal opening then transition to relevant biblical insight and encouragement for a life of faith rooted in the key verse."

REFLECTING GOD

PO Box 419427, Kansas City, MO 64141 | 816-931-1900
dbrush@thefoundrypublishing.com | reflectinggod.com
Duane Brush, editor

Denomination: Nazarene
Parent company: The Foundry Publishing
Audience: adults
Type: print; also website, podcast, email
Frequency: print, quarterly; website, daily
Submissions: Send a couple of sample devotions to fit the format and request an assignment. Length: 180–200 words.
Payment: $115 for seven
Tip: "Our purpose is the pursuit to embrace holy living. We want to foster discussion about what it means to live a holy life in the 21st century."

REJOICE!

718 N. Main St., Newton, KS 67114 | 316-281-4412

RejoiceEditor@MennoMedia.org | www.mennomedia.org/rejoice

April Yamasaki, editor

Denomination: Mennonite
Parent company: MennoMedia
Audience: adults
Type: print
Frequency: quarterly
Submissions: Devotions on assignment only. Length: 240–265 words. Rights: first, electronic. Bible: prefers NRSVue. Also accepts devotional articles, 700 words, eight per year; poems, free verse, light verse, 60 characters, eight per year, submit three maximum.
Payment: devotions, $100–125 for seven; articles, $50; poems, $25; on publication
Tip: "Don't apply for an assignment unless you are familiar with the publication and Anabaptist theology."

THE SECRET PLACE

1075 First Ave., King of Prussia, PA 19406 | 610-768-2084

thesecretplace@judsonpress.com | www.judsonpress.com

Katelyn Morgan, administrator

Denomination: American Baptist
Parent company: Judson Press
Audience: adults
Type: print
Frequency: quarterly
Submissions: Accepts freelance submissions; does not give assignments. Length: 250 words. Rights: first. Bible: NRSV updated.
Guidelines: *tinyurl.com/ynf6zhfu*
Payment: $20 each
Tip: "Write for comfort, inspiration, and hope in people's everyday lives."

TAKE 5 PLUS

1445 N. Boonville Ave., Springfield, MO 65802 | 417-862-2781

wquick@ag.org | myhealthychurch.com

Wade Quick, team leader

Denomination: Assemblies of God
Parent company: Gospel Publishing House
Audience: teens
Type: print
Frequency: quarterly
Submissions: Assignment only. Request writers guidelines and sample assignment (unpaid) via email. After samples are approved, writers will be added to the list for assignments. Length: 210–235 words. Rights: all. Bible: NIV.
Payment: $25 each, on acceptance
Tip: "Study the publication before attempting the sample assignment."

THESE DAYS: Daily Devotions for Living by Faith

100 Witherspoon St., Louisville, KY 40202 | 800-624-2412
mlindberg@presbypub.com | *www.thethoughtfulchristian.com/Pages/ Item/59264/These-Days.aspx*

Denomination: Presbyterian
Parent company: Presbyterian Publishing Corporation
Audience: adults
Type: print
Frequency: quarterly
Submissions: Accepts freelance submissions. Length: 190 words. Rights: first. Bible: NRSV.
Payment: $100 or $150 worth of books for seven
Tip: "Write thoughtful entries based on a Scripture passage, use gender-inclusive language for God and humanity, and include a brief closing prayer."

UNLOCKED

2060 43rd St. SE, Grand Rapids, MI 49508 | 616-647-4500
editorial@unlocked.org | *unlocked.org*
Hannah Howe, editor

Parent company: Keys for Kids Ministries
Audience: teens
Type: print; also website, podcast
Frequency: quarterly
Submissions: Accepts only freelance submissions. Rights: all. Publishes devotional essays, 200–315 words (personal stories, book-of-the-Bible summaries, church history pieces, tough topics, etc.); fiction, 200–350 words (primarily looking for

allegorical fiction, especially sci-fi and fantasy; sometimes accepts contemporary fiction stories with characters, situation, and dialogue that are not too young; when in doubt, write for an older audience, not a younger one); and poetry, 16–23 lines. Takes teen writers. Bible: CSB, NIV, NLT, WEB. Sample: *unlocked.org/about*.

Guidelines: *unlocked.org/writers-guidelines*

Payment: $30 on acceptance

Tip: "We recommend all interested writers sign up for our writer's newsletter for monthly updates and more details about the kinds of submissions we are looking for (topics, genres, etc.): *unlocked.org/writers-newsletter*."

THE UPPER ROOM

1908 Grand Ave., Nashville, TN 37212 | 615-340-6000

ureditorial@upperroom.org | *upperroom.org*

Lindsay Gray, editorial director

Parent company: The Upper Room

Audience: adults

Type: print, also website

Frequency: bimonthly

Submissions: Accepts freelance submissions. Length: 300 words, which include everything on the printed page. Rights: first, electronic. Bible: NIV, NRSV, CEB, KJV. Submit through the website form (preferred), by mail, or by email.

Guidelines: *submissions.upperroom.org/guidelines*

Payment: $30, on publication

Tip: "*The Upper Room* is meant for an international, interdenominational audience. We want to encourage Christians in their personal life of prayer and discipleship. We seek to build on what unites us and to connect Christians together in prayer around the world."

THE WORD IN SEASON

411 N. Washington Ave., Minneapolis, MN 55401 | 800-328-4648

dancingturtle15@gmail.com | *www.augsburgfortress.org*

Rochelle Melander. managing editor

Denomination: Evangelical Lutheran Church in America

Parent company: Augsburg Fortress/1517 Media

Audience: adults

Type: print, also Amazon ebook

Frequency: quarterly

Submissions: Assignment only; gives assignments based on samples. Request guidelines, and write three trial devotions. Length: 215 words. Rights: all. Bible: NRSV.

Guidelines: download from *tinyurl.com/4ujb7yaw*

Payment: $40

Tip: "Know Lutheran theology, especially the concept of grace."

12

DRAMA

CHRISTIAN PUBLISHERS, LLC

PO Box 248, Cedar Rapids, IA 52406 | 844-841-6387

editor@christianpub.com | www.christianpub.com

Audiences: adult, children, teens

Types: children's Christmas and Easter pageants, full-length musicals, full-length plays, one-act musicals, one-act plays

Submissions: Publishes plays for the Christian market, including but not limited to elementary through high school, adults, and youth groups. Submit complete script through the website form. Response time varies according to the time of the year.

Payment: 10% royalty, often to a fixed amount; no advance

Guidelines: *www.christianpub.com/default.aspx?pg=ag*

Tip: "Be sure your play builds. People have short attention spans, and if the story is too bogged down in excessive dialogue, or if the play wanders aimlessly, they will simply tune out. If the comedy or suspense doesn't build from scene to scene, if we're not involved with the main character(s) or the dramatic question, then the play isn't going anywhere."

CSS PUBLISHING COMPANY, INC.

5450 N. Dixie Hwy., Lima, OH 45807 | 419-227-1818

editor@csspub.com | www.csspub.com

Audiences: adult, children, teens

Types: monologues, one-act plays, reader's theatre, short skits, skit compilations

Submissions: Publishes five to ten skits per year. Receives 20–30 submissions per year. Length: 15 minutes. Primarily interested in Advent/Christmas/Epiphany, and Lent/Easter. Doesn't publish lengthy dramatic works. Contact: email or mail query letter or complete script. Responds in six months. Simultaneous submissions OK.

Payment: negotiated, no advance

Guidelines: *store.csspub.com/page.php?Custom%20Pages=10*

Tip: "Content needs to be fresh and imaginative."

DRAMA MINISTRY

2814 Azalea Pl., Nashville, TN 37204 | 866-859-7622

service@dramaministry.com | www.dramaministry.com

Vince Wilcox, general manager

Audiences: adult, children, teens

Types: monologues, reader's theatre, short skits

Submissions: Open to all topics, including seasonal/holidays, for children, youth, and adults. Email or mail script. Buys all rights.

Guidelines: *www.dramaministry.com/faq*

ELDRIDGE CHRISTIAN PLAYS AND MUSICALS

PO Box 4904, Lancaster, PA 17604 | 850-385-2463

editorial@histage.com | www.95church.com

Susan Shore, senior editor

Audiences: adult, children, teens

Types: full-length musicals, full-length plays, monologues, one-act plays, reader's theatre, skit compilations

Submissions: Publishes 15 scripts per year; receives 300 submissions annually. Length: plays and musicals, minimum 30 minutes, maximum two hours. Submit complete script via email attachment with cover letter in the body of the message. Simultaneous OK. Responds in two months.

Payment: 50% royalty plus 10% copy sales, no advance

Guidelines: *95church.com/submission-guidelines*

Tip: "We like all kinds of plays and are always open to new ideas. Generally speaking, our customers like plays with more female than male roles or flexible casting in which roles can be played by either men or women. This is not a hard-and-fast rule, however. We like easy costuming and scenery, if possible, as many church budgets are limited."

WORDCRAFTS THEATRICAL PRESS

912 E. Lincoln, Tullahoma, TN 37388 | 615-397-8376

wordcraftspress@gmail.com | wordcrafts.net

Mike Parker, publisher

Audience: Adult

Types: full-length plays, one-act plays

Details: Publishes two to four plays per year. Receives 25 submissions. Email query letter or complete script, or submit through the website. Accepts simultaneous submissions. Responds in two to four weeks.

Payment: royalty, no advance

Guidelines: *www.wordcrafts.net/how-to-submit*

Tip: "Make sure your play is producible."

13

GREETING CARDS
AND GIFTS

BLUE MOUNTAIN ARTS

Editorial Dept., PO Box 1007, Boulder, CO 80306 | 303-449-0536

editorial@sps.com | www.sps.com

Audience: adult

Product: greeting cards

Submissions: General card publisher with some inspirational cards. Not looking for rhymed poetry, religious verse, or one-liners. Length: 50 to 300 words. Buys all rights. Accepts freelance submissions by email (no attachments), website form, or mail. Responds in two months or not interested. Holiday deadlines: Christmas and general holidays, June 15; Valentine's Day, August 12; Easter, October 8; Mother's Day and graduation, November 13; Father's Day, January 7.

Guidelines: *www.sps.com/greeting-card-guidelines-submissions*

Tip: "Because our cards capture genuine emotions on topics such as love, friendship, family, missing you, and other real-life subjects, we suggest that you have a friend, relative, or someone else in your life in mind as you write. Writings on special occasions (birthday, anniversary, congratulations, etc.), as well as the challenges, difficulties, and aspirations of life, are also considered."

CHRISTIAN ART PUBLISHING

359 Longview Dr., Bloomingdale, IL 60108 | 800-521-7807

info@christianartpublishing.com | www.christianartpublishing.com

Rob Teigen, vice president of publishing

Audiences: adult, children, teens

Products: Bibles, box of blessings, coloring books, devotionals, gift books, gifts, journals, mugs

Submissions: Looking for books with an uplifting, biblical message that meets the strong felt needs of readers. Not looking for fiction or traditional chapter books; but interested in devotionals, prayer books, seasonal books, and kids resources. Submit query through the website form. Buys all rights. See product lines at *www.christianartgifts.com*.

Payment: 10-14% royalty, sometimes offers advance

Guidelines: *christianartpublishing.com/get-started*

Tip: "Looking for devotionals, kids devotionals, prayer books, and thoughtful gift books."

DICKSONS, INC.

709 B Ave. E, Seymour, IN 47274 | 812-522-1308

submissions@dicksonsgifts.com | *www.dicksonsgifts.com*

Thom Hunter, director of product development

Audience: adult

Products: gifts

Submissions: Two to eight lines, maximum 16, suitable for plaques, bookmarks, etc. Email submission. Responds in three months. Subjects can cover any gift-giving occasion and Christian, inspirational, and everyday social-expression topics. Phrases or acrostics of one or two lines for bumper stickers are also considered. Buys reprint rights.

Payment: royalty, negotiable

Tip: Looking for religious verses.

ELLIE CLAIRE

6100 Tower Cir., Ste. 210, Franklin, TN 37067 | 615-932-7600

www.hachettebookgroup.com/imprint/hachette-nashville/worthy-books/ellie-claire-gifts/?lens=worthy-books

Jeana Ledbetter, acquisitions editor

Audience: adult

Products: devotionals, gift books, journals

Submissions: Submit through agents only. Buys all rights.

Payment: flat fee, royalty

Tip: "We operate in the gift market, and the writing will need to reflect that. We are not interested in Bible studies but in inspirational and encouraging devotions, funny stories with a spiritual component, and compilations from a Christian worldview."

INK & WILLOW

10807 New Allegiance Dr., Ste. 500, Colorado Springs, CO 80921 | *719-590-4999*

info@waterbrookmultnomah.com | *waterbrookmultnomah.com/ink-and-willow*

Jamie Lapeyrolerie, acquisitions editor

Audience: adult

Products: coloring books, inspirational cards, journals, planners

Submissions: Takes submissions only from agents.

Tip: "Ink & Willow encompasses a line of interactive products that infuse contemplation and inspiration into the regular spiritual practice of creative-minded Christians, wherever they are in their faith journey. Each thoughtfully curated gift product is based in biblical truth and sparks a reminder of how God reveals beauty in the midst of our ordinary."

WARNER CHRISTIAN RESOURCES

2902 Enterprise Dr., Anderson, IN 46013 | 800-741-7721

editors@warnerpress.org | *www.warnerpress.org*

Julie Campbell, product and acquisitions editor

Audiences: adult, children

Products: greeting cards

Submissions: Themes include birthday, anniversary, baby congratulations, sympathy, get well, kid's birthday and get well, thinking of you, friendship, Christmas, praying for you, encouragement. Use a conversational tone with no lofty poetic language, such as *thee, thou, art.* Don't preach or use a negative tone. Strive to share God's love and provide a Christian witness. Length: average of four lines. Responds in six to eight weeks. Email as attachment. Buys all rights. Deadlines: everyday, July 31; Christmas, October 1.

Guidelines: *www.warnerpress.org/submission-guidelines*

Payment: $25

Tip: "Visit our website and view the greeting cards we currently offer before submitting. We publish material for boxed cards, not counter-line cards."

14

TRACTS

The following companies publish gospel tracts but do not have writers guidelines. If you are interested in writing for them, email or phone to find out if they currently are looking for submissions. Also check your denominational publishing house to see if it publishes tracts.

FELLOWSHIP TRACT LEAGUE
3733 Snook Rd., Morrow, OH 45152 | 513-494-1075
mail@fellowshiptractleague.org | *fellowshiptractleague.org*

GOOD NEWS PUBLISHERS
1300 Crescent St., Wheaton, IL 60187 | 630-682-4300
info@crossway.org | *www.crossway.org/tracts*

GOSPEL TRACT SOCIETY, INC.
1105 S. Fuller, Independence, MO 64050 | 816-461-6086
gospeltractsociety@gmail.com | *www.gospeltractsociety.org*

GRACE VISION PUBLISHERS
321-745-9966 (text only)
www.gracevision.com

MOMENTS WITH THE BOOK
PO Box 322, Bedford, PA 15522 | 814-623-8737
email through the website | *mwtb.org*

TRACT ASSOCIATION OF FRIENDS
1501 Cherry St., Philadelphia, PA 19102
info@tractassociation.org | *tractassociation.org*

15

BIBLE CURRICULUM

This list includes only the major, nondenominational curriculum publishers. If you are in a denominational church, also check its publishing house for curriculum products. Plus some organizations, like Awana and Pioneer Clubs, produce curriculum for their programs.

Since Bible curriculum is written on assignment only, you'll need to get samples for age groups you want to write for (from the company's website, large Christian bookstores, or your church) and study the formats and pieces. Look for editors' names on the copyright pages of teachers manuals, or call the publishing house for this information.

Then write query letters to specific editors. Tell why you're qualified to write curriculum for them, include a sample of curriculum you've written or other sample of your writing, and ask for a trial assignment. Since the need for writers varies widely, you may not get an assignment for a year or more.

Some of these companies also publish undated, elective curriculum books that are used in a variety of ministries. Plus some book publishers publish lines of Bible-study guides. (See "Traditional Book Publishers.") These are contracted like other books with a proposal and sample chapters.

DAVID C COOK

4050 Lee Vance Dr., Colorado Springs, CO 80918 | 719-536-0100
davidccook.org/curriculum

Type: Sunday school

Imprints: The Action Bible, Bible-in-Life, Echoes, Gospel Light, HeartShaper, Scripture Press, SEEN Youth, Standard Lesson, Tru, Wonder Ink

GROUP PUBLISHING

1515 Cascade Ave., Loveland, CO 80538 | 800-447-1070
submissions@group.com | www.group.com

Types: Sunday school, vacation Bible school, children's worship
Imprints: BE BOLD, DIG IN, FaithWeaver NOW, Fearless
Conversation, Following Jesus, Hands-On Bible Curriculum, LIVE,
Simply Loved, KidsOwn Worship, Play-n-Worship

PENSACOLA CHRISTIAN COLLEGE
PO Box 17900, Pensacola, FL 32522-7900 | 877-356-9385
www.joyfullifesundayschool.com

Type: Sunday school
Imprint: Joyful Life

UNION GOSPEL PRESS
19695 Commerce Pkwy., Cleveland, OH 44130 | 216-749-2100
editorial@uniongospelpress.com | *www.uniongospelpress.com*

Type: Sunday school

UMI (URBAN MINISTRIES, INC.)
1551 Regency Ct., Calumet City, IL 60409-5448 | 800-860-8642
support@urbanministries.com | *urbanministries.com*

Types: Sunday school, vacation Bible school

16

MISCELLANEOUS

These companies publish a variety of books and other products that fall into the specialty-markets category, such as puzzle books, game books, children's activity books, craft books, charts, church bulletins, and coloring books.

BARBOUR PUBLISHING
See entry in "Traditional Book Publishers."

BEAMING BOOKS
See entry in "Traditional Book Publishers."

BROADSTREET PUBLISHING
See entry in "Traditional Book Publishers."

CF4K
See entry in "Traditional Book Publishers."

CSS PUBLISHING GROUP, INC.
See entry in "Traditional Book Publishers."

DAVID C COOK
See entry in "Traditional Book Publishers."

GROUP PUBLISHING
1515 Cascade Ave., Loveland, CO 80538 | 970-669-3836
www.group.com/writer-submissions

> **Submissions:** Looking for innovative children's ministry experts who are interested in being contract writers to contribute to books,

online articles, and curriculum. Complete the online form to get an assignment.

JUST FOR KIDS

2 Overlea Blvd., Toronto, ON M4H 1P4, Canada | 416-425-2111
justforkids@salvationarmy.ca | salvationist.ca/editorial/just-for-kids/2023-back-issues
Abbigail Oliver, editor

> **Parent company:** The Salvation Army in Canada and Bermuda
> **Audience:** ages 5–12
> **Type:** weekly activity page
> **Submissions:** Puzzles that relate to a biblical story or concept, common themes (seasons, holidays, sports, animals, etc.), and Salvation Army distinctives (junior soldiers, Salvation Army flag, etc.); jokes and tongue twisters; general knowledge and Salvation Army trivia questions; news photo (junior soldier enrollment, achievement or recognition of a young person or group of young people, a corps activity for or by young people, etc.) with caption of 75 words maximum.
> **Payment:** none
> **Guidelines:** *salvationist.ca/files/salvationarmy/Magazines/Writers_ Guidelines_2023/Writers_Guidelines_-Just_for_Kids_23-04-27_.pdf*

PAULINE BOOKS AND MEDIA

See entry in "Traditional Book Publishers."

ROSE PUBLISHING

See entry in "Traditional Book Publishers."

ROSEKIDZ

See entry in "Traditional Book Publishers."

WARNER CHRISTIAN RESOURCES

2902 Enterprise Dr., Anderson, IN 46013 | 800-741-7721
editors@warnerpress.org | www.warnerpress.org

> **Church bulletins:** Short devotions that tie into a visual image and incorporate a Bible verse. Especially interested in material for holidays and special Sundays, such as Christmas, New Year's Day, Palm Sunday, Easter, Pentecost, and Communion. General themes are also welcome. Length: 250 words maximum. Submission period:

January 1–March 15 annually. Buys all rights. Payment varies.

Children's coloring and activity books: Most activity books focus on a Bible story or biblical theme, such as love and forgiveness. Ages range from preschool (ages 2–5) to upper elementary (ages 8–10). Include activities and puzzles in every upper-elementary book. Coloring-book manuscripts should present a picture idea and a portion of the story for each page. Deadlines: May 1 and October 1. Payment varies.

Children's teaching resources: Books with skits, science experiments, and crafts. Length: 48-144 pages. Activities must be interesting for kids, teach important biblical lessons, and be easy to use in a class. Payment varies.

Guidelines: *www.warnerpress.org/submission-guidelines*

PART 5

SUPPORT
FOR
WRITERS

17

LITERARY AGENTS

Asking editors and other writers is a great way to find a reliable agent. You may also want to visit *www.sfwa.org/other-resources/for-authors/writer-beware/agents* for tips on avoiding questionable agents and choosing reputable ones.

The general market has the Association of American Literary Agents (*aalitagents.org*), also known as AALA. To be a member, the agent must agree to a code of ethics. The website has a searchable list of agents. Some listings below indicate at least one agent belongs to the AALA. Lack of such a designation, however, does not indicate the agent is unethical; most Christian agents are not members.

A DROP OF INK LITERARY AGENCY

8587 Green Valley Rd. SE, Caledonia, MI 49316 | 616-443-1993
tomdean@adropofink.pub | *www.adropofink.pub*

Agent: Tom Dean
Agency: Established in 2020. Represents 20 clients. Also does publishing and marketing consulting.
Types of books: adult nonfiction
New clients: Open to well-established book authors and writers met at conferences. First contact: website form, referral from current client. Responds in five to seven business days.
Commission: 15%
Tip: "Be as thorough as possible in your initial proposal draft."

AKA LITERARY MANAGEMENT

11445 Dallas Rd., Peyton, CO 80831 | 719-339-0077
terrie@akaliterary.com | *akalm.net*

Agent: Terrie Wolf
Agency: Established in 2009. Represents 35+ clients. Member of Association of American Literary Agents. Responds in eight weeks;

feel free to nudge after then. Specializes in manuscript to film/TV/ media adaptation but does not take scripts or screenplays.

Types of books: adult fiction, adult nonfiction, children's fiction, children's nonfiction, general-market children's, general-market fiction, general-market nonfiction

New clients: Open to all writers except self-published. First contact: website form, referral from current client. Query first via the instructions on the website through Submittable or Query Manager, then full proposal. Simultaneous OK.

Commission: 15%

Tip: "Visit our website, then make sure to carefully follow instructions for how to submit your project. Please provide concise and applicable information regarding your manuscript, and show us nothing short of your very best work."

ALIVE LITERARY AGENCY

5001 Centennial Blvd. #50742, Colorado Springs, CO 80908

admin@aliveliterary.com | www.aliveliterary.com

Agents: Bryan Norman, Lisa Jackson, Rachel Jacobson, Kathleen Kerr
Agency: Established in 1989.
Types of books: adult nonfiction
New clients: Open only to well-established book writers. Contact through the website. Response time varies.
Commission: 15%
Tip: "We only accept manuscripts by request or referral."

AMBASSADOR LITERARY

PO Box 50358, Nashville, TN 37205 | 615-370-4700

wes@AmbassadorAgency.com | www.AmbassadorAgency.com

Agent: Wes Yoder
Agency: Established in 1993. Represents 20 clients. Also offers national media representation for select clients.
Types of books: adult nonfiction, religious
New clients: Open only to well-established book writers. Contact by email with a full proposal. Responds in two weeks.
Commission: 15%
Tip: "Looking for great storytellers!"

AUTHORIZEME LITERARY FIRM

PO Box 1816, South Gate, CA 90280 | 310-508-9860

AuthorizeMeNow@gmail.com | www.AuthorizeMe.net

Agent: Dr. Sharon Norris Elliott

Agency: Established in 2020. Represents 60+ clients. Other services: See entry in "Editorial Services."

Types of books: adult fiction, Bible study, board books, Christian living, devotionals, early readers, picture books, women's issues

New clients: Open to writers from established to those seeking their first contract. Contact: email with one-sheet. Responds in one to three months.

Commission: 15%

Tip: "Love Jesus; be teachable, patient, and humble; possess a strong desire to reach for excellence; smile a lot."

BANNER LITERARY

PO Box 1828, Winter Park, CO 80482

mike@mikeloomis.co | www.mikeloomis.co

Agent: Mike Loomis

Agency: Established in 2004. Represents 48 clients. Other services: See listings in "Editorial Services" and "Publicity and Marketing Services."

Types of books: adult nonfiction, business, inspiration, politics, self-help

New clients: Open to writers who have not published a book and self-published writers. Contact through email or website form. Responds in two weeks.

Commission: 15%

Tip: "Send your web address with query."

BBH LITERARY

david@bbhliterary.com | www.bbhliterary.com

Agents: David Bratt; Laura Bardolph, *laura@bbhliterary.com*

Agency: Established in 2021. Represents 30 clients. Other services: See listings in "Editorial Services" and "Publicity and Marketing Services."

Types of books: adult nonfiction

New clients: Open to all book writers. Contact: email, website form, referral from current client. Accepts simultaneous submissions. Responds in one week.

Commission: 15%

Tip: "Please tell us why your book has some urgency to its message.

We are most interested in books that speak to real life in a complicated world with nuance and wisdom."

THE BINDERY

2727 N. Cascade Ave., Ste. 170, Colorado Springs, CO 80207

info@thebinderyagency.com | *www.thebinderyagency.com*

Agents: Alex Field, Andrea Heinecke, Trinity McFadden, Ingrid Beck, John Blase, Morgan Strehlow

Agency: Established in 2017. Represents 200+ clients. Member of Association of American Literary Agents.

Types of books: adult fiction, adult nonfiction, biography, Christian living, cultural issues, culture, history, memoir, mental health, parenting, poetry, pop culture, psychology, relationships, self-help, social issues, spirituality

New clients: Open to all book writers. Initial contact: email, referral from current client, website form. Query first, or send full proposal. Accepts simultaneous submissions. Responds in 10–12 weeks or is not interested.

Commission: 15%

Tip: "Before sending a query, you can find out what each agent is seeking on the About page of our website. We will read every query to determine whether it's a fit for our agency. However, due to the volume of email queries we receive, we have to be incredibly selective; and, as a result, we won't reply to every submission. If one of our agents would like to read more of your manuscript or discuss your project with you, they will reach out to you directly."

THE BLYTHE DANIEL AGENCY, INC.

PO Box 64197, Colorado Springs, CO 80962-4197

blythe@theblythedanielagency.com | *www.theblythedanielagency.com*

Agents: Blythe Daniel; Stephanie Alton, *stephanie@ theblythedanielagency.com*

Agency: Established in 2005. Represents 115 clients. In addition to literary representation, it offers marketing services. For more information, email the projects manager, Rebecca George, at *rebecca@theblythedanielagency.com*. See listing in "Publicity and Marketing Services."

Types of books: adult fiction (a few titles in women's, romance, romantic suspense, historical, suspense, and military; no adult fantasy or science fiction), business, Christian living, crafts/DIY, current events, devotionals, early readers, family, friendship, gift books, leadership, marriage, middle grade, military, parenting, picture books, prophecy, social issues, spiritual growth, women's issues

New clients: We represent authors who have previously published, never published before, and have had an agent previously. We meet writers at conferences and take referrals from current clients. We represent writers-conference directors whose conferences we attend. Contact: email. Responds in 8–12 weeks.

Commission: 15%

Tip: "We want to work with authors who are open to feedback and suggestions and are willing to work hard. We are looking for writers who are saying something no one else is saying, are committed to becoming authors who are building their audience, and with whom we can build a relationship with over time."

BOOKS & SUCH LITERARY MANAGEMENT

representation@booksandsuch.com | www.booksandsuch.com

Agents: Janet Kobobel Grant, *janet@booksandsuch.com;* Wendy Lawton, *wendy@booksandsuch.com;* Rachel Kent, *rachel@ booksandsuch.com;* Cynthia Ruchti, *cynthia@booksandsuch.com;* Barb Roose, *barb@booksandsuch.com;* Debbie Alsdorf, *debbie@ booksandsuch.com*

Agency: Established in 1996. Represents 275 clients.

Types of books: adult fiction, adult nonfiction, children's fiction, children's nonfiction, Christian living, devotionals, discipleship, family, health/wellness, leadership, marriage, middle grade, ministry, teen/YA fiction, teen/YA nonfiction

New clients: Open to writers who have not published a book. Contact by email with query first. Responds in one month.

Commission: 15%

Tip: "We're especially interested in writers who have developed a social-media presence and have a website."

CHRISTIAN LITERARY AGENT

PO Box 428, Newburg, PA 17257 | 717-423-6621

keith@christianliteraryagent.com | www.christianliteraryagent.com

Agent: Keith Carroll

Agency: Established in 2010. Represents 10–15 new clients annually. Other service: writer coach.

Types of books: adult nonfiction

New clients: Open to first-time book authors and self-published writers. Initial contact: email, phone, website form. Responds in two to four weeks.

Commission: 10%

Tip: "I try to help you make your material more of an effective read."

THE CHRISTOPHER FEREBEE AGENCY

submissions@christopherferebee.com | *christopherferebee.com*

Agents: Christopher Ferebee, Angela Scheff, Jana Burson, Jonathan Merritt

Agency: Established in 2011.

Types of books: adult fiction, adult nonfiction

New clients: Submit query letter and proposal as email attachment. Responds in four weeks.

Tip: "As a small agency, we focus our efforts on a very select group of authors. Our primary focus and attention is always on existing client relationships. But we are looking for the right authors with important ideas."

CREATIVE MEDIA AGENCY

query@cmalit.com | *cmalit.com*

Agent: Paige Wheeler

Agency: Established in 1997. Represents 20–30 clients. Member of Association of American Literary Agents. Looking for women's fiction, book-club fiction, romance, mystery/thrillers, young adult, middle grade, and select nonfiction. For more information, visit *cmalit.com/paige-wheeler.*

Types of books: adult fiction, adult nonfiction, middle grade, young adult

New clients: Open to all querying authors. Query by email. Responds in four to six weeks; but due to the pandemic backlog, they've been responding a little slower.

Commission: standard

Tip: "Make sure you include an interesting hook in your query! I'm particularly drawn to unique voices and immersive stories. We have some wonderful submission tips on our website at *cmalit. com/submit.*"

C.Y.L.E. AGENCY (Cyle Young Literary Elite)

PO Box 1, Clarklake, MI 49230 | 330-651-1604

submissions@cyleyoung.com | *cyleyoung.com*

Agents: Cyle Young, Tessa Emily Hall, Del Duduit, Megan Burkhart, Bethany Jett, Antwan Houser, Andy Clapp

Agency: Established in 2018. Represents 80 clients. Member of Association of American Literary Agents. Specialty: children's and nonfiction. Acquires general-market books too.

Types of books: adult fiction, adult nonfiction, children's fiction, children's nonfiction, middle grade, teen/YA fiction, teen/YA nonfiction

New clients: Some of the agents are currently closed to queries and proposals except when meeting writers at a conference or an online writing event. Check the website to see who is open to submissions. Simultaneous submissions OK. Responds in three months or not interested.

Commission: 15%

Tip: "We look for projects with great writing, big ideas, and great platform."

DUNAMIS WORDS

www.cherylricker.com/dunamis-words

Agent: Cheryl Ricker

Agency: Established in 2015. Represents 15 clients.

Types of books: adult fiction, business, Charismatic, Christian living, current events, devotionals, gift books, leadership, marriage, memoir, ministry, parenting, social issues, women's issues

New clients: Accepts queries—maximum of six pages—only through the website. If interested, will ask for more information and sample chapters.

Tip: "One's heart matters as much as one's calling and ability to write. These authors work diligently at growing their craft and tuning their antennae to the Creator and wellspring of life. From a deep abiding relationship with Christ flows the richest substance and wisdom."

EMBOLDEN MEDIA GROUP

PO Box 953607, Lake Mary, FL 32795

submissions@emboldenmediagroup.com | *emboldenmediagroup.com*

Agents: Jevon Bolden, Quantrilla Ard, Cynthia Crawford

Agency: Established in 2017. Represents 42 clients. Also offers content development, editorial, writing coaching.

Types of books: adult fiction, adult nonfiction, African American, Charismatic, children's fiction, children's nonfiction, Christian living, devotionals, health/wellness, leadership, memoir

New clients: Open to writers at every level, including self-published. Contact: email query, website form, or current client referral. Accepts simultaneous submissions. Responds in 8–12 weeks.

Commission: 15%

Tip: "Follow us and our agents on social media, keep up with the kind of authors we represent and themes that catch our hearts and eyes."

GARDNER LITERARY, LLC

rachellegardner.com

Agents: Rachelle Gardner, Kristy Cambron, Ashley Hong

Agency: Established in 2021. Represents 85 clients.

Types of books: adult fiction, adult nonfiction, general-market fiction, general-market nonfiction

New clients: Open to any writer. First contact by email query at *querymanager.com/query/GardnerLiterary.* Responds in one month.

Commission: 15%

Tip: "Read 'What We're Looking For' on our submission page to see if we will consider your project."

THE GATES GROUP

sarah@the-gates-group.com | *www.the-gates-group.com*

Agents: Don Gates, Sarah Coverstone

Agency: Established in 2012. Represents more than 50 authors.

Types of books: nonfiction

New clients: Open to writers who have not published a book and well-established book writers. Initial contact: email. Responds in two days.

Commission: 15%

Tip: "We can collaborate with you and your ministry and publisher to get the most out of your marketing and publicity efforts. We have the expertise and experience to deliver results."

GOLDEN WHEAT LITERARY

goldenwheatliterary.com

Agents: Jessica Schmeidler, *jessica@goldenwheatliterary.com;* Susan Nystoriak, *susan@goldenwheatliterary.com*

Agency: Established in 2015. Also sells to the general market.

Types of books: adult fiction, devotionals, general-market fiction, memoir, middle grade, picture books, teen/YA nonfiction

New clients: Email query letter and first three chapters, all in body of message; no attachments. If no response in six months, assume the agent is not interested.

Tip: "If our lack of response has been due merely to a time availability issue, then we have been known to respond to queries that have gone unanswered for six months or longer. So, if you do not wish to receive a response after a certain time, for your own sanity and/or record-keeping reasons, please note that in your initial query. Likewise, if your manuscript is no longer available for consideration, please do remember to withdraw the submission."

HEART SONG LITERARY AGENCY

heartsongliterary@gmail.com | *www.heartsongliterary.com*

Agent: Patricia Riddle-Gaddis

Agency: Established in 2023. Especially interested in sweet romance, cozy mysteries (think Hallmark), and young-adult categories. Other services: additional consulting and referrals to further your publishing goals if work is not accepted, comprehensive editing services at competitive rates.

Types of books: adult fiction, adult nonfiction, clean general-market fiction, young adult

New clients: Open to selected unpublished authors, published authors, and referrals. Initial contact: email proposal per guidelines, referral. Responds in three months or not interested.

Tip: "For the most part, Heart Song works with domestic (living in the United States or Canada) authors, but international writers are considered on an individual basis."

ILLUMINATE LITERARY AGENCY

submissions@illuminateliterary.com | *illuminateliterary.com*

Agent: Jenni Burke

Agency: Established in 2006. Represents 30 clients. Specialty: faith-based nonfiction.

Types of books: Bible studies, business, children's fiction, Christian living, church and ministry, culture, devotionals, family, gift books, leadership, lifestyle, memoir, personal development, relationships, spiritual growth

New clients: Open to writers with a strong platform, clear writing, and a powerful message. Initial contact: website form, referral from current client, full proposal. Responds in one month.

Commission: 15%

Tip: "Please review our website thoroughly, including what Jenni is looking for; and follow submission guidelines closely. Fast Track option is available for client referrals and sizable platforms."

LINDA S. GLAZ LITERARY AGENCY

51670 Washington St., New Baltimore, MI 48047

linda@lindasglaz.com | lindasglaz.com

Agent: Linda S. Glaz

Agency: Established in 2022. Represents 35 clients.

Types of books: adult fiction, adult nonfiction, general-market fiction, general-market nonfiction

New clients: Open to most authors but primarily those met at conferences or referred by other authors. First contact: email with full proposal, referral through current client. Accepts simultaneous submissions. Responds in one month; after that feel free to nudge.

Commission: 15%

Tip: "Be sure you send your best work that is exactly what I ask for and only in genres that I represent."

LITERARY MANAGEMENT GROUP

150 Young Way, Richmond Hill, GA 31324 | 615-812-4445

brucebarbour@literarymanagementgroup.com | www.literarymanagement-group.com

Agent: Bruce R. Barbour

Agency: Established in 1996. Represents 100 clients.

Types of books: adult nonfiction

New clients: Open only to previously published authors with traditional publishers. Contact: email proposal according to the website template and sample chapters. Accepts simultaneous submissions. Responds in four to six weeks.

Commission: 15%

Tip: "Proposals and sample chapters should not be formatted or sent as PDF. Simple Word or Google documents allow me to reply with comments."

MACGREGOR AND LEUDEKE

PO Box 1316, Manzanita, OR 97130 | 503-389-4803

submissions@macgregorliterary.com | www.MacGregorLiterary.com

Agents: Amanda Luedeke, *amanda@macgregorliterary.com;* Chip MacGregor, *chip@macgregorliterary.com;* Alina Mitchell, *alina@macgregorliterary.com;* Elisa Saphier, *elisa@macgregorliterary.com;* Colleen Oefelein, *colleen@macgregorliterary.com*

Agency: Established in 2006. Member of Association of American

Literary Agents. Represents 100 clients.

Types of books: adult fiction, Christian living, deeper life, marriage, parenting, prescriptive, self-help

New clients: Open to published writers, including self-published, with a platform. Initial contact: website form, referral from a current client. No simultaneous submissions. Responds in one to two months.

Commission: 15%

Tip: "Take the time to finish your work. Most rejected projects are rejected because they are not really complete—they are 60% complete. As a writer, you'll find you have more success if you polish, listen to experienced advice, revise, rework, go back and look again, then finish the manuscript to the best of your abilities. A rough draft rarely sells. A polished work of a salable idea, presented by an author with a platform to help market and sell copies, is a winning combination."

MARY DEMUTH LITERARY

2150 Heather Glen Dr., Rockwall, TX 75087 | 214-475-9083

mary@marydemuthliterary.com | *marydemuthliterary.com*

Agent: Mary DeMuth

Agency: Established in 2022; former agent with Books & Such Literary Management. Represents 38 clients. Specialty: Christian living. Other service: coaching in platform (free).

Types of books: art-based, Christian living, cookbook, design, gift books, global church, theology, well-written surprising topics

New clients: Open to well-established book writers, writers met at conferences, and writers who have agents and are looking for a new one. First contact: email, website form, referral from current client. Query first. Simultaneous OK. Responds in one week.

Commission: 15%

Tip: "Know the publishing industry, and have a robust platform."

PAPE COMMONS

11327 Rill Pt., Colorado Springs, CO 80921 | 719-648-4019

don@papecommons.com | *papecommons.com*

Agent: Don Pape

Agency: Established in 2021. Represents 50 clients. Also does publishing-industry consulting.

Types of books: adult fiction, adult nonfiction, general-market fiction, general-market nonfiction

New clients: Open to writers serious about their craft and a long-term engagement with publishing. Contact: query first, website form. Responds in one week.

Commission: 15%

Tip: "Be serious about the craft and willing to be part of a community of writers."

THE SEYMOUR AGENCY

4100 Corporate Sq., Ste. 140, Naples, FL 34104 | 239-398-8209

querymanager.com/JulieGwinn | www.theseymouragency.com

Agent: Julie Gwinn

Agency: Established in 1992. Primarily a general-market agency; Julie handles the Christian books.

Types of books: adult fiction

New clients: Open to writers who have not published a book and self-published writers. First contact: Query Manager. Responds in three weeks or not interested.

Commission: 15%

Tip: "Hone your craft. Take advantage of writers groups, critique partners, etc., to polish your manuscript into the best shape it can be."

THE STEVE LAUBE AGENCY

24 W. Camelback Rd. A-635, Phoenix, AZ 85013 | 602-336-8910

info@stevelaube.com | www.stevelaube.com

Agents: Steve Laube, *krichards@stevelaube.com;* Tamela Hancock Murray, *ewilson@stevelaube.com;* Bob Hostetler, *rgwright@stevelaube. com;* Dan Balow, *vseem@stevelaube.com;* Megan Brown, *jsanders@ stevelaube.com;* Lynette Eason, *ehumphries@stevelaube.com*

Agency: Established in 2004. Represents more than 300 clients. See website blog post by each agent for what he or she is looking for. Not actively pursuing children's picture book projects at this time.

Types of books: adult fiction, adult nonfiction

New clients: Open to unpublished authors. Email proposal as attachment according to the guidelines on the website. Steve Laube also will take proposals by mail. Accepts simultaneous submissions. Responds in 8–12 weeks.

Commission: 15%; foreign, 20%

Tip: "Please follow the guidelines! Since your book proposal is like a job application, you want to present yourself in the most professional manner possible. Your proposal will be a simple vehicle to convey your idea to us and, ultimately, to a publisher. Don't call the office to pitch your book idea. We'd rather read the proposal."

WILLIAM K. JENSEN LITERARY AGENCY
119 Bampton Ct., Eugene, OR 97404 | 541-688-1612
queries@wkjagency.com | www.wkjagency.com

Agents: William K. Jensen, Teresa Evenson
Agency: Established in 2005. Represents more than 50 clients.
Types of books: adult nonfiction
New clients: Open to unpublished authors. Contact by email only; no attachments. See the website for complete query details. Accepts simultaneous submissions. Responds in one month or not interested.
Commission: 15%
Tip: "Due to the changes in book retailing over the last ten years, publishers will only accept authors with a robust social-media and/or speaking platforms. That being the case, we can only consider queries by writers with at least 20,000 online followers and/or a dynamic speaking ministry."

WINTERS & KING
2448 E. 81st St., Ste. 5900, Tulsa, OK 74137-4259 | 918-494-6868
alalourse@wintersking.com | wintersking.com/practice-areas/publishing-agent-services

Agents: Thomas J. Winters, Alyssa M. LaCourse
Agency: Established in 1983. Represents 150 clients. Part of a law firm. Other services: legal review of publishing contracts, drafting of work-for-hire agreements to contract writer/editor services, copyright/trademark filing.
Types of books: adult fiction, adult nonfiction
New clients: Open to writers with a story to tell. Contact: email or website form. Responds in two weeks.
Commission: 15%
Tip: "Submissions should be carefully edited and free of typos. Accompanying manuscripts or sample chapters for presentation to publishers should be edited, typo-free, and basically print-ready."

WOLGEMUTH & ASSOCIATES
info@wolgemuthandassociates.com | www.wolgemuthandassociates.com

Agents: Andrew Wolgemuth, Erik Wolgemuth, Austin Wilson
Agency: Established in 1992. Represents 150 clients.
Types of books: adult nonfiction, Bible studies, children's fiction,

children's nonfiction

New clients: Open only to authors who have at least one book commercially published or are referred by a client or close contact. Contact: emailed query with writing sample. Responds in two weeks if interested.

Commission: 15%

WORDSERVE LITERARY GROUP

700 Colorado Blvd. #318, Denver, CO 80206

admin@wordserveliterary.com | *www.wordserveliterary.com*

Agents: Greg Johnson; Keely Boeving, *Keely@wordserveliterary.com*

Agency: Established in 2003. Represents 175 clients. General-market nonfiction is limited to military, history, business, health, and wellness. Other services: movie options.

Types of books: adult fiction, adult nonfiction, Bible studies, children's fiction, children's nonfiction, general-market nonfiction, gift books

New clients: Open to writers who have not published a book yet and self-published writers. Contact: emailed query first or referral from a current client. Accepts simultaneous submissions. Responds in two to four weeks.

Commission: 15%

Tip: "Go to our website to learn more. Follow instructions on submissions."

WORDWISE MEDIA SERVICES

4083 Avenue L, Ste. 255, Lancaster, CA 93536

www.wordwisemedia.com/agency

Agents: Steven Hutson, David Fessenden, Michelle S. Lazurek

Agency: Established in 2011. Member of Association of American Literary Agents. Represents 60 clients.

Types of books: almost everything

New clients: Open to unpublished book authors. Contact: Submit query form as email attachment. Accepts simultaneous submissions. Responds in one month; OK to nudge after then.

Commission: 15%, more for movie deals

Tip: "Follow directions carefully. Meet us at a conference. Specify the agent's name in the email subject line if you have a preference."

WTA MEDIA

321 Billingsly Ct., Ste. 7, Franklin, TN 37067

info@wta.media | *thewtagroup.com*

Agents: David Schroeder, Jenaye Merida

Types of books: adult fiction, adult nonfiction, children's fiction, children's nonfiction, curriculum, devotionals

YATES & YATES

1551 N. Tustin Ave., Ste. 710, Santa Ana, CA 92705 | 714-480-4000

email@yates2.com | www.yates2.com

Agents: Sealy Yates, Matt Yates, Curtis Yates, Mike Salisbury, Karen Yates

Agency: Established in 1989. Represents fewer than 50 clients.

Types of books: adult nonfiction

New clients: No unpublished authors. Contact: email with full proposal. Responds in one to two months. Other services: author coaching and courses.

Commission: negotiable

Tip: "We serve passionate, articulate, gifted Christian communicators, using our strengths to guide, counsel, and protect them, fiercely advocate for them, and help them advance life- and culture-transforming messages for the sake of the Kingdom."

18

WRITERS CONFERENCES AND SEMINARS

This chapter is divided by states, international countries, and online, each section in alphabetical order. Many directors had not set dates for 2024 when this book went to print.

ALABAMA

BLUE LAKE CHRISTIAN WRITERS RETREAT
Andalusia, AL | March 20–23 | *bluelakecwr.com*

Director: Marilyn Turk, 107 Bermuda Way, Niceville, FL 32578; 850-225-2466; *marilynturkwriter@yahoo.com*

Description: Blue Lake Christian Writers Retreat is a small, Christian writers conference in a retreat-like setting, offering a variety of classes, both fiction and nonfiction for writers of all levels.

Special tracks: advanced writers, speaking, teens

Faculty includes: agents, editors, publishers

Scholarships: partial

Attendance: 85

Contests/awards: Living Water Awards for published and unpublished writers in poetry, devotions, articles, nonfiction books, novels, children's, and YA books.

SOUTHERN CHRISTIAN WRITERS CONFERENCE
Leeds, AL (Birmingham area) | June | *southernchristianwriters.my.canva.site*

Director: Cheryl Wray, PO Box 3057, Hueytown, AL 35023; 205-

534-0595; *scwritersconference@gmail.com*

Description: The SCWC is a two-day conference for beginners or experienced writers that focuses on several genres: nonfiction books, magazines, fiction, grammar, business aspects, legal aspects, etc.

Faculty includes: agents, editors

Attendance: 160-200

ARIZONA

FAITH, HOPE AND LOVE CHRISTIAN WRITERS CONFERENCE

Phoenix, AZ | September | *fhlchristianwriters.com/conference*

Director: *president@fhlchristianwriters.com*

Description: Focused on writing and selling romantic fiction.

Faculty includes: agents, authors, editors

CALIFORNIA

VISION CHRISTIAN WRITERS CONFERENCE

Mt. Hermon, CA (near Santa Cruz) | March 22–26 | *vcwconf.com*

Director: Robynne Elizabeth Miller, 530-217-8233, *director@vcwconf.com*

Description: Vision is a full-service premier conference, featuring top agents, editors, and publishers from across the country, as well as more than 50 workshops, tracks, and speakers. One-on-one appointments with agents, editors, publishers, and industry experts are free (as are the gorgeous redwoods).

Faculty includes: agents, editors, publishers

Plenary speaker: Robin Jones Gunn

Scholarships: full, partial

Attendance: 200

Contests/awards: Most Promising Writer, Most Encouraging, and more.

WEST COAST CHRISTIAN WRITERS CONFERENCE

Sacramento or San Francisco, CA | October | *www.westcoastchristianwriters.com*

Director: Susy Flory, 1750 Prairie City Rd., Ste. 130, #689, Folsom, CA 95630; 800-660-0747; *info@westcoastchristianwriters.com*

Description: West Coast Christian Writers (WCCW) is a strong community of writers with writing events known for high value, expert speakers and teachers, and hands-on help for writers at all levels. A legacy conference of nearly 30 years with a flair for innovation and forward thinking, WCCW is committed to serving the community of Christian writers in all of its richness and diversity. We want to help our writers thrive by taking the next faith-filled step in their unique writing journeys.

Special tracks: advanced writers, speaking

Faculty includes: agents, editors, publishers

Scholarships: full, partial

Attendance: 250–300

Contests/awards: We give out Goldie Awards and host a writing contest for multiple genres, including nonfiction, fiction, memoir, poetry, children's/YA, and bad writing (!). We also have a Call Me Ishmael award for best opening line and a Best in Conference award.

COLORADO

COLORADO CHRISTIAN WRITERS CONFERENCE

Estes Park, CO | May 15–18 | *colorado.writehisanswer.com*

Director: Marlene Bagnull, 951 Anders Rd., Lansdale, PA 19446; 267-436-2503; *mbagnull@aol.com*

Description: We plan to be back in person at the YMCA of the Rockies for our 26th conference. Six powerful keynotes, eight continuing sessions, approximately 50 workshops, panels, one-on-one appointments, and more in a magnificent retreat setting.

Special track: teens

Faculty includes: agents, editors, publishers

Scholarships: full, partial

Attendance: 200

Contests/awards: Poetry (12–30 lines) or prose (500–800 words) on our conference theme, "Write His Answer"—not only how He is calling you to "write His answer" but also what you have found to be His answer in the struggles you have faced as you have sought to "live His answer." Published and not-yet published writers are judged in separate categories. The four first-place winners receive $50 off next year's registration fee.

WRITE IN THE SPRINGS

Colorado Springs, CO | April 19–20 | *acfwcosprings.net*

Director: Susan G. Mathis, 3820 N. 30th St., Colorado Springs, CO 80904; *info@acfwcosprings.com*

Description: Write in the Springs is a small, personal, in-depth Christian writers conference at Glen Eyrie Conference Center.
Special tracks: advanced writers, teens
Faculty includes: editors, publishers
Plenary speaker: Misty Beller
Scholarships: partial
Attendance: 75

FLORIDA

FLORIDA CHRISTIAN WRITERS CONFERENCE

Leesburg, FL | October 15–20 | *Word-Weavers.com/FloridaEvents*

Director: Eva Marie Everson, PO Box 520224, Longwood, FL 32752; 407-414-8188; *WordWeaversInternational@gmail.com*
Description: Florida Christian Writers Conference offers 10 continuing classes, approximately 60 one-hour workshops, five three-hour workshops, special workshops (Book Proposal Studio, The 1000-Books-a-Month Workshop, etc.), VIP breakfasts (with speakers), a yearly genre-focused intensive (2024: children's), and a keynote speaker. Writers of all levels are welcome.
Special tracks: advanced writers, speaking
Faculty includes: agents, editors, publishers
Plenary speaker: Saundra Dalton-Smith
Scholarships: full, partial
Attendance: 250
Contests/awards: See website for details.

ILLINOIS

WRITE TO PUBLISH CONFERENCE

Wheaton, IL (Chicago area) | June 11–14 | *writetopublish.com*

Director: Dan Balow, *dan@christianwritersinstitute.com*
Description: Since 1971, Write to Publish has been training, inspiring, and encouraging writers, connecting them with editors to help them improve their craft, with publishers who are looking for good books to publish, and with literary agents who can represent them. No matter where you are in your writing career—beginning the journey to becoming a published writer, exploring the process of becoming a working writer, or an experienced professional

desiring to stay connected and growing—the Write to Publish Conference is key to reaching those goals.

Faculty includes: agents, editors, publishers
Scholarships: full, partial
Attendance: 300

INDIANA

TAYLOR UNIVERSITY'S PROFESSIONAL WRITERS' CONFERENCE

Upland, IN | July | *taylorprofessionalwritersconference.weebly.com*

Director: Linda K. Taylor, 1846 Main St., Upland, IN 46989; 765-998-5591; *taylorPRWConference@gmail.com*
Description: Hear from agents, editors, and authors who will inspire and encourage you.
Special tracks: advanced writers, teens
Faculty includes: agents, editors, publishers
Attendance: 100

IOWA

CEDAR FALLS CHRISTIAN WRITERS CONFERENCE

Cedar Falls, IA | June 6–8 | *cfcwc.org*

Director: Mary Potter Kenyon, 1720 Rhomberg Ave., Dubuque, IA 52001; 563-235-9408; *marypotterkenyon@gmail.com*
Description: Annual conference for writers of all levels to connect, be inspired, and learn.
Faculty includes: editors
Plenary speaker: Susie Finkbeiner
Scholarships: partial
Attendance: 35

KENTUCKY

EVANGELICAL PRESS ASSOCIATION ANNUAL CONVENTION

Lexington, KY | April 21–23 | *www.epaconvention.com*

Director: Lamar Keener, PO Box 1787, Queen Creek, AZ 85142;

480-868-2466; *director@evangelicalpress.com*

Description: Christian media convention for editors, writers, designers, digital content managers, etc., who create content in the print/digital periodical industry. Note: This conference changes locations every year.

Faculty includes: editors

Plenary speakers: Nona Jones, Russell Moore

Attendance: 200

Contests/awards: Freelance writers may submit articles and/or blog entries into Awards of Excellence and Higher Goals in Journalism, which require EPA membership.

KENTUCKY CHRISTIAN WRITERS CONFERENCE

Elizabethtown, KY | October | *www.kychristianwriters.com*

Director: Gregg Bridgeman, PO Box 2719, Elizabethtown, KY 42702; *info@kychristianwriters.com*

Description: Our purpose is to provide an annual, interdenominational event to equip and encourage writers in their quest for publication. The conference provides a safe environment where writers can discover their gifts and share their work.

Faculty includes: agents, editors, publishers

Attendance: 75

LOUISANA

ACFW CONFERENCE

New Orleans, LA | September 5–8 | *www.acfw.com-conference*

Director: Robin Miller, PO Box 101066, Palm Bay, FL 32910-1066; *director@acfw.com*

Description: Continuing education sessions and workshop electives specifically geared for five levels of fiction-writing experience from beginner to advanced. Note: This conference changes locations every year.

Special track: advanced writers

Faculty includes: agents, editors

Scholarships: full

Attendance: 500

Contests/awards: The Genesis Contest is for unpublished writers whose Christian fiction manuscript is completed. The Carol Awards honor the best of Christian fiction from the previous calendar year.

MARYLAND

REALM MAKERS WINTER RETREAT

North East, MD, plus online | February 16–20 | *www.realmmakers.com*

Director: Rebecca Minor, *becky@realmmakers.com*

Description: The Realm Makers Winter Retreat seeks to gather writers of all experience levels in an encouraging, intimate setting where they can learn from a master writer and experience fellowship along the way. Writers will enjoy time gaining new skills, as well as opportunities to focus on the manuscript of their choosing.

Plenary speaker: James L. Rubart

Attendance: 40

MICHIGAN

MARANATHA WRITERS RETREAT

Muskegon, MI | February 16–19 | *www.maranathachristianwriters.com*

Director: Shayne Moore, 4759 Lake Harbor Rd., Norton Shores, MI 49441; 231-798-2161; *info@maranathachristianwriters.com*

Description: We focus on the Christian woman writer in an intimate community, so writing flows from a place of deep purpose grounded in Christ. We facilitate discipleship through small groups, one-on-ones, and encouraging relationships to continue through our social-media communities.

Plenary speaker: Ann Swindell

Scholarships: partial

Attendance: 80

SPEAK UP CONFERENCE

Grand Rapids, MI | July 11–13 | *speakupconference.com*

Director: Bonnie Emmorey, 1320 N. Topeka, Wichita, KS 67214; 316-882-9400; *bonnie@speakupconference.com*

Description: The Speak Up Conference equips emerging Christian speakers and writers to create global ministry impact.

Faculty includes: agents, editors, publishers

Scholarships: partial

Attendance: 280

MISSOURI

REALM MAKERS WRITERS CONFERENCE

St. Louis, MO | July 18–20 | *www.realmmakers.com*

Director: Becky Minor, *becky@realmmakers.com*

Description: Are you a creative person who loves science fiction and fantasy, but also makes your spiritual growth a high priority? Have you found that you're a little too weird for the usual church crowd, but don't exactly fit in with the sci-fi convention set either? Now there's a place for you to learn, share your talents, and commune with people a lot like yourself. Find your tribe at Realm Makers.

Special tracks: advanced writers, teens

Faculty includes: agents, editors, publishers

Scholarships: full, partial

Attendance: 400

Contests/awards: The Realm Awards is open to all Christian authors of speculative fiction with a book published the previous calendar year. Not limited to attendees of the conference. Submissions open January 1–21 each year.

NEW YORK

reNEW—SPIRITUAL RETREAT FOR WRITERS AND SPEAKERS

Speculator, NY | April 26–28 | *renewwriting.com*

Director: Rachel Britton, 978-758-9574, *rachel@renewwriting.com*

Description: reNEW is a community of Christ-following writers and speakers, both beginners and seasoned, growing inwardly so we can be effective outwardly.

Special track: speaking

Scholarships: partial

Attendance: 100

NORTH CAROLINA

ASHEVILLE CHRISTIAN WRITERS CONFERENCE

Asheville, NC | February 23–25 | *www.ashevillechristianwritersconference.com*

Director: Cindy Sproles, 377 Woodcrest Dr., Kingsport, TN 37663; 423-384-4821; *cindybootcamp@gmail.com*

Description: Teaching the writing craft and helping writers to hear and understand their call.

Special track: advanced writers

Faculty includes: agents, editors, publishers

Plenary speakers: Bob Hostetler, Eva Marie Everson

Scholarships: partial

Attendance: 119

Contests/awards: Sparrow Award Book Contest for unpublished manuscripts

BLUE RIDGE MOUNTAINS CHRISTIAN WRITERS CONFERENCE

Black Mountain, NC | May 26–30 | *www.BlueRidgeConference.com*

Director: Edie Melson, 604 S. Almond Dr., Simpsonville, SC 29681; 864-373-4232; *ediegmelson@gmail.com*

Description: This is a multidiscipline conference that caters to writers of all levels. In addition to outstanding craft/industry instruction, there is a strong focus on preparing spiritually to follow God as He directs our words for His glory.

Special tracks: advanced writers, speaking, teens

Faculty includes: agents, editors, publishers

Scholarships: partial

Attendance: 550

Contests: Selah Awards (industry-wide published books), Directors' Choice Awards (for former attendees and those in attendance at the 2024 event), Foundation Awards (restricted to unpublished writers who are attending the 2024 event).

MOUNTAINSIDE NOVELIST RETREAT

Black Mountain, NC | October | *www.BlueRidgeConference.com/ mountainside-retreats*

Director: Edie Melson, 604 S. Almond Dr., Simpsonville, SC 29681; 864-373-4232; *ediegmelson@gmail.com*

Description: Through small-group instruction and hands-on exercises from bestselling writers, the craftsman is able to focus on building strengths from challenges. Writers developing all levels of their careers will benefit from one-on-one consultations, brainstorming, and instruction. This event is a guided intensive where all participants have the opportunity to practice what they're learning under experienced team leaders.

Attendance: 40

SHE SPEAKS CONFERENCE

Charlotte, NC | July 18–20 | *shespeaksconference.com*

Director: Lisa Allen, 630 Team Rd. #100, Matthews, NC 28105; 704-849-2270; *shespeaks@Proverbs31.org*

Description: Speaking and writing tracks. For women only.

Special track: speaking

Faculty includes: agents, editors

Attendance: 700

WRITING FOR YOUR LIFE

Durham or Charlotte, NC | late April/May | *writingforyourlife.com/conferences*

Director: Kate Rademacher, *info@writingforyourlife.com*

Description: If you write or read books that matter—books with substance and soul—then this is the place for you. Writing for Your Life produces writing conferences featuring leading authors and industry experts presenting on various topics in the areas of how to write, how to get published, and how to market.

Faculty includes: agents, editors

Attendance: 70

OREGON

CASCADE CHRISTIAN WRITERS CONFERENCE

Canby, OR (Portland area), plus online | June 23–26 | *oregonchristianwriters.org*

Director: Christina Suzann Nelson, PO Box 862, Philomath, OR 97371; 541-760-2322; *summerconf@oregonchristianwriters.org*

Description: Set in the beautiful Willamette Valley, the Cascade Christian Writers Conference is an annual gathering that provides a supportive and educational platform for Christian writers to network, learn from industry professionals, and enhance their writing skills. Attendees are surrounded by encouraging individuals who seek to foster a community rooted in faith and creativity.

Special tracks: advanced writers, speaking, teens

Faculty includes: agents, editors, publishers

Scholarships: partial

Attendance: 130

Contests/awards: The Cascade Awards

OREGON CHRISTIAN WRITERS FALL ONE-DAY CONFERENCE

Salem, OR | October | *www.oregonchristianwriters.org*

Director: *contact@oregonchristianwriters.org*

Description: Two morning keynote addresses and two one-hour workshop sessions in the afternoon with four choices in each session, a great time to further the craft of writing.

Plenary speaker: Cynthia Ruchti

Attendance: 120

OREGON CHRISTIAN WRITERS SPRING ONE-DAY CONFERENCE

Tualatin, OR (Portland area) | March 16 | *www.oregonchristianwriters.org*

Director: *contact@oregonchristianwriters.org*

Description: Two morning keynote addresses and two one-hour workshop sessions in the afternoon with four choices in each session, a great time to further the craft of writing.

Plenary speaker: Matt Mikalatos

Attendance: 120

PENNSYLVANIA

MONTROSE CHRISTIAN WRITERS CONFERENCE

Montrose, PA | July | *www.montrosebible.org*

Director: Marsha Hubler, 1833 Dock Hill Rd., Middleburg, PA 17842; 570-837-0002; *marshahubler@outlook.com*

Description: In a family atmosphere at the restored home and conference center of evangelist R.A. Torrey, the conference always offers a faculty of best-selling authors, agents, editors, and publishers who present classes for beginners as well as published authors, teaching fiction, nonfiction, children's fiction and nonfiction, marketing, poetry, music, drama, and numerous subgenres. Private critiques are always offered, as well as works-in-progress sessions.

Special tracks: advanced writers, teens

Faculty includes: agents, editors, publishers

Scholarships: partial

Attendance: 70

Contests/awards: The Shirley Brinkerhoff Scholarship Fund offers $200 to the best entry of a 300-piece submission based on the year's theme.

ST. DAVIDS CHRISTIAN WRITERS' CONFERENCE

Meadville, PA | June 19–23 | *www.stdavidswriters.com/conference*

Director: Sue Boltz, *treasurer@stdavidswriters.com*
Faculty includes: agents, editors
Scholarships: full, partial
Attendance: 45
Contests/awards: See detailed list on the website.

SOUTH CAROLINA

CAROLINA CHRISTIAN WRITERS CONFERENCE

Spartanburg, SC | March 7–9 | *www.fbs.org/writers*

Director: Linda Gilden, 250 E. Main St., Spartanburg, SC 29306; *linda@lindagilden.com*
Description: Conference is for older teens to all ages of adults. Focus is on learning to write to reach the world we live in with the love of Jesus. Special features include "Lightning Learning"; panel discussions; and appointments with publishers, editors, agents, and professional writers. Friday is Pastors and Ministry Leaders Day.
Special tracks: advanced editors, pastors, speaking
Faculty includes: agents, editors, publishers
Scholarships: full
Attendance: 125
Contests/awards: Kudos contest for book and article writers, published and unpublished

TENNESSEE

THE ART OF WRITING

Nashville, TN | November | *thechristyaward.com*

Director: Cindy Carter, ECPA, 5801 S. McClintock Dr., Ste. 104, Mesa, AZ 85283; 480-966-3998; *TheChristyAward@ecpa.org*
Description: The Art of Writing is a conference for writers, storytellers, and publishing curators that is run in conjunction with The Christy Award program. It features four timely sessions for authors and publishing professionals. Networking and learning from featured authors and high-level publishing professionals sets this conference apart. The Christy Award Gala celebrating

excellence in Christian fiction by naming the year's best in nine categories follows the conference. Bundle pricing is available.
Faculty includes: agents, editors, publishers
Attendance: 200

MID-SOUTH CHRISTIAN WRITERS CONFERENCE

Collierville, TN (Memphis area) | March 15 | *midsouthconferenceonline.com*

Director: Beth Gooch, 346 Landen Cir., Byhalia, MS 38611; 901-277-5525; *midsouthchristianwriters@gmail.com*

Description: Conference is 9 a.m. to 5 p.m. Saturday, and registration fee includes lunch as well as a Friday-night meet-and-greet gathering. There are also optional Friday afternoon workshops for an additional fee.

Special track: advanced writers
Faculty includes: agents, editors
Plenary speakers: Patricia Bradley, Katara Patton
Scholarships: full, partial
Attendance: 100

WASHINGTON

NORTHWEST CHRISTIAN WRITERS RENEWAL

Bellevue, WA | May | *nwchristianwriters.org/Conference*

Director: Charles Harris, PO Box 2706, Woodinville, WA 98072; 206-250-6885; *renewal@nwchristianwriters.org*

Description: This conference is where writers, editors, and publishers can connect, network, and collaborate. Conferees will sharpen their skills, learn strategies, and form connections to boost their success on the writing journey.

Faculty includes: agents, editors, publishers
Scholarships: full
Attendance: 130

WISCONSIN

FAITH FORWARD WRITERS WORKSHOP

Sparta, WI | April 18–20 | *sparrowsnest-abbey.com/facility-calendar*

Director: Collette Schultz, 17304 Havenwood Rd., Sparta, WI 54656; 608-853-1435; *acresofhope.sna@gmail.com*

Description: Provides a peaceful, God-centered space for anyone who wants to put pen to paper. From blogs to books. From journaling to capturing your journey. From fiction to nonfiction. This is the place to bring your ideas, desires, and stories. Collaborate with inspired writers, learn new tips and strategies, write from your heart, and learn about everything from genres to publishing.
Special track: advanced writers
Faculty includes: editors, publishers
Scholarships: partial
Attendance: 50

AUSTRALIA

OMEGA WRITERS CONFERENCE

Sydney, Australia | September 20–22 | *omegawriters.com.au/events*

Director: Penny Reeve, *info@aomegawriters.org*
Description: Omega Writers Conference offers focused craft workshops, genre groups, networking opportunities, as well as sessions on essential skills for writers like time management, psychology marketing, and more. Participants also benefit from the opportunity for one-on-one appointments with editors, agents, and publishers and walk away with friendships and Christian encouragement, unlike any other conference in Australia.
Attendance: 70

CANADA

InSCRIBE CHRISTIAN WRITERS' FELLOWSHIP CONFERENCE

Fort Qu'Appelle, SK, Canada | September | *inscribe.org/fall-conference*

Director: Box 68025, Edmonton, AB T6C 4N6, Canada; *president@ inscribe.org*
Description: InScribe's Fall Conference features a seasoned author, publisher, or other expert as the keynote speaker; plus we offer a variety of workshop topics and presenters. It's a weekend where writers—whether they are seasoned or beginning—can connect for fellowship, encouragement, and support.
Scholarships: partial
Contests/awards: See *www.inscribe.org/contests.*

NEW ZEALAND

NZ CHRISTIAN WRITERS RETREAT

Whitianga, New Zealand | April | *www.nzchristianwriters.org*

> **Director:** Justin St. Vincent, 179B St. Johns Rd., St. Johns, Auckland, North Island, New Zealand 1072; *editor@xtrememusic.org*
> **Description:** Our seminar speakers will inspire, refresh, and upskill each of us on our writing journey.
> **Faculty includes:** editors, publishers
> **Attendance:** 40

ONLINE

CASCADE CHRISTIAN WRITERS CONFERENCE

See listing in Oregon.

MT ZION RIDGE PRESS ONLINE WRITING CONFERENCE

May 16-18 | *www.mtzionridgepress.com/writing-off-the-beaten-path-confere*

> **Director:** Penny McGinnis, 4280 Hickory Park Ln., Batavia, OH 45103; 937-402-0782; *penny.frost.mcginnis@gmail.com*
> **Description:** The online conference with an in-person experience.
> **Faculty includes:** agents, editors, publishers
> **Attendance:** 60

PENCON EDITORS' CONFERENCE

May 1-3 | *PENCONeditors.com*

> **Director:** *director@PENCONeditors.com*
> **Description:** PENCON is the only annual conference for Christian editors and proofreaders. Our goal is to provide networking, education, and inspiration for Christians in the publishing industry.
> **Faculty includes:** editors, publishers
> **Scholarships:** full, partial
> **Attendance:** 75

PUBLISHING IN COLOR

March and October | *publishingincolor.com*

> **Director:** Joyce Dinkins, PO Box 150, Grand Junction, MI 49056; *JoyceDinkinsPublishing@gmail.com*

Description: Publishing in Color (PIC) is a bridge for Black and Indigenous People of Color (BIPOC) striving to publish content that shares biblical truths with everyone. Through its conferences and network, PIC helps connect creatives with publishers addressing historic underrepresentation.
Faculty includes: agents, editors, publishers
Plenary speaker: Joyce Dinkins
Scholarships: full
Attendance: 100

REALM MAKERS WINTER RETREAT
See listing in Maryland.

ROYAL WRITERS VIRTUAL CONFERENCE
November 1–2 | *acfwvirginia.com/writers-conference*
Director: Kelly Goshorn, ACFW VA, 1019B Edwards Ferry Rd. #1159, Leesburg, VA 20176; *acfwvirginia@gmail.com*
Description: The Royal Writers Virtual Conference will extend your knowledge of the business and craft of writing, fill you with inspiration, and provide the tools you need to write for God's glory. Your registration fee for this two-day event includes two keynote sessions; Ask the Experts Panel; workshops for beginner, intermediate, and advanced writers; 90-day post conference video access to all 24 instructional sessions; and the opportunity for faculty appointments. Winners of The Crown Award are announced at the conference.
Special track: advanced writers
Faculty includes: agents, editors, publishers
Attendance: 260

WRITE HIS ANSWER CONFERENCE (formerly Greater Philly)
End of July or early August | *philadelphia.writehisanswer.com*
Director: Marlene Bagnull, 951 Anders Rd., Lansdale, PA 19446; 267-436-2503; *mbagnull@aol.com*
Description: Approximately 100 hours of live video content (available to view through the end of the year), plus small-group breakouts, round tables, critique sessions, live chats, appointments with editors and agents, and preconference webinars.
Faculty includes: agents, editors
Scholarships: partial

Attendance: 200

Contests/awards: Poetry (12–30 lines) or prose (500–800 words) on our conference theme, "Write His Answer"—not only how He is calling you to "write His answer" but also what you have found to be His answer in the struggles you have faced as you have sought to "live His answer." Published and not-yet published writers are judged in separate categories.

WRITE2IGNITE MASTER CLASSES

April and September | *write2ignite.com*

Director: Jean Matthew Hall, 704 W. Madison St., Ware Shoals, SC 29692; 704-578-0858; *jeanmatthewhall@outlook.com*

Description: Master Classes are designed to educate, inspire, and encourage Christian writers of literature for children and young adults.

Faculty includes: agents, editors

Attendance: 30

19

WRITERS GROUPS

In addition to the groups listed here, check the writers organizations for new groups in your area and information about starting a group.

WRITERS ORGANIZATIONS

540 WRITERS COMMUNITY

540writerscommunity.com

Contact: Becky Antkowiak, PO Box 133, Sutherland, VA, 23885; *Info@540writerscommunity.com*

Services: "The 540 Writers Community is a 501c3 nonprofit dedicated to educating, equipping, and encouraging writers to create clean, clear, compelling, life-changing contact. We seek to remove barriers for writers by providing free virtual opportunities to access stellar education. We provide educational sessions, opportunities to write with others, and a thriving online community."

Members: 1,200+

Membership fee: none

AMERICAN CHRISTIAN FICTION WRITERS

acfw.com

Contact: Robin Miller, PO Box 101066, Palm Bay, FL 32910-1066; *director@acfw.com*

Services: Email loop, genre Facebook pages, online courses, critique groups, and local and regional chapters. Sponsors contests for published and unpublished writers and conducts the largest Christian fiction writers conference annually.

Members: 2600+
Membership fee: $75 to join, $49/year to renew

CHRISTIAN AUTHORS NETWORK

ChristianAuthorsNetwork.com

Contact: Susan U. Neal, *contact@christianauthorsnetwork.com*
Services: "CAN is a group of traditionally published Christian authors who have joined together in a supportive association to spread the news about books to book lovers everywhere. We operate as a cooperative, Christ-centered marketing organization, to encourage and teach one another, and get the word out about CAN authors' books to readers, retailers, and librarians. Membership is open to authors with two or more published books. One must be a Christian book published by a traditional royalty-paying publisher (with no financial input by the author), whose books are currently available in publication (in any and all formats) at the date of the membership application."
Members: 140
Membership fee: $90/year

CHRISTIAN INDIE AUTHOR NETWORK

www.christianindieauthors.com

Contact: Mary C. Findley, 918-805-0669, *mjmcfindley@gmail.com*
Services: Provides a readers site to connect independently published books to readers, several Facebook groups for both authors and readers, and book promotion opportunities.
Members: 400+
Membership fee: none

THE CHRISTIAN PEN: PROOFREADERS AND EDITORS NETWORK

www.TheChristianPEN.com

Contact: *Director@TheChristianPEN.com*
Services: "The Christian PEN: Proofreaders and Editors Network provides aspiring, beginning, established, and professional editors and proofreaders with networking, community, and industry discounts. If you are an editor or proofreader, or are thinking about becoming one, join this community of like-minded professionals who share our knowledge and experience with one another."
Members: 200
Membership fee: $25-90/year

FAITH, HOPE AND LOVE CHRISTIAN WRITERS

fhlchristianwriters.com

> **Contact:** Nancy J. Farrier, *president@fhlchristianwriters.com*
> **Services:** "To promote excellence in Christian fiction and/or fiction written from a Christian worldview. To help Christian writers establish their careers and to provide continuing support for writers within the fiction-publishing industry. We accomplish this stated purpose through our email groups, our online programs, our contests and awards, etc."
> **Membership fee:** $35

INSPIRE CHRISTIAN WRITERS

www.inspirewriters.com

> **Contact:** Robynne Miller, 530-217-8233, *inspiredirectors@gmail.com*
> **Services:** "Through Inspire you'll find a community of writers working together to achieve writing and publication goals. By taking advantage of our online and in-person critique groups, you'll give and receive feedback and grow in your craft. We offer web-based and local training through workshops and conferences to help you navigate publishing decisions, create your online presence, and polish your writing until it shines. You'll have opportunities to network with other writers— multi-published as well as those just starting out." Sponsors the Vision Christian Writers Conference at Mt. Hermon.
> **Members:** 150
> **Membership fee:** $50/year

REALM MAKERS

www.realmmakers.com

> **Contact:** Scott Minor, *scott@realmmakers.com*
> **Services:** "Realm Makers supports writers and artists who create science fiction and fantasy in their journeys from idea to marketplace. Whether participating artists wish to gear their content for inspirational or mainstream audiences, Realm Makers seeks to encourage them from a faith-friendly perspective." Offers a membership program, where authors can connect throughout the year, critique one another's work, and participate in periodic webinars to keep their writing and marketing toolkits sharp. Sponsors the Realm Makers conference.
> **Members:** 100
> **Membership fee:** ranges from $4.99/month or $49.99/year to $24.99/month or $249.99/year

WORD WEAVERS INTERNATIONAL, INC.
www.Word-Weavers.com
> **Contact:** Eva Marie Everson, CEO, *WordWeaversInternational@aol.com*
> **Services:** Local traditional chapters and Zoom online pages for manuscript critiquing. Sponsors Florida Christian Writers Conference.
> **Members:** 1,000
> **Membership fee:** $50/year, traditional or online; $65/year, traditional plus online

WORDGIRLS
www.kathycarltonwillis.com/wordgirls
> **Contact:** Kathy Carlton Willis, 956-642-6319, *kathy@kathycarltonwillis.com*
> **Services:** "WordGirls is a special sisterhood of writing support for women writing from a biblical worldview (whether for the faith market or general market). Services include one-on-one coaching, topical monthly video sessions, writing accountability, prayer support, and more. In-person and virtual getaways are hosted several times a year. Sessions offer how-tos for the nonwriting side of the writing business, as well as honing writing skills. From want-to-be a writer to the multipublished experienced professional, WordGirls helps each writer get to the next step of her writing journey. Membership is limited in order to customize services to the needs of the group. WordGirls is a group of fun, female believers from across America who are serious about writing."
> **Members:** 30-50
> **Membership fee:** $300/year

NATIONAL AND INTERNATIONAL ONLINE GROUPS

ACFW BEYOND THE BORDERS
www.facebook.com/groups/ACFWBeyondtheBorders
> **Contact:** Iola Goulton, *BeyondBorders@acfwchapter.com*
> **Members:** 100, in all countries outside the US
> **Membership fee:** national fee
> **Affiliation:** American Christian Fiction Writers

ACFW CHILDREN'S AUTHORS
www.facebook.com/groups/acfwkidlit
> **Contact:** Bettie Boswell, *acfwkidlit@acfwchapter.com*

Members: 38
Membership fee: national fee
Affiliation: American Christian Fiction Writers

ACFW QIP AUTHORS

www.facebook.com/groups/ACFWQIPAuthors

Contact: Hallee Bridgeman
Members: only for Qualified Independently Published writers who are current ACFW members
Membership fee: national fee
Affiliation: American Christian Fiction Writers

WORD WEAVERS ONLINE GROUPS

www.Word-Weavers.com

Meetings: online via Zoom, times vary, two hours
Contact: Eva Marie Everson, 407-414-8188, *WordWeaversInternational@aol.com*
Members: 400
Membership fee: $50/year
Affiliation: Word Weavers

ALABAMA

WORD WEAVERS NORTH ALABAMA

www.facebook.com/groups/936711453176211

Meetings: Hartsell, email for information; third Thursdays, 10:00 a.m.-noon
Contact: Bonita McCoy, *byvette.mccoy@gmail.com*
Members: 7
Membership fee: $50/year
Affiliation: Word Weavers

ARIZONA

ACFW ARIZONA

www.christianwritersofthewest.com

Meetings: Denny's Restaurant, 3315 N. Scottsdale Rd., Scottsdale; second Saturdays, noon-2:00 p.m.

Contact: Pamela Tracy, *arizona@acfwchapter.com*
Members: 30
Membership fee: $15/year plus national fee
Affiliation: American Christian Fiction Writers

CHANDLER WRITERS' GROUP
chandlerwriters.wordpress.com
> **Meetings:** Panera Bread, 3426 E. Baseline Rd., Gilbert; first Fridays, 9:00–11:30 a.m.
> **Contact:** Peggy Morris, 480-507-0421, *peggysuemor29@gmail.com*
> **Members:** 12
> **Membership fee:** none

FOUNTAIN HILLS CHRISTIAN WRITERS' GROUP
> **Meetings:** Fountain Hills Presbyterian Church, 13001 N. Fountain Hills Blvd., Fountain Hills; second Fridays, 9:00 a.m.–noon
> **Contact:** JoAnne Crosby, 763-242-9181, *joannecrosby40@yahoo.com*
> **Members:** 12
> **Membership fee:** $10/year

MESA CHRISTIAN WRITERS
> **Meetings:** Redemption Gilbert Church, 1820 W. Elliot Rd., Gilbert; second Wednesdays, 9 a.m.
> **Contact:** Peggy Morris, 480-507-0421, *peggysuemor29@gmail.com*
> **Members:** 10–25
> **Membership fee:** none

READY WRITERS PSALM 45:1
www.facebook.com/ReadyWritersPsalm451
> **Meetings:** Pantano Christian Church (sometimes local libraries), 1755 S. Houghton Rd., Tucson; twice monthly Saturdays, 2:00–3:30 p.m.
> **Contact:** Charity Plumb, 520-255-3020, *cplumbwrites@gmail.com*
> **Members:** 10
> **Membership fee:** none

WORD WEAVERS NORTHERN ARIZONA
> **Meetings:** Verde Community Church, 102 S. Willard, Cottonwood; second Saturdays, 9:30–11:30 a.m.
> **Contact:** Alice Klies, *Alice.Klies@Gmail.com*
> **Membership fee:** $50/year

Affiliation: Word Weavers

WORD WEAVERS SOUTHEAST ARIZONA
Meetings: Pantano Christian Church, 1755 S. Houghton Rd., Tuscan; third Saturdays, 10:00 a.m.–noon
Contact: Charity Plumb, *cplumbwrites@gmail.com*
Membership fee: $50/year
Affiliation: Word Weavers

ARKANSAS

ACFW NW ARKANSAS
www.facebook.com/groups/127662834752320
Meetings: Springdale; first Mondays, 5:30 p.m.
Contact: Robyn Hook, *NWArkansas@acfwchapter.com*
Members: 20
Membership fee: national fee
Affiliation: American Christian Fiction Writers

CALIFORNIA

ACFW ORANGE COUNTY
www.acfwoc.com
Meetings: varies from North OC to South OC; second Thursdays, 7:00 p.m.
Contact: Susan K. Beatty, *orangecounty@acfwchapter.com*
Members: 12
Membership fee: $10/year plus national fee
Affiliation: American Christian Fiction Writers

WORD WARRIORS
www.facebook.com/wordwarriorswriters
Meetings: online, Castro Valley; first Tuesdays September–June, 7:00 p.m.
Contact: Debbie Jones Warren, *debbiencj@aim.com*
Members: 10
Membership fee: none

WORD WEAVERS VENTURA COUNTY
Meetings: Lucky Llama Coffee Shop, 5100 Carpinteria Ave.,
  Carpinteria; third Mondays, 9:00–11:00 a.m.
Contact: Norma Bennett, *normajeanbennett@gmail.com*
Membership fee: $50/year
Affiliation: Word Weavers

COLORADO

ACFW COLORADO SPRINGS
acfwcosprings.net
Meetings: Fervent Church, 3337 N. Academy Blvd., Colorado Springs;
  first Saturdays, 10:00–11:30 a.m.
Contact: Susan G. Mathis, *info@acfwcosprings.com*
Members: 60
Membership fee: $25/year plus national fee
Affiliation: American Christian Fiction Writers

HIGHLANDS RANCH CREATIVES
www.facebook.com/groups/1509730649342640
Meetings: 9912 Sylvestor Rd., Highlands Ranch; first Thursdays, 6:30 p.m.
Contact: Mike Klassen, *mklassen@illumifymedia.com*
Membership fee: none
Affiliation: Writers on the Rock

POWER OF THE PEN: EAST DENVER CREATIVES
writersontherock.com/groups
Meetings: email for time and place; quarterly
Contact: Linda Eskridge, *lyeskridge@gmail.com*
Membership fee: none
Affiliation: Writers on the Rock

WOLF CREEK CHRISTIAN WRITERS NETWORK
wolfcreekwriters.com
Meetings: Grace in Pagosa, 264 Village Dr., Pagosa Springs and online
  via Zoom; Mondays except holidays, 9:00–11:00 a.m.
Contact: Cathy McIver, 970-946-3554, *allynschuylerink@gmail.com*
Members: 35
Membership fee: $30/year

WORD WEAVERS PIKES PEAK

Meetings: 2650 Leoti Dr., Colorado Springs; third Saturdays, 9:30–11:30 a.m.
Contact: Tez Brooks, 407-797-4408, *tezwrites@gmail.com*
Members: 12
Membership fee: $50/year
Affiliation: Word Weavers

WORD WEAVERS WESTERN SLOPE

www.facebook.com/groups/568085077249557

Meetings: The Rock Church, 2170 Broadway Ave., Grand Junction; third Saturdays, 9:30 a.m.–noon
Contact: Templa Melnick, 970-261-7230, *templa.melnick@gmail.com*
Members: 10
Membership fee: $50/year
Affiliation: Word Weavers

WRITERS ON THE ROCK ARVADA

www.facebook.com/groups/281086379291783

Meetings: email or call for location, Arvada; last Thursdays, 6:30–8:30 p.m.
Contact: Sue Roberts, 303-467-0286, *srobertswithjoy@yahoo.com*
Membership fee: none
Affiliation: Writers on the Rock

WRITERS ON THE ROCK CASTLE ROCK

www.facebook.com/groups/193369214634778

Meetings: Phillip Miller Library, 100 S. Wilcox St., Castle Rock; third Mondays, 6:30 p.m.
Contact: Amber Baughman, *amberjbaughman@gmail.com*
Membership fee: none
Affiliation: Writers on the Rock

WRITERS ON THE ROCK COLORADO SPRINGS

www.facebook.com/groups/1916955675297782

Meetings: Penrose Library, 20 N. Cascade Ave., Colorado Springs; second Thursdays, 6:30 p.m.
Contact: April Musekamp, 719-650-1480
Membership fee: none
Affiliation: Writers on the Rock

WRITERS ON THE ROCK LAKEWOOD
www.writersontherock.com/groups

Meetings: Green Mountain Recreation Center, 13198 W. Green Mountain Dr., Lakewood; fourth Tuesdays, 7:00–8:30 p.m.
Contact: Amy Young, *amy.young@swissmail.org*
Membership fee: none
Affiliation: Writers on the Rock

WRITERS ON THE ROCK NORTH METRO DENVER
www.facebook.com/groups/1110986532338485

Meetings: Crossroads Church, 10451 Huron St., Northglenn; first Mondays, 6:30–8:30 p.m.
Contact: Marla Lindstrom Bentroth, *tellyourstorytoo@msn.com*
Membership fee: none
Affiliation: Writers on the Rock

WRITERS ON THE ROCK NORTHERN COLORADO
www.facebook.com/groups/445776855860806

Meetings: Panera Bread, 1550 Fall River Dr., Loveland; third Thursdays, 7:00–8:30 p.m.
Contact: Jen Grams, *jennygrams@gmail.com*
Membership fee: none
Affiliation: Writers on the Rock

DELAWARE

DELMARVA CHRISTIAN WRITERS' ASSOCIATION
www.facebook.com/groups/219751814716191

Meetings: third Saturdays, 9:00 a.m.–noon
Members: 20
Membership fee: none

WORD WEAVERS DELMARVA
Meetings: Laurel Wesleyan Church, 30186 Seaford Rd. #3836, Laurel; fourth Saturdays, 9:00–11:00 a.m.
Contact: Andrew Jackson, *info@aejackson.com*
Membership fee: $50/year
Affiliation: Word Weavers

FLORIDA

ACFW CENTRAL FLORIDA
www.facebook.com/CFACFW
> **Meetings:** Longwood; third Saturdays
> **Contact:** Dorothy Mays, *centralflorida@acfwchapter.com*
> **Membership fee:** national fee
> **Affiliation:** American Christian Fiction Writers

SUNCOAST CHRISTIAN WRITERS GROUP
> **Meetings:** The Haus Coffee Shop, 12199 Indian Roacks Rd., Largo;
> third Wednesdays, 10:00 a.m.
> **Contact:** Elaine Creasman, 727-251-3756, *emcreasman@aol.com;*
> contact her before attending first meeting
> **Members:** 10–20
> **Membership fee:** none

WORD WEAVERS BREVARD COUNTY
> **Meetings:** Freedom Christian Center, 7250 Lake Andrew Dr.,
> Melbourne; first Saturdays, 10:00 a.m.–noon
> **Contact:** Sally Friscea, *sfriscea@gmail.com*
> **Members:** 5
> **Membership fee:** $50/year
> **Affiliation:** Word Weavers

WORD WEAVERS CLAY COUNTY
www.facebook.com/groups/WordWeaversClayCounty
> **Meetings:** Panera Bread, 1510 County Rd. 220, Fleming Island;
> second Saturdays, 9:00 a.m.
> **Contact:** Victoria Roberts, *carpediem4christ@gmail.com*
> **Members:** 13
> **Membership fee:** $50/year
> **Affiliation:** Word Weavers

WORD WEAVERS DESTIN
> **Meetings:** Crosspoint Church Bluewater, 4400 Highway 20 E, Ste.
> 600, Niceville; second Saturdays, 9:30 a.m.
> **Contact:** Alice Murray, *pstyre@aol.com*
> **Members:** 17
> **Membership fee:** $50/year

Affiliation: Word Weavers

WORD WEAVERS GAINESVILLE
Meetings: 5003 N.W. 13th Ave., Gainesville; second Sundays, 2:00–4:30 p.m.
Contact: Lori Roberts, *authorLorilynRoberts@gmail.com*
Members: 6
Membership fee: $50/year
Affiliation: Word Weavers

WORD WEAVERS JENSEN BEACH
Meetings: Coastal Style Kitchens, conference room, 11274 Business Park Pl., Jensen Beach; third Saturdays, 9:30 a.m.–noon
Contact: Penny Cooke, *LifeCoachPenny@yahoo.com*
Membership fee: $50/year
Affiliation: Word Weavers

WORD WEAVERS LAKE COUNTY
www.facebook.com/groups/1790245144535020
Meetings: Leesburg Public Library, 100 E. Main, Leesburg; third Saturdays, 9:30 a.m.
Contact: M. L. Anderson, 678-477-3649, *andersonwriter@gmail.com*
Members: 25
Membership fee: $50/year
Affiliation: Word Weavers

WORD WEAVERS OCALA CHAPTER
Meetings: Belleview Public Library, 13145 S.E. County Highway 484, Belleview; second Fridays, 10:00 a.m.–12:30 p.m.
Contact: Yeny Rowley, *yenyrowley@yahoo.com*
Members: 10+
Membership fee: $50/year
Affiliation: Word Weavers

WORD WEAVERS ORLANDO
www.facebook.com/groups/216603998394619
Meetings: Calvary Chapel, 5015 Goddard Ave., Orlando; second Saturdays, 10:00 a.m. –12:30 p.m.
Contact: Julie Payne, *info@juliamargaretauthor.com*
Members: 60
Membership fee: $50/year

Affiliation: Word Weavers

WORD WEAVERS PENSACOLA

Meetings: Hillcrest Baptist Church, 800 E. Nine Mile Rd., Pensacola; second Tuesdays, 5:30–8:00 p.m.
Contact: Gretchen Huesmann, *gretchenjoy4884@gmail.com*
Members: 9
Membership fee: $50/year
Affiliation: Word Weavers

WORD WEAVERS SARASOTA

Meetings: First United Methodist Church, 104 S. Pineapple Ave., Sarasota; fourth Sundays, 2:00–4:00 p.m.
Contact: Sam Wright, *drsamwright@comcast.net*
Members: 10
Membership fee: $50/year
Affiliation: Word Weavers

WORD WEAVERS SOUTH FLORIDA

www.facebook.com/groups/132148070172748

Meetings: Gracepoint Church, 5590 N.E. 6th Ave., Fort Lauderdale; second Tuesdays, 9:00 a.m.
Contact: Patricia Hartman, *Patricia@PatriciaHartman.net*
Members: 15
Membership fee: $50/year
Affiliation: Word Weavers

WORD WEAVERS TAMPA

Meetings: 1901 S. Village Ave., Tampa; first Saturdays, 9:30 a.m.–12:30 p.m.
Contact: Carol Pierce, *cboyd7116@gmail.com*
Members: 25
Membership fee: $50/year
Affiliation: Word Weavers

WORD WEAVERS TREASURE COAST

www.facebook.com/groups/480150568723000

Meetings: First Church of God Vero Beach, 1105 58th Ave., Vero Beach; first Saturdays, 9:30 a.m.–noon
Contact: Del Bates, *Del@DelBates.com*
Members: 10

Membership fee: $50/year
Affiliation: Word Weavers

WORD WEAVERS VOLUSIA COUNTY

www.facebook.com/groups/227447203952675

> **Meetings:** Faith Church, 4700 S. Clyde Morris Blvd., Port Orange; first Mondays, 7:00 p.m.
> **Contact:** Jessica Jackson, *Jessica@GeriWestfallre.com*
> **Members:** 18
> **Membership fee:** $50/year
> **Affiliation:** Word Weavers

GEORGIA

ACFW GEORGIA

acfwga.com

> **Meetings:** Buford First United Methodist Church, 285 E. Main St., Buford; second Tuesdays, 6:30–8:30 p.m.
> **Contact:** Janette Johnson Melson, 770-973-6081, *georgia@ acfwchapter.com*
> **Members:** 59
> **Membership fee:** $15 plus national fee
> **Affiliation:** American Christian Fiction Writers

CHRISTIAN AUTHORS GUILD

www.christianauthorsguild.org

> **Meetings:** Sojourn Woodstock, 8816 Main St., Woodstock; first Mondays, 7:00 p.m.
> **Contact:** Deborah Crawford, *deborahrdcrawford@gmail.com*
> **Members:** 30
> **Membership fee:** $30/year

WORD WEAVERS BROOKHAVEN

www.facebook.com/groups/200656040663612

> **Meetings:** Westminster Presbyterian Church, 1438 Sheridan Rd. NE, Atlanta; second Saturdays, 10:00 a.m.–12:30 p.m.
> **Contact:** Elizabeth Buttimer, *epb1205@gmail.com*
> **Members:** 8
> **Membership fee:** $50/year

Affiliation: Word Weavers

WORD WEAVERS COLUMBUS

www.facebook.com/groups/541016626433688

> **Meetings:** Cornerstone Church of God, 7701 Lloyd Rd., Columbus;
> third Mondays, 6:30 p.m.
> **Contact:** Terri Miller, *wordweaverscolumbus@gmail.com*
> **Members:** 8
> **Membership fee:** $50/year
> **Affiliation:** Word Weavers

WORD WEAVERS CONYERS

www.facebook.com/groups/638509006538934

> **Meetings:** Bethel Christian Church, 1930 Bethel Rd. NE, Conyers;
> second Saturdays, 10:00 a.m.–noon
> **Contact:** Leigh DeLozier, *LeighDeLozier@Bellsouth.net*
> **Members:** 8
> **Membership fee:** $50/year
> **Affiliation:** Word Weavers

WORD WEAVERS GREATER ATLANTA

> **Meetings:** 4541 Vendome Pl. NE, Roswell; first Saturdays, 9:30 a.m.
> **Contact:** Kathleen Metzger, *mkmetzger45@hotmail.com*
> **Members:** 15
> **Membership fee:** $50/year national fee
> **Affiliation:** Word Weavers

WORD WEAVERS MACON-BIBB

www.facebook.com/groups/173188826644758

> **Meetings:** Central City Church, 621 Foster Rd., Macon; second
> Sundays, 3:00–5:30 p.m.
> **Contact:** Robin Dance, *RobinDance.me@gmail.com*
> **Members:** 45
> **Membership fee:** $50/year
> **Affiliation:** Word Weavers

WORD WEAVERS VALDOSTA

> **Meetings:** Corinth Baptist Church, 4089 Corinth Church Rd., Lake
> Park; third Saturdays, 2:00–4:00 p.m.
> **Contact:** Christy Adams, *ChristyAdams008@gmail.com*
> **Membership fee:** $50/year

Affiliation: Word Weavers

ILLINOIS

ACFW CHICAGO

chicagoacfw.org

Meetings: Schaumburg Township District Library, 130 S. Roselle Rd., Schaumburg; second Fridays, 6:30–8:30 p.m.
Contact: Lori Davis, *chicago@acfwchapter.com*
Members: 20
Membership fee: $35 plus national fee
Affiliation: American Christian Fiction Writers

WORD WEAVERS LAND OF LINCOLN

Meetings: Open Arms, chapel, 1321 State Route 10, Lincoln; second Saturdays, 10:00 a.m.–noon
Contact: Robin McClallen, *ramtwm@msn.com*
Members: 10
Membership fee: $50/year
Affiliation: Word Weavers

WORD WEAVERS ON THE BORDER

Meetings: Panera Bread, 254 East Rollins Rd., Round Lake; fourth Thursdays, 7:00–8:30 p.m.
Contact: Mark Drinnenberg, *WritingsbyMark@gmail.com*
Members: 10
Membership fee: $50/year
Affiliation: Word Weavers

INDIANA

ACFW INDIANA

www.hoosierink.blogspot.com

Meetings: various places in Indiana and Zoom; four to six times per year
Contact: Rebecca Reed, *acfwindianachapter@gmail.com*
Members: 40
Membership fee: $15/year plus national fee
Affiliation: American Christian Fiction Writers

HEARTLAND CHRISTIAN WRITERS
www.heartlandchristianwriters.com
> **Meetings:** Mount Pleasant Christian Church, 381 N. Bluff Rd.,
> Greenwood; third Mondays, 10:00 a.m. and 6:30 p.m.
> **Contact:** John Matthew Walker, *admin@heartlandchristianwriters.com*
> **Members:** 10
> **Membership fee:** none

WORD WEAVERS INDY
> **Meetings:** Carmel-Clay Public Library, 425 E. Main St., Carmel; third
> Tuesdays, 6:30–8:30 p.m.
> **Contact:** Mandy Young, *wwindychap@gmail.com*
> **Membership fee:** $50/year
> **Affiliation:** Word Weavers

IOWA

WORD WEAVERS DES MOINES
www.facebook.com/groups/495808943830132
> **Meetings:** The Church at Union Park, 821 Arthur Ave., Des Moines;
> last Mondays, 6:30–8:00 p.m.
> **Contact:** Judy Hagey, *Judy.Hagey@gmail.com*
> **Members:** 12
> **Membership fee:** $50/year
> **Affiliation:** Word Weavers

KANSAS

HEART OF AMERICA CHRISTIAN WRITERS NETWORK
www.hacwn.org
> **Meetings:** Colonial Presbyterian Church, 12501 W. 137th St.,
> Overland Park; second Thursdays, 7:00 p.m.
> **Contact:** Karen Morerod, *HACWN@earthlink.net*
> **Members:** 150
> **Membership fee:** active member, $35/year; professional member,
> $45/year

KENTUCKY

ACFW LOUISVILLE
acfwlouisville.com

Meetings: Southeast Christian Church, room WC 448, 920 Blankenbaker Pkwy., Louisville; fourth Saturdays, 10:30 a.m.–noon
Contact: Crystal Caudill, *louisville@acfwchapter.com*
Members: 30
Membership fee: national fee
Affiliation: American Christian Fiction Writers

WORD WEAVERS BOONE COUNTY

Meetings: Grace Fellowship Church, 9379 Gunpowder Rd., Florence; first Saturdays, 10:30 a.m.–12:30 p.m.
Contact: Karisa Moore, 859-380-3449, *karisam660@gmail.com*
Members: 15
Membership fee: $50/year
Affiliation: Word Weavers

LOUISIANA

ACFW LOUISIANA
www.facebook.com/pages/ACFW-Louisiana/1525862364304046

Meetings: Bossier City; last Saturdays
Contact: Charles Sutherland, *louisiana@acfwchapter.com*
Membership fee: national fee
Affiliation: American Christian Fiction Writers

SOUTHERN CHRISTIAN WRITERS
scwguild.com

Meetings: Gospel Bookstore, 91 Westbank Expressway, Gretna; third Saturdays except November and December, 10:30 a.m.
Contact: Teena Myers, *scwg@cox.net*
Members: 23
Membership fee: $50/year

MICHIGAN

ACFW GREAT LAKES
acfwgreatlakes.wordpress.com
>**Meetings:** various and online; monthly
>**Contact:** Beth Foreman, *acfwgreatlakes@gmail.com*
>**Members:** 35
>**Membership fee:** $10/year plus national fee
>**Affiliation:** American Christian Fiction Writers

WORD WEAVERS WEST MICHIGAN–HOLLAND ZEELAND
>**Meetings:** City on a Hill, 100 Pine St., Zeeland; first and third Tuesdays, noon–2:00 p.m.
>**Contact:** Gene Koon, *koongene@gmail.com*
>**Members:** 10
>**Membership fee:** $50/year
>**Affiliation:** Word Weavers

WORD WEAVERS WEST MICHIGAN–MUSKEGON/ NORTON SHORES
>**Meetings:** Hendrick Meijer Library, Muskegon Community College, 221 S. Quarterline Rd., Muskegon; first and third Tuesdays, 6:00–8:00 p.m.
>**Contact:** Gene Koon, *koongene@gmail.com*
>**Members:** 10
>**Membership fee:** $50/year
>**Affiliation:** Word Weavers

WORD WEAVERS WEST MICHIGAN–NORTH GRAND RAPIDS
>**Meetings:** Russ' Restaurant, 3531 Alpine Ave. NW, Walker; first and third Tuesdays, 6:00–8:00 p.m.
>**Contact:** Gene Koon, *koongene@gmail.com*
>**Members:** 12
>**Membership fee:** $50/year
>**Affiliation:** Word Weavers

MINNESOTA

ACFW MINNESOTA N.I.C.E.
www.acfwmnnice.com
> **Meetings:** Ridgewood Church, 4420 County Rd. 101, Minnetonka; fourth Sundays, 6:00–8:00 p.m.
> **Contact:** Michelle Aleckson, *minnesota@acfwchapter.com*
> **Members:** 25
> **Membership fee:** $25/year plus national fee
> **Affiliation:** American Christian Fiction Writers

MINNESOTA CHRISTIAN WRITERS GUILD
www.mnchristianwriters.com
> **Meetings:** Oak Knoll Lutheran Church, 600 Hopkins Crossroad, Minnetonka; second Mondays, September–May, 7:00–8:30 p.m.
> **Contact:** Jason Sisam, *info@mnchristianwriters.com*
> **Members:** 50
> **Membership fee:** $80/year or $15/meeting

MISSISSIPPI

MID-SOUTH CHRISTIAN WRITERS ROUNDTABLE
www.facebook.com/groups/145426569547064
> **Meetings:** various locations, Memphis metro area; third Saturdays
> **Contact:** William G. Hill, 901-212-8020
> **Members:** 10
> **Membership fee:** none

MISSOURI

ACFW MOZARKS
www.facebook.com/MozArksACFW
> **Meetings:** The Library Center, 4653 S. Campbell Ave., Springfield; third Saturdays, 10:30 a.m.
> **Contact:** Erin Miffin, 417-251-1587, *mozarks@acfwchapter.com*
> **Members:** 10
> **Membership fee:** $10 plus national fee
> **Affiliation:** American Christian Fiction Writers

ACFW ST. LOUIS
acfwstl.wordpress.com

> **Meetings:** Festus Public Library, 400 W. Main St., Festus; second Saturdays, 11:30 a.m.
> **Contact:** Karen Sargent, 573-450-0514, *stlouis@acfwchapter.com*
> **Members:** 20
> **Membership fee:** $15 plus national fee
> **Affiliation:** American Christian Fiction Writers

OZARKS CHAPTER OF AMERICAN CHRISTIAN WRITERS
www.OzarksACW.org

> **Meetings:** University Heights Baptist Church, 1010 S. National, Springfield; second Saturdays, September–May, 10:00 a.m.–noon
> **Contact:** Dr. Jeanetta Chrystie, 417-832-8409, *OzarksACW@yahoo.com*
> **Members:** 50
> **Membership fee:** $20/year; family, $30; newsletter only, $10

NEBRASKA

MY THOUGHTS EXACTLY WRITING WORKSHOP
mythoughtsexactlywriters.wordpress.com

> **Meetings:** Keene Memorial Library, 1030 N. Broad St., Fremont; third Mondays, 6:30–8:00 p.m.
> **Contact:** Cheryl, *mythoughtse@gmail.com*
> **Membership fee:** none

NEW JERSEY

ACFW NY/NJ
www.facebook.com/groups/955365637934907

> **Meetings:** online; first Saturdays October–June, 10 a.m.–noon; critique groups at other times
> **Contact:** Cherlyn Gatto, *nynj@acfwchapter.com*
> **Members:** 65
> **Membership fee:** $20/year plus national fee
> **Affiliation:** American Christian Fiction Writers

NORTH JERSEY CHRISTIAN WRITERS GROUP

www.njcwg.blogspot.com

Meetings: varies, North Haledon; first Saturdays except holidays, 10:00 a.m.–noon

Contact: Barbara Higby, *bhigby9323@gmail.com*

Members: 10

Membership fee: none

NEW YORK

WORD WEAVERS NEW HAVEN

Meetings: 245 Sundown Rd., Fulton; third Thursdays, 9:00 a.m.–noon

Contact: Mary Curcio, *mathmary56@gmail.com*

Membership fee: $50/year

Affiliation: Word Weavers

WORD WEAVERS WESTERN NEW YORK

Meetings: 2458 Rush Mendon Rd., Honeoye Falls; third Thursdays, 5:00–8:00 p.m.

Contact: Karen Rode, 585-571-7124, *karen.a.rode@gmail.com*

Members: 7

Membership fee: $50/year

Affiliation: Word Weavers

NORTH CAROLINA

ACFW NORTH CAROLINA

www.facebook.com/groups/336801510020700

Meetings: Raleigh

Contact: Vince Vezza, *northcarolina@acfwchapter.com*

Membership fee: national fee

Affiliation: American Christian Fiction Writers

WORD WEAVERS CHARLOTTE

Meetings: Hunter & Chandler Law Group, 10800 Sikes Pl., Ste. 105, Charlotte; first Saturdays, 10:00 a.m.–noon

Contact: Kim Dent, *cltwordweavers@yahoo.com*

Members: 15

Membership fee: $50/year
Affiliation: Word Weavers

WORD WEAVERS HICKORY-NEWTON
www.facebook.com/groups/2328785447421711
> **Meetings:** Vertical Life Church, 111 W. 8th St., Newton; first
> Saturdays, 10:00 a.m.
> **Contact:** Norma Poore, *NormaPoore464@gmail.com*
> **Members:** 6
> **Membership fee:** $50/year
> **Affiliation:** Word Weavers

WORD WEAVERS MAGGIE VALLEY
> **Meetings:** Woodland Baptist Church, 545 Crabtree Rd., Waynesville;
> second Saturdays, 9:30–11:30 a.m.
> **Contact:** Linda Summerford, *Juleps2@yahoo.com*
> **Membership fee:** $50/year
> **Affiliation:** Word Weavers

WORD WEAVERS PIEDMONT TRIAD
> **Meetings:** 510 Holyoke Rd., Pleasant Garden; third Saturdays, 10:00
> a.m.–noon
> **Contact:** Renee Leonard Kennedy, *Reneeleonardkennedy@gmail.com*
> **Members:** 10
> **Membership fee:** $50/year
> **Affiliation:** Word Weavers

WORD WEAVERS WILMINGTON
> **Meetings:** Panera Bread, 2506 Oleander Dr., Wilmington; second
> Tuesdays, 6:30 p.m.
> **Contact:** Laurel Senick, *contact@laurelsenick.com*
> **Members:** 5
> **Membership fee:** $50/year
> **Affiliation:** Word Weavers

WORD WEAVERS WINSTON-SALEM
> **Meetings:** 1038 Pine Place Dr., Germanton; second Saturdays,
> 9:30–11:30 a.m.
> **Contact:** Diane Virginia Cunio, *Diane@dianevirginia.com*
> **Membership fee:** $50/year
> **Affiliation:** Word Weavers

OHIO

ACFW OHIO
www.facebook.com/groups/220166801456380
> **Meetings:** Etna United Methodist Church, 500 Pike St., Etna; first Saturdays
> **Contact:** Bettie Boswell, *ohio@acfwchapter.com*
> **Members:** 65
> **Membership fee:** national fee
> **Affiliation:** American Christian Fiction Writers

COLUMBUS CHRISTIAN WRITERS ASSOCIATION
www.facebook.com/profile.php?id=100057586834554
> **Meetings:** Zoom; second Sundays, 3:00–5:00 p.m.
> **Contact:** Mina R. Raulston, 614-507-7893, *m_raulston@hotmail.com*
> **Members:** 5
> **Membership fee:** none

DAYTON CHRISTIAN SCRIBES
www.facebook.com/DaytonChristianScribes
> **Meetings:** Kettering Seventh-day Adventist Church, 3939 Stonebridge Rd., Kettering; second Thursdays, 7:00–9:00 p.m.
> **Contact:** Kim D. Villalva, 512-680-8729, *Kdanisk@yahoo.com*
> **Members:** 20
> **Membership fee:** $15/year

MIDDLETOWN AREA CHRISTIAN WRITERS (MAC WRITERS)
middletownwriters.blogspot.com
> **Meetings:** Healing Word Assembly of God, 5303 S. Dixie Hwy., Franklin; second Tuesdays, 7:00–8:30 p.m.
> **Contact:** Donna J. Shepherd, 513-373-5671, *donna.shepherd@gmail.com*
> **Members:** 25
> **Membership fee:** $30/year or $5/meeting

WORD WEAVERS NORTHEAST OHIO
> **Meetings:** Good Shepherd Villa, 726 Center St., Ashland; first Thursdays, 6:30–8:30 p.m.
> **Contact:** Cherie Martin, *kitties395@yahoo.com*

Members: 10
Membership fee: $50/year
Affiliation: Word Weavers

OKLAHOMA

ACFW OKLAHOMA CITY

www.okchristianfictionwriters.com

> **Meetings:** New Hope Church of Christ, 700 W. 2nd St., Edmond; third Saturdays, 1:00–3:00 p.m.
> **Contact:** Chris Tarpley, *OCFWchapter@gmail.com*
> **Members:** 35
> **Membership fee:** $20/year plus national fee
> **Affiliation:** American Christian Fiction Writers

FELLOWSHIP OF CHRISTIAN WRITERS

fellowshipofchristianwriters.org

> **Meetings:** Kirk of the Hills Presbyterian Church, 4102 E. 61st St., Tulsa; second Tuesdays, 6:30–8:00 p.m.
> **Contact:** Cheryl Barker, *cheryl@cherylbarker.net*
> **Members:** 33
> **Membership fee:** $30

WORDWRIGHTS

www.wordwrights-ok.com

> **Meetings:** The Last Drop Coffee Shop, 5425 N. Lincoln Blvd., Oklahoma City; second Saturdays, 10:00 a.m.
> **Contact:** *info@wordwrightsok.com*
> **Members:** 30
> **Membership fee:** $20/year

OREGON

OREGON CHRISTIAN WRITERS

www.oregonchristianwriters.org

> **Meetings:** Portland metro area and Salem, OR
> **Contact:** President, 503-393-3356, *president@oregonchristianwriters.com*
> **Services:** Sponsors two Saturday conferences and a summer coaching

conference each year.
Membership fee: $75/year; two family members, $100/year; students and seniors (62+), $45/year

PENNSYLVANIA

LANCASTER CHRISTIAN WRITERS
lancasterchristianwriters.org
Meetings: varies, see website; third Saturdays every other month, 9:30 a.m.–noon
Contact: Cheryl Weber, through the website
Members: 450
Membership fee: none

WORD WEAVERS HARRISBURG
Meetings: Living Water Community Church, 206 Oakleigh Ave., Harrisburg; second Saturdays, 1:30–3:30 p.m.
Contact: Mae Spradley, *Mae@2c1ministries.org*
Membership fee: $50/year
Affiliation: Word Weavers

WRITE HIS ANSWER CRITIQUE GROUPS
writehisanswer.com/critiquegroups
Meetings: online; every other Thursday, 8:00 a.m. and alternating Thursdays, 8:00 p.m.
Contact: Marlene Bagnull, 267-436-2503, *mbagnull@aol.com*
Members: 15 each group
Membership fee: none

SOUTH CAROLINA

ACFW SOUTH CAROLINA LOWCOUNTRY
www.facebook.com/groups/ACFWSCLowCountry
Meetings: Seacoast Church, 750 Long Point Rd., Mt. Pleasant; fourth Saturdays, 10:00 a.m.–noon
Contact: Cristina Sinisi, *sclowcountry@acfwchapter.com*
Members: 14
Membership fee: $20/year plus national fee
Affiliation: American Christian Fiction Writers

ACFW UPSTATE SC
ACFWUpstateSC.com
> **Meetings:** Cross Roads Baptist Church, 705 Anderson Ridge Rd., Greer; second Saturdays, 10:00 a.m.–1:00 p.m.
> **Contact:** Christine Boatwright, *upstatesc@acfwchapter.com*
> **Members:** 25
> **Membership fee:** $20 plus national fee
> **Affiliation:** American Christian Fiction Writers

WORD WEAVERS AIKEN
> **Meetings:** Trinity United Methodist Church, 2724 Whiskey Rd., Aiken; second Tuesdays, 7:00–9:00 p.m.
> **Contact:** Lee Allen-Russ, *AikenWordWeavers@gmail.com*
> **Members:** 5
> **Membership fee:** $50/year
> **Affiliation:** Word Weavers

WORD WEAVERS CHARLESTON
www.facebook.com/groups/2112701302307131
> **Meetings:** St John's Parish Church, Resurrection Hall, 1811 Paulette Dr., Johns Island; third Saturdays, 10:00 a.m.–noon
> **Contact:** Timothy Griggs, *timothygriggs@gmail.com*
> **Members:** 20
> **Membership fee:** $50/year
> **Affiliation:** Word Weavers

WORD WEAVERS LEXINGTON, SC
LexingtonWordWeavers.com
> **Meetings:** Trinity Baptist Church, 2003 Charleston Hwy., Cayce; second Mondays, 6:45–9:00 p.m.
> **Contact:** Jean Wilund, *Jwilund@icloud.com*
> **Members:** 40
> **Membership fee:** $50/year
> **Affiliation:** Word Weavers

WRITING 4 HIM
> **Meetings:** Spartanburg First Baptist Church, The Hanger, 250 E. Main St., Spartanburg; second Thursdays, 9:45 a.m.
> **Contact:** Linda Gilden, *linda@lindagilden.com*
> **Members:** 25
> **Membership fee:** none

TENNESSEE

ACFW KNOXVILLE
www.facebook.com/groups/341397182924371
>**Meetings:** Parkway Baptist Church, 401 S. Peters Rd., Knoxville;
>second Tuesdays
>**Contact:** Jenny Lynn Keller, *knoxville@acfwchapter.com*
>**Members:** 20
>**Membership fee:** national fee
>**Affiliation:** American Christian Fiction Writers

ACFW MEMPHIS
facebook.com/groups/699561666820044
>**Meetings:** M.R. Davis Library, 8554 Northwest Dr., Southaven; first
>Saturdays except December, 10:15 a.m.–noon
>**Contact:** Jessica Patch, *memphis@acfwchapter.com*
>**Members:** 20
>**Membership fee:** $20/year plus national fee
>**Affiliation:** American Christian Fiction Writers

ACFW MID-TENNESSEE
www.facebook.com/groups/250177678658399
>**Meetings:** Nashville; first Saturdays, 10:00 a.m.–noon
>**Contact:** Suzie Waltner, *midtennessee@acfwchapter.com*
>**Members:** 30
>**Membership fee:** $24/year plus national fee
>**Affiliation:** American Christian Fiction Writers

WORD WEAVERS KNOXVILLE
www.facebook.com/groups/336414403544597
>**Meetings:** Rio Revolution Church, 3419 E. Lamar Alexander Pkwy.,
>Maryville; third Saturdays, 9:30 a.m.–noon
>**Contact:** Beth Boring, 865-679-3370, *boringb@bellsouth.net*
>**Members:** 12
>**Membership fee:** $50/year
>**Affiliation:** Word Weavers

WORD WEAVERS NASHVILLE
>**Meetings:** Goodletsville Public Library, 205 Rivergate Pkwy.,
>Goodlettsville; second Saturdays, 10:00 a.m.–noon

Contact: Kim Aulich, *KAAfterGodsOwnHeart@gmail.com*
Members: 10
Membership fee: $50/year
Affiliation: Word Weavers

WORD WEAVERS SOUTH MIDDLE TENNESSEE
www.facebook.com/groups/323376445183667
> **Meetings:** Edgemont Baptist Church, 150 Fairfield Pike, Shelbyville; third Saturdays, 10:00 a.m.
> **Contact:** Amanda West, *awestwrites@outlook.com*
> **Members:** 8
> **Membership fee:** $50/year
> **Affiliation:** Word Weavers

TEXAS

67 WRITERS
roaringwriters.org/groups-locations
> **Meetings:** A H Meadows Library, Bluebonnet Room, 922 S. 9th St., Midlothian; second Saturdays except December, 2:00-3:45 p.m.
> **Contact:** Jan Johnson, email through the website
> **Membership fee:** none
> **Affiliation:** Roaring Writers

ACFW ALAMO CITY
www.facebook.com/groups/243114107289
> **Meetings:** San Antonio; second Saturdays, 10 a.m.-noon
> **Contact:** Allison Pittman, *alamocity@acfwchapter.com*
> **Members:** 15
> **Membership fee:** national fee
> **Affiliation:** American Christian Fiction Writers

ACFW DFW READY WRITERS
acfwdfwtx.com, www.facebook.com/DFWReadyWriters
> **Meetings:** Arlington Community Church, 1715 Randol Mill Rd., Arlington; second Saturdays, 10:00 a.m.-noon
> **Contact:** Paula Peckham, *acfwdfw@gmail.com*
> **Members:** 40
> **Membership fee:** national fee
> **Affiliation:** American Christian Fiction Writers, Roaring Writers

ACFW THE WOODLANDS

wotsacfw.blogspot.com

> **Meetings:** The Woodlands; second Saturdays
> **Contact:** Linda Kozar, *wotsacfw@gmail.com*
> **Members:** 40
> **Membership fee:** $20/year plus national fee
> **Affiliation:** American Christian Fiction Writers

GOD'S GARDEN WRITERS

roaringwriters.org/groups-locations

> **Meetings:** The Marina in Hideaway, 1373 Hideaway Ln. W, Hideaway; twice monthly Mondays, 1:00–4:00 p.m.; phone for dates
> **Contact:** Sandi Tomkins, 903-330-7852
> **Membership fee:** none
> **Affiliation:** Roaring Writers

HEART AND SOUL WRITERS

roaringwriters.org/groups-locations

> **Meetings:** Alsbury Baptist Church, 500 N.E. Alsbury Blvd., Burleson; third Tuesdays 7:00–9:00 p.m.
> **Contact:** Lisa Bell, email through the website
> **Membership fee:** none
> **Affiliation:** Roaring Writers

INSPIRATIONAL WRITERS ALIVE! CENTRAL HOUSTON

www.centralhoustoniwa.com

> **Meetings:** Houston's First Baptist Church, 7474 Katy Fwy., Houston; monthly, see website for details
> **Contact:** Diana Battista, *centralhoustoniwaweb@gmail.com*
> **Members:** 15
> **Membership fee:** see the website

LIVING WATERS

roaringwriters.org/groups-locations

> **Meetings:** Hood County Library, Pecan Room, 222 N. Travis, Granbury; second Fridays, 2:00–4:00 p.m.
> **Contact:** Lisa Bell, email through the website
> **Membership fee:** none
> **Affiliation:** Roaring Writers

ROARING WRITERS MENTORING WITH FRANK BALL

roaringwriters.org/roaring-writers-mentoring

> **Meetings:** Roaring Lambs, upstairs conference room, 17110 Dallas Pkwy., Ste. 284, Dallas; third Saturdays. 9:30 a.m.–12:30 p.m.
> **Contact:** Frank Ball, email through the website
> **Membership fee:** $30 per session, $95 for four-month season
> **Affiliation:** Roaring Writers

ROCKWALL CHRISTIAN WRITERS GROUP

www.facebook.com/groups/rockwallchristianwritersgroup

> **Meetings:** Lake Pointe Church, room 212, 701 E. Interstate 30, Rockwall; third Wednesdays except December, 7:00–9:00 p.m.
> **Contact:** Leslie Wilson, 214-505-5336, *leslieporterwilson@gmail.com*
> **Members:** 15–20 in person, 300+ on Facebook page
> **Membership fee:** none
> **Affiliation:** Roaring Writers

WACO CHRISTIAN WRITERS WORKSHOP

roaringwriters.org/groups-locations

> **Meetings:** First Woodway Baptist Church, room 210-211, 101 Ritchie Rd., Woodway; Sundays except November and December, 5:30–7:00 p.m.
> **Contact:** Michelle Ruddell, *mruddell21@gmail.com*
> **Members:** 25
> **Membership fee:** none
> **Affiliation:** Roaring Writers

WITNESS WRITERS

roaringwriters.org/groups-locations

> **Meetings:** Plainview; email for location and days
> **Contact:** Carole Bell, *caroleabell@gmail.com*
> **Membership fee:** none
> **Affiliation:** Roaring Writers

WRITE WITH GRACE

roaringwriters.org/groups-locations

> **Meetings:** Twin Oaks Ranch, 20131 FM Rd. 16, Garden Valley; twice monthly Wednesdays, 6:30–9:00 p.m.
> **Contact:** Sandi Tomkins, 903-330-7852

Membership fee: none
Affiliation: Roaring Writers

VIRGINIA

ACFW VIRGINIA

acfwvirginia.com

> **Meetings:** Leesburg, Chesapeake, Fredericksburg, Lynchburg, Woodbridge; check website for days and times; plus monthly webinars
> **Contact:** Deena Adams, *acfwvirginia@gmail.com*
> **Members:** 75
> **Membership fee:** $15/year plus national fee
> **Affiliation:** American Christian Fiction Writers

CAPITAL CHRISTIAN WRITERS FELLOWSHIP

ccwritersfellowship.org

> **Meetings:** Centreville Presbyterian Church and virtual, 15450 Lee Hwy., Centreville; quarterly in-person meetings, Saturday mornings; off-months virtual, Wednesdays, 8:00 p.m.
> **Contact:** Sarah Hamaker, *president@ccwritersfellowship.org*
> **Members:** 60
> **Membership fee:** $40

WORD WEAVERS WOODBRIDGE

> **Meetings:** varies, email for locations, Woodbridge; second Saturdays, 11:00 a.m.
> **Contact:** Lauren Craft, *laurenchristianauthor@gmail.com*
> **Members:** 4
> **Membership fee:** $50/year
> **Affiliation:** Word Weavers

WASHINGTON

VANCOUVER CHRISTIAN WRITERS

> **Meetings:** email for address, Vancouver; first Mondays, 9:00 a.m.
> **Contact:** Jon Drury, 510-909-0848, *jondrury2@yahoo.com*
> **Members:** 8
> **Membership fee:** none
> **Affiliation:** Oregon Christian Writers

WISCONSIN

ACFW WI SOUTHEAST

www.facebook.com/wiseacfw

Meetings: first Thursdays, 6:30–8:30 p.m.
Contact: Laura DeNooyer Moore, *wisconsinSE@acfwchapter.com*
Members: 25
Membership fee: $25/year plus national fee
Affiliation: American Christian Fiction Writers

PENS OF PRAISE CHRISTIAN WRITERS

www.susanmarlene.com/writers-pens

Meetings: Faith Evangelical Free Church, 2201 S. 42nd St.,
Manitowoc; various Tuesdays except December and holidays,
1:30–3:00 p.m.
Contact: Susan Marlene Kinney, 920-242-3631, *susanmarlenewrites@
gmail.com*
Members: 10
Membership fee: none

WORD AND PEN CHRISTIAN WRITERS

wordandpenchristianwriters.com

Meetings: St. Thomas Episcopal Church, April–November; Zoom,
January–March, 226 Washington St., Menasha; second Mondays,
7:30 p.m.
Contact: Chris Stratton, 920-739-0752, *gcefsi@new.rr.com*
Members: 18
Membership fee: $10/year

WORD WEAVERS ST. CROIX

Meetings: Selah Vie Coffee Bistro, 208 N. Main St., River Falls;
second Saturdays, 10:00 a.m.–noon
Contact: Erin Maruska, *erin.maruska@gmail.com*
Membership fee: $50/year
Affiliation: Word Weavers

AUSTRALIA AND NEW ZEALAND

AUSTRALASIAN CHRISTIAN WRITERS
australasianchristianwriters.com
> **Contact:** Narelle Atkins, Jenny Blake, Iola Goulton; email through the website
> **Services:** Online group of writers in Australia, New Zealand, and beyond. Weekly Tuesday book chats.
> **Members:** 700

NEW ZEALAND CHRISTIAN WRITERS
www.nzchristianwriters.org
> **Meetings:** various places, see website
> **Contact:** Justin St. Vincent, *president@nzchristianwriters.org*
> **Services:** "NZ Christian Writers is a nationwide collective of over 330 authors, bloggers, editors, lyricists, poets, publishers, songwriters, storytellers, and writers throughout New Zealand. Along with our bimonthly magazines and competitions, we offer inspiring seminars and writers retreats to encourage, inspire, and upskill people in their writing. NZ Christian Writers' vision is to encourage and inspire Christian writers throughout New Zealand. We welcome both beginner and experienced writers to join us."
> **Members:** 330+

OMEGA WRITERS
omegawriters.com.au
> **Contact:** *membership@omegawriters.org*
> **Services:** Australian group with local and online chapters across the country and New Zealand. See the website for locations. Also sponsors an annual conference and the CALEB Award to recognize the best in Australasian Christian writing, published and unpublished.
> **Members:** 125
> **Membership fee:** $60/year

CANADA

InSCRIBE CHRISTIAN WRITERS' FELLOWSHIP
inscribe.org
> **Contact:** Sheila Webster, email through the website
> **Services:** Canadian group with chapters across the country. See the website for locations. Also sponsors workshops, a fall conference, and contests and produces the quarterly magazine *FellowScript* that is included with membership.
> **Members:** 160
> **Membership fee:** varies, see website

MANITOBA CHRISTIAN WRITERS ASSOCIATION
> **Meetings:** Bleak House, 1637 Main St., Winnipeg; first Saturdays except second Saturdays in January and February, 1:30–4:00 p.m.
> **Contact:** Frieda Martens, 204-770-8023, *friedamartens1910@gmail.com*
> **Members:** 20–23
> **Membership fee:** $30
> **Affiliation:** InScribe Christian Writers' Fellowship

THE WORD GUILD
www.thewordguild.com
> **Contact:** Box 77001, Markham ON L3P 0C8, Canada; 800-969-9010; *info@thewordguild.com*
> **Services:** "The Word Guild is a growing community of Canadian writers, editors, speakers, publishers, booksellers, librarians and other interested individuals who are Christian. From all parts of Canada and many denominational and cultural backgrounds, we affirm a common statement of faith and are united in our passion for the written word." Sponsors regional chapters across Canada and contests and awards for Canadian Christian writers.
> **Members:** 325
> **Membership fee:** $65/year; professional, $105; student, $30

SOUTH SUDAN

WORD WEAVERS CENTRAL EQUATORIA SOUTH SUDAN

Meetings: ACROSS Compound, Buluk off Ministries Rd., Juba; third Saturdays, 2:00-4:00 p.m.

Contact: Teresa Janzen, WhatsApp: +6162325480, *teresajanzen@gmail.com*

Membership fee: $50/year

Affiliation: Word Weavers

20

EDITORIAL SERVICES

Entries in this chapter are for information only, not an endorsement of editing skills. Before hiring a freelance editor, ask for references if they are not posted on the website; and contact two or three to help determine if this editor is a good fit for you. You may also want to pay for an edit of a few pages or one chapter before hiring someone to edit your complete manuscript.

A LITTLE RED INK | BETHANY KACZMAREK
115 1st St., Somerset, WI 54025 | 715-907-5144
contact@bethanykaczmarek.com | *www.bethanykaczmarek.com/little-red-ink2*
> **Contact:** website
> **Services:** copyediting, manuscript evaluation, substantive/ developmental editing
> **Types of manuscripts:** adult, middle grade, novels, teen/YA
> **Charges:** hourly rate
> **Credentials/experience:** "An ACFW Editor of the Year finalist (2015), Bethany enjoys working with both traditional and indie authors. Several of her clients are award-winning and best-selling authors, though she does work with aspiring authors as well. She has edited speculative fiction for Enclave Fiction and Gilead, and general fiction for Sunrise Publishing."

A LITTLE RED INK | ERYNN NEWMAN
1 Fairway One, Taylors, SC 29687 | 919-229-1357
ErynnNewman@gmail.com | *www.ALittleRedInk.com*
> **Contact:** email, website
> **Services:** copyediting, proofreading, substantive/developmental editing
> **Types of manuscripts:** adult, novels, teen/YA

Charges: hourly rate

Credentials/experience: "I specialize in helping authors find their unique voice, deepening point of view, and bringing characters to life. I'm an unapologetic grammar nerd, but I don't take anything (except the Oxford Comma) too seriously. I have edited over 100 published novels including several *NYT* and *USA Today* best sellers, have authored two award-winning novels of my own, and won the National Readers' Choice Award and the Rita Award for editing."

A WORD IN SEASON | SAMANTHA HANNI

3400 Windsor Ter., Oklahoma City, OK 73122 | 405-642-7855
samantha.hanni@mrshanni.com | *mrshanni.com/work-with-me*

Contact: email, website

Services: copyediting, manuscript evaluation, substantive/developmental editing

Types of manuscripts: adult, articles, Bible studies, curriculum, devotions, nonfiction books, teen/YA

Charges: flat fee, word rate

Credentials/experience: "I am passionate about wielding words for good, whether it be writing my own or refining the words of others. For the past decade, I've had the privilege of writing and editing, helping individuals and businesses share the content that's most important to them. As a freelance writer and editor, I have self-published four books for Christian teens and edited dozens of manuscripts for Christian authors, many of them debut authors. I have provided copy editing services for two Christian publishing houses and for The Odyssey Online. Specialty: non-fiction."

AB WRITING SERVICES, LLC | ANN BYLE

annbyle@gmail.com | *www.annbylewriter.com*

Contact: email

Services: articles, back-cover copy, consulting, copyediting, discussion questions for books, ghostwriting, manuscript evaluation, press releases

Types of manuscripts: adult, articles, book proposals, devotionals, nonfiction books, novels, query letters

Charges: hourly rate

Credentials/experience: "Ann's experience includes years as a newspaper copy editor, freelance journalist for newspapers and magazines including *Publishers Weekly*, writing her own books including *Christian Publishing 101*, and co- and ghost-writing book projects."

ABOVE THE PAGES | PAM LAGORMARSINO
abovethepages@gmail.com | www.abovethepages.com

> **Contact:** email, website
> **Services:** back-cover copy, copyediting, discussion questions for books, manuscript evaluation, proofreading, substantive/developmental editing, writing coach
> **Types of manuscripts:** academic, adult, Bible studies, book proposals, curriculum, devotionals, easy readers, gift books, middle grade, nonfiction books, novels, query letters, short stories, teen/YA
> **Charges:** flat fee, word rate
> **Credentials/experience:** "Pam has edited, proofread, or beta-read Christian fiction and nonfiction books, devotionals, sermons, Bible studies, homeschool curriculum, and children's books since 2015. Additional experience includes working in a rural library for twenty years, being a sales rep of children's books, and home teaching her children through high school. Her college coursework included English, literature, library science, and child development. Pam is familiar with the Bible and Christian doctrine and teachings. Some editing courses include: Essential Skills for Editing Nonfiction, Editing Children's Books, Editing Nonfiction, Proofreading, and Editing Devotionals."

ACEVEDO WORD SOLUTIONS, LLC | JENNE ACEVEDO
editor@jenneacevedo.com | www.jenneacevedo.com

> **Contact:** email
> **Services:** back-cover copy, copyediting, discussion questions for books, project management, proofreading, substantive/developmental editing, writing coach
> **Types of manuscripts:** adult, Bible studies, book proposals, curriculum, devotionals, gift books, middle grade, nonfiction books, query letters, teen/YA
> **Charges:** hourly rate, word rate
> **Credentials/experience:** "Consultant for private and corporate clients, proofreader for publishers. Cofounder of Christian Editors Association, former director of The Christian PEN, former director of PENCON, member of Christian Editor Connection, instructor for The PEN Institute, Editors' Choice Award judge. Founder and former director of Chandler Writers' Group."

AMBASSADOR COMMUNICATIONS | CLAIRE HUTCHINSON

13733 W. Gunsight Dr., Sun City West, AZ 85375 | 812-390-7907
clairescreenwriter@gmail.com | *www.clairehutchinson.net*

Contact: email
Services: coauthoring, copyediting, proofreading, screenwriting, substantive/developmental editing, writing coach
Types of manuscripts: scripts
Charges: flat fee
Credentials/experience: "M.A. English, Professional Program in Screenwriting UCLA, produced and award-winning screenwriter and producer and script analyst."

AMI EDITING | ANNETTE IRBY

editor@AMIediting.com | *www.AMIediting.com*

Contact: email
Services: copyediting, critiquing, manuscript evaluation (fiction only), proofreading, substantive/developmental editing
Types of manuscripts: novellas, novels, short stories
Charges: page rate
Credentials/experience: "Annette spent 5 years working as an acquisitions editor for a Christian book publisher. She has 20 years of experience editing freelance in the CBA marketplace. Her clients have included several well-known authors and publishers. She is a long-time member of ACFW and has served as a judge for their contests, including final-round evaluation. As a fiction author herself, she has published books of various lengths. Over the years, her writing has achieved top-three status in competitions, as well as placing first in BRMCWC's 2019 Selah Contest. In 2009, she founded Seriously Write, a co-hosted blog, which ran for 10 years with active participation from the Christian writing community. See her editing website for testimonials."

ANDREA MERRELL

60 McKinney Rd., Travelers Rest, SC 29690 | 864-616-5889
AndreaMerrell7@gmail.com | *www.AndreaMerrell.com*

Contact: email, website
Services: back-cover copy, copyediting, proofreading
Types of manuscripts: adult, articles, devotionals, nonfiction books, novels, short stories

Charges: hourly rate

Credentials/experience: "Professional freelance editor. Associate editor for LPC Books and Christian Devotions Ministries. Member of The Christian PEN: Proofreaders and Editors Network."

ANN KROEKER, WRITING COACH

ann@annkroeker.com | annkroeker.com/writing-coach

Contact: email, website

Services: writing coach

Types of manuscripts: adult, articles, blog posts, book proposals, nonfiction books, query letters, social-media content

Charges: flat fee, hourly rate, word rate

Credentials/experience: "A writing coach, author, speaker, and host of the *Ann Kroeker, Writing Coach* podcast, Ann works with clients one-to-one, through programs and courses like The Art & Craft of Writing, and through Your Platform Matters (YPM), her platform membership program. Her website has landed on *The Write Life*'s annual '100 Best Websites for Writers' list six years in a row thanks to years of valuable writing-related content. She leverages over three decades of experience in the writing and publishing world to support writers looking for input and confidence to advance their careers. Ann's clients have achieved personal goals, landed contracts, hit bestseller lists, and won awards. She's presented at conferences, retreats, and summits; coauthored *On Being a Writer: 12 Simple Habits for a Writing Life that Lasts*; and authored *Not So Fast: Slow-Down Solutions for Frenzied Families* and *The Contemplative Mom*."

ARMOR OF HOPE WRITING & PUBLISHING SERVICES |
DENISE M. WALKER

info@armorofhopewritingservices.com | www.armorofhopewritingservices.com

Contact: email

Services: copyediting, proofreading, writing coach

Types of manuscripts: Bible studies, board/picture books, devotionals, easy readers, nonfiction books

Charges: flat fee, word rate

Credentials/experience: "I have been in business for over five years and have copyedited and/or proofread 100+ nonfiction, children's picture books, and easy readers. In addition, I serve as a writing coach, assisting nonfiction authors with organizing and developing their thoughts. I am also a full-service nonfiction self-publishing coach and an author of middle grades/YA fiction, women's Christian fiction, and Bible literacy journals. I have attended several book writing and editing workshops. I am also certified in middle grades English language arts and have taught English for over 20 years."

AUTHOR AS ENTREPRENEUR | MICHAEL L. WHITE

PO Box 8277, Mobile, AL 36689 | 251-643-6985

mwhite@authorasentrepreneur.com | *www.authorasentrepeneur.com*

Contact: email, website

Services: back-cover copy, proofreading, substantive/developmental editing

Types of manuscripts: articles, Bible studies, nonfiction books, novels, poetry

Charges: custom

Credentials/experience: "Dual B.S. degree in English and history from Troy University. Master of Divinity degree from Emory University's Candler School of Theology. 40+ years as a freelance writer. 27+ years of experience as a pastor before retiring. Retired with 30+ years of service as a Chaplain Assistant and a Chaplain in the U.S. Army and Alabama Army National Guard. 17+ years of experience as the founder and managing editor for the independent Christian publishing company, Parson Place Press."

AUTHOR GATEWAY | CALEB BREAKEY

424 W. Bakerview Rd., Ste. 105, Bellingham, WA 98226

team@authorgateway.com | *www.authorgateway.com*

Contact: email

Services: book proposals, writing coach

Types of manuscripts: books of all kinds and all ages

Charges: $3,500–5,500

Credentials/experience: "Backed by more than 200 years of experience, HarperCollins Christian Publishing's Author Gateway provides the best team in the country dedicated to helping men and women of faith land a prominent literary agent and sign with a major Christian publisher. We serve authors who are looking to up their game when it comes to pitching to literary agents and acquisition editors."

AUTHORIZEME LITERARY FIRM, LLC | SHARON NORRIS ELLIOTT

PO Box 1816, South Gate, CA 90280 | 310-508-9860

AuthorizeMeNow@gmail.com | lifethatmatters.net/authorizeme

> **Contact:** email, website
>
> **Services:** back-cover copy, book-contract evaluation, copyediting, discussion questions for books, ghostwriting, manuscript evaluation, proofreading, substantive/developmental editing, writing coach
>
> **Types of manuscripts:** adult, articles, Bible studies, board/picture books, book proposals, devotionals, easy readers, gift books, nonfiction books, novels, poetry, short stories
>
> **Charges:** hourly rate, page rate, word rate
>
> **Credentials/experience:** "I am a 36-year veteran English and writing instructor with over 20 years of experience as a professional editor for publishing companies and private clients. I now work full time as a book developer, writing coach, ghostwriter, and editor hired by royalty publishing houses and private clients." Also offers AuthorizeMe Academy Masterclass Series.

AUTHORS WHO SERVE | RACHEL HILLS

rachel@authorswhoserve.com | authorswhoserve.com

> **Contact:** website
>
> **Services:** copyediting, ghostwriting, manuscript evaluation, substantive/developmental editing, writing coach
>
> **Types of manuscripts:** adult, articles, devotionals, nonfiction books, novels, query letters, teen/YA
>
> **Charges:** flat fee, word rate
>
> **Credentials/experience:** "Twenty plus years of experience editing with certificates in copyediting, developmental editing, and ghostwriting."

AVODAH EDITORIAL SERVICES | CHRISTY DISTLER

www.avodaheditorialservices.com

> **Contact:** website
>
> **Services:** copyediting, manuscript evaluation, proofreading, substantive/developmental editing
>
> **Types of manuscripts:** adult, devotionals, easy readers, nonfiction books, novels, picture books, poetry, short stories
>
> **Charges:** word rate

Credentials/experience: "Educated at Temple University and University of California–Berkeley. Thirteen years of editorial experience, both as an employee and a freelancer. Currently works mostly for publishing houses but accepts freelance work as scheduling allows."

BANNER LITERARY | MIKE LOOMIS
mike@mikeloomis.co | www.MikeLoomis.co

Contact: email, website

Services: back-cover copy, book-contract evaluation, coauthoring, copyediting, discussion questions for books, ghostwriting, manuscript evaluation, substantive/developmental editing, writing coach

Types of manuscripts: articles, book proposals, devotionals, nonfiction books, query letters

Charges: custom, flat fee

Credentials/experience: "I have ghostwritten two *NYT* bestsellers, and advised internationally-known authors. But I truly enjoy helping aspiring authors develop their books, brands, and business."

BARBARA KOIS
barbara.kois@gmail.com

Contact: email

Services: back-cover copy, copyediting, ghostwriting, manuscript evaluation, proofreading, substantive/developmental editing, writing coach

Types of manuscripts: adult, Bible studies, devotionals, gift books, middle grade, nonfiction books, novels, short stories, teen/YA

Charges: hourly rate, word rate

Credentials/experience: "Barbara has worked as a writer, ghostwriter, editor, teacher, coach, corporate communication consultant and journalist, and served as Writer in Residence at Tyndale House Publishers. She has written or co-written ten books, published more than 600 articles in the *Chicago Tribune*, and edited more than 250 books for various publishers and authors. Barbara has helped dozens of writers to prepare for the publication of their books, including both those who have published with traditional publishers and those who have chosen to self-publish. Her goals include making writing clear, memorable and even humorous where appropriate."

BBH LITERARY | DAVID BRATT

david@bbhliterary.com | *www.bbhliterary.com/developmental-editing*

Contact: email, website

Services: manuscript evaluation, substantive/developmental editing

Types of manuscripts: academic, articles, book proposals, nonfiction books, query letters

Charges: hourly rate

Credentials/experience: "Twenty-one years editing for Eerdmans Publishing; Ph.D. in American religion (Yale University, 1999)."

BECCA WIERWILLE EDITING AND COACHING SERVICES

becca@beccawierwille.com | *beccawierwille.com/editing-services*

Contact: email, website

Services: copyediting, manuscript evaluation, proofreading, substantive/developmental editing, writing coach

Types of manuscripts: adult, book proposals, devotionals, easy readers, middle grade, novels, query letters, short stories, teen/YA

Charges: word rate

Credentials/experience: "Becca Wierwille is a freelance editor and writing coach who has worked with writers of various genres and experience levels. As a former newspaper reporter and avid critique group member, she has years of experience doing edits at every level. She loves partnering with authors to help make their stories shine and focuses on editing clean fiction, with a specialization in middle grade and YA. Her editing portfolio and testimonials are available upon request."

BESTSELLING BOOK SHEPHERD | PAMELA GOSSIAUX

pam@pamelagossiaux.com | *BestsellingBookShepherd.com*

Contact: email

Services: back-cover copy, coauthoring, copyediting, discussion questions for books, ghostwriting, manuscript evaluation, proofreading, substantive/developmental editing, writing coach

Types of manuscripts: adult, articles, Bible studies, board/picture books, book proposals, devotionals, easy readers, gift books, middle grade, nonfiction books, novels, query letters, short stories, teen/YA

Charges: custom, flat fee, hourly rate, packages

Credentials/experience: "30 years experience writing, editing, journalism, book PR. Dual degree in Creative Writing & English

Language and Literature from University of Michigan. International bestselling author. Have coached and promoted authors to Amazon, *USA Today* and *Wall Street Journal* bestsellers."

BLACK DOG AUTHOR SERVICES | VICTORIA MERKIEL
blackdogeditor@gmail.com | *blackdogauthors.com*

Contact: email
Services: copyediting, substantive/developmental editing
Types of manuscripts: adult, middle grade, novels, query letters, synopsis, teen/YA
Charges: word rate
Credentials/experience: "Victoria, owner of Black Dog Author Services, has years of experience editing manuscripts for self-published and traditionally-published authors and has sat on the other side of the table as an author herself. She brings together both experiences for a unique service tailored to each individual author's needs."

BOOKHOUND EDITING | KATY SCHLOMACH
katy@bookhoundediting.com | *www.bookhoundediting.com*

Contact: email, website
Services: copyediting, manuscript evaluation, proofreading
Types of manuscripts: adult, novels, short stories, teen/YA
Charges: flat fee, packages, word rate
Credentials/experience: "Katy Schlomach specializes in proofreading, copyediting, and line editing fiction. Her goal is to refine and polish while carefully preserving the author's voice. She has a BA in communication (technical writing) and a passion for the craft of editing fiction so it is clear, correct, consistent, and compelling for readers. She completed training through Edit Republic and The PEN Institute and is a member of the Christian Editor Connection. Her love of language has turned into a career that allows her to help writers communicate their stories clearly."

BOOKOX | THOMAS WOMACK
165 S. Timber Creek Dr., Sisters, OR 97759 | 541-788-6503
Thomas@BookOx.com | *www.BookOx.com*

Contact: email
Services: copyediting, discussion questions for books, manuscript evaluation, proofreading, substantive/developmental editing, writing coach
Types of manuscripts: adult, Bible studies, curriculum, devotionals,

easy readers, middle grade, nonfiction books, novels, short stories

Charges: word rate

Credentials/experience: "My decades of editing experience have centered on Christian books published by Crossway, Zondervan, Multnomah, WaterBrook, NavPress, Harvest House, David C. Cook, and other publishing houses. These have included numerous titles in the categories of spiritual nurture and care, spiritual disciplines and devotion, Bible study and theology, and marriage and family, as well as memoirs, fiction, and business and leadership books."

BREAKOUT EDITING | DORI HARRELL

doriharrell@gmail.com | doriharrell.wixsite.com/breakoutediting

Contact: email

Services: copyediting, proofreading, substantive/developmental editing, website text

Types of manuscripts: adult, articles, devotionals, middle grade, nonfiction books, novels, picture books, query letters, short stories, teen/YA

Charges: word rate

Credentials/experience: "Dori is a multiple-award-winning writer and a highly experienced editor who freelance edits full time and has edited more than 300 novels and nonfiction books. Breakout authors final in awards or win awards almost every year! She edits for publishers, including Gemma Halliday Publishing and Kregel Publications, and as an editor, she releases more than twenty books annually."

BROOKSTONE CREATIVE GROUP | JOHN HERRING

100 Missionary Ridge, Birmingham, AL 35242 | 302-514-7899

www.brookstonecreativegroup.com

Contact: website

Services: book proposals, copyediting, ghostwriting, one-sheets, proofreading, substantive/developmental editing, writing coach

Types of manuscripts: books of all kinds and all ages

Charges: flat fee

Credentials/experience: "Brookstone Creative Group is changing the landscape for how writers, authors, speakers, pastors, musicians, and other creatives navigate the ever-changing landscape of platform development. Through true and tested solutions, training, and community-building, Brookstone Creative Group guides their clients in the who, where, when, and how to inspirational success."

BUTTERFIELD EDITORIAL SERVICES | DEBRA L. BUTTERFIELD

4810 Gene Field Rd., Saint Joseph, MO 64506 | 816-752-2171

deb@debralbutterfield.com | *themotivationaleditor.com*

Contact: email

Services: copyediting, substantive/developmental editing

Types of manuscripts: adult, book proposals, nonfiction books, novels

Charges: word rate

Credentials/experience: "Debra began her writing career as a copywriter for Focus on the Family. She has been editing manuscripts since 2010."

C. S. LAKIN EDITORIAL SERVICES

20406 Tiger Tail Rd., Grass Valley, CA 95949 | 530-200-5466

cslakin@gmail.com | *www.livewritethrive.com, www.critiquemymanuscript.com*

Contact: email

Services: back-cover copy, copyediting, critiquing, manuscript evaluation, proofreading, substantive/developmental editing, writing coach

Types of manuscripts: academic, adult, articles, Bible studies, book proposals, curriculum, devotionals, easy readers, gift books, middle grade, nonfiction books, novels, poetry, query letters, short stories, teen/YA

Charges: hourly rate, page rate

Credentials/experience: "I've been a freelance book copyeditor and writing coach for 18 years, having worked with more than a thousand writers in six continents. I do more than 200 manuscript critiques a year and have coached thousands of writers via my online school at *cslakin.teachable.com*."

CATHY STREINER

South Carolina

Cathy@thecorporatepen.com | *thecorporatepen.com*

Contact: email

Services: back-cover copy, coauthoring, copyediting, discussion questions for books, proofreading, substantive/developmental editing, writing coach

Types of manuscripts: academic, adult, articles, Bible studies, devotionals, easy readers, gift books, middle grade, nonfiction books, novels, scripts, short stories, technical material, teen/YA

Charges: custom, flat fee, hourly rate, word rate

Credentials/experience: "Author of a Christian novel, I have experience with the start-to-finish self-publishing process. I also have extensive experience working with writers who need editing and proofreading services as well as limited coaching with constructive feedback."

CELTICFROG EDITING | ALEX MCGILVERY

Kamloops, BC, Canada

thecelticfrog@gmail.com | celticfrogediting.com

Contact: email, website

Services: manuscript evaluation, writing coach

Types of manuscripts: adult, articles, devotionals, middle grade, nonfiction books, novels, short stories, teen/YA

Charges: word rate

Credentials/experience: "I have been reviewing and critiquing books for more than three decades, and editing since 2014. One client compared my work favourably with the editors at a traditional publisher."

CHERI FIELDS EDITING

1232 Garfield Ave. NW, Grand Rapids, MI 49504 | 269-953-4271

Cherifieldsediting@gmail.com | Cherifields.com

Contact: email

Services: copyediting, manuscript evaluation, substantive/ developmental editing, writing coach

Types of manuscripts: academic, articles, Bible studies, board/ picture books, book proposals, curriculum, devotionals, easy readers, middle grade, nonfiction books, teen/YA

Charges: word rate

Credentials/experience: "Gold member of the Christian PEN for nonfiction and children's editing."

CHRISTIAN COMMUNICATOR MANUSCRIPT CRITIQUE SERVICE | SUSAN TITUS OSBORN

3133 Puente St., Fullerton, CA 92835 | 714-313-8651

susanosb@aol.com | www.christiancommunicator.com

Contact: email, phone, website

Services: back-cover copy, book-contract evaluation, coauthoring, copyediting, discussion questions for books, ghostwriting, manuscript evaluation, proofreading, writing coach

Types of manuscripts: academic, adult, articles, Bible studies, book proposals, curriculum, devotionals, easy readers, gift books, middle grade, nonfiction books, novels, picture books, poetry, query letters, scripts, short stories, technical material, teen/YA

Charges: hourly rate, page rate

Credentials/experience: "Our critique service, comprised of 14 professional editors, has been in business for almost 40 years. We are recommended by ECPA, the Billy Graham Association, and a number of publishing houses and agents."

CHRISTIAN EDITOR CONNECTION

PO Box 9243, Brea, CA 92822

director@ChristianEditor.com | *www.ChristianEditor.com*

Contact: website

Services: copyediting, ghostwriting, indexing, manuscript evaluation, proofreading, substantive/developmental editing, writing coach

Types of manuscripts: academic, adult, articles, Bible studies, board/picture books, book proposals, curriculum, devotionals, easy readers, gift books, middle grade, nonfiction books, novels, poetry, query letters, short stories, technical material, teen/YA

Charges: hourly rate, page rate, word rate

Credentials/experience: "Christian Editor Connection is a matchmaking service that connects Christian authors, project managers, agents, and publishers with vetted, professional Christian editors."

CHRISTIANBOOKPROPOSALS.COM | CINDY CARTER

ccarter@ecpa.org | *ChristianBookProposals.com*

Contact: website

Services: online proposal-submission service

Types of manuscripts: books of all kinds and all ages

Charges: $98 for six months

Credentials/experience: "Operated by the Evangelical Christian Publishers Association (ECPA), it is the only manuscript service created by the top Christian publishers looking for unsolicited manuscripts in a traditional, royalty-based relationship. It allows authors to submit their manuscript proposals in a secure, online format for review by editors from publishing houses that are members of ECPA."

CLAIRE KOHLER

clairekohlerbooks@yahoo.com | *www.clairekohlerbooks.com/services*

Contact: website
Services: copyediting, proofreading
Types of manuscripts: devotionals, novels
Charges: word rate
Credentials/experience: "I worked as an English teacher in a public school for two years before becoming an online English teacher to students overseas. I completed a rigorous proofreading course in 2022 and have worked as a professional editor since then. I am also a published author with two books and a third in progress."

COLLABORATIVE EDITORIAL SOLUTIONS | ANDREW BUSS

info@collaborativeeditorial.com | *collaborativeeditorial.com*

Contact: email
Services: copyediting, proofreading
Types of manuscripts: academic, adult, articles, Bible studies, devotionals, nonfiction books, technical material
Charges: hourly rate, page rate
Credentials/experience: "I'm a professional editor with more than five years of full-time experience working with authors and scholarly publishers such as InterVarsity Press, Reformation Heritage, P&R Publishing, Georgetown University Press, and Baylor University Press. Although I primarily work in the genre of scholarly nonfiction, I'm always keen to work with creative and thoughtful authors, whatever the topic or genre. I'm a member of the Editorial Freelancers Association and the Society of Biblical Literature."

COMMUNICATION ASSOCIATES | KEN WALKER

729 Ninth Ave. #331, Huntington, WV 25701 | 304-525-3343
kenwalker33@gmail.com | *www.KenWalkerWriter.com*

Contact: email
Services: back-cover copy, coauthoring, discussion questions for books, ghostwriting, substantive/developmental editing
Types of manuscripts: adult, articles, Bible studies, devotionals, nonfiction books
Charges: flat fee, hourly rate
Credentials/experience: "Started freelancing in 1983 and went full-time in 1990. Experienced ghostwriter and developmental book editor. Have been doing more book editing the past nine years.

Written, edited or contributed to more than 90 books."

CORNERSTONE-INK EDITING | VIE HERLOCKER

vherlock@yahoo.com | www.cornerstone-ink.com

Contact: email, website

Services: copyediting, manuscript evaluation, substantive/developmental editing

Types of manuscripts: adult, articles, book proposals, devotionals, gift books, middle grade, nonfiction books, novels, query letters, short stories, teen/YA

Charges: word rate

Credentials/experience: "Vie Herlocker provides 'Tough-Love Editing with a Tender Touch.' She is a member of Christian Editor Connection, Christian Proofreaders and Editors Network, ACFW, and Word Weavers, Int. Her experience includes: editing for a small Christian publisher (10 years), editing for a regional magazine, judging a national writing contest, and freelance editing. She uses *The Chicago Manual of Style, Christian Writers' Manual of Style*, and *Merriam-Webster* 11th."

COULTER CHRISTIAN EDITING SERVICES | KAY COULTER

806 Hopi Trail, Temple, TX 76504 | 254-718-9045

bkcoulter1@att.net | coulterchristianeditingservices.net

Contact: email, website

Services: back-cover copy, copyediting, ghostwriting, proofreading, substantive/developmental editing

Types of manuscripts: academic, adult, Bible studies, devotionals, gift books, nonfiction books, novels, short stories, teen/YA

Charges: hourly rate

Credentials/experience: "I am a published author myself and am a certified copyeditor. I have worked with authors on over 350 projects the last 21 years. I have continued to learn by taking many different editing courses. I have also worked as a contract editor for several publishing companies, most recently Iron Stream Media. I'm a member of Christian Editor Connection and Christian PEN."

CREATIVE CORNERSTONES | CAYLAH COFFEEN

creativecornerstones@gmail.com | creativecornerstones.com/editing-2

Contact: email, website

Services: back-cover copy, copyediting, ghostwriting, manuscript evaluation, substantive/developmental editing, writing coach

Types of manuscripts: adult, articles, novels, scripts, teen/YA

Charges: hourly rate, word rate

Credentials/experience: "Caylah Coffeen will give you the tools you need to make your fantasy or sci-fi novel shine! Don't be one in millions of 3 star books. Caylah will give your story a health checkup (manuscript evaluation), help you write characters that make readers laugh and cry (developmental edit), and make your turns of phrase clear and compelling (line edit). A member of the Editorial Freelancers Association, she has several years of freelance editing experience and also works with Monster Ivy Publishing and Eschler Editing. She is the founder of Creative Cornerstones, a book publishing services company which guides authors at each stage in the publishing journey: writing, design, and sales. Our team will take your story from 'great,' and elevate it to unforgettable."

CREATIVE EDITORIAL SOLUTIONS | CLAUDIA VOLKMAN

cvolkman@mac.com

Contact: email

Services: back-cover copy, book-contract evaluation, copyediting, discussion questions for books, ghostwriting, indexing, manuscript evaluation, proofreading, substantive/developmental editing, writing coach

Types of manuscripts: adult, Bible studies, devotionals, gift books, nonfiction books, novels

Charges: flat fee, word rate

Credentials/experience: "I have more than 35 years of experience in the publishing world, most of it in Christian and Catholic trade publishing. Now as owner of Creative Editorial Solutions, I offer author coaching, developmental editing, and copyediting to entrepreneurs, coaches, speakers, and authors."

CREATIVE ENTERPRISES STUDIO | MARY HOLLINGSWORTH

1507 Shirley Way, Ste. A, Bedford, TX 76022-6737 | 817-312-7393

ACreativeShop@aol.com | *CreativeEnterprisesStudio.com*

Contact: email

Services: coauthoring, copyediting, discussion questions for books, ghostwriting, manuscript evaluation, proofreading, substantive/developmental editing

Types of manuscripts: adult, book proposals, curriculum, devotionals, easy readers, gift books, middle grade, nonfiction books, novels, picture books, short stories, teen/YA

Charges: custom

Credentials/experience: "CES is a publishing services company, hosting more than 150 top Christian publishing freelancers. We work with large, traditional Christian publishers on books by best-selling authors. We also produce custom, first-class books on a turnkey basis for independent authors, ministries, churches, and companies."

DENICA MCCALL EDITING

denica@denicamccall.com | denicamccall.com/copyediting-services

Contact: email, website form

Services: copyediting, manuscript evaluation, proofreading

Types of manuscripts: adult, articles, devotionals, easy readers, middle grade, nonfiction books, novels, poetry, short stories, teen/YA

Charges: flat fee, word rate

Credentials/experience: "I am a graduate of the trade books copyediting course and the copyediting mentorship course through Editorial Arts Academy. I have also been writing fiction and poetry for over sixteen years and am a current intern for Twenty Hills Publishing. I've been offering freelance editorial services since March 2023 and have worked with young adult and children's fiction."

DENISE HARMER

1695 Dorothea Ave., Fallbrook, CA 92028 | 760-505-0531
dharmeredits@gmail.com | www.deniseharmer.weebly.com

Contact: email

Services: copyediting, proofreading

Types of manuscripts: novels, short stories, teen/YA

Charges: word rate

Credentials/experience: "My editing experience began in 1990 with editing court transcripts. In 2010 I started copyediting fiction manuscripts, and I currently freelance for many Christian authors. I am a Gold member of the Christian PEN: Proofreaders and Editors Network, the Christian Editor Connection, ACFW (American Christian Fiction Writers), and ACES: The Society for Editing. I very much enjoy being a part of helping others reach their publication goals."

DESERT RAIN EDITING | GLENIECE LYTLE

PO Box 8163, Hualapai, AZ 86412 | 928-715-7125
desert.rain.editing@gmail.com | desertrainediting.com

Contact: email, website

Services: back-cover copy, copyediting, proofreading, substantive/developmental editing

Types of manuscripts: Bible studies, book proposals, business books, devotionals, memoir, nonfiction books

Charges: word rate

Credentials/experience: "For over six years, I have edited memoir, devotionals, Bible studies, Christian living, health and wellness, and business books from a Christian perspective for self-publishing authors. Every one of these projects taught me something new about editing and about life. I am a silver member of the Christian PEN: Proofreaders and Editors Network and use the current versions of the *Chicago Manual of Style, Merriam-Webster's Collegiate Dictionary,* and the *Christian Writer's Manual of Style.* I look forward to partnering with my clients, taking the vision they held for their manuscripts and nurturing their books to full bloom."

DONE WRITE EDITORIAL SERVICES | MARILYN A. ANDERSON

127 Sycamore Dr., Louisville, KY 40223 | 502-244-0751

shelle12@aol.com

Contact: email, phone

Services: copyediting, proofreading, substantive/developmental editing, writing coach

Types of manuscripts: academic, adult, articles, Bible studies, book proposals, children, curriculum, devotionals, gift books, nonfiction books, novels, poetry, query letters, short stories, technical material

Charges: hourly rate

Credentials/experience: "I am qualified by both bachelor's and master's degrees in English. I am also qualified because I have tutored more than thirty English/writing students since 2004. Most of them have been English-language learners. Also, I have taught English/writing as a classroom teacher. I have additionally conducted business-project editing for several corporations over the years. I currently copyedit for nonfiction and fiction independent writers, as well as for publishers and a few Christian ministries and am in the process of mentoring several other writers/editors. I copyedit both books (such as memoirs) and doctoral dissertations, theses, and other academic journal articles and papers.

"I offer a free sample edit, and my rates are both reasonable and competitive. I am a Gold charter member of The Christian PEN proofreaders and editors' network, along with a tested member of the Christian Editor Connection."

ECHO CREATIVE MEDIA | BRENDA NOEL
bnoel@thewordeditor.com | echocreativemedia.com

> **Contact:** email
> **Services:** copyediting, discussion questions for books, ghostwriting, proofreading, substantive/developmental editing
> **Types of manuscripts:** adult, articles, book proposals, curriculum, devotionals, easy readers, gift books, nonfiction books, picture books, short stories, teen/YA
> **Charges:** flat fee, hourly rate
> **Credentials/experience:** "Sixteen years of experience in the Christian publishing industry."

EDIT RESOURCE, LLC | ERIC STANFORD
19265 Lincoln Green Ln., Monument, CO 80132 | 719-290-0757
info@editresource.com | www.editresource.com

> **Contact:** email
> **Services:** back-cover copy, book proposals, coauthoring, copyediting, discussion questions for books, ghostwriting, indexing, manuscript evaluation, proofreading, substantive/developmental editing, writing coach
> **Types of manuscripts:** adult, Bible studies, book proposals, curriculum, devotionals, middle grade, nonfiction books, novels, query letters, teen/YA
> **Charges:** depends on the service
> **Credentials/experience:** "Owners Eric and Elisa have a combined 40 years of experience and have worked with numerous bestselling authors and books. They also represent a team of other top writing and editing professionals."

EDIT WITH CLAIRE | CLAIRE TUCKER
PO Box 3072, Ladysmith, KwaZulu Natal 3370, South Africa
editor@editwithclaire.com | www.editwithclaire.com

> **Contact:** email
> **Services:** back-cover copy, copyediting, proofreading
> **Types of manuscripts:** adult, devotionals, nonfiction books, novels, short stories
> **Charges:** hourly rate, word rate
> **Credentials/experience:** "My aim with editing is to work with authors to achieve excellence, and I am committed to education and encouragement in my edits. Some of my editing strengths are

developing author and character voice and heightening tension. I am experienced with the *Chicago Manual of Style,* the *Christian Writers Manual of Style,* and *New Hart's Rules* (UK style). Books I've edited include Southern fiction, contemporary fiction, suspense, fantasy, science fiction, devotionals, and Christian nonfiction for indie authors and authors pursuing traditional publishing."

EDITING BY LUCY | LUCY CRABTREE

editingbylucy@gmail.com | editingbylucy.com

Contact: email, website
Services: copyediting, discussion questions for books, manuscript evaluation, proofreading, substantive/developmental editing
Types of manuscripts: academic, adult, articles, Bible studies, devotionals, gift books, nonfiction books, novels, teen/YA
Charges: word rate
Credentials/experience: "I have been a communications professional since 2007—at a national syndicate, a public university, and even an art museum. So when I say I've edited a little bit of everything ... I do mean everything! Crossword puzzles, faculty manuscripts, advice columns, political commentaries, comic strips, university websites, grant proposals, promotional copy—you name it, I've (probably) read it."

EDITING GALLERY, LLC | CAROL L. CRAIG

2622 Willona Dr., Eugene, OR 97408 | 541-735-1834
kf7orchid@gmail.com | www.editinggallery.com

Contact: email
Services: back-cover copy, coauthoring, copyediting, manuscript evaluation, substantive/developmental editing, writing coach
Types of manuscripts: adult, book proposals, easy readers, middle grade, novels, query letters, teen/YA
Charges: hourly rate
Credentials/experience: "University of Oregon, English Major, 20+ years of editing for well-known Christian Authors."

eDITMORE EDITORIAL SERVICES | TAMMY DITMORE

501-I S. Reino Rd. #194, Newbury Park, CA 91320 | 805-630-6809
tammy@editmore.com | www.editmore.com

Contact: email

Services: copyediting, discussion questions for books, manuscript evaluation, proofreading, substantive/developmental editing, writing coach

Types of manuscripts: academic, adult, articles, Bible studies, curriculum, devotionals, gift books, nonfiction books, teen/YA

Charges: hourly rate

Credentials/experience: "Tammy Ditmore offers editing, proofreading, and coaching services to publishers, authors, businesses, organizations, and scholars. Two of her Christian authors recently won Benjamin Franklin awards from the Independent Book Publishers Association, and one of those authors has worked with Tammy while publishing dozens of articles in national and international periodicals and websites. An editor for more than 40 years, Tammy specializes in nonfiction, with an emphasis on Christian and spiritual topics, personal histories, current events, and material on aging and Alzheimer's disease."

EDITOR WORLD: EDITING AND PROOFREADING SERVICES | PATTI FISHER

11815 Fountain Way, Ste. 300, Newport News, VA 23606 | 614-500-3348

info@editorworld.com | *www.editorworld.com*

Contact: website

Services: copyediting, proofreading

Types of manuscripts: academic, adult, articles, Bible studies, board/picture books, book proposals, curriculum, devotionals, easy readers, gift books, middle grade, nonfiction books, novels, poetry, query letters, scripts, short stories, technical material, teen/YA

Charges: word rate

Credentials/experience: "We are a U.S.-based editing and proofreading services company. All editors at Editor World are native English speakers who have passed a stringent test of their editing and proofreading skills. We have expert editors available 24/7 to help you improve your writing."

ELOQUENT EDITS | DENISE ROEPER

1025 Third St., Port Orange, FL 32129 | 386-290-4117

denise.eloquentedits@gmail.com | *www.eloquentedits.com*

Contact: email

Services: copyediting, proofreading

Types of manuscripts: easy readers, middle grade, novels, short stories, teen/YA

Charges: word rate
Credentials/experience: "Fiction is my passion. I love to read it. I love to edit it. My clients will receive my full attention when I work on their creation."

EXEGETICA PUBLISHING | CATHY CONE

312 Greenwich #112, Lee's Summit, MO 64082

editor@exegeticapublishing.com | exegeticapublishing.com/editing

Contact: website
Services: copyediting, manuscript evaluation, proofreading, substantive/developmental editing
Types of manuscripts: academic, articles, Bible studies, curriculum, devotionals, nonfiction books
Charges: page rate
Credentials/experience: "Exegetica editorial staff have more than 30 years editing experience with diverse media and publishers."

EXTRA INK EDITS | MEGAN EASLEY-WALSH

Ireland

Megan@ExtraInkEdits.com | www.ExtraInkEdits.com

Contact: email
Services: back-cover copy, copyediting, discussion questions for books, manuscript evaluation, proofreading, substantive/developmental editing, writing coach
Types of manuscripts: academic, adult, articles, Bible studies, devotionals, easy readers, gift books, middle grade, nonfiction books, novels, picture books, poetry, query letters, short stories, teen/YA
Charges: flat fee, word rate
Credentials/experience: "Megan Easley-Walsh, PhD History, is an author of historical fiction, a researcher, and a writing consultant and editor at Extra Ink Edits. She is an award-winning writer and has taught college writing in the UNESCO literature city of Dublin, Ireland. She is a dual American and Irish citizen and lives in Ireland with her Irish husband. Megan is a Professional Member of the Irish Writers' Centre, a Full Member of the Irish Writers' Union, a member of the Historical Novel Society, a Full Member of ACES: The Society for Editing, a member of the Irish Association of Professional Historians, and a member of the American Historical Association. Additionally, she was shortlisted for the 2021 Hammond House International Literary Prize in Poetry."

FAITH EDITORIAL SERVICES | REBECCA FAITH

PO Box 184, Novelty, OH 44072 | 216-906-0205

rebecca@faitheditorial.com | *www.faitheditorial.com*

Contact: email, website

Services: copyediting, manuscript evaluation, proofreading

Types of manuscripts: academic, adult, articles, Bible studies, book proposals, curriculum, devotionals, medical, nonfiction books, technical material

Charges: hourly rate

Credentials/experience: "My experience editing in the Christian market includes six years as managing editor for a Christian nonprofit, another eight years editing/transcribing content for a global Christian ministry, and copyediting nonfiction Christian books and devotionals. In addition I have eleven years experience editing technical, engineering, medical, and educational material for university presses, journal publishers, and independent clients. I hold membership in the EFA, the Christian PEN (Gold), and the Christian Editor Connection."

FAITHWORKS EDITORIAL & WRITING, INC. | NANETTE THORSEN SNIPES

PO Box 1596, Buford, GA 30518 | 770-945-3093

nsnipes@bellsouth.net | *www.faithworkseditorial.com*

Contact: email, website

Services: copyediting, manuscript evaluation, proofreading, work-for-hire projects

Types of manuscripts: adult, articles, business materials, devotionals, easy readers, gift books, memoir, middle grade, nonfiction books, picture books, poetry, query letters, short stories

Charges: hourly rate, page rate

Credentials/experience: "Member: The Christian PEN (Proofreaders & Editors Network), Christian Editor Connection, Christian Editor Network. Proofreader for corporate newsletters, thirteen years. Published writer for more than twenty-five years. Published hundreds of articles in magazines and stories in more than sixty compilation books, including Guideposts, B&H, Regal, and Integrity. Twelve years of editorial experience in both adult and children's short fiction and books, memoirs, short stories, devotions, articles, business. Rates are generally by page but, under specific circumstances, by the hour. Editorial clients have published with such houses as Zondervan, Tyndale, and Revell."

FINAL TOUCH PROOFREADING & EDITING | HEIDI MANN

mann.heidi@gmail.com | www.FinalTouchProofreadingAndEditing.com

Contact: email

Services: copyediting, proofreading

Types of manuscripts: devotionals, middle grade, nonfiction books, picture books, teen/YA

Charges: flat fee, hourly rate

Credentials/experience: "In addition to my editing expertise, I bring experience as a Lutheran pastor and seminary training in Bible and theology."

THE FOREWORD COLLECTIVE | MOLLY HODGIN

1726 Charity Dr., Brentwood, TN 37027 | 615-497-4322

molly.hodgin@theforewordcollective.com | www.theforewordcollective.com

Contact: email, website

Services: back-cover copy, book-contract evaluation, coauthoring, discussion questions for books, ghostwriting, manuscript evaluation, substantive/developmental editing, writing coach

Types of manuscripts: adult, apps, board/picture books, book proposals, cookbooks, devotionals, easy readers, gift books, middle grade, nonfiction books, novels, query letters, style books, teen/YA

Charges: flat fee, hourly rate

Credentials/experience: "Molly Hodgin has over twenty years of publishing experience. She served as the Associate Publisher for the Specialty Division of HarperCollins Christian Publishing, the Editorial Director for Zondervan Gift, Thomas Nelson Gift Books, Tommy Nelson Kids Books, and The Thomas Nelson New Media Division, a Senior Editor for Scholastic Inc. and an editor for Penguin Young Readers Group. Molly has extensive experience in acquiring and editing gift books, cookbooks, style books, devotionals, trade nonfiction books, YA and middle grade fiction, and children's picture books and board books. Her specialty is helping authors craft a book proposal that will stand out to land them an agent or publishing deal. She has also written, ghost written, and co-authored over seventy-five books.

"If Molly isn't the right fit for your book, well, The Foreword Collective also employs a number of highly experienced industry professionals from all areas of Christian publishing. Whether you are an experienced author looking for editorial help or brand building or a new author who wants to make the leap into traditional publishing, The Foreword Collective is here to help!"

FRENCH AND ENGLISH COMMUNICATION SERVICES |
DIANE GOULLARD

3104 E. Camelback Rd., PMB 124, Phoenix, AZ 85016-4502 | 602-870-1000

RequestFAECS2008@cox.net | *frenchandenglish.com*

> **Contact:** email, phone, website
> **Services:** copyediting, English to French translation, French to English translation, proofreading
> **Types of manuscripts:** academic, adult, articles, Bible studies, book proposals, curriculum, devotionals, easy readers, gift books, middle grade, nonfiction books, novels, poetry, query letters, scripts, short stories, technical material, teen/YA
> **Charges:** custom, flat fee, hourly rate, page rate, word rate
> **Credentials/experience:** "Experience + academic + occupational training. MA, BA, Certificates, Experience, Skills."

GEMMA WRITING SERVICES | JESSICA BURCHFIELD

5527 110th Ave. N, M104, Pinellas Park, FL 33782 | 727-418-9906

jelainek@gmail.com

> **Contact:** email
> **Services:** articles, back-cover copy, coauthoring, copyediting, ghostwriting, manuscript evaluation, proofreading
> **Types of manuscripts:** articles, Bible studies, curriculum, devotionals, easy readers, gift books, novels, scripts, short stories
> **Charges:** hourly rate
> **Credentials/experience:** "Jessica is a high school theatre and photography teacher with over 20 years of experience in education. She has written curriculum for Accelerated Christian Education, as well as Clearwater Christian College. She was a ghostwriter for a prominent family with a regular column in *TwoTen Magazine* and her articles can be found on their website. She works with teen through adult writers of Christ-centered content for magazines, websites, and publication."

GRACE BRIDGES

4/11 Hall Rd., Glenfield, Auckland 0629, New Zealand | 64224722301

www.gracebridges.kiwi/hire-me

> **Contact:** website
> **Services:** copyediting, proofreading, substantive/developmental editing, writing coach
> **Types of manuscripts:** middle grade, nonfiction books, novels, short

stories, teen/YA
Charges: word rate
Credentials/experience: Listed at *gracebridges.kiwi/hire-me/
experience.html.*

THE GRAMMAR QUEEN | RENEE GARRICK
1503 S. Park St., Red Wing, MN 55066 | 651-327-9686
renee@thegrammarqueen.net | TheGrammarQueen.net

Contact: email
Services: copyediting, proofreading, substantive/developmental
editing
Types of manuscripts: Bible studies, devotionals, memoir, nonfiction
books
Charges: hourly rate
Credentials/experience: "Since 2014 I've edited 7 books and
proofed 3 more for TRISTAN Publishing in Minneapolis, MN; 3 of
the editing projects have won a total of 4 awards. During the same
time period, I've also edited for more than a dozen self-publishing
authors and personal historians, along with providing services for
4 books for one 'boutique' publisher."

HANEMANN EDITORIAL | NATALIE HANEMANN
1865 Gunner Ln., Chapel Hill, TN 37034
nathanemann@gmail.com | www.nataliehanemann.com

Contact: website
Services: coauthoring, ghostwriting, substantive/developmental
editing, writing coach
Types of manuscripts: academic, nonfiction books, novels
Charges: custom
Credentials/experience: "After working in publishing for 20 years
doing many forms of editing, I've honed my skillset to co-authoring,
ghostwriting, and coaching. Will do developmental edits if it's a
challenging manuscript that needs massive work (I'm a sucker
for problem-solving!). Preferred categories include Catholic
or Orthodox, academic (i.e. books with lots of footnotes and
citations), social justice (poverty, disenfranchised people groups)
and novels (adventure, general, historical, women's, biblical). Not
accepting projects that are 'light reads' or strictly 'entertaining.'
I like books that are well-thought out with deep messages that
promote social change ... or change of heart."

HEATHER KLEINSCHMIDT

hkleinschmidt@pm.me | tiny.cc/christian-ghost

Contact: email

Services: back-cover copy, coauthoring, copyediting, discussion questions for books, ghostwriting, indexing, manuscript evaluation, proofreading, substantive/developmental editing, writing coach

Types of manuscripts: academic, adult, articles, curriculum, nonfiction books, technical material

Charges: flat fee, word rate

Credentials/experience: "For a 10% discount, use 'CWMG' in your email subject line (or mention that this is where you found me)! Nonfiction: I specialize in emotionally nuanced or complicated topics—or issues that are just generally difficult to articulate. Genres I work in include Health & Wellness, Psychology & Mental Health, Business & Finance. Academic: I've worked with universities and researchers to create high-impact curricula and research communications for both general and academic audiences."

HEATHER PUBOLS

heather.pubols@gmail.com | heatherpubols.com/editing-services

Contact: email, website

Services: copyediting, substantive/developmental editing

Types of manuscripts: academic, articles, Bible studies, nonfiction books, technical material

Charges: hourly rate

Credentials/experience: "More than 20 years of editorial experience working in corporate communications for Christian missions organizations. Freelance editor since 2018."

HENRY MCLAUGHLIN

921 Silver Streak Dr., Saginaw, TX 76131 | 817-703-9875

henry@henrymclaughlin.org | www.henrymclaughlin.org

Contact: email

Services: back-cover copy, coauthoring, copyediting, discussion questions for books, ghostwriting, manuscript evaluation, proofreading, substantive/developmental editing, writing coach

Types of manuscripts: adult, book proposals, novels, short stories

Charges: page rate

Credentials/experience: "Over 20 years as a novelist, coach/mentor, editor, teacher. Prize winning novelist. Successful ghostwriter.

Teaching the craft at conferences, workshops, writers groups. Coaching and editing several clients to publication."

HONEST EDITING | WILLIAM CARMICHAEL
PO Box 2437, Sisters, OR 97759
www.honestediting.com
> **Contact:** website
> **Services:** copyediting, manuscript evaluation, proposal creation, substantive/developmental editing
> **Types of manuscripts:** academic, adult, Bible studies, book proposals, devotionals, easy readers, gift books, middle grade, nonfiction books, novels, query letters, teen/YA
> **Charges:** flat fee
> **Credentials/experience:** "A professional editor with years of experience in Christian editing is assigned."

INKSNATCHER | SALLY HANAN
429 S. Avenue C, Elgin, TX 78621 | 512-265-6403
bookhelp@inksnatcher.com | inksnatcher.com
> **Contact:** email, website
> **Services:** back-cover copy, coauthoring, copyediting, discussion questions for books, ghostwriting, manuscript evaluation, proofreading, substantive/developmental editing
> **Types of manuscripts:** adult, devotionals, nonfiction books, novels
> **Charges:** custom
> **Credentials/experience:** "A full-service provider for self-publishing authors, Inksnatcher is a vetted and verified member of the Alliance of Independent Authors, the Christian Editor Connection, and Reedsy. Sally is also a self-published author of five books in multiple genres and coauthor of two."

THE INKY BOOKWYRM | GINA KAMMER
1054 Deer Ridge Ct. NW, Lonsdale, MN 55046 | 507-381-1887
ginakammer@inkybookwyrm.com | www.inkybookwyrm.com
> **Contact:** website
> **Services:** copyediting, manuscript evaluation, proofreading, query/submissions coaching, substantive/developmental editing, writing coach
> **Types of manuscripts:** adult, easy readers, middle grade, novels, query letters, teen/YA

Charges: monthly fee, word rate

Credentials/experience: "Gina Kammer specializes in editing and book coaching for science fiction and fantasy. She is a former Capstone editor and Bethany Lutheran College writing/journalism instructor with 10+ years of experience in fiction and children's nonfiction. Using brain science hacks, hoarded craft knowledge, and solution-based direction, this book dragon helps science-fiction and fantasy authors get their stories—whether on the page or still in their heads—ready to enchant their readers."

INSPIRATION FOR WRITERS, INC. | SANDY TRITT

1527 18th St., Parkersburg, WV 26101 | 304-428-1218

IFWeditors@gmail.com | *Inspirationforwriters.com/editorial-services*

Contact: email

Services: copyediting, ghostwriting, manuscript evaluation, proofreading, substantive/developmental editing, writing coach

Types of manuscripts: academic, adult, articles, Bible studies, book proposals, devotionals, gift books, memoir, middle grade, nonfiction books, novels, query letters, short stories, teen/YA

Charges: word rate

Credentials/experience: "Since 1998, Inspiration for Writers has provided editing and writing services for hundreds of clients. Our editors are all published writers (including *NY Times* bestselling) and are active in the writing world. We believe in treating our clients with dignity and honesty—and 90% of our business is repeat business. We love our clients and they love us."

JAMI'S WORDS | JAMI BENNINGTON

jami@jamiswords.com | *jamiswords.com*

Contact: email

Services: copyediting, manuscript evaluation, proofreading

Types of manuscripts: adult, articles, Bible studies, curriculum, devotionals, nonfiction books, novels, short stories, teen/YA

Charges: word rate

Credentials/experience: "After spending over twenty years as a teacher of language arts, Jami launched her editing business in 2017. She is a graduate of UC San Diego's copyediting certificate program, is a fan of continuing education, and is a member of The Christian PEN."

JAMIE CHAVEZ

jamie.chavez@gmail.com

> **Contact:** email
> **Services:** copyediting, substantive/developmental editing
> **Types of manuscripts:** nonfiction books, novels
> **Charges:** flat fee
> **Credentials/experience:** "Jamie Chavez worked for more than ten years in the Christian publishing industry (and more than twenty as a freelance copywriter) before she found her niche as an independent writer and editor in 2004. Specializing in content and line/copy editing, Chavez counts many national publishing houses as clients, many authors and agents as friends, and spends her days in the swanky second-floor office in the pink house with the green door making good books better."

JEANETTE GARDNER LITTLETON, PUBLICATION SERVICES

3706 N.E. Shady Lane Dr., Gladstone, MO 64119-1958 | 816-459-8016
jeanettedl@earthlink.net | *www.linkedin.com/in/jeanette-littleton-b1b790101*

> **Contact:** email
> **Services:** back-cover copy, book-contract evaluation, copyediting, discussion questions for books, indexing, manuscript evaluation, proofreading, substantive/developmental editing
> **Types of manuscripts:** adult, articles, Bible studies, book proposals, curriculum, devotionals, gift books, nonfiction books, novels, query letters, short stories, technical material, teen/YA
> **Charges:** flat fee, hourly rate, page rate
> **Credentials/experience:** "I've been a full-time editor and writer for more than thirty years for a variety of publishers. I've written five thousand articles and edited thousands of articles and dozens of books. Please see my profile at LinkedIn."

JEANETTE HANSCOME

jeanette@jeanettehanscome.com | *jeanettehanscome.com/services-for-writers*

> **Contact:** email, website
> **Services:** writing coach
> **Types of manuscripts:** devotionals, memoir, novels
> **Charges:** custom, hourly rate
> **Credentials/experience:** "Jeanette is a multi-published author with almost thirty years of writing experience. She has written, edited, and coached authors in a variety of genres and enjoys helping writers grow."

JENNIFER EDWARDS COMMUNICATIONS

2839 Sleeping Bear Rd., Montrose, CO 81401 | 916-768-4207

mail.jennifer.edwards@gmail.com | *www.jedwardsediting.net*

Contact: email

Services: back-cover copy, coauthoring, copyediting, manuscript evaluation, substantive/developmental editing, writing coach

Types of manuscripts: adult, articles, Bible studies, book proposals, curriculum, devotionals, memoir, nonfiction books, short stories

Charges: hourly rate

Credentials/experience: "Jennifer Edwards is a professional editor, author coach, and self-publishing consultant serving Christian nonfiction authors and publishers. She has worked with numerous authors and Christian publishers over the past ten years, including Penguin Random House, Lexham Press, Redemption Press, PTLB Publishing, BMH Books, Compel/She Speaks, and more. Her master's degree in Biblical and Theological Studies from Western Seminary has proven invaluable in helping Christian authors with their manuscripts by providing a critical eye for content, a thorough understanding of Scripture, and insightful theological thinking."

JENNIFER WESTBROOK

14030 Connecticut Ave. #6813, Silver Spring, MD 20916

support@jenwestwriting.com | *www.jenwestwriting.com/book-marketing*

Contact: email

Services: back-cover copy

Types of manuscripts: Bible studies, devotionals, nonfiction books, novels

Charges: flat fee

Credentials/experience: "As a copywriter with over 20 years of experience, I write back cover copy for book authors that motivates readers to buy. I do this by crafting copy that taps into your readers' needs and desires so they'll instantly connect with your book."

JHWRITING+ | NICOLE HAYES

jhwritingplus@yahoo.com | *www.jhwritingplus.com*

Contact: email, website

Services: coauthoring, copyediting, discussion questions for books, ghostwriting, manuscript evaluation, proofreading, substantive/developmental editing, writing coach

Types of manuscripts: adult, articles, curriculum, devotionals, gift books, nonfiction books, novels, poetry, short stories, technical material, teen/YA

Charges: flat fee, word rate

Credentials/experience: "Bachelor's degree in English; PhD in education. Although I do most writing, editing, and proofreading projects, my niche is creative nonfiction (engaging, dramatic, factual prose). I have been writing and editing for more than twenty-five years."

JK PAYLEITNER & ASSOCIATES | JAY PAYLEITNER

629 N. Tyler Rd., Saint Charles, IL 60174 | 630-377-7899

jaypayleitner@me.com | www.jaypayleitner.com

Contact: email, phone

Services: back-cover copy, coauthoring, ghostwriting

Types of manuscripts: adult, book proposals, gift books, nonfiction books, scripts

Charges: flat fee

Credentials/experience: "Author of 38 books. Thousands of radio scripts. National speaker. Two decades as an advertising copywriter. Keynote for Writer's Conferences: "Fourteen Book Writing Secrets I Don't Want to Tell You" (and other talks on creativity and storytelling). I can write anything."

JOHN D. LOEWEN EDITING SERVICE | JOHN DAVID LOEWEN

12720 Robindale Dr., Rockville, MD 20853 | 202-536-7688

authorjohndloewen@gmail.com

Contact: email, phone

Services: back-cover copy, book-contract evaluation, coauthoring, copyediting, discussion questions for books, ghostwriting, manuscript evaluation, proofreading, substantive/developmental editing, writing coach

Types of manuscripts: academic, adult, articles, Bible studies, book proposals, curriculum, devotionals, easy readers, gift books, middle grade, nonfiction books, novels, poetry, scripts, short stories, technical material, teen/YA

Charges: custom, flat fee, hourly rate, word rate

Credentials/experience: "As a *Cum Laude* graduate in both Geography and Civil Engineering and with a nomination to the Phi Beta Kappa Honor Society, John cut his teeth writing in the upper echelons of academia. Later on, after being born-again, God gave John an anointing to write a wide variety of genres, which he has since used to transition into the world of editing. As the editor of more than twenty published books, including the award winning, *Be Made Whole,* (Kathy

Armstrong, Xulon Press, 2007), John has also authored two of his own published books (*Breakthrough and Breakout!* and *The Battle*)."

JOHN SLOAN, LLC
830 Grey Eagle Cir. N, Colorado Springs, CO 80919 | 719-888-0365
jsjohnsloan@gmail.com | sloanhinds.com
Contact: email
Services: coauthoring, substantive/developmental editing, writing coach
Types of manuscripts: academic, adult, Bible studies, devotionals, easy readers, gift books, nonfiction books, short stories, teen/YA
Charges: flat fee, hourly rate, word rate
Credentials/experience: "I have worked in publishing and editorial roles for 40 years, with Multnomah Press and HarperCollins Christian Publishing, Zondervan. I am offering my services for freelance work in the areas of book development, collaboration, writer coaching, book doctoring, macro editing, content editing. I have worked with a broad spectrum of book and author types: I have edited the literary and general market works of authors like Philip Yancey and Frederick Buechner; the popular issues volumes of writers like Chuck Colson; the high visibility authors like Lee Strobel and Ben Carson; the broader market authors and pastors like John Ortberg and Mark Batterson; and I've worked in the area of the popular academic works."

JOT OR TITTLE EDITORIAL SERVICES | SAMUEL RYAN KELLY
sam@jotortittle.com | jotortittle.com
Contact: email
Services: copyediting, manuscript evaluation, proofreading, substantive/developmental editing, writing coach
Types of manuscripts: academic, adult, articles, Bible studies, devotionals, nonfiction books, novels, short stories
Charges: hourly rate
Credentials/experience: "Sam has a double BA in English and biblical and religious studies and an MA in theology. He specializes in academic writing and has a background in biblical languages, but he likes to bring his expertise to a variety of projects. In addition to his freelance work, Sam does research for pastors and churches at Docent Research Group and serves as an associate editor with Wordsmith Writing Coaches."

JOY MEDIA | JULIE-ALLYSON IERON
PO Box 413, Mt. Prospect, IL 60056

j-a@joymediaservices.com | www.joymediaservices.com

Contact: email

Services: back-cover copy, coauthoring, copyediting, discussion questions for books, ghostwriting, manuscript evaluation, substantive/developmental editing, writing coach

Types of manuscripts: adult, articles, Bible studies, book proposals, devotionals, gift books, nonfiction books, novels, query letters, teen/YA

Charges: hourly rate

Credentials/experience: "Julie was a mentor/master craftsman with the Jerry B. Jenkins Christian Writers Guild. She mentored more than 100 professional writers through Guild studies. Her students reached their writing goals of signing publishing contracts and seeing articles published. Julie was lead writer for the Guild's Writing Essentials and Apprentice curriculum in 2010. She works with late-teen through senior-adult writers of Christ-centered materials."

JUDITH ROBL
PO Box 802, Lyons, KS 67554 | 620-257-3143

jrlight620@yahoo.com | www.judithrobl.com/editing-2

Contact: email

Services: back-cover copy, copyediting, discussion questions for books, proofreading, writing coach

Types of manuscripts: adult, Bible studies, devotionals, gift books, novels, query letters, short stories

Charges: custom

Credentials/experience: "Educated as a secondary English teacher decades ago, I've edited for people for many years. My first major accomplishment in editing was published in 2010. I use *The Chicago Manual of Style* unless another style guide is required. A sample edit lets me see if the author and I are a good fit and allows me to determine the appropriate fee. While perfection in writing is the goal, it must be done with absolute respect for the author's voice."

KAREN APPOLD
kappold@msn.com

Contact: email

Services: copyediting, proofreading

Types of manuscripts: academic, articles, curriculum

Charges: flat fee, hourly rate, word rate

Credentials/experience: "I am an award-winning journalist with a BA from Penn State University in English (Writing). I have more than 25 years of professional editorial experience. I mainly write on healthcare/medical and retail, but welcome Christian-themed work."

KATHY IDE WRITER SERVICES

Kathy@KathyIde.com | www.KathyIde.com

Contact: email

Services: coauthoring, copyediting, ghostwriting, manuscript evaluation, proofreading, substantive/developmental editing, writing coach

Types of manuscripts: adult, articles, Bible studies, book proposals, curriculum, devotionals, gift books, nonfiction books, novels, query letters, screenplays, scripts, short stories, technical material, teen/YA

Charges: hourly rate

Credentials/experience: "Kathy Ide is the author of *Proofreading Secrets of Best-Selling Authors* and *Editing Secrets of Best-Selling Authors* and the editor/compiler of the Fiction Lover's Devotional series. She's been a professional freelance editor for 20+ years, and in 2022 started proofreading screenplays for Pinnacle Peak/PureFlix. Kathy owns Christian Editor Network, parent organization to the four divisions she founded: The Christian PEN: Proofreaders and Editors Network, The PEN Institute, PENCON, and Christian Editor Connection. CEN sponsors the Editors' Choice Award."

KATIE PHILLIPS CREATIVE SERVICES

1500 E. Tall Tree Rd. #6206, Derby, KS 67037-6033 | 316-293-9202

katie@katiephillipscreative.com | www.katiephillipscreative.com

Contact: email

Services: back-cover copy, branding, copyediting, substantive/developmental editing, writing coach

Types of manuscripts: adult, book proposals, middle grade, novels, query letters, short stories, teen/YA

Charges: hourly rate, word rate

Credentials/experience: "Edited six award-finalist novels in multiple categories, including the winners of the Realm Award for Book of the Year, Reader's Choice, and Fantasy. Instructor for The Author Conservatory, run by bestselling and award-winning authors Brett Harris and Kara Swanson. Over ten years industry experience writing and editing both fiction and non-fiction. Bachelor of Arts in Journalism."

KIM PETERSON

1114 Buxton Dr., Knoxville, KY 37922

petersk.ktp@gmail.com | *naturewalkwithgod.wordpress.com/about-kim*

Contact: email

Services: back-cover copy, copyediting, create brochures and newsletters, discussion questions for books, manuscript evaluation, proofreading, substantive/developmental editing, write curriculum/lesson plans, writing coach

Types of manuscripts: academic, adult, articles, Bible studies, blog posts, book proposals, curriculum, devotionals, easy readers, gift books, middle grade, nonfiction books, novels, poetry, query letters, short stories, technical material, teen/YA

Charges: hourly rate

Credentials/experience: "College writing instructor (30+ years), freelance writer (40+ years), freelance editor (15 years), conference speaker (16 years), contest judge (11 years), and former agent's fiction reader (9 years). MA in print communication."

KRISTEN STIEFFEL

kristen@kristenstieffel.com | *www.kristenstieffel.com*

Contact: email

Services: coauthoring, copyediting, ghostwriting, manuscript evaluation, proofreading, substantive/developmental editing, writing coach

Types of manuscripts: novels, short stories, teen/YA

Charges: flat fee, word rate

Credentials/experience: "Kristen Stieffel specializes in Sci-Fi and Fantasy and has edited more than 80 books for more than 60 clients in her 20-plus years as a freelancer. Kristen is also a writing instructor—teaching is her primary gift, so she approaches editing as an opportunity to educate. Her writing includes the fantasy novel *Alara's Call* and a steampunk book, *Tales of the Phoenix.*"

LEE WARREN COMMUNICATIONS

leewarrenjr@outlook.com | *www.leewarren.info/editing*

Contact: email

Services: copyediting, proofreading

Types of manuscripts: adult, articles, devotionals, gift books, nonfiction books, novels, short stories

Charges: word rate

Credentials/experience: "Lee Warren has twenty-plus years of experience in the Christian publishing industry (both traditional and indie publishing) and has been a contract editor for various publishers. He's also written 19 books (a mixture of nonfiction and fiction), as well as worked as a freelance journalist."

LESLIE L. MCKEE EDITING

lmckeeediting@gmail.com | lmckeeediting.wixsite.com/lmckeeediting

Contact: email

Services: back-cover copy, copyediting, discussion questions for books, proofreading, substantive/developmental editing

Types of manuscripts: adult, Bible studies, devotionals, easy readers, middle grade, nonfiction books, novels, poetry, short stories, teen/YA

Charges: flat fee, page rate, word rate

Credentials/experience: "Freelance editor and proofreader with various publishing houses (large and small) since 2012. I work with traditionally published and self-published/indie authors. I'm a member of The Christian PEN and American Christian Fiction Writers. See my website for details on services offered, as well as testimonials and a portfolio."

LESLIE SANTAMARIA

PO Box 195861, Winter Springs, FL 32719 | 407-497-5365

www.lesliesantamaria.com

Contact: website

Services: copyediting, manuscript evaluation, proofreading, substantive/developmental editing, writing coach

Types of manuscripts: easy readers, middle grade, teen/YA

Charges: page rate

Credentials/experience: "Leslie Santamaria specializes in children's literature. With over 200 pieces published in periodicals, including *Highlights for Children, Pockets,* and *Spider,* and a picture book, Leslie earned a Master of Fine Arts in Creative Writing for Children from Spalding University. A longtime freelance editor for publishers, businesses, ministries, and individuals, she is a frequent contest judge and workshop presenter. Leslie has coached many writers to publication and would love to help you, too."

LIBBY GONTARZ

libbygontarz@gmail.com | libbygontarz.com

Contact: email, phone

Services: copyediting, substantive/developmental editing

Types of manuscripts: adult, articles, Bible studies, curriculum, devotionals, nonfiction books

Charges: custom, page rate, word rate

Credentials/experience: "After a career of teaching and nationwide educational training, I accepted a curriculum development position at an educational publishing company. Writing lessons and assessments gradually led into editing. Since 2015, I have focused on Christian nonfiction, editing for various publishers and individuals. Earned 2022 Excellence in Editing award for copyediting winning book, *On Wings Like Eagles*. Worked on editing team for two other award-winning books—a devotional and a business book. Your project deserves professional editing!"

LIFE LAUNCH ME | JANE RUBIETTA

9030 Federal Ct., Des Plaines, IL 60016 | 847-363-6364

jane@lifelaunchme.com | www.LifeLaunchMe.com

Contact: email, phone

Services: coauthoring, copyediting, discussion questions for books, ghostwriting, manuscript evaluation, proofreading, substantive/ developmental editing, writing coach

Types of manuscripts: adult, articles, book proposals, devotionals, nonfiction books, novels, query letters

Charges: hourly rate

Credentials/experience: "The author of 21 books and hundreds of articles and devotionals, Jane has helped launch many writing careers as a writing coach and editor. Her writing savvy and marketing background help writers find their own voices and progress in their callings. She can turn one idea into 100 articles and numerous books."

LIGHTHOUSE EDITING | DR. LON ACKELSON

13326 Community Rd. #11, Poway, CA 92064 | 858-748-9258

Isaiah68la@sbcglobal.net | lighthouseedit.com

Contact: website

Services: back-cover copy, book-contract evaluation, coauthoring, copyediting, ghostwriting, manuscript evaluation, substantive/ developmental editing

Types of manuscripts: adult, Bible studies, book proposals, curriculum, devotionals, nonfiction books, query letters

Charges: flat fee, hourly rate, page rate

Credentials/experience: "A professional editor for thirty-four years and a published writer for forty years."

LIGHTNING EDITING SERVICES | DENISE LOOCK
699 Golf Course Rd., Waynesville, NC 28786 | 908-868-5854
denise@lightningeditingservices.com | *www.lightningeditingservices.com*

Contact: email
Services: coauthoring, copyediting, discussion questions for books, ghostwriting, manuscript evaluation, proofreading, substantive/developmental editing
Types of manuscripts: adult, articles, Bible studies, book proposals, devotionals, nonfiction books, teen/YA
Charges: flat fee, hourly rate
Credentials/experience: "Former high school English teacher and college instructor Denise Loock is a general editor for Iron Stream Media and also accepts freelance projects. With thirty years of experience in the academic world coupled with ten years in the publishing industry, she helps writers produce books that attract publishers and engage readers."

LISA BARTELT
lmbartelt@gmail.com | *lisabartelt.com/the-work*

Contact: website
Services: back-cover copy, coauthoring, copyediting, manuscript evaluation, proofreading
Types of manuscripts: nonfiction books, novels
Charges: hourly rate
Credentials/experience: "20 years of experience including 8 years as a newspaper editor/reporter, 4 years as a contest judge for a well-known writing organization, ACFW contest judging, 2 co-authored books, avid reader of all kinds of books, middle school reading teacher's aide."

LISSA HALLS JOHNSON EDITORIAL
13926 Double Girth Ct., Matthews, NC 28105 | 479-220-8662
lissahallsjohnson@gmail.com | *lissahallsjohnson.com*

Contact: email, website
Services: manuscript evaluation, substantive/developmental editing, writing coach
Types of manuscripts: memoir, novels, teen/YA

Charges: hourly rate

Credentials/experience: "Editor for fiction, nonfiction narrative, memoir for 20+ years. Some writers have received Christy Award finalist awards or nominations, been on bestselling lists, received *Publishers Weekly* starred reviews."

LOGOS WORD DESIGNS, LLC | LINDA NATHAN

PO Box 735, Maple Falls, WA 98266-0735 | 360-599-3429

editor@logosword.com | www.logosword.com

Contact: email

Services: back-cover copy, copyediting, discussion questions for books, ghostwriting, manuscript evaluation, proofreading, substantive/developmental editing

Types of manuscripts: academic, adult, articles, Bible studies, book proposals, devotionals, gift books, nonfiction books, novels, query letters, short stories, technical material, teen/YA

Charges: custom, flat fee, hourly rate, page rate, word rate

Credentials/experience: "Linda Nathan has over 30 years of experience as a professional independent freelance writer, editor, and publishing consultant, working with authors and institutions on a wide range of projects. She is a published author with 10 years of experience in the legal field and has spoken on the radio and at conferences and seminars. Since 1992 she has run her own company, Logos Word Designs, LLC. Linda has a B.A. in Psychology from the University of Oregon and master's level work. She is a freelance staff editor with Redemption Press, a Gold member of the Christian Editor Connection, and a member of four other professional writers' and editors' associations."

LOUISE M. GOUGE, COPYEDITOR

900 Jamison Loop #105, Kissimmee, FL 34744 | 407-694-5765

Louisemgouge@aol.com | louisemgougeauthor.blogspot.com

Contact: email

Services: copyediting, substantive/developmental editing

Types of manuscripts: novels

Charges: word rate

Credentials/experience: "Louise M. Gouge is a retired college English professor and the author of twenty-eight novels. For editing, she utilizes *CMOS* and *CWMoS*. Copyediting includes checking grammar, punctuation, spelling, and phrasing. Substantive editing includes making sure character arcs are balanced, the story is well-paced, and the conclusion is satisfying. Checking a client's research will raise the cost, the amount depending upon how much research is required. Novel editing $2,000–3000, depending on word count and services required."

LUCIE WINBORNE

116 Hickory Rd., Longwood, FL 2750-2708 | 321-439-7743
lwinborne704@gmail.com | *www.bluetypewriter.com*

Contact: email
Services: copyediting, proofreading
Types of manuscripts: adult, devotionals, middle grade, nonfiction books, novels, poetry, short stories, teen/YA
Charges: hourly rate
Credentials/experience: "Conversant with *Chicago Manual of Style, Merriam-Webster Collegiate Dictionary*, Google Docs and Microsoft Word, with experience in fiction, nonfiction, educational, and business documents. Demonstrated adherence to deadlines and excellent communication and organizational skills."

LYNNE TAGAWA

5606 Onyx Way, San Antonio, TX 78222 | 210-544-4397
lbtagawa@gmail.com | *www.lynnetagawa.com/editing*

Contact: email
Services: back-cover copy, copyediting
Types of manuscripts: adult, articles, novels, short stories, teen/YA
Charges: word rate
Credentials/experience: "I am an author, educator, and editor. Experienced with ministry materials as well as Christian fiction. I use the *Chicago Manual of Style* and Hudson's *The Christian Writer's Manual of Style*. My specialty is historical fiction."

MEGHAN STOLL EDITING

meghanstollediting.com

Contact: website
Services: copyediting, manuscript evaluation, substantive/developmental editing
Types of manuscripts: devotionals, nonfiction books, novels
Charges: hourly rate, word rate
Credentials/experience: "For the past six years, I've been helping independent authors bring their books to a high level of excellence.

It's a great joy to aid them in producing works that are true to their vision and valuable and enjoyable to their audience. Please see my website for more information."

MG LITERARY SERVICES | MEGAN GERIG

mgliteraryservices@gmail.com | mgliteraryservices.com

Contact: website
Services: copyediting, proofreading, substantive/developmental editing
Types of manuscripts: middle grade, teen/YA
Charges: word rate
Credentials/experience: "I am a proofreader for Enclave Publishing and have also performed several developmental edits for a Penguin Random House imprint. I've also worked with several incredible self-published and aspiring authors to bring their manuscripts to the next level. Client testimonials are available on my website."

MIDWEST PROOFREADING SERVICES | TRACY ADAMS

midwest-proofreading-services.com

Contact: website
Services: copyediting, proofreading
Types of manuscripts: adult, articles, easy readers, middle grade, novels, short stories, teen/YA
Charges: word rate
Credentials/experience: "I am a passionate proofreader and copy editor, dedicated to helping authors create clean and polished manuscripts. With a keen eye for detail and a love for language, I thrive on refining written content to ensure clarity and coherence. Throughout my career, I have honed my skills in grammar, punctuation, and style, allowing me to meticulously polish texts across various genres and industries. My commitment to maintaining the author's voice while enhancing readability has earned me a reputation for delivering exceptional results. I find immense satisfaction in collaborating with writers, offering insightful suggestions and constructive feedback to bring their stories to life in the most impactful way. If you're seeking a meticulous proofreader and copy editor to elevate your work, I am eager to embark on this rewarding partnership with you."

MISSION AND MEDIA | MICHELLE RAYBURN

info@missionandmedia.com | www.missionandmedia.com

Contact: email

Services: copyediting, discussion questions for books, ghostwriting, proofreading, substantive/developmental editing
Types of manuscripts: Bible studies, nonfiction books
Charges: flat fee, hourly rate, word rate
Credentials/experience: "Michelle Rayburn has been a freelance writer for more than 20 years and has edited for Christian publishers as well as for indie authors. Has also worked in the marketing and public relations industry. Michelle has an MA in ministry leadership and has published hundreds of articles and Bible studies as well as five books. She specializes in Christian living, Bible study, humor, and self-help."

MOUNTAIN CREEK BOOKS | KARA STARCHER
PO Box 93, Chloe, WV 25235 | 330-705-3399
mountaincreekbooks.com

Contact: website
Services: copyediting, ghostwriting, manuscript evaluation, proofreading, substantive/developmental editing, writing coach
Types of manuscripts: academic, adult, Bible studies, curriculum, devotionals, middle grade, nonfiction books, novels, teen/YA
Charges: flat fee, word rate
Credentials/experience: "BA in Publishing; 20+ years of editing and publishing experience for independent authors and small presses."

NEXT INDEX SERVICES | JESSICA MCCURDY CROOKS
jessica@JessicaCrooks.com | *www.next-index.com*

Contact: email, website
Services: indexing, proofreading, website text
Types of manuscripts: adult, articles, devotionals, middle grade, nonfiction books, novels, teen/YA
Charges: flat fee, hourly rate, page rate, word rate
Credentials/experience: "My training as a librarian and records manager gives me an eye for detail and finding information. I also know how readers tend to search for information, a skill that helps me arrive at keywords and phrases for the indexes I write. I have more than twenty years of indexing experience."

NOBLE CREATIVE, LLC | SCOTT NOBLE
PO Box 131402, St. Paul, MN 55113 | 651-494-4169
snoble@noblecreative.com | *www.noblecreative.com*

Contact: email
Services: copyediting, ghostwriting, manuscript evaluation, proofreading, substantive/developmental editing, writing coach
Types of manuscripts: adult, articles, book proposals, curriculum, devotionals, nonfiction books, query letters
Charges: flat fee
Credentials/experience: "Nearly twenty years of experience as an award-winning journalist, writer, editor, and proofreader. More than 1,000 published articles, many of them prompting radio and television appearances. Won several awards from Evangelical Press Association. Worked with dozens of published authors and other public figures, as well as first-time authors and small businesses. Have a BA and MS from St. Cloud State University and an MA from Bethel Seminary."

NOVEL IMPROVEMENT EDITING SERVICES | JEANNE MARIE LEACH
PO Box 552, Hudson, CO 80642

jeanne@novelimprovement.com | novelimprovement.com

Contact: website
Services: substantive/developmental editing, writing coach
Types of manuscripts: book proposals, novels, query letters
Charges: flat fee
Credentials/experience: "Jeanne Marie Leach is a multi-published Christian fiction author, freelance editor, and a writing and editing coach. She is also a staff editor at Elk Lake Publishing, Inc. She has edited over 150 books in fifteen years, and many of her clients have gone on to win Christian writer's awards and make bestseller's lists. She is a Gold member of The Christian PEN: Proofreaders and Editors Network and is an editor with the Christian Editor Connection."

OASHEIM EDITING SERVICES, LLC | CATHY OASHEIM
Central Florida | 202-389-8207

cathy@cathyoasheim.com | www.cathyoasheim.com

Contact: email, website
Services: copyediting, discussion questions for books, manuscript evaluation, proofreading, substantive/developmental editing, writing coach
Types of manuscripts: academic, articles, Bible studies, curriculum, devotionals, devotions, doctoral dissertations/theses, nonfiction books, novels, query letters, short stories, technical material
Charges: custom, flat fee, hourly rate, page rate, word rate

Credentials/experience: "Cathy is a professional freelance editor since 2012, blogger, and writing coach who specializes in nonfiction, true fiction, and fiction for Indy authors. She has judged over 1,000 Indie books for the Next Generation Indie Book Awards since 2016. Her services also include academic editing and fact checking for doctoral candidates (all have passed their boards), and blogs. A BS degree in Applied Psychology from Regis University allows Cathy to 'Refine Your Masterpiece.' Earlier engineering and military experiences support highly technical work and complex storytelling to get the rough draft manuscript out of the head, to the heart, and out of the plume to a polished product for the readers.

"Organizations: Author Alliance of Independent Authors, Journal Storage, National Association of Independent Writers & Editors, Nonfiction Authors Association, Toastmasters International—Distinguished Toastmaster, and The Christian PEN Proofreaders and Editors Network—Silver Member."

PAGE & PIXEL PUBLICATIONS | SUSAN MOORE

pageandpixelpublications@gmail.com | pageandpixelpublications.com

Contact: email

Services: back-cover copy, coauthoring, copyediting, discussion questions for books, ghostwriting, indexing, manuscript evaluation, proofreading, substantive/developmental editing

Types of manuscripts: academic, adult, articles, Bible studies, book proposals, curriculum, devotionals, easy readers, gift books, middle grade, nonfiction books, novels, poetry, query letters, scripts, short stories, technical material, teen/YA

Charges: hourly rate

Credentials/experience: "Whether your project requires extensive reworking or simple proofreading, with more than 30 years of editing experience I can put that professional edge on your publication. Your full length manuscript or article can be edited for continuity and grammar to industry standards so that it's ready to submit to your publisher. If your manuscript is only in the idea stage and you can't get started . . . If you suspect you need additional assistance beyond traditional editing . . . If you have a project or assignment that you just can't get to . . . If your research is complete but you don't know where to go from there—let's talk. I am accepting freelance assignments on a variety of topics."

PENCIL SHAVINGS | CHRISTINA FENNELL
lifeofawriter2@gmail.com

Contact: email

Services: manuscript evaluation, substantive/developmental editing, writing coach

Types of manuscripts: adult, articles, Bible studies, board/picture books, devotionals, easy readers, middle grade, nonfiction books, novels, scripts, short stories, teen/YA

Charges: custom, flat fee

Credentials/experience: "Bachelor's in English, junior high and high school English teacher, freelance editor work for an independent book publisher."

PERPEDIT PUBLISHING INK | BECKY LYLES
PO Box 190246, Boise, ID 83719 | 208-562-1592

beckylyles@beckylyles.com | www.beckylyles.com

Contact: email

Services: copyediting, ghostwriting, manuscript evaluation, proofreading, writing coach

Types of manuscripts: adult, articles, Bible studies, book proposals, devotionals, nonfiction books, novels, query letters, short stories, teen/YA

Charges: flat fee, hourly rate, word rate

Credentials/experience: "15 years creating/proofing/editing articles, newsletters and magazines for government and corporate entities and 15 years freelance-editing fiction and nonfiction, including Bible studies, white papers, résumés, novels and short stories."

PICKY, PICKY INK | SUE MIHOLER
1075 Willow Lake Rd. N, Salem, OR 97303

suemiholer@comcast.net

Contact: email

Services: back-cover copy, copyediting, proofreading

Types of manuscripts: articles, Bible studies, devotionals, nonfiction books

Charges: hourly rate

Credentials/experience: "Line editing for 20+ years for both publishers and individuals."

PRAIRIE FALLS BOOKS | DEBRA L. BUTTERFIELD and TAMARA CLYMER

4810 Gene Field Rd. #2, St. Joseph, MO 64506 | 816-752-2171

prairiefallsbooks.com

Contact: website

Services: back-cover copy, copyediting, proofreading, substantive/developmental editing

Types of manuscripts: adult, articles, board/picture books, book proposals, devotionals, easy readers, gift books, middle grade, nonfiction books, novels, short stories, teen/YA

Charges: word rate

Credentials/experience: "An award-winning editorial team with decades of experience in Christian writing, editing, and publishing."

PRATHER!NK LITERARY SERVICES | VICKI PRATHER

20 Parkview Rd., Clinton, MS 39056 | 601-573-4295

pratherINK@gmail.com | pratherink.wordpress.com

Contact: email

Services: coauthoring, copyediting, discussion questions for books, proofreading

Types of manuscripts: academic, articles, Bible studies, curriculum, devotionals, easy readers, gift books, middle grade, nonfiction books, novels, poetry, scripts, short stories, teen/YA

Charges: custom, flat fee, hourly rate, word rate

Credentials/experience: "I've been assisting first-time and experienced authors since 2014 in taking their writing to the next level, whether that means general advice or proofreading or being by their side through publishing. My first love is Christian works of any kind. I've authored and coauthored curriculums, Bible studies, and memoirs, as well as children's books & fiction. Before transitioning into freelance work, I wrote procedures manuals in my secretarial years, then taught writing skills and study skills and Bible to middle schoolers for a decade. If I'm *not* right for your editing needs, I'll tell you!"

PROFESSIONAL PUBLISHING SERVICES | CHRISTY CALLAHAN

professionalpublishingservices@gmail.com | professionalpublishingservicesus.weebly.com

Contact: email

Services: copyediting, discussion questions for books, French to English translation, French-language editing, manuscript evaluation, proofreading, substantive/developmental editing

Types of manuscripts: academic, adult, articles, Bible studies, curriculum, devotionals, easy readers, gift books, middle grade, nonfiction books, novels, teen/YA

Charges: custom

Credentials/experience: "Christy graduated Phi Beta Kappa from Carnegie Mellon University and then earned her MA in Intercultural Studies from Fuller Seminary. A gold member of The Christian PEN: Proofreaders and Editors Network and certified by the Christian Editor Connection and Reedsy, she also completed the 40-hour Foundational Course (Christian track) with the Institute for Life Coach Training."

PROVISION EDITING | NINA HUNDLEY

mrshundley14@gmail.com | ninahundley.com

Contact: email, website

Services: copyediting, manuscript evaluation, substantive/ developmental editing

Types of manuscripts: adult, articles, Bible studies, book proposals, devotionals, middle grade, nonfiction books, novels, query letters, teen/YA

Charges: flat fee, word rate

Credentials/experience: "Freelance editor with a focus on fiction manuscripts. Member of the Editorial Freelancers Association and silver member of The Christian Pen: Proofreaders and Editors Network."

PWC EDITING | PAUL W. CONANT

527 Bayshore Pl., Dallas, TX 75217-7755 | 214-289-3397

pwcediting@gmail.com | PWC-editing.com

Contact: email

Services: copyediting, proofreading

Types of manuscripts: academic, adult, articles, Bible studies, business materials, devotionals, nonfiction books, novels, poetry, short stories, technical material, textbooks

Charges: hourly rate, word rate

Credentials/experience: "Book editor since '94; textbook editor for 1.5 years; academic editor since 2001; Silver member of The Christian PEN (Proofreaders and Editors Network); contract editor for Holy Fire Publishing; copyeditor for Christian Editing & Design, Redemption Press, and Creative Enterprises Studio."

READ. WRITE. PRAY. CARE, LLC | MARTI PIEPER
246 Maple Grove Rd., Seneca, GA 29678 | 352-409-3136
marti@martipieper.com | www.martipieper.com
   Contact: website
   Services: copyediting, ghostwriting, manuscript evaluation, proofreading, substantive/developmental editing, writing coach
   Types of manuscripts: adult, articles, book proposals, curriculum, devotionals, nonfiction books, query letters
   Charges: custom
   Credentials/experience: "I have served as ghostwriter/collaborative writer for eight traditionally published books, including a CBA bestseller, and edited many more. I have written and edited for both print and digital magazines, all of these in the Christian market."

REBECCA LUELLA MILLER'S EDITORIAL SERVICES
rluellam@yahoo.com | rewriterewordrework.wordpress.com
   Contact: email, website
   Services: back-cover copy, copyediting, manuscript evaluation, proofreading, substantive/developmental editing, writing coach
   Types of manuscripts: academic, adult, articles, devotionals, middle grade, nonfiction books, novels, query letters, short stories, teen/YA
   Charges: page rate, word rate
   Credentials/experience: "I became an editor as a direct result of my work as a critique partner. Behind that were the thirty years I spent as an English teacher evaluating student writing. Since 2004 I have had the privilege of working with numerous traditionally published authors, self-published authors, and aspiring authors alike."

REFINE SERVICES, LLC | KATE MOTAUNG
kate@refineservices.com | www.refineservices.com
   Contact: email
   Services: copyediting, proofreading
   Types of manuscripts: academic, adult, articles, Bible studies, board/picture books, book proposals, curriculum, devotionals, easy readers, gift books, middle grade, nonfiction books, novels, poetry, query letters, scripts, short stories, teen/YA
   Charges: word rate
   Credentials/experience: "Kate Motaung is the owner of Refine Services, LLC. She has been offering copyediting services since 2015 and enjoys serving a variety of authors. Visit *refineservices.com/reviews* to read testimonials from past clients."

REVISIONS BY RACHEL, LLC | RACHEL E. BRADLEY

1512 Lynhaven Ave., Richmond, VA 23224 | 918-207-2833

editor@RevisionsbyRachel.com | *www.RevisionsbyRachel.com*

Contact: email

Services: back-cover copy, coauthoring, copyediting, ghostwriting, indexing, manuscript evaluation, proofreading, substantive/developmental editing

Types of manuscripts: adult, Bible studies, curriculum, nonfiction books, novels, teen/YA

Charges: custom, flat fee, hourly rate, word rate

Credentials/experience: "Rachel holds a BS degree in Paralegal Studies from Northeastern State University in Oklahoma. She graduated *summa cum laude* in 2006 and has been awarded the Advanced Certified Paralegal designation by the National Association of Legal Assistants. She is a gold member of the Christian PEN: Proofreaders and Editors Network, is an established freelance editor with the Christian Editor Connection, is an instructor with the PEN Institute, and has served as a judge for the Excellence in Editing Award and as faculty for PENCON, the only conference for editors in the Christian market."

RICK STEELE EDITORIAL SERVICES

26 Dean Rd., Ringgold, GA 30736 | 706-937-8121

rsteelecam@gmail.com | *steeleeditorialservices.myportfolio.com*

Contact: website

Services: back-cover copy, book-contract evaluation, copyediting, manuscript evaluation, proofreading, substantive/developmental editing, writing coach

Types of manuscripts: academic, adult, articles, Bible studies, book proposals, curriculum, devotionals, middle grade, nonfiction books, novels, query letters, short stories, teen/YA

Charges: flat fee

Credentials/experience: "To fulfill your dream to be that great author, you may find you need some professional publishing help. Rick Steele Editorial Services has the experience and know-how to provide the attention you need, whether it involves coaching or more hands-on editing. Can help with all aspects of both traditional and custom publishing, including editorial critiques, query letter and proposal coaching services, developmental editing, and copyediting."

ROBIN L. REED

1857 Alcan Dr., Medford, OR 97504 | 541-301-0869

robin@robinlreed.com | robinlreed.com

> **Contact:** email
> **Services:** copyediting, proofreading
> **Types of manuscripts:** academic, adult, Bible studies, curriculum, devotionals, easy readers, middle grade, nonfiction books, novels, short stories, teen/YA
> **Charges:** word rate
> **Credentials/experience:** "I'm an experienced editor who specializes in helping independent authors get their books into print with the highest possible quality. My priority is to preserve and strengthen my clients' original writing voice and support them through the editing process. I've received training through the PEN Institute and Proofread Anywhere as well as earning a master's degree in history from UC Riverside."

SARA ELLA EDITING

saraellawrites@gmail.com | saraella.com/editorial-services

> **Contact:** email, website
> **Services:** copyediting, substantive/developmental editing, writing coach
> **Types of manuscripts:** adult, book proposals, middle grade, novels, query letters, teen/YA
> **Charges:** word rate
> **Credentials/experience:** "Seven+ years experience as a freelance editor, specializing in developmental and line edits. Copywriter and editor for School Webmasters. Editor for Enclave Publishing. High School creative writing instructor. Experienced writing conference instructor and keynote speaker. Multi-published, award-winning author of 6 novels."

SARA LAWSON

sarareneelawson@gmail.com | www.sarasbooks.com

> **Contact:** website
> **Services:** copyediting, substantive/developmental editing
> **Types of manuscripts:** adult, Bible studies, devotionals, middle grade, novels, teen/YA
> **Charges:** word rate
> **Credentials/experience:** "Sara Lawson has over a decade of freelance editing experience working with fiction and nonfiction. She has also

served at churches from various denominations and ethnic groups, so she understands a variety of ministry contexts. She loves to help writers because she believes that everyone has a story to tell and no one should have to let technical writing abilities get in the way of telling their story."

SARAH HAMAKER

sarah@sarahhamaker.com | sarahhamakerfiction.com/editorial-services
   Contact: email
   Services: copyediting, ghostwriting, proofreading, substantive/ developmental editing, writing coach
   Types of manuscripts: articles, Bible studies, book proposals, easy readers, middle grade, nonfiction books, novels, query letters, short stories
   Charges: custom
   Credentials/experience: "Sarah is a certified writers and speakers coach through the Advanced Writers & Speakers Association (AWSA) who has helped many writers with their manuscripts. Her clients have gone on to publish nonfiction works on spirituality and prayer, as well as fantasy, historical, contemporary, suspense and other forms of fiction."

SARAH HAYHURST EDITORIAL, LLC

1441 Haynescrest Ct., Grayson, GA 30017 | 470-825-2905
sarah@sarahhayhurst.com | www.sarahhayhurst.com
   Contact: email, website
   Services: copyediting, proofreading, substantive/developmental editing
   Types of manuscripts: articles, Bible studies, curriculum, devotionals, nonfiction books, short stories
   Charges: word rate
   Credentials/experience: "Sarah is a gold-level member of The Christian PEN and Christian Editor Network with whom she passed extensive testing and demonstrated expertise in the substantive editing, copyediting, and proofreading of both fiction and nonfiction manuscripts. Sarah has over ten years of editing experience and started her editorial company in 2014."

SCRIBELANCE | VALARI WESTEREN

valari.westeren@scribelance.com
   Contact: email

Services: copyediting, indexing, proofreading

Types of manuscripts: academic, adult, articles, Bible studies, nonfiction books, novels

Charges: page rate, word rate

Credentials/experience: "Valari helps Christian authors and scholars become authoritative voices in their fields with meticulous proofreading that Grammarly can't provide. Her academic studies have spanned both English and theology, and her skills have served academic Christian presses such as B&H Academic, debut authors publishing under Wipf & Stock, and theology professors submitting PhD-level work."

SCRIPTS4C.COM | DAVID M. HYDE
scripts4c@icloud.com | *Scripts4c.com*

Contact: email, website

Services: copyediting, manuscript evaluation, novel adaptation, substantive/developmental editing

Types of manuscripts: scripts

Charges: flat fee

Credentials/experience: "Kairos Prize, multi-optioned, produced screenwriter."

SCRIVEN COMMUNICATIONS | KATHIE SCRIVEN
22 Ridge Rd. #220, Greenbelt, MD 20770 | 240-542-4602
KathieScriven@yahoo.com

Contact: email, phone

Services: back-cover copy, coauthoring, copyediting, discussion questions for books, ghostwriting, manuscript evaluation, proofreading, substantive/developmental editing, writing coach

Types of manuscripts: academic, adult, articles, Bible studies, book proposals, devotions, easy readers, gift books, middle grade, nonfiction books, poetry, query letters, short stories, technical material, teen/YA

Charges: custom

Credentials/experience: "I specialize in offering editing and coaching services related to self-publishing and marketing books. Have completed over 95 nonfiction Christian book-editing assignments. Former editor of three Christian publications and freelance writer for mostly secular publications. Bachelor's degree in Mass Communication (concentration in journalism) from Towson University. I'm happy to send anyone interested a document that goes over my background, credentials and the services I offer in greater detail. Discount for those in full-time ministry."

SETTINGS CHRISTIAN EDITING | REBEKAH MCKAMIE

editor@settingschristian.com | www.settingschristian.com

Contact: website

Services: manuscript evaluation, substantive/developmental editing, writing coach

Types of manuscripts: adult, Bible studies, devotionals, nonfiction books, novels, poetry

Charges: custom, word rate

Credentials/experience: "I am a published author and poet with decades of writing experience, and have edited dozens of Christian works. I hold a Master of Arts in Composition (& Rhetoric) from Liberty University."

STICKS AND STONES | JAMIE CALLOWAY-HANAUER

snsedits@gmail.com | www.snsedits.com

Contact: email

Services: book-contract evaluation, coauthoring, copyediting, discussion questions for books, ghostwriting, manuscript evaluation, proofreading, substantive/developmental editing, writing coach

Types of manuscripts: adult, articles, book proposals, curriculum, devotionals, easy readers, middle grade, nonfiction books, novels, poetry, query letters, short stories, teen/YA

Charges: flat fee

Credentials/experience: "Jamie has eighteen years of experience in the editing field. Previously a full-time public interest attorney who also edited part-time, she is now the owner/operator of Sticks and Stones, where she specializes in academic, legal, and faith-based fiction and nonfiction for adults and teens; ghostwriting; and proposal and query review and development."

SUE A. FAIRCHILD, EDITOR

sueafairchild74@gmail.com | www.sueafairchild.wordpress.com

Contact: email, website

Services: copyediting, manuscript evaluation, proofreading, substantive/developmental editing, writing coach

Types of manuscripts: devotionals, gift books, middle grade, nonfiction books, novels, teen/YA

Charges: hourly rate

Credentials/experience: "Gold Member editor of the Christian Editor Connection, editor for Elk Lake Publishing Inc., writing coach/editor with Redemption Press."

SUSAN KING EDITORIAL SERVICES

1113 Brookside Dr., Nashville, TN 37069 | 615-202-6019

susankingedits.com

Contact: website

Services: coauthoring, copyediting, discussion questions for books, ghostwriting, manuscript evaluation, proofreading, substantive/ developmental editing, writing coach

Types of manuscripts: academic, adult, articles, Bible studies, book proposals, devotionals, gift books, nonfiction books, novels, poetry, query letters, short stories, teen/YA

Charges: hourly rate

Credentials/experience: "Of my more than 30 years in the industry, I served 24 years as an editor for *The Upper Room,* the world's premier daily devotional guide reaching 3 million subscribers in 100 countries and 35 languages. For the past 21 years, I have trained writers at over one hundred Christian writers' conferences in the U.S. and Canada. My professional life has also included teaching freshman English, American literature, and feature-writing classes at Lipscomb University, Biola University, and Abilene Christian University for a total of 27 years. Currently, I am the compiler and editor of the Short and Sweet anthology series."

SUSAN RESCIGNO

PO Box 336, Fort Montgomery, NY 10922 | 914-844-5217

srescigno7.wixsite.com/mysite

Contact: website

Services: copyediting, proofreading

Types of manuscripts: nonfiction books

Charges: hourly rate

Credentials/experience: "I have 25+ years of experience copyediting and proofreading nonfiction books. My clients have included such Christian publishers as CLC Ministries, Orbis Books, and Twenty-third Publications. I have also worked with author and pastor Jean Max St. Louis on his manuscripts. My hourly fee is $20 per hour, and I will give you an initial estimate based on your ten-page, double-spaced sample set in 12-point type. I can used MS Word

Track Changes but have found that it's easier for authors if I simply make the necessary edits to capitalization, grammar, punctuation, spelling, etc. without this feature. I will provide you with an individualized style sheet so that there is consistency throughout your book."

TANDEM SERVICES | JENNIFER CROSSWHITE
PO Box 220, Yucaipa, CA 92399 | 414-465-2567
www.tandemservicesink.com
> **Contact:** website
> **Services:** back-cover copy, copyediting, copywriting, manuscript evaluation, proofreading, substantive/developmental editing, writing coach
> **Types of manuscripts:** adult, devotionals, middle grade, nonfiction books, novels, teen/YA
> **Charges:** custom, flat fee
> **Credentials/experience:** "Jennifer Crosswhite is owner and CEO of Tandem Services. Her experience spans both sides of the publishing desk, from author to former managing editor of a Big 5 publisher for over 20 years. She and her team have worked with hundreds of authors at every stage to help them tell the story of their heart."

THREE FATES EDITING | SARAH GRACE LIU
28 Close Hollow Dr., Hamlin, NY 14464
sarah.grace@threefatesediting.com | *www.threefatesediting.com*
> **Contact:** email, website
> **Services:** copyediting, ghostwriting, manuscript evaluation, proofreading, substantive/developmental editing
> **Types of manuscripts:** academic, adult, Bible studies, middle grade, nonfiction books, novels, poetry, short stories, teen/YA
> **Charges:** word rate
> **Credentials/experience:** "I have an MA in Creative Writing and have run my own editing business since 2012. My true specialization is speculative fiction. For nonfiction, I am more comfortable with progressive texts."

TINSY WINSY STUDIO | BRENDA WILBEE
7959 Birch Bay Dr. #2, Blaine, WA 98230 | 360-389-6895
Brenda@BrendaWilbee.com | *BrendaWilbee.com*
> **Contact:** email

Services: back-cover copy, copyediting, manuscript evaluation, substantive/developmental editing, writing coach

Types of manuscripts: adult, gift books, nonfiction books, novels

Charges: flat fee, hourly rate, page rate

Credentials/experience: "I'm an award-winning writer, author of 11 books (fiction and nonfiction), and have sold over 700,000 copies. In addition, I hold an MA in Professional Writing, a BA in Creative Writing, and an AA in Visual Communications. For seven years, I taught college and university English (99 [grammar], 101 [essay], 201 [academic writing], and 104 [research]). My skill set has seen me teaching at writers conferences, historical societies, and elder hostels in both the US and Canada, and serving on the board for the Pacific NW Writers Association. For 20–30 years I've been working with authors and small publishing houses as an editor, book packager, cover designer, and spin-off marketing products.

"I specialize in historical/biographical fiction, literary novels, memoir, and family histories that integrate narrative and imagery. In nonfiction, I work with themes of wounded women and hope."

TISHA MARTIN EDITORIAL, LLC

www.tishamartin.com

Contact: website

Services: back-cover copy, copyediting, discussion questions for books, ghostwriting, manuscript evaluation, proofreading, self-publishing packages, substantive/developmental editing, writing coach

Types of manuscripts: adult, articles, curriculum, deaf subject matter, devotionals, gift books, memoir, nonfiction books, novels, query letters, scripts, teen/YA

Charges: custom, hourly rate, word rate

Credentials/experience: "I partner with brilliant, insightful authors to write and edit their best stories. Fiction, nonfiction, and creative memoir. Themes: redemption, faith, love, relationships, inspiration, leadership. Encouraging is my middle name. Joy and peace are my superpowers. Together, we work from a place of rest and grace, dedication and determination, patience and prayer."

TRAILBLAZE EDITORIAL | SARAH BARNUM

sarah@trail-blazes.com | *trail-blazes.com*

Contact: website

Services: back-cover copy, book-contract evaluation, coauthoring, copyediting, manuscript evaluation, substantive/developmental editing, writing coach

Types of manuscripts: adult, articles, book proposals, devotionals, gift books, nonfiction books, short stories

Charges: flat fee, page rate, word rate

Credentials/experience: "Sarah Barnum is an award-winning freelance writer and editor. She holds a bachelor's degree with highest honors, and in 2022, she earned the Christian Editor Connection's Excellence in Editing award. Sarah's short stories have been featured in five Chicken Soup for the Soul anthologies and in Revell's *The Horse of My Heart* and *The Horse of My Dreams*. Sarah serves as the Administrative Director for the West Coast Christian Writers Conference, where she also teaches on faculty."

TUPPANCE ENTERPRISES | JAMES PENCE
PO Box 99, Greenville, TX 75403 | 469-730-6478
james@pence.com | jamespence.com/writing-services

Contact: email, phone, website

Services: coauthoring, copyediting, ghostwriting, manuscript evaluation, proofreading, substantive/developmental editing, writing coach

Types of manuscripts: adult, articles, Bible studies, book proposals, devotionals, middle grade, nonfiction books, novels, query letters, short stories, technical material, teen/YA

Charges: flat fee, hourly rate, word rate

Credentials/experience: "James has been writing and editing professionally since 2000, and is a traditionally published author of ten books. Publishers include Osborne/McGraw-Hill, Tyndale, Kregel, Baker (co-author), Thomas Nelson (ghostwriter), and Mountainview Books. Published works include textbooks, how-to, novels (adult and YA), Christian living, and memoir."

TURN THE PAGE CRITIQUES | CINDY THOMSON
PO Box 298, Pataskala, OH 43062 | 614-354-3904
cindyswriting@gmail.com | cindyswriting.com/index.php/critique-service

Contact: email

Services: critiquing, manuscript evaluation, proofreading

Types of manuscripts: articles, book proposals, novels, query letters

Charges: flat fee

Credentials/experience: "Published author both traditionally and independently of fiction and non-fiction, author of numerous magazine articles, and a former mentor with the Jerry B. Jenkins Christian Writers Guild, I can help you get a solid footing as you prepare to publish."

WHALIN & ASSOCIATES | W. TERRY WHALIN

170 Ambroise, Newport Coast, CA 92657 | 516-900-5711

terry@terrywhalin.com | *terrywhalin.blogspot.com*

Contact: email
Services: coauthoring, discussion questions for books, ghostwriting, substantive/developmental editing
Types of manuscripts: adult, book proposals, devotionals, gift books, nonfiction books
Charges: flat fee
Credentials/experience: "Terry has written more than sixty books for traditional publishers, including one book that has sold more than 100,000 copies. He has written for more than fifty publications and worked in acquisitions at three publishing houses."

WORDMELON | MARGOT STARBUCK

308-B Northwood Cir., Durham, NC 27701 | 919-321-5440

wordmelon@gmail.com | *www.wordmelon.com*

Contact: email
Services: coauthoring, discussion questions for books, ghostwriting, manuscript evaluation, substantive/developmental editing, writing coach
Types of manuscripts: articles, Bible studies, book proposals, devotionals, gift books, nonfiction books, query letters
Charges: flat fee, word rate
Credentials/experience: "Margot has written over thirty books, one *New York Times* bestseller, and has worked alongside countless publishers and authors. She is a graduate of Westmont College and Princeton Seminary."

WORDPOLISH EDITORIAL SERVICES | YVONNE KANU

yvonne@wordpolish.net | *www.wordpolish.net*

Contact: email, website
Services: copyediting, discussion questions for books, manuscript evaluation, proofreading, writing coach
Types of manuscripts: academic, Bible studies, devotionals, easy readers, nonfiction books, novels, short stories, teen/YA

Charges: word rate

Credentials/experience: "Over 10 years of experience in publishing, business communication, and technical writing. BA degree in English, and certificates in Editing, Publishing, and Technical Writing."

WORDPRO COMMUNICATION SERVICES | LIN JOHNSON

9118 W. Elmwood Dr., Ste. 1G, Niles, IL 60714-5820 | 847-296-3964

ljohnson@wordprocommunications.com | *wordprocommunications.com*

Contact: email

Services: back-cover copy, book-contract evaluation, copyediting, discussion questions for books, proofreading, small-group Bible study guides

Types of manuscripts: adult, Bible studies, curriculum, devotionals, nonfiction books

Charges: flat fee, hourly rate

Credentials/experience: "I've worked in Christian publishing for more than four decades as an in-house and freelance Bible curriculum editor and writer; award-winning writer of more than 70 books and hundreds of articles, devotions, and reviews; former managing editor of *Christian Communicator, Advanced Christian Writer,* and *Church Libraries;* and freelance editor and proofreader for traditional and independent publishing houses, organizations, and authors. Clients have praised me for being accurate, detailed, thorough, and deadline oriented.

"In addition, I've trained thousands of writers at conferences, as an adjunct writing instructor at Taylor University, and in international settings. I have an English minor from Adrian College, a BA in Christian education from Cedarville University, a BA in Bible-theology from Moody Bible Institute, and an MS in adult and continuing education from National-Louis University."

WORDS FOR WRITERS | GINNY L. YTTRUP

PO Box 1651, Lincoln, CA 95648 |

ginny@wordsforwriters.net | *wordsforwriters.net*

Contact: email, website

Services: manuscript evaluation, substantive/developmental editing, writing coach

Types of manuscripts: adult, book proposals, devotionals, novels, query letters, teen/YA

Charges: hourly rate, word rate

Credentials/experience: "Ginny is an award-winning author, a writing coach who received a certificate in coaching through Western Seminary, and a developmental editor who has trained under other editors, taken courses through UC Berkeley's Extension program in editing, and has had the honor of editing several award-winning or bestselling manuscripts."

WRITE BY LISA | LISA THOMPSON

200 Laguna Dr. S, Litchfield Park, AZ 85340 | 623-258-5258
writebylisa@gmail.com | *www.writebylisa.com*

Contact: website
Services: back-cover copy, copyediting, discussion questions for books, ghostwriting, manuscript evaluation, proofreading, substantive/developmental editing, writing coach
Types of manuscripts: academic, adult, articles, Bible studies, board/ picture books, book proposals, curriculum, devotionals, easy readers, middle grade, nonfiction books, novels, query letters, short stories, teen/YA
Charges: flat fee, hourly rate, word rate
Credentials/experience: "I have a degree in elementary education and a minor in English and Spanish. I have been editing since 2009. Nearly everything I edit is Christian content. I also subcontract for a fairly large Christian publisher and several smaller indie publishers in addition to editing for many Christian leaders, pastors, and lay people."

WRITE CONCEPTS, LLC | ALICE B. CRIDER

590 Highway 105 #107, Monument, CO 80132 | 719-651-0160
editoralicecrider@gmail.com | *www.alicecrider.com*

Contact: email
Services: back-cover copy, coauthoring, ghostwriting, manuscript evaluation, substantive/developmental editing, writing coach
Types of manuscripts: adult, book proposals, nonfiction books, query letters
Charges: custom
Credentials/experience: "I am a certified life coach and author coach with more than ten years of experience in helping individuals and authors achieve their dreams and goals. I am also a non-fiction editor with 20+ years of experience in book publishing, including eight years in a division of Random House. I specialize in developmental, content, and line editing. I am skilled at analyzing a manuscript's strengths and weaknesses, and at suggesting improvements and

revisions. I love strategizing and brainstorming ideas with writers. Most recently, I have been a collaborative writer for authors who don't have the time or talent to write their own books."

THE WRITE FLOURISH | TIM and NOLA PASSMORE

nola@thewriteflourish.com.au | www.thewriteflourish.com.au

Contact: email

Services: copyediting, manuscript evaluation, mentoring, proofreading, substantive/developmental editing

Types of manuscripts: academic, adult, articles, book proposals, devotionals, memoir, nonfiction books, novels, poetry, short stories, teen/YA

Charges: hourly rate

Credentials/experience: "Tim and Nola Passmore each have more than 20 years of experience as university academics. Nola also has a degree in creative writing. They founded The Write Flourish in 2014 and have edited a wide range of manuscripts across a variety of styles and genres. They have also had many of their own short pieces published including fiction, poetry, devotions, memoir, nonfiction and academic articles. They would love to help you add the right flourish to your manuscript."

WRITE HIS ANSWER MINISTRIES | MARLENE BAGNULL

951 Anders Rd., Lansdale, PA 19446 | 267-436-2503

mbagnull@aol.com | writehisanswer.com/editingmentoring

Contact: email

Services: copyediting, manuscript evaluation, proofreading, substantive/developmental editing

Types of manuscripts: adult, articles, devotionals, nonfiction books, novels

Charges: flat fee, hourly rate

Credentials/experience: "More than forty years of experience in publishing, leading critique groups, and directing writers conferences; author of fourteen books and more than a thousand sales to Christian periodicals; editor, typesetter, and publisher of twelve Ampelos Press books."

WRITE JUSTIFIED | JUDY HAGEY

10628 Sharon Cir., Urbandale, IA 50322 | 386-562-7192

judy.hagey@gmail.com | judy@judyhagey.com

Contact: email

Services: back-cover copy, copyediting, proofreading, writing coach
Types of manuscripts: academic, adult, Bible studies, devotionals, nonfiction books, novels
Charges: word rate
Credentials/experience: "Freelance editor with more than a dozen years of experience editing and proofreading for Christian publishers, self-publishing/independent authors, and academics with projects ranging from Christian nonfiction, Bible studies, and devotionals to adult and middle grade novels. Currently nonfiction managing editor for Elk Lake Publishing, Inc. Proficient in *CMS* and *CWMS*. Professional memberships include ACES, Christian Editors Association (CEA), and Gold Member of Christian Editor Connection. I can ensure your manuscript uses the right word at the right time in the right way."

WRITE NOW EDITING | KARIN BEERY

PO Box 31, Elk Rapids, MI 49629
karin@karinbeery.com | writenowedits.com

Contact: email
Services: back-cover copy, copyediting, ghostwriting, manuscript evaluation, substantive/developmental editing, writing coach
Types of manuscripts: adult, novels, teen/YA
Charges: page rate, word rate
Credentials/experience: "Member of The Christian Proofreaders and Editors Network and the Christian Editor Network; PEN Institute instructor."

WRITE PATHWAY EDITORIAL SERVICES | ANN KNOWLES

annknowles03@aol.com | write-pathway.blogspot.com

Contact: email
Services: coauthoring, copyediting, ghostwriting, proofreading, Spanish translation, transcription, writing coach
Types of manuscripts: adult, articles, book proposals, curriculum, devotionals, easy readers, gift books, middle grade, nonfiction books, novels, picture books, poetry, query letters, short stories, teen/YA
Charges: custom
Credentials/experience: "Retired educator, MA in education, certified ESL and Spanish; ESL training consultant for public schools and community colleges. I joined The Christian PEN: Proofreaders and Editors Network in 2005 and started Write

Pathway in 2007. I have taken numerous courses from The Christian PEN, American Christian Fiction Writers, Write Integrity Press, and Christian Writers International."

THE WRITE STUFF EDITING | TODD WILLIAMS

4062 Greenwich Rd., Norton, OH 44203 | 330-631-8387
expectdoublechecks@gmail.com | *thewritestuffediting.com*

Contact: email, website

Services: copyediting, manuscript evaluation, proofreading, substantive/developmental editing

Types of manuscripts: academic, adult, articles, Bible studies, curriculum, devotionals, easy readers, middle grade, nonfiction books, short stories

Charges: hourly rate, word rate

Credentials/experience: "My last 30+ years have been spent editing, writing, and proofreading Bible exposition, teaching materials, and scholarly biblical resources, including Sunday school literature, devotionals, short stories, study Bibles, and even a Koine Greek dictionary. The Lord has allowed me to do a great deal of biblical research and gain much knowledge as I prepared these materials for publication (in conjunction with my own Bible teaching and preaching). Now it is my joy to help authors do their best writing for publication."

WRITE WAY | PEGGYSUE WELLS

3419 E. 1000 N Roanoke, IN 46783 | 260-433-2817
peggysuewells@gmail.com | *www.PeggySueWells.com*

Contact: email, website

Services: back-cover copy, book proposals, coauthoring, discussion questions for books, ghostwriting, substantive/developmental editing, writing coach

Types of manuscripts: adult, articles, Bible studies, book proposals, curriculum, devotionals, easy readers, gift books, middle grade, nonfiction books, novels, picture books, query letters, scripts, short stories, teen/YA

Charges: custom, flat fee, hourly rate

Credentials/experience: "Bestselling author of 34 books, collaborator of many more. She also polishes manuscripts to be publish-ready, drafts proposals, and prepares manuscripts to publish independently."

WRITE WAY COPYEDITING, LLC | DIANA SCHRAMER

diana@writewaycopyediting.com | *www.writewaycopyediting.com*

    Contact: email

    Services: copyediting, manuscript evaluation

    Types of manuscripts: Bible studies, devotionals, gift books, memoir, nonfiction books, novels

    Charges: hourly rate

    Credentials/experience: "I started my business in 2010 and have copyedited 100+ book-length manuscripts and have reviewed 200+ manuscripts. In addition, I have copyedited and reviewed front- and back-cover copy as well as business-related documents and blogs."

WRITERS' COACH | EDDIE JONES

2333 Barton Oaks Dr., Raleigh, NC 27614

writerscoach.us@gmail.com | *writerscoach.us*

    Contact: email, website

    Services: back-cover copy, book-contract evaluation, coauthoring, discussion questions for books, ghostwriting, manuscript evaluation, proofreading, substantive/developmental editing, writing coach

    Types of manuscripts: adult, Bible studies, board/picture books, book proposals, devotionals, easy readers, gift books, middle grade, nonfiction books, novellas, query letters, scripts, short stories, teen/YA

    Charges: custom, flat fee, monthly fee

    Credentials/experience: "Do you need help with your novel or nonfiction project? Do you have a book idea but are not sure where to start? Book your free Introductory Coaching Session at *writerscoach.us*. With 30-plus years of experience in Christian publishing (agenting, editing, book publishing), our team can help you turn your stories, talks, sermons, life lessons, and podcasts into a book."

WRITER'S EDGE SERVICE, LLC

PO Box 310, Sisters, OR 97759

www.writersedgeservice.com

    Contact: website

    Services: manuscript evaluation

    Types of manuscripts: academic, adult, Bible studies, book proposals, devotionals, easy readers, gift books, middle grade, nonfiction books, novels, teen/YA

    Charges: $99

    Credentials/experience: "Manuscripts evaluated by professional

Christian editors who've worked for major publishers." If the manuscript is approved, it's referred to more than 75 traditional publishers in the monthly or bimonthly newsletter.

WRITER'S TABLET, LLC | TERRI WHITMIRE

3155 Hembree Trace Dr., Marietta, GA 30062 | 770-331-4326
Twhitmire@writerstablet.org | *www.Writerstablet.org*

Contact: email

Services: back-cover copy, copyediting, discussion questions for books, ghostwriting, indexing, manuscript evaluation, proofreading, substantive/developmental editing, writing coach

Types of manuscripts: academic, adult, articles, Bible studies, curriculum, devotionals, easy readers, middle grade, nonfiction books, novels, picture books, poetry, scripts, short stories, teen/YA

Charges: page rate

Credentials/experience: "Writers Tablet, LLC has been helping aspiring writers become authors for over seven years, including three bestselling authors. With well over 60 years of combined experience, the Writers Tablet Team consists of highly sought-after editors, publishers, poets, illustrators, and graphic artists who are industry experts. As a Christian assisted self-publishing agency, we pray with and for your project and attribute all of our success to our Father in heaven. With certifications in literature, editing, and graphic artists, the Writers Tablet team has received numerous awards, accolades, and recognition for its service to the writing community."

WRITING PURSUITS | KATHRESE MCKEE

27708 Tomball Pkwy., PMB 107, Tomball, TX 77375
kmckee@writingpursuits.com | *www.writingpursuits.com*

Contact: website

Services: copyediting, manuscript evaluation, substantive/developmental editing

Types of manuscripts: adult, middle grade, novels, short stories, teen/YA

Charges: flat fee, hourly rate

Credentials/experience: "Kathrese McKee has edited fiction professionally since 2014 in the following genres: urban and paranormal fantasy, fairytale retellings, dystopian and military science fiction, women's fiction, and contemporary and historical romance. She hosts the *Writing Pursuits* podcast and writes and produces a weekly newsletter, *Writing Pursuits Tips for Authors*."

YO PRODUCTIONS, LLC | YOLONDA SANDERS

7185 E. Main St., Unit 1242, Reynoldsburg, OH 43068 | 614-452-4920
info_4u@yoproductions.net | *www.yoproductions.net*

Contact: email, phone, website

Services: back-cover copy, coauthoring, copyediting, discussion questions for books, ghostwriting, manuscript evaluation, proofreading, substantive/developmental editing, writing coach

Types of manuscripts: academic, adult, articles, Bible studies, curriculum, devotionals, easy readers, gift books, middle grade, nonfiction books, novels, poetry, query letters, scripts, short stories, technical material, teen/YA

Charges: custom, flat fee, hourly rate, word rate

Credentials/experience: "Owned by author and scholar, Yolonda Tonette Sanders, PhD., Yo Productions, LLC, has provided editorial services since 2008. Yolonda has worked with new and established authors, small and large organizations, and those who are still trying to discover if they even like writing! Yolonda and her team provide personalized services and offer customizable packages."

21

PUBLICITY AND MARKETING SERVICES

THE ADAMS GROUP | GINA ADAMS
6688 Nolensville Rd. 108-149, Brentwood, TN 37027 | 615-776-1590
gina@adamsprgroup.com | *www.adamsprgroup.com*

> **Contact:** email, phone, website form
> **Services:** public relations, publicity campaigns, press releases, press-release distribution, press-kit creation, contributed content, video production
> **Books:** all genres
> **Charges:** flat fee
> **Credentials/experience:** "Honored by the prestigious Communicator Awards in 2019, 2020, and 2022, The Adams Group has represented faith-based authors for over three decades. Gina received her B.S. degree in business and marketing from Murray State University. She is a member of the National Religious Broadcasters and the Evangelical Press Association and serves on the Publicity Committee for the Arts of Southern Kentucky. Gina has also earned an Expert Rating Certification in Social Media Marketing and is a Hootsuite Certified Professional in Social Marketing."

ANCHOR PROJECT MANAGEMENT | MELISSA CLUTTER
PO Box 574, Anoka, MN 55303
melissa@anchorprojectmanagement.com | *www.anchorprojectmanagement.com*

> **Contact:** email, website form
> **Services:** support for launching new books and products, from prelaunch to post-release
> **Books:** no preference, previous experience with nonfiction and children's
> **Charges:** flat fee, hourly rate
> **Credentials/experience:** "Owner, Melissa Clutter, has more than a

decade of experience in managing projects and events, such as conferences, film festivals, new brand launches, and concerts. Melissa has skills and a keen understanding of the value of social media and email marketing."

AUDRA JENNINGS PR | AUDRA JENNINGS
2609 Sandy Ln., Corsicana, TX 75110 | 903-874-8363
ajenningspr@gmail.com | *www.audrajennings.com*

Contact: email
Services: publicity, blog tours, social-media management, graphics packages
Specialty: Christian books to Christian media
Books: nonfiction, fiction, children's
Charges: flat fee, hourly rate
Credentials/experience: "I have worked as a publicist in the Christian market since 2002. For 16 years, I worked for two different agencies before going freelance on my own and have worked with every major Christian publisher over the years."

BANNER CONSULTING | MIKE LOOMIS
mike@mikeloomis.co | *www.mikeloomis.co*

Contact: email, website form
Services: book-launch planning, branding, article curation and placement, web development, PR
Specialty: branding and marketing strategy
Books: nonfiction
Charges: custom
Credentials/experience: "I've worked with internationally known brands and *New York Times* bestsellers. I've helped clients get breakthrough PR, speaking engagements, and bestseller lists."

BBH LITERARY | LAURA BARDOLPH
616-319-1641
laura@bbhliterary.com | *bbhliterary.com/publicity*
David Bratt, david@bbhliterary.com

Contact: email, website form
Services: book publicity
Books: nonfiction
Charges: flat fee
Credentials/experience: "Nine years on staff in the marketing department at Eerdmans Publishing, with roles that included

publicist, publicity manager, and director of marketing and publicity."

BBS PUBLISHING AND COMMUNICATIONS, LLC |
PAMELA GOSSIAUX

734-846-0112

pam@pamelagossiaux.com | *BestsellingBookShepherd.com*

Contact: email

Services: marketing, newsletters, blurbs, press kits, blogs, social media and more

Specialty: bestseller campaigns

Books: fiction, nonfiction

Charges: custom, flat fee, hourly rate, package rates

Credentials/experience: "I've promoted authors to Amazon, *USA Today* and *Wall Street Journal* bestsellers. I have dual degrees in Creative Writing and English Language and Literature from University of Michigan and am a speaker and international bestselling author."

BLUE RIDGE READER CONNECTION | EDIE MELSON
604 S. Almond Dr., Simpsonville, SC 29681 | 864-373-4232

ediegmelson@gmail.com | *blueridgereaderconnections.com*

Debb Hackett, brreaderconnection@gmail.com
Darlene Franklin, brreaderconnection@gmail.com
Heather Kreke, brreaderconnection@gmail.com

Contact: website form

Services: connecting authors to readers

Books: all clean reads in all genres

Charges: flat fee

Credentials/experience: "Our aim is to create a place for readers and book clubs to take their reading experience deeper. This is more than opening a new book. This is where you can find new authors or rediscover old favorites and interact with them, check out new writers, and hear about upcoming releases." BRRC falls under the Blue Ridge Mountains Christian Writers Conference.

THE BLYTHE DANIEL AGENCY, INC. | BLYTHE DANIEL
PO Box 64197, Colorado Springs, CO 80962-4197

www.theblythedanielagency.com

Blythe Daniel, blythe@theblythedanielagency.com
Stephanie Alton, stephanie@theblythedanielagency.com

Contact: email

Services: customized pitches to appropriate media: radio, TV, podcasts, websites, magazines, blogs, launch teams, and newspapers/journals

Specialty: placing different genres of books with appropriate media and also with clients we represent who have media platforms; our relationships as literary agents of authors who interview guests has given us additional opportunities

Books: adult nonfiction, children's nonfiction and fiction, some adult fiction

Charges: custom

Credentials/experience: "Blythe Daniel managed the publicity for Thomas Nelson, a division of Harper Collins Christian Publishing, for 7 years and led the publicity team in media relations. She has 26 years of experience managing relationships with traditional media and is also an author and conducts her own publicity and marketing campaigns as well for clients. Stephanie Alton leads the launch teams, blog network, and podcast network for the agency's marketing clients."

BROOKSTONE CREATIVE GROUP | JOHN HERRING

100 Missionary Ridge, Birmingham, AL 35242 | 888-811-9934
www.brookstonecreativegroup.com

Contact: website form

Services: Amazon optimization, social-media assessment and consulting, video interviews, email and digital marketing, search-engine optimization, Facebook and Google ad management

Books: all

Charges: custom, flat fee

Credentials/experience: "Brookstone Creative Group is changing the landscape for how writers, authors, speakers, pastors, musicians, and other creatives navigate the ever-changing landscape of platform development. Through true and tested solutions, training, and community-building, Brookstone Creative Group guides their clients in the who, where, when, and how to inspirational success."

CELEBRATE LIT PUBLICITY | SANDRA BARELA

45459 Stockton St., Beaumont, CA 92223 | 909-520-8603
Celebratelit@celebratelit.com | *www.celebratelit.com*
Denise Barela, editor.deniseb@gmail.com

Contact: email

Services: book tours, epic book-launch promos, social-media building promos

Specialty: book tours, book launches

Books: any Christian or clean fiction and nonfiction

Charges: flat fee

Credentials/Experience: "Our ministry began in 2015. We complete between 28 and 35 promos a month and have over 700,000 views per book tour on average. Both Denise and Sandra have master's degrees in English, which include marketing classes. We have scholarships available."

CHOICE MEDIA & COMMUNICATIONS | HEATHER ADAMS

404-423-8411

hello@choicemediacommunications.com | www.choicemediacommunications.com

Allie Ellers, senior publicist, Allie@ChoiceMediaCommunications.com

Devon Brown, senior publicist, Devon@ChoiceMediaCommunications.com

Emily Taylor, associate publicist, Emily@ChoiceMediaCommunications.com

Contact: website form

Services: media relations, branding and strategy, social media, events, podcast production

Books: nonfiction

Charges: flat fee, retainer-based partnership

Credentials/experience: "Choice Media & Communications is a boutique media and communications business dedicated to providing clients with quality public relations. Choice helps authors create a clear communications plan, gain media coverage, and receive guidance they won't get anywhere else. With more than two decades of high-level professional communications experience across varying industries and with many of today's tastemakers and thought leaders, Choice founder Heather Adams created a public relations business marked with warmth and enthusiasm, strategic development, clear communication, detailed execution, and thorough reporting."

CHRISTIAN INDIE PUBLISHING ASSOCIATION |
SUSAN NEAL

PO Box 481022, Charlotte, NC 28269 | 704-277-7194

cipa@christianpublishers.net | www.christianpublishers.net

Contact: email, website form

Services: resources and tools for publishing and marketing for independent authors

Specialty: marketing services

Books: all genres

Credentials/experience: "Our mission is to support, strengthen, and promote independent authors and small publishers in the Christian marketplace. We have been doing this since 2004."

CREATIVE CORNERSTONES | CAYLAH COFFEEN

Huntsville, AL

creativecornerstones@gmail.com | *creativecornerstones.com*

Contact: email, website form

Services: digital marketing—social media, Facebook and Amazon advertising—media kits, brand advising

Books: fiction

Charges: custom, flat fee, hourly rate

Credentials/experience: "Currently I work as the marketing manager for Monster Ivy Publishing and have also helped multiple indie authors to reach nearly 10K followers and bring in reviews. Using Amazon ad campaigns and keyword metrics, in just a couple months I made one author's novel rise from rank #1,484 to #283 in Religious Science Fiction and Fantasy. The Kindle deal I ran brought it to #2 in free Christian Futuristic Fiction. In the past I've also worked as the marketing manager for The Philips Museum of Art."

EABOOKS PUBLISHING | CHERI COWELL

5840 Red Bug Lake Rd., Winter Springs, FL 32708 | 407-712-3431

yourpartner@eabookspublishing.com | *www.eabookspublishing.com*

Rhonda Robinson, Rhonda@eabookspublishing.com

Contact: email, website form

Services: social-media and email campaigns, book launch, blog tour, electronic media kit, radio and YouTube interviews

Books: fiction, nonfiction, devotional, memoir, children's, Bible study

Charges: flat fee

Credentials/experience: "Serving Christian authors with integrity since 2010."

EPIC—A RESULTS AGENCY | JENNIFER WILLINGHAM

Murfreesboro, TN 615-829-6441

hello@epic.inc | *epic.inc*

Contact: email, phone, website form

Services: social-media management, email marketing, publicity campaigns, press materials, media training, platform development

Credentials/experience: Group of PR and marketing specialists with years of experience.

JONES LITERARY | JASON JONES

2233 Surrey Dr., Murfreesboro, TN 37129-1043 | 512-720-2996
jason@jonesliterary.com | jonesliterary.com
Mark Breta, mark@jonesliterary.com
Marianna Gibson, marianna@jonesliterary.com

Contact: email

Services: literary publicity/PR and consulting, website buildouts, social-media management, speaking engagements, podcast production

Specialty: publicity for books at the intersection of faith and culture, full-service PR campaigns for traditionally published authors, DIY PR tools for self-published authors

Books: nonfiction, fiction, traditionally published, self-published

Charges: custom

Credentials/experience: "Jason led campaigns for HarperCollins Christian/Thomas Nelson's top nonfiction books, brands, and authors between 2007–2013. For many years since he has run one of the nation's most successful literary publicity agencies, having directed PR campaigns for over 400 books and 12 *New York Times* bestsellers. He was also host of *The Book Publicist Podcast* and is an author."

McWRITING SERVICES | SHARON CARTER JENKINS

2162 Spring Stuebner Rd., Ste. 140-1018 , Spring, TX 77389 |
832-930-0604
sharon@mcwritingservices.com | www.mcwritingservices.com

Contact: email, phone, website form

Services: digital marketing services and public relations support

Specialty: helping aspiring authors develop a marketing plan and strategy that fits their specific Kingdom calling

Books: fiction, nonfiction, children's, inspirational

Charges: custom

Credentials/experience: "Sharon C. Jenkins is the inspirational principal for The Master Communicator's Writing Services. Her business provides writing and coaching services to small businesses, nonprofits, and authors. Her professional experience ranges from working as an editor for a major minority communications and marketing company to being an author's virtual coach. She is also a certified authors assistant and life coach. She's hosted events, such as the Authors Networking Summit, America's Favorite Author, and Write Your Book in 90 Days at Alpine Resort, and is the founder of the Authorpreneur Coach Certification Program."

MEDIA CONNECT | SHARON FARNELL

1675 Broadway, New York, NY 10019 | 212-593-6337
sharon.farnell@finnpartners.com | www.media-connect.com

Contact: email

Services: full-service book publicity firm with custom campaigns for each title/author, offering satellite TV tours, radio tours, media tours, as well as outreach to national and local media

Books: all types

Charges: custom, package rates

Credentials/experience: "We are a full-service book publicity agency; and for over 50 years, we've worked with publishers, authors, artists, organizations, and more."

REDEMPTION PRESS | ATHENA DEAN HOLTZ

1602 Cole St., Enumclaw, WA 98022 | 360-226-3488
info@redemption-press.com | www.redemption-press.com
Shelly Brown, shellyb@redemption-press.com

Contact: email, website form

Services: Amazon bestseller campaign, relaunch strategy, influence platform coaching, focused media pitch

Specialty: developing companion-product strategy to relaunch published works

Books: 70% nonfiction, 15% fiction, 15% children's

Charges: custom

Credentials/experience: "Working with indie authors for over 30 years, finding and vetting marketing and publicity services is of the utmost importance."

SIDE DOOR COMMUNICATIONS | DEBBIE LYKINS

224-234-6699
deb@sidedoorcom.net | www.sidedoorcom.net

Contact: website form

Services: media relations, press-kit creation, consulting, publicity-plan development

Books: primarily nonfiction, also children's and fiction but highly selective, no self-published novels, few self-published nonfiction

Charges: custom

Credentials/experience: "Side Door Communications is a national publicity agency that connects faith-based publishers and personalities with national and local media outlets as well as bloggers, with the goal of obtaining coverage in newspapers and magazines, and on radio, television, and the Internet. Based in the Milwaukee area, founder Debbie Lykins has more than two decades of experience in marketing, publicity, and communications."

VERITAS COMMUNICATIONS | DON S. OTIS

318 Huppert Ln., Sandpoint, ID 83864 | 719-275-7775
don@veritasincorporated.com | *www.veritasincorporated.com*

Contact: email

Services: author and ministry publicity and promotion

Specialty: interviews, writing media materials

Books: nonfiction, issues-driven fiction

Charges: flat fee

Credentials/experience: "Thirty years of publicity experience exclusively in the Christian media community. Published author of five books, radio host, producer, and station manager."

WESTWIND BOOK MARKETING | SCOTT LORENZ

1310 Maple St., Plymouth, MI 48170 | 734-667-2090
scottlorenz@westwindcos.com | *www.westwindbookmarketing.com*

Contact: website form

Services: publicity

Books: memoir, business, Christian, fiction, finance

Charges: monthly retainer

Credentials/experience: "With 30+ years as a book publicist, Scott Lorenz knows the service its successful clients want most is publicity—not reports. Westwind clients want a high-level point of contact, and that is why he is actively involved in your book marketing campaign from start to finish. In a world where branding is crucial, Westwind Book Marketing has a powerful social-media presence that gives them the reach needed to move the needle: Twitter followers = 47,800; LinkedIn connections = 6,000; YouTube Channel = 100 book trailers; blog posts about book publishing = 200+. It's important today to have a social-media footprint because so many story ideas are pitched via Twitter, Facebook and LinkedIn and less and less via phone and email. Lorenz is also the author of a 27-time award-winning, bestselling *Book Title Generator: A Proven System in Naming Your Book.*"

WILDFIRE MARKETING | ROB EAGAR

3625 Chartwell Dr., Suwanee, GA 30024 | 770-887-1462
Rob@StartaWildfire.com | www.StartaWildfire.com

Contact: phone, website form

Services: all facets of book marketing, including book launches, author websites, email marketing, social media, public speaking, and author-revenue growth

Specialty: book marketing

Books: all genres

Charges: flat fee

Credentials/experience: "Rob Eagar is the founder of Wildfire Marketing, a consulting practice that has coached more than 1,000 authors and helped books hit *The New York Times* best-seller list in three different categories: new fiction, new nonfiction, and backlist nonfiction. His company has attracted numerous bestselling authors, including Dr. Gary Chapman, Lysa TerKeurst, DeVon Franklin, Wanda Brunstetter, and Dr. John Townsend."

22

LEGAL AND ACCOUNTING SERVICES

CAROL TOPP, CPA

10288 Amberwood Ct., Cincinnati, OH 45241 | 513-290-4730

Carol@TaxesforWriters.com | TaxesForWriters.com

> **Contact:** email, phone
> **Services:** business consulting, consultations, tax review
> **Charges:** hourly rate
> **Credentials/Experience:** "I am a certified public accountant and author of 15 books both self-published and small publishers, including *Business Tips and Taxes for Writers*. I do one-on-one consultations via phone or email with writers to discuss their business set up, operation, and taxes. I am no longer accepting clients for individual tax preparation."

CHRIS MORRIS, CPA, LLC

623-451-8182

cmorris@chrismorriscpa.com | chrismorriscpa.com

> **Contact:** email, website form
> **Services:** accounting, taxes
> **Charges:** flat fee, hourly rate
> **Credentials/experience:** "I have been working with creative entrepreneurs as a certified public accountant for the last decade, with about 65% of my business in the author space. Clients include publishers, agents, authors, editors, and various others related to this space. I know the tax and accounting codes related to this space because I've dedicated the last decade to it. I'm also a published author myself, so I have even more motivation to learn everything well."

TOM UMSTATTD, CPA

13276 Research Blvd., Austin, TX 78750 | 512-250-1090

tom@taxmantom.com | *www.taxmantom.com*

Contact: email, phone, website form
Services: accounting, taxes
Charges: hourly rate
Credentials/experience: Forty years of experience in accounting and taxes.

WINTERS & KING

2448 E. 81st St., Ste. 5900, Tulsa, OK 74137 | 918-494-6868

wintersking.com/attorneys/thomas-j-winters

Contact: phone, website form
Service: contract negotiation
Credentials/experience: "We understand that negotiating with major publishers can feel like a lopsided process, and we work hard to level the playing field. Our experience in the publishing industry allows us to negotiate comprehensive and ironclad publishing contracts based on the realities of the industry. Our goal is to help our clients tell their stories on their own terms and receive the rightful benefits of their hard work through royalties and advances."

23

SPEAKING SERVICES

ADVANCED WRITERS AND SPEAKERS ASSOCIATION (AWSA)

PO Box 6421, Longmont, CO 80501
ReachOut2Linda@gmail.com | awsa.com

Director: Linda Evans Shepherd

Contact: email

Services: website directory, coaching, online training and community, speaking and publishing courses, annual conference prior to the opening of Christian Product Expo, Golden Scroll and Christian Market Book Awards, daily devotion, and *Leading Hearts* magazine

Qualifications: main membership: two major forms of communication from this list: national media (column, blog, podcast, radio or TV show), published book, speaking more than twice a year outside your community, making movies, acting; protégé membership for beginning to intermediate communicators; women only

Fees: $50/year, optional fees for extra benefits

CHRISTIAN COMMUNICATORS CONFERENCE

contact@christiancommunicators.com | www.ChristianCommunicators.com

Directors: Tammy Whitehurst, Lori Boruff

Contact: email

Service: annual conference to educate, validate, and launch speakers to the next level for beginning or seasoned speakers

CHRISTIAN SPEAKER NETWORK

christianspeaker.net

Contact: website form

Service: web page that is listed in the online database

Fee: $39.95/year

CHRISTIAN SPEAKERS BOOT CAMP

PO Box 150473, Grand Rapids, MI 49505 | 616-363-4608
robyn@robyndykstra.com | *christianspeakersbootcamp.com/csbc/bootcamp*

Director: Robyn Dykstra
Contact: website form
Service: a personalized program to catapult your speaking skills and opportunities, teaching you to craft a full-length signature talk that promotes your book, book engagements, negotiate fees, and handle contracts
Fee: custom

CHRISTIAN WOMEN'S SPEAKERS DIRECTORY

877-774-6986
viamarnie@gmail.com | *womenspeakers.com*

Director: Marnie Swedberg
Contact: website form
Services: list speakers on the website, free and paid training
Qualifications: Christian woman older than 18
Fees: free; $49.99/month or $499/year for higher ranking, extra features and benefits; $1598/one time for highest level of promotion
Representation: nonexclusive

DECLARE

info@wearedeclare.com | *wearedeclare.com*

Directors: Eryn Hall, Megan Fish
Contact: email, website form
Services: annual retreat, blog, podcasts, coaching, local events, and webinars

NEXT STEP COACHING SERVICES

amy@amycarroll.org | *amycarroll.org/coaching*

Director: Amy Carroll
Contact: website form
Services: coaching for women speakers, quarterly newsletter

NORTHWEST CHRISTIAN SPEAKERS

Bellingham, WA | 360-966-0203
www.christianspeakersnw.com

Director: Christie Miller

Contact: website form
Services: speakers bureau, not limited to the Northwest; speaker
   training
Requirement: attend training workshops/evaluation session

SHE SPEAKS CONFERENCE

See entry in "Writers Conferences and Seminars."

SPEAK UP SPEAKER SERVICES

3141 Winged Foot Dr., Lakeland, FL 33803 | 586-481-7661
gene4speakup@aol.com | speakupspeakerservices.com

Director: Carol Kent
Contact: mail
Services: speakers bureau, fee negotiation, contracts for services,
   speech and interview coaching, SpeakUp Conference (see listing in
   "Writers Conferences and Seminars")
Qualifications: at least two books or CDs currently available in the
   Christian market and regularly speaking nationally; see list of
   application details to mail
Representation: exclusive, nonexclusive

24

WRITING EDUCATION RESOURCES

ANN KROEKER, WRITING COACH

annkroeker.com/podcasts

> **Type:** podcast
>
> **Host:** Ann Kroeker
>
> **Description:** "These writing podcast episodes offer practical tips and motivation for writers at all stages. . . . Tune in for solutions addressing anything from self-editing and goal-setting . . . to administrative and scheduling challenges."

AUTHOR CONSERVATORY

www.authorconservatory.com

> **Type:** organization, courses
>
> **Directors:** Brett Harris, Kara Swanson Matsumoto
>
> **Description:** "An online, college alternative focused on writing craft and entrepreneurship. Learn the writing and business skills you need to pursue publication and avoid becoming a starving artist. Download our syllabus and apply for a free consultation on our website."

AUTHOR SCHOOL

authorschool.com/courses

> **Type:** courses
>
> **Director:** Rachelle Gardner
>
> **Description:** Giving you the tools you need while pursuing publishing and blogging. Courses are jam-packed with information and resources to help you take the next step toward publishing or building and growing an author blog.

THE BOOK PUBLICIST PODCAST

podcasts.apple.com/us/podcast/the-book-publicist-podcast/id1503562889

> **Type:** podcast
> **Host:** Jason Jones
> **Description:** "Helping authors become their own publicist. Join long-time literary agent/publicist/host Jason Jones as he asks authors, publicists, and media the key questions." No new episodes.

CHRISTIAN EDITORS ASSOCIATION

www.ChristianEditorsAssociation.com

> **Type:** organization
> **Director:** Kathy Ide, *KathyIde@ChristianEditorsAssociation.com*
> **Description:** "Our goal is to equip, empower, and encourage editors in the Christian market through our four divisions. Join a community of like-minded professionals at The Christian PEN. Advance your knowledge and skills through The PEN Institute. Attend the PENCON editors conference. Once you're established, apply to join Christian Editor Connection to get more job leads. Christian Editors Association also sponsors the Editors' Choice Award, honoring superbly written and well-edited recently published books."

CHRISTIAN INDIE WRITERS' PODCAST

christianindiewriters.net/category/podcast

> **Type:** podcast
> **Hosts:** Jenifer Carll-Tong, Christina Cattane, Rhonda Hagerman, Jamie Hershberger
> **Description:** "We inform, encourage and support Christian indie writers on the journey toward publication."

CHRISTIAN PUBLISHING SHOW

christianpublishingshow.com

> **Type:** podcast
> **Host:** Thomas Umstattd, Jr.
> **Description:** "The *Christian Publishing Show* is a podcast to help Christian authors change the world. We talk about how to improve in the craft of writing, how to get published, and how to market effectively. Get expert advice from industry insiders."

CHRISTIAN WRITERS INSTITUTE
christianwritersinstitute.com

> **Type:** organization, courses
> **Directors:** Steve Laube, president; Alana Terry, program director; Dan Balow, conference director
> **Description:** "The Christian Writers Institute was created to help Christians become proficient in the skills, craft, and business of writing. To build the Kingdom of God word-by-word. It does so by providing audio and video courses taught by some of the industry's best teachers. In addition, the Institute publishes a number of books on writing for writers, including *The Christian Writers Market Guide*. Originally founded in 1945, it is estimated that over **30,000** students have been trained by the Christian Writers Institute. It also runs the Write-to-Publish Conference held in Wheaton, IL."

CREATE IF WRITING
createifwriting.com/podcast-and-show-notes

> **Type:** podcast
> **Host:** Kirsten Oliphant
> **Description:** "*Create If Writing* is a podcast for writers and bloggers dealing with authentic platform building online. You will hear from experts on list-building, connecting through Twitter, and how to utilize Facebook. But tools for building an audience would feel empty without a little inspiration, so these training episodes are balanced with inspirational interviews with writers who share their creative process, ups and downs, and how they have dealt with success or failure." No new episodes.

CREATIVELY CHRISTIAN
theophanymedia.com/creativelychristian

> **Type:** podcast
> **Hosts:** Brannon Hollingsworth, Andrea Sandefur, Dave Ebert, Rachel Oxborough
> **Description:** "*Creatively Christian* is a podcast for artists and creatives of all types! *Creatively Christian* explores the intersection of faith and creativity by interviewing believers who use their God-given gifts in unique ways. Through the lives of directors, musicians, artists, writers, and more we inspire, inform, educate, and empower the next generation of creative Christians."

THE DAILY WRITER

dailywriterlife.com/podcast

> **Type:** podcast
> **Host:** Kent Sanders
> **Description:** "*The Daily Writer* podcast helps you cultivate the mindset and habits for creative success. Each weekday, author and ghostwriter Kent Sanders brings you a short lesson on writing inspired by some of history's greatest artists, authors, and thinkers, both past and present. The weekend edition features listener Q&A, conversations with notable writers and creatives, and teaching to help you take a deeper dive as a writer."

DECLARE PODCAST

podcasts.apple.com/us/podcast/declare/id867933809

> **Type:** podcast
> **Host:** Anne Watson
> **Description:** "The mission of Declare is to equip women to walk in their callings as Christian communicators." No new episodes.

FIGHTWRITE PODCAST

www.fightwrite.net/podcast

> **Type:** podcast
> **Host:** Carla Hoch
> **Description:** "A writer's resource for writing believable action and fight scenes." No new episodes.

THE GATECRASHERS PODCAST

gatecrasherspodcast.libsyn.com

> **Type:** podcast
> **Hosts:** Amanda Luedeke, Charis Crowe
> **Description:** "Teaming up to talk about both sides of publishing (self-publishing and traditional), Amanda and Charis share their combined twenty years of experience in the industry from both sides of the desk. They offer a glimpse behind the 'gates' as they share the realities, opportunities, and difficulties of the publishing world." No new episodes.

GRACEWRITERS PODCAST

gracewriters.libsyn.com

> **Type:** podcast

Hosts: Belinda Pollard, Donita Bundy, Alison Joy
Description: "Discussions and interviews that encourage and equip Christian writers who are called to influence popular culture through books, blogs, songwriting, poetry, scriptwriting, copywriting and other forms—whether writing for Christian or mainstream audiences."

THE HABIT
thehabit.co/the-habit-podcast
Type: podcast
Host: Jonathan Rogers
Description: "Conversations with writers about writing."

HOME ROW: JUST KEEP WRITING
homerowpod.com
Type: podcast
Host: J. A. Medders
Description: "Get inspired to write from some of today's best writers. Listen. Learn. Just keep writing. You might learn how to get a book deal, write a best-seller, or quit your day job. Maybe you'll get that nudge you need to . . . write the blog, article, or book you've been thinking on for far too long. As Christians, our aim is to write in such a way that Jesus is made much of and the Church is encouraged to follow our risen Lord." No new episodes.

JERRY JENKINS
jerryjenkins.com/online-creative-writing-courses
Type: courses
Director: Jerry Jenkins
Description: Jerry Jenkins, the author of more than 200 books with sales of more than 73 million copies, including the bestselling Left Behind series and The Chosen novels, offers online courses to help you "become the best writer you can be." Most courses are recordings of live workshops, and all come with lifetime access. Plus he gives away a number of free writing guides by email.

THE JERRY JENKINS WRITERS GUILD
jerrysguild.com
Type: organization, courses
Director: Jerry Jenkins

Description: "The Writers Guild is like a writing conference you can access from anywhere 24/7. Instant access to video training on any writing topic. Additionally, several times each month Jerry answers your questions live, hosts new writing workshops, interviews industry experts, and so much more." Membership is open only periodically; email *wecare@jerryjenkins.com* for the next open period.

THE KEEP WRITING PODCAST
podcasts.apple.com/us/podcast/the-keep-writing-podcast/id1071732977?mt=2

Type: podcast
Host: Nika Maples
Description: "Nika Maples is a writer, speaker, and lupus and stroke survivor who loves to help Christian writers conquer what's holding them back so they can finish, publish, and market their amazing books."

KINGDOM WRITERS
authors.libsyn.com/podcast

Type: podcast
Hosts: CJ and Shelley Hitz
Description: "CJ and Shelley Hitz are passionate about equipping and empowering Christian writers of all genres to share their unique gifts with the world. This podcast is filled with spiritual encouragement as well as prayers to help you overcome the resistance you face as a writer. Your story matters! We believe that you have a specific role to play in the kingdom of heaven to impact lives for eternity. And because of this, we will pour out our lives encouraging writers like you to not only tell your stories but to take the courageous step of self-publishing your stories in books that will outlive you and leave behind a powerful legacy."

NOVEL MARKETING PODCAST
authormedia.com/novel-marketing

Type: podcast
Host: Thomas Umstattd Jr.
Description: "This is the show for writers who want to build their platform, sell more books, and change the world with writing worth talking about. Whether you self-publish or are with a traditional house, this podcast will make book promotion fun and easy. Thomas Umstattd Jr. interviews publishers, indie authors and bestselling traditional authors about how to get published and sell more books."

PASTOR WRITER

pastorwriter.com/episodes

Type: podcast

Host: Chase Replogle

Description: "Join me as I interview pastors, authors, and writing experts in my journey to better understand the calling and the craft of writing, reading, and living the Christian life."

THE PEN INSTITUTE

PENInstitute.com

Type: courses

Director: Susan K. Stewart

Description: "Whether you are just beginning your editing career or are looking for an advanced class to update your skills, The PEN Institute has training opportunities for you. We offer group courses, one-on-one instruction, webinars, videos, lesson packs, and individual mentoring for aspiring and established freelance and in-house editors. Instructors are all experienced industry professionals."

THE PORTFOLIO LIFE WITH JEFF GOINS

podcasts.apple.com/us/podcast/the-portfolio-life-with-jeff-goins/id844091351

Type: podcast

Host: Jeff Goins

Description: "Jeff Goins shares thoughts & ideas that will help you to pursue work that matters, make a difference with your art & discover your true voice!" No new episodes.

THE PROLIFIC CREATOR

podcasts.apple.com/us/podcast/the-art-of-paying-attention/id1185387038

Type: podcast

Host: Ryan Pelton

Description: "*The Prolific Creator* is about life, art, and doing the generous thing. Follow writer, artist, and publisher Ryan J. Pelton as he discusses processes and strategies for writing lots of words, creating lots of art, and the motivation driving the whole thing. TPC podcast also interviews fellow prolific creators, writers, artists, and entrepreneurs as they discuss tips, tricks, and motivation for making art, and doing the generous thing in the world."

THE PURPOSEFUL PEN

www.amylynnsimon.com/purposeful-pen-podcast

    Type: podcast

    Host: Amy Lynn Simon

    Description: "*The Purposeful Pen* podcast is for you if you struggle to understand how to use your writing to glorify God and serve others. We talk about all those thoughts that bounce around in your head telling you that you aren't good enough; what the Bible has to say about earning money for your work; why it's important to know who your ideal reader is and what exactly you have to offer him or her; how to think outside the box and figure out what you really want to accomplish through your writing; how to create a writing life that brings joy to you, glory to God, and benefit to others."

ROB EAGAR MARKETING CONSULTANT

www.startawildfire.com

    Type: courses

    Director: Rob Eagar

    Description: Rob offers a private Book Marketing Master Course anytime and two online video courses—Mastering Amazon for Authors and Sell Books on a Shoestring Budget—at various times during the year.

SERIOUS WRITER

seriouswriter.com

    Type: organization, courses

    Directors: Cyle Young, Bethany Jett

    Description: "The mission of Serious Writer is to build community, create networking opportunities, share current industry information, and provide free and affordable instruction, training, and best practices for writing, marketing, and publishing."

SERIOUS WRITER PODCAST

seriouswriterpodcast.buzzsprout.com

    Type: podcast

    Hosts: Cyle Young, Bethany Jett

    Description: "No matter where you are in your writing journey— just starting out, working on proposals, looking for an agent, or marketing your book—we're happy you're here and we're happy to help." No new episodes.

THE STORY BLENDER PODCAST
www.thestoryblender.com
Type: podcast
Host: Steven James
Description: "We are passionate about well-told, impactful stories. We love to listen to them. Watch them. Create them. So, we decided to talk with premier storytellers from around the country. Hear their stories and get their insights. From novelists to comedians to film makers to artists. Stories are told through a variety of people in a variety of ways. And here they are. The secrets of great storytelling from great storytellers."

THE STORY EMBERS PODCAST
storyembers.org/podcast
Type: podcast
Host: James Noller
Description: "A discussion-based podcast where Story Embers staff members explore how to glorify God through storytelling. New episodes are released every third Monday of the month and cover all areas of story craft, including plot, theme, characters, and more."

THE STORYTELLER'S MISSION WITH ZENA DELL LOWE
www.buzzsprout.com/872170
Type: podcast
Host: Zena Dell Lowe
Description: "Zena Dell Lowe is a seasoned and engaging teacher with a passion for writers and storytellers. Her focused, concise, and practical episodes (all under 20 minutes) not only explore the nuts and bolts of the craft, but also dive deep into the inner life of the artist and the 'why' behind creativity. If you believe that story matters, you'll want to give this podcast a listen."

TAYLOR UNIVERSITY ONLINE PROFESSIONAL WRITING
www.taylor.edu/online/courses/content-areas/communication-writing
Type: courses
Director: Linda Taylor
Description: "Online program with both certificate and AA offerings. One-to-one ratio, flexible schedule, and open enrollment. Work with professionals as your instructors."

THE YOUNG WRITER

www.theyoungwriter.com/workshop

Type: organization, courses

Directors: Brett Harris, Josiah DeGraaf

Description: "A supportive online Christian community for young writers. Learn how to write more, hone your craft, and finish projects you're proud of—all while connecting with published authors and like-minded peers. Enrollment opens every January, May, and August."

WRITE FOR A REASON

writeforareason.buzzsprout.com

Type: podcast

Host: Janet Wilson

Description: "For Christians new to writing novels for kids and teens. Creative writing tips, encouragement and inspiration." No new episodes.

WRITE FROM THE DEEP

writefromthedeep.com/write-from-the-deep-podcast

Type: podcast

Hosts: Karen Ball, Erin Taylor Young

Description: "Encouragement, refreshment, and truth from writers, for writers. Every writer, at some point, faces the deep places of crushing trials and struggles. But the deep is also a place where we can learn to abide in God as never before. This podcast reminds writers they're not alone, and equips and helps them to embrace the deep, to discover their truest voice and message, and to share it with refined craft and renewed passion."

WRITE2IGNITE MASTER CLASSSES

write2ignite.com

Type: courses

Director: Jean Matthew Hall

Description: Write2Ignite offers two master classes a year to target specific skills and genres to help Christians who write for children and young adults to master those skills.

A WRITER'S DAY

podcasts.apple.com/us/podcast/a-writers-day/id1472104073

Type: podcast

Host: R. A. Douthitt

Description: "A podcast to help writers learn more about the craft, talk with published authors, and learn more about the publishing industry in order to have a competitive edge. Today, it takes more than just a good story to become a successful writer. You must know about marketing strategies, publishing options, and platforms that will help you stand out from the millions of writers out there. This podcast will help you."

THE WRITERLY LIFE

podcasts.apple.com/us/podcast/the-writerly-life/id914574328

Type: podcast

Host: hope*writers

Description: "Each episode of *The Writerly Life* offers you practical tips and interviews with publishing pros to help you skip the long learning curve and put you ahead of the game. *The Writerly Life* is all about balancing the art of writing with the business of publishing so that you can hustle without losing heart. Listen in and be inspired to keep putting your pen to the page. We'll help you find clarity to take the next step in your writing journey. You have words, and your words matter. Let's get them out into the world!" No new episodes.

WRITING AT THE RED HOUSE

www.writingattheredhouse.com/podcast-2

Type: podcast

Host: Kathi Lipp

Description: "The podcast is for those who love God and want to share His story through writing, speaking, social media—and yes—even marketing. . . . The refreshing and honest take on the 'industry' do's and don'ts, as well as insight on what makes you stand out from the rest, will not only entertain, but will serve in helping you propel your career to the next level."

WRITING FOR YOUR LIFE

writingforyourlife.com

Type: organization

Director: Kate Rademacher

Description: "Writing for Your Life is committed to offering a wide variety of useful resources and services to support spiritual writers. We offer online and in-person conferences featuring leading spiritual writers and publishing industry experts. Authors discuss and teach about various aspects of spiritual writing. Industry experts offer advice on how to get published and how to market. We also provide a host of services and free resources to support your spiritual writing. We cannot guarantee that you will become a best-selling author, but we will help you take your best shot. Learn to tell your own story; write for your life!"

WRITING PURSUITS

www.writingpursuits.com/podcast

Type: podcast
Host: Kathrese McKee
Description: "*Writing Pursuits* is a weekly podcast for authors who drink too much coffee, endure judgmental looks from their furry writing companions, and struggle for words. If you are a writer seeking encouragement, information, and inspiration, this podcast is for you."

YOUR BEST WRITING LIFE

www.buzzsprout.com/1127762

Type: podcast
Host: Linda Goldfarb
Description: "Christian writing industry experts share weekly content for all levels of Christian writers. Whether you're a beginner or bestseller, you receive practical information and how-to application you can use to grow your writing career as a faith-based author. Each week, Linda Goldfarb and her guests cover various topics, including the craft of writing, fiction topics, nonfiction topics, self-care for writers, and the business of writing to name a few. If you're an aspiring Christian writer, we have content to help you grow. Published writers, we have current content to make your next book proposal, manuscript editing, speaking event, and writer's conference worth your time and energy."

25

CONTESTS AND AWARDS

A listing here does not guarantee endorsement of the contest. For guidelines on evaluating contests, go to *www.sfwa.org/other-resources/for-authors/writer-beware/contests.*

Note: Dates may not be accurate since many sponsors had not posted their 2024 dates before press time.

CHILDREN AND TEENS

CORETTA SCOTT KING BOOK AWARD
www.ala.org/awardsgrants/awards/24/apply

> **Description:** Sponsored by Coretta Scott King Task Force, American Library Association. Annual award for children's books published the previous year by African-American authors and/or illustrators. Books must promote an understanding and appreciation of the "American Dream" and fit one of these categories: preschool to grade 4, grades 5-8, grades 9-12.
> **Deadline:** December 1
> **Entry fee:** none
> **Prizes:** $1,000 and plaque

SOCIETY OF CHILDREN'S BOOK WRITERS AND ILLUSTRATORS
www.scbwi.org/awards/grants/for-authors

> **Description:** Sponsors a variety of contests and grants.
> **Deadline:** varies
> **Entry fee:** none
> **Prizes:** vary

WORDS AND MUSIC WRITING COMPETITION
wordsandmusic.org/contest

Description: Sponsored by *Peauxdunque Review*. Categories: poetry, fiction, creative nonfiction, and short story by a high-school student, plus multigenre "Beyond the Bars" for incarcerated juveniles. Previously unpublished work only.
Deadline: August 1
Entry fee: varies by category
Prizes: $500–750, depending on category, plus publication in *Peauxdunque Review*

FICTION

AMERICAN CHRISTIAN FICTION WRITERS CONTESTS
acfw.com/acfw-contests

Description: Genesis Contest for unpublished Christian fiction writers in a number of categories/genres. First Impressions Contest for unpublished writers. Carol Awards for best Christian fiction published the previous year.
Deadline: varies by contest
Entry fee: varies by category and membership status
Prizes: vary by contest

AWP PRIZE FOR THE NOVEL
www.awpwriter.org/contests/awp_award_series_overview

Description: Sponsored by Association of Writers and Writing Programs. Open to published and unpublished authors. Length: at least 60,000 words.
Deadline: submit between January 1 and February 28
Entry fee: $15 for members, $30 for nonmembers
Prizes: $2,500 and publication by the University of Nebraska Press

THE BARD FICTION PRIZE
www.bard.edu/bfp

Description: Sponsored by Bard College. Awarded to a promising, emerging young writer of fiction, 39 years or younger and an American citizen. Entries must be previously published.
Deadline: June 15
Entry fee: none

Prizes: $30,000 and appointment as writer-in-residence for one semester at Bard College, Annandale-on-Hudson, New York

BOSTON REVIEW AURA ESTRADA SHORT STORY CONTEST

www.bostonreview.net/contests

Description: Previously unpublished short stories no longer than 5,000 words.
Deadline: June 30
Entry fee: $20
Prizes: $1,000 plus publication

BULWER-LYTTON FICTION CONTEST

www.bulwer-lytton.com

Description: Sponsored by San Jose State University English Department. For the worst opening line to a novel. Each submission must be a single sentence; multiple entries allowed. Entries will be judged by categories: general, detective, western, science fiction, romance, etc. Overall winners, as well as category winners.
Deadline: June 30
Entry fee: none
Prizes: publication on the website

THE CROWN AWARD

acfwvirginia.com/acfw-virginia-the-crown

Description: Sponsored by ACFW Virginia. Gives unpublished writers the opportunity to have those all-important, first five pages of their Christian fiction manuscript evaluated by industry professionals. Requires a one-page synopsis, which is not scored. Categories: contemporary, contemporary romance, historical/historical romance/historical romantic suspense, mystery/thriller/suspense/romantic suspense, speculative, young adult/middle grade.
Deadline: submit between July 10 and August 9
Entry fee: chapter members, $20; nonmembers, $25
Prizes: badge, certificate, and crown lapel pin or tie clip for each category winner

FAITH, HOPE AND LOVE READER'S CHOICE AWARD

fhlchristianwriters.com/fhlcw-readers-choice-award

Description: Sponsored by Faith, Hope and Love Christian Writers

(FHLCW). For Christian romances or Christian novels with romantic elements in print form. FHLCW defines Christian fiction as "stories written by writers whose worldview, influenced by their faith in the God of the Bible, is woven into the fabric of the book or manuscript." Entries should not include inappropriate or gratuitous demonstration of sin, whether in language (profanity), violence, or sexual situations.

Deadline: March 1
Entry fee: $25 for FHLCW members, $35 for nonmembers
Prizes: winner in each category: engraved box; finalists in each category: certificate

FLANNERY O'CONNOR AWARD FOR SHORT FICTION

www.ugapress.org/index.php/series/FOC

Description: Sponsored by University of Georgia Press. For collections of short fiction. Length: 40,000–75,000 words. Contestants must be residents of North America.
Deadline: submit between April 1 and May 31
Prizes: $1,000 plus publication under a royalty book contract

GET PUBBED

scriveningspress.com/get-pubbed

Description: Sponsored by Scrivenings Press. Entries will be divided among four broad categories: speculative, historical, contemporary, and mystery/suspense. Submit the first ten pages.
Deadline: varies, check the website
Entry fee: $25
Prizes: grand prize, publishing contract, paid registration for annual author retreat, thorough critique of up to 25 pages of the manuscript, and $75 Amazon gift card; entry with the highest score in each genre will receive a critique of up to 25 pages of the manuscript and $25 Amazon gift card

GRACE PALEY PRIZE FOR SHORT FICTION

www.awpwriter.org/contests/awp_award_series_overview

Description: Sponsored by Association of Writers and Writing Programs. Short-story collections. May contain stories previously published in periodicals. Length: 150–300 pages.
Deadline: submit between January 1 and February 28
Entry fee: $25
Prizes: $5,500 and publication

HAVOK

gohavok.com/submission-guidelines

Description: Sponsored by Havok Publishing. For flash fiction 300–1,000 words. Havok operates as an ongoing publishing contest, with monthly themes and deadlines, seasonal awards, and smaller prizes randomly throughout the year ("Best Story Title," "Most Prolific Author," etc.). Publishes stories in five major genres (mashups allowed): science fiction, fantasy, mystery, thriller, and comedy. Each month, 20 stories win the website publication round. Then each six-month season, 30 of those published stories win their way into print and ebook anthologies (with payment varying by season as company grows; minimum $30). Top two stories in each six-month season are awarded $100 each.

Deadline: monthly

Entry fee: free

Prizes: $100 Readers' Choice Award, $100 Editors' Choice Award, and more

JAMES JONES FIRST NOVEL FELLOWSHIP

tinyurl.com/v8ee2t8v

Description: Sponsored by Wilkes University. For a first novel or novel-in-progress by a US writer who has not published a novel. Submit a two-page outline and the first 50 pages of an unpublished novel.

Deadline: submit between October 1 and March 15

Entry fee: $30 plus $3 processing fee

Prizes: first place, $10,000; first runner-up, $2,000; second runner-up, $1,000

KATHERINE ANNE PORTER PRIZE FOR FICTION

untpress.unt.edu/authors/porter-prize-submissions

Description: Sponsored by University of North Texas Press. Quality unpublished fiction by emerging writers of contemporary literature. Can be a combination of short-shorts, short stories, and novellas from 100 to 200 pages (27,500–50,000 words). Material should be previously unpublished in book form.

Deadline: submit between May 1 and June 30

Entry fee: $25

Prizes: $1,000 and publication by UNT Press

NOVEL STARTS

scriveningspress.com/novel-starts

Description: Sponsored by Scrivenings Press. For an unfinished novel in four genres: speculative, historical, contemporary, and mystery/suspense. Submit the first five pages.

Deadline: varies, check the website

Entry fee: $25

Prizes: grand prize, author retreat, invitation to submit novel for consideration by Scrivenings Press once it is finished, thorough critique of up to 25 pages of the manuscript, and $75 Amazon gift card; entry with the highest score in each genre will receive a critique of up to 25 pages of the manuscript and $25 Amazon gift card

THE REALM AWARDS

www.realmmakers.com/enter-the-awards

Description: Sponsored by The Faith and Fantasy Alliance. Genre awards in these categories: science fiction, fantasy, supernatural, paranormal, horror, young adult, middle grade, short fiction, audio, and specialty. Children's and graphic novels every other year. Length: novels, 60,000 words minimum; YA, 50,000 words minimum; middle grade, 20,000 words minimum; short stories, 9,999 words minimum; novellas, 10,000 words up to the category minimum.

Deadline: submit between January 1 and 21

Entry fee: $15–35, depending on category

Prizes: commemorative award, award stickers, promotional opportunities, and the opportunity to be carried in the Realm Makers Mobile Bookstore and Bookish bookstore

REALM MAKER'S READERS' CHOICE AWARD

www.realmmakers.com/realm-award-readers-choice-alliance-award

Description: Sponsored by The Faith and Fantasy Alliance to give readers their say in what speculative fiction novels they enjoyed most in the preceding year. Only readers may nominate books in this contest. Books may be traditionally published or self-published.

Deadline: submit between April 1 and 15

Entry fee: none

Prize: certificate of recognition

SERENA MCDONALD KENNEDY AWARD

www.snakenationpress.org/snakenation

Description: Sponsored by Snake Nation Press. Novellas up to 50,000 words or short-story collections up to 200 pages, published or unpublished.
Deadline: August 31
Entry fee: $30
Prizes: $1,000 and publication

TOBIAS WOLFF AWARD FOR FICTION

www.bhreview.org/general-submissions-guidelines

Description: Sponsored by Western Washington University's *Bellingham Review*. Length: 5,000 words maximum.
Deadline: submit between December 1 and March 15
Entry fee: $20
Prizes: $1,000 plus publication

ZOETROPE: ALL-STORY SHORT FICTION COMPETITION

www.zoetrope.com/contests

Description: For all genres of literary fiction. Entries must be unpublished and strictly 5,000 words or fewer. More than one entry allowed.
Deadline: October 2
Entry fee: $30
Prizes: first place, $1,000; second place, $500; third place, $250; plus publication of winning story and consideration for agency representation

MULTIPLE GENRES

ANGEL BOOK AWARDS

ffbookfestival.com

Description: Sponsored by Faith & Fellowship Book Festival to promote excellent books with a Christian worldview. The awards are open to all writers whose Christian fiction or nonfiction books were originally published between January 1 and June 30. Books entered must be written from a Christian worldview. There should be no profanity, gratuitous violence, graphic sex, or other objectionable material not accepted by Christian publishing standards.
Deadline: June 30
Entry fee: $50

Prizes: certificate and logo that can be uploaded to blogs, used on memes, etc., for each winner; first place winners also receive a display award; most entries will receive judges' feedback

BLUE RIDGE MOUNTAINS CHRISTIAN WRITERS CONFERENCE CONTESTS

www.blueridgeconference.com/contest-info

Description: Sponsors three book contests for fiction or nonfiction: Foundation Awards, Directors' Choice Awards, and The Selah Awards. Look for details about guidelines, deadlines, and entry fees on the website after January 1.

Deadline: varies by contest

Entry fee: $35–40

THE BRAUN BOOK AWARDS

wordalivepress.ca/pages/the-braun-book-awards

Description: Sponsored by Word Alive Press. For unpublished Christian books written by Canadian citizens and permanent residents in Canada. Categories: nonfiction and fiction.

Deadline: March 15

Entry fee: none

Prizes: one fiction and one nonfiction manuscript will each receive a royalty-based book publishing contract; select number of secondary winners will also receive prizes, including credit toward publishing

CASCADE WRITING CONTEST

www.oregonchristianwriters.org

Description: Sponsored by Oregon Christian Writers. Open to anyone with emphasis on unpublished works. All contestants receive three score sheets from the judges reviewing their work, and finalists receive an additional two score sheets.

Deadline: submit between January 15 and February 15

Entry fee: $35 for members, $45 for nonmembers

Prizes: certificates to all finalists; pins to the winners

CHRISTIAN INDIE AWARDS

www.christianaward.com

Description: Sponsored by Christian Indie Publishing Association. This award is designed to promote and bring recognition to quality Christian books by small publishers and independently published authors. Books must be printed in English, for sale in the United States, and promote the Christian faith. Awards are offered in 18 categories. Publishers and authors may nominate titles.

Deadline: October 1

Entry fee: $89–109, depending on submission date

Prizes: promotion

EDITORS' CHOICE AWARD

christianeditorsassociation.com/eca

Description: This award (which ran for seven years as Excellence in Editing Award) celebrates the authors, editors, and publishers behind books that are superbly written, well edited, and published by a Christian publisher or self-published by a Christian author. Each year's contest is open to books published the previous calendar year. Winners announced at PENCON. Judges' notes provided on request.

Deadline: December 31

Entry fee: $60 before November 15, $75 after; discounts for members of The Christian PEN and Christian Editor Connection

Prizes: promotion of finalist and winning books on websites and social media, digital emblems, printed stickers, certificates, blog and newsletter interviews; winning authors and editors receive select benefits from divisions of Christian Editors Association

ERIC HOFFER BOOK AWARD

www.hofferaward.com

Description: Eighteen categories for books from small, academic, and micro presses, including self-published, ebooks, and older books. The prose category is for creative fiction and nonfiction fewer than 10,000 words.

Deadline: January 21

Entry fee: varies by category

Prizes: $2,500 grand prize, other prizes awarded in categories

HIGHER GOALS AWARDS

www.evangelicalpress.com/contest

Description: Sponsored by Evangelical Press Association. Awards are given in a variety of categories for periodical manuscripts published in the previous year. Although most submissions are made by publication staff members, associate EPA members may also submit their articles.

Deadline: submit between mid-November and January 23
Entry fee: $27
Prizes: certificate

NARRATIVE CONTESTS
www.narrativemagazine.com/submit-your-work

Description: Biannual contests in a variety of categories, including short stories, essays, memoirs, poetry, and literary nonfiction. Entries must be previously unpublished. Length: varies by category.
Deadline: varies
Entry fee: varies
Prizes: vary by category

NATIONAL WRITERS ASSOCIATION CONTESTS
www.nationalwriters.com/page/page/2734945.htm

Description: Sponsors five contests: novel, young writers, poetry, short short, and David Raffelock Award for Publishing Excellence.
Deadline: varies by contest
Entry fee: varies by contest
Prizes: vary by contest

NEW LETTERS EDITOR'S CHOICE AWARD
www.newletters.org/editors-choice-award

Description: Sponsored by *New Letters*. For short narratives, whether they are stories, essays, poems, or hybrid forms. Length: maximum 1,000 words.
Deadline: submit between July 1 and October 16
Entry fee: $20
Prizes: $1,000 and publication in magazine

NEW MILLENNIUM WRITING AWARDS
newmillenniumwritings.submittable.com/submit

Description: Sponsored by New Millennium Writings. Fiction and nonfiction, 6,000 words maximum; flash fiction (short-short story), 1,000 words maximum; poetry, three poems to five pages total. No restrictions as to style or subject matter.
Deadline: November 30
Entry fee: $20, $35 for two entries, $45 for three entries, $60 for four entries, $80 for five entries
Prizes: $1,000 plus publication for each category

TENNESSEE WILLIAMS/NEW ORLEANS LITERARY FESTIVAL

tennesseewilliams.net/contests

Description: Tennessee Williams gained some early recognition by entering a writing contest. The festival that bears his name now sponsors writing contests in poetry, fiction, very short fiction, and one-act playwriting.

Deadline: varies according to genre

Entry fee: varies

Prizes: vary by category

THE WORD GUILD CHRISTIAN WRITING AWARDS

thewordguild.com/contests

Description: The Word Awards recognize the best work published in the previous year in a wide variety of categories and are open to all Canadian writers who are Christian. You do not need to be a member of The Word Guild to submit an entry, but members save money on their entry fees.

Deadline: varies according to award

Entry fee: varies according to award

Prizes: vary according to award

THE WRITER 500-WORD CONTEST

www.writermag.com/the-writer-contests

Description: Any genre, fiction or nonfiction. Multiple submissions allowed. Length: maximum 500 words.

Deadline: submit between March 28 and May 16

Entry Fee: $25

Prizes: first place, $1,000, publication in *The Writer* and on website, one-year VIP membership; second place, $500, publication on the website, and one-year VIP membership; third place, $250, publication on the website, and one-year VIP membership

WRITER'S DIGEST COMPETITIONS

www.writersdigest.com/writers-digest-competitions

Description: Every other month, *Writer's Digest* presents a creative challenge for fun and prizes, providing a short, open-ended prompt for short-story submissions based on that prompt. Winner receives publication in *Writer's Digest*. Also sponsors annual contests for a wide variety of genres, including inspirational, feature articles,

short stories, poetry, personal essays, and self-published books.
Deadline: varies according to contest
Entry fee: varies
Prizes: vary

THE WRITERS' UNION OF CANADA AWARDS & COMPETITIONS
www.writersunion.ca/content/awards

Description: Short Prose Competition for Developing Writers in fiction or nonfiction by an author who has not yet published a book. Length: 2,500 words maximum. Danuta Gleed Literary Award for the best first collection of short fiction.
Deadline: varies
Entry fee: varies
Prizes: Short Prose, $2,500; Danuta, $10,000 plus two finalist awards of $1,000 each

NONFICTION

ANNIE DILLARD AWARD
bhreview.org/general-submissions-guidelines

Description: Sponsored by Western Washington University's *Bellingham Review*. Unpublished essays on any subject. Length: 5,000 words maximum.
Deadline: submit between December 1 and March 15
Entry fee: $20 for first submission, $10 each additional one
Prize: $1,000

BECHTEL PRIZE
www.twc.org/publications/bechtel-prize

Description: Sponsored by Teachers & Writers Collaborative. For unpublished essays describing a creative writing teaching experience, project, or activity that demonstrates innovation in creative writing instruction. Length: 2,500 words maximum.
Deadline: January 15
Entry fee: $20
Prizes: $1,000 and publication

EVENT NON-FICTION CONTEST

www.eventmagazine.ca/contest-nf

Description: Unpublished creative nonfiction. Length: 5,000 words maximum.

Deadline: October 15

Entry fee: $34.95, includes a one-year subscription to *EVENT*

Prizes: first place, $1,500; second place, $1,000; third place, $500 plus publication

GUIDEPOSTS WRITERS WORKSHOP CONTEST

guideposts.org/writers-workshop-contest

Description: Contest is held in even years. Submit an original, unpublished, true, first-person story (your own or ghostwritten for another person) about an experience that changed your life. Show how faith made a difference. Length: 1,500 words maximum.

Deadline: mid-June

Entry fee: none

Prizes: all-expenses-paid, weeklong writers workshop in New York to learn about inspirational storytelling and writing for Guideposts publications for 12 winners

INTREPID TIMES TRAVEL WRITING COMPETITION

intrepidtimes.com/competitions

Description: Sponsored by Exisle Publishing. *Intrepid Times* has a proud history of running narrative, travel-writing contests that focus on stories, places, and people.

Deadline: varies

Entry fee: free

Prizes: first place, $150, publication on website, and possible publication in anthology; runners-up, $50

RICHARD J. MARGOLIS AWARD

www.margolisaward.org

Description: Sponsored by Blue Mountain Center. Given annually to a promising young journalist or essayist whose work combines warmth, humor, wisdom, and concern with social justice. Submit at least two examples of published or unpublished work and a short biographical note, including a description of current and anticipated work. Length: 30 pages maximum.

Deadline: July 1

Entry fee: none
Prizes: first place, $5,000 plus a one-month residency at the Blue
   Mountain Center in Blue Mountain Lake, New York; finalists, $1,000

THE SUE WILLIAM SILVERMAN PRIZE FOR CREATIVE NONFICTION

www.awpwriter.org/contests/awp_award_series_overview

Description: Sponsored by Association of Writers and Writing
   Programs. Open to published and unpublished authors. Book
   collection of nonfiction manuscripts.
Deadline: submit between January 1 and February 28
Entry fee: $15 for members, $30 for nonmembers
Prizes: $2,500 and publication with the University of Georgia Press

THE WRITER ESSAY CONTEST

www.writermag.com/the-writer-contests

Description: Nonfiction essay on any theme, subject, or genre.
   Length: under 2,000 words.
Deadline: submit between January 10 and February 28
Entry Fee: $25
Prizes: first place, $1,000, publication in *The Writer* and on website,
   one-year VIP membership; second place, $500, publication on
   the website, and one-year VIP membership; third place, $250,
   publication on the website, and one-year VIP membership

PLAYS/SCRIPTS/SCREENPLAYS

ACADEMY NICHOLL FELLOWSHIPS IN SCREENWRITING

www.oscars.org/nicholl/about

Description: International contest open to any writer who has not
   optioned or sold a treatment, teleplay, or screenplay for more than
   $35,000. May submit up to three scripts. Length: 70–160 pages.
Deadline: submit between March 1 and May 1
Entry fee: $50–90, depending on submission date
Prizes: up to five $35,000 fellowships; recipients will be expected to
   complete at least one original feature-film screenplay during the
   fellowship year

AMERICAN ZOETROPE SCREENPLAY CONTEST

www.zoetrope.com/contests

> **Description:** To find and promote new and innovative voices in cinema. For screenplays and television pilots. No entrant may have earned more than $5,000 as a screenwriter for theatrical films or television or for the sale of, or sale of an option to, any original story, treatment, screenplay, or teleplay. Prizes, fellowships, awards, and other contest winnings are not considered earnings and are excluded from this rule. Length: film scripts, 70–130 pages; one-hour television pilot scripts, 45–65 pages; half-hour television scripts, 22–34 pages.
> **Deadline:** September 5
> **Entry fee:** $40–50, depending on submission date
> **Prizes:** first place, $5,000 plus consideration for film option and development; nine finalists will also get this consideration

AUSTIN FILM FESTIVAL SCREENWRITERS COMPETITION

austinfilmfestival.com/submit

> **Description:** Offers a number of contest categories, including narrative feature, narrative short, documentary feature, documentary short for screenplays, screenplay, teleplay, and scripted digital competition.
> **Deadline:** varies by type
> **Entry fee:** $35–70, varies by type and submission date
> **Prizes:** $1,000–5,000

KAIROS PRIZE FOR SPIRITUALLY UPLIFTING SCREENPLAYS

www.kairosprize.com

> **Description:** Sponsored by Movieguide. For feature-length screenplays. Judges consider not only a script's entertainment value and craftsmanship, but also whether it is uplifting, inspirational, and spiritual and if it teaches lessons in ethics and morality. Length: 87–130 pages; will accept scripts up to 150 pages (not counting the title page) for an additional $20.
> **Deadline:** submit between July 20 and October 31
> **Entry fee:** varies, depending on submission date
> **Prizes:** $15,000 each for first-time and professional screenwriters

MILDRED AND ALBERT PANOWSKI PLAYWRITING COMPETITION

www.nmu.edu/forestrobertstheatre/playwritingcompetition

> **Description:** Sponsored by Forest Roberts Theatre, Northern Michigan

421

University. Unpublished, unproduced, full-length plays. Award to encourage and stimulate artistic growth among educational and professional playwrights. Provides students and faculty members the opportunity to mount and produce an original work on the university stage.

Deadline: submit between October 1 and November 1

Entry fee: none

Prizes: $2,000, a summer workshop, a fully mounted production, and transportation to Marquette, Michigan

MOONDANCE INTERNATIONAL FILM FESTIVAL COMPETITION

www.moondancefilmfestival.com

Description: Offers a variety of awards for films, screenplays, librettos, and features that raise awareness about social issues.

Deadline: October 31

Entry fee: $25–50

Prizes: promotion to film companies for possible option

SCRIPTAPALOOZA SCREENPLAY COMPETITION

www.scriptapalooza.com/competition/how-to-enter

Description: Any screenplay from any genre considered; must be the original work of the author (multiple authorship acceptable). Shorts competition: screenplays fewer than 40 pages.

Deadline: submit between December 12 and April 3

Entry fee: $30–75, depending on category and deadline

Prizes: first place, $10,000; each genre winner, $500; plus access to more than 50 producers through Scriptapalooza's network

SCRIPTAPALOOZA TV COMPETITION

www.scriptapaloozatv.com/competition

Description: Scripts for television pilots, one-hour dramas, reality shows, and half-hour sitcoms. Length: pilots, 30–60 pages; one-hour drama, 50–60 pages; reality show, one- to five-page treatment; half-hour sitcom, 25–35 pages.

Deadline: submit between September 6 and October 10

Entry fee: $45–55, varies with deadline

Prizes: first place, $500; second place, $200; third place, $100 in each category; plus access to more than 50 producers through Scriptapalooza's network

POETRY

49TH PARALLEL AWARD FOR POETRY

bhreview.org/general-submissions-guidelines

Description: Sponsored by Western Washington University's *Bellingham Review*. Up to three poems in any style or on any subject.
Deadline: submit between December 1 and March 15
Entry fee: $20; international entries, $30
Prizes: $1,000 and publication

ACADEMY OF AMERICAN POETS

poets.org/academy-american-poets/american-poets-prizes

Description: See the website for a list of multiple contests and prizes.

BALTIMORE REVIEW POETRY CONTEST

baltimorereview.submittable.com/submit

Description: All styles and forms of poetry, directed toward an announced theme. Maximum of three entries.
Deadline: November 30
Entry fee: none
Prizes: $100–500 and publication

BARBARA MANDIGO KELLY PEACE POETRY AWARDS

www.peacecontests.org/#poetry

Description: Sponsored by Nuclear Age Peace Foundation. Awards to encourage poets to explore and illuminate positive visions of peace and the human spirit. Poems must be original, unpublished, and in English. May submit up to three poems for one entry fee.
Deadline: July 1
Entry fee: adults, $15; youth ages 13–18, $5; ages 12 and under, none
Prizes: adult winner, $1,000; youth winner, $200; ages 12 and under, $200

BOSTON REVIEW ANNUAL POETRY CONTEST

www.bostonreview.net/about/contests

Description: Submit up to five unpublished poems; no more than ten pages total. Submit manuscripts in duplicate with cover note.
Deadline: May 31/June 30
Entry fee: $20, includes a subscription to *Boston Review*
Prizes: $1,000 plus publication

CAVE CANEM POETRY PRIZE

cavecanempoets.org/prizes/cave-canem-poetry-prize

Description: Sponsored by Cave Canem Foundation. Supports the work of black poets of African descent with excellent manuscripts and who have not found a publisher for their first book. Offered every other year. Length: 48–75 pages.

Deadline: January 31

Entry fee: none

Prizes: $1,000 plus publication by a national press and copies of the book, with a feature reading in New York City

THE DONALD HALL PRIZE FOR POETRY

www.awpwriter.org/contests/awp_award_series_overview

Description: Sponsored by Association of Writers and Writing Programs. Open to published and unpublished authors. Length: 48 pages maximum.

Deadline: submit between January 1 and February 28

Entry fee: $15 for members, $30 for nonmembers

Prizes: $5,500 and publication by University of Pittsburgh Press

HOLLIS SUMMERS POETRY PRIZE

www.ohioswallow.com/poetry_prize

Description: Sponsored by Ohio University Press. For an unpublished collection of original poems, 60–95 pages. Open to both those who do not have a published book-length collection and to those who have.

Deadline: December 31

Entry fee: $30

Prizes: $1,000 plus publication in book form by Ohio University Press

JAMES LAUGHLIN AWARD

www.poets.org/academy-american-poets/james-laughlin-award-guidelines

Description: Sponsored by Academy of American Poets. To recognize a second full-length print book of original poetry by a US citizen, permanent resident, or person who has DACA/TPS status, forthcoming within the next calendar year. Author must have published one book of poetry in English in a standard edition (48 pages or more) in the United States or under contract and scheduled for publication during the current calendar year;

publication of chapbooks (less than 48 pages) does not disqualify. Length: 48–100 pages.
Deadline: submit between August 1 and October 1
Entry fee: none
Prizes: $5,000 plus publication

JESSIE BRYCE NILES CHAPBOOK CONTEST

comstockreview.org/comstock-writers-group-chapbook-award-for-2014

Description: Sponsored by Comstock Review, Inc. Submissions must be unpublished as a collection, but individual poems may have been published previously in journals. Length: 25–34 pages. Poems may run longer than one page.
Deadline: submit between August 1 and October 31
Entry fee: $30
Prizes: $1,000 plus publication and author copies

KATE TUFTS DISCOVERY AWARD

arts.cgu.edu/tufts-poetry-awards

Description: Sponsored by Claremont Graduate University. Award presented annually for a first poetry volume published in the preceding year by a poet of genuine promise.
Deadline: June 30
Entry fee: none
Prize: $10,000

KINGSLEY TUFTS POETRY AWARD

arts.cgu.edu/tufts-poetry-awards

Description: Sponsored by Claremont Graduate University. Presented annually for a published book of poetry by a midcareer poet to both honor the poet and provide the resources that allow artists to continue working toward the pinnacle of their craft.
Deadline: June 30
Entry fee: none
Prizes: $100,000 and one week residence at Claremont Graduate University

MURIEL CRAFT BAILEY MEMORIAL POETRY AWARD

comstockreview.org/annual-contest

Description: Sponsored by *Comstock Review*. Unpublished poems up to 40 lines. No limit on number of submissions.

Deadline: submit between April 1 and July 15
Entry fee: postal, $5 per poem for up to five poems; online, $27.50 for five poems
Prizes: first place, $1,000; second place, $250; third place, $100

PATRICIA CLEARY MILLER AWARD FOR POETRY

www.newletters.org/patricia-cleary-miller-award-for-poetry

Description: Sponsored by *New Letters*. A single poetry entry may contain up to six poems, and the poems need not be related.
Deadline: submit between November 21 and May 22
Entry fee: $24 each entry; if entering online, add a $5 service charge to entry fee; includes a one-year subscription to *New Letters*
Prize: $2,500 for best group of three to six poems

PHILIP LEVINE PRIZE FOR POETRY

cah.fresnostate.edu/english/centers-projects/levineprize/index.html

Description: Sponsored by the Creative Writing Program at California State University, Fresno. An annual book contest for original, previously unpublished, full-length poetry manuscripts. Length: 48–80 pages with no more than one poem per page.
Deadline: submit between July 1 and September 30
Entry fee: $25
Prizes: $2,000 and publication by Anhinga Press

POETRY SOCIETY OF VIRGINIA POETRY CONTESTS

www.poetrysocietyofvirginia.org/adult-contests

Description: More than twenty-five categories for adults and students. Form and length limit of entries vary according to the contests. All entries must be unpublished, original, and not scheduled for publication before the winners of the competition are announced.
Deadline: January 19
Entry fee: members, none; nonmembers, $6 per poem
Prizes: vary by specific competition

SLIPSTREAM ANNUAL POETRY CHAPBOOK COMPETITION

www.slipstreampress.org/contest.html

Description: Sponsored by Slipstream Press. Entries may be any style, format, or theme. Length: 40 pages maximum.

Deadline: December 1
Entry fee: $20
Prizes: $1,000 plus 50 published copies of chapbook

TOI DERRICOTTE & CORNELIUS EADY CHAPBOOK PRIZE

cavecanempoets.org/prizes/toi-derricotte-cornelius-eady-chapbook-prize

Description: Sponsored by Cave Canem Foundation. Dedicated to the discovery of exceptional chapbook-length manuscripts by black poets. Presented in collaboration with the O, Miami Poetry Festival and The Center for the Humanities at the CUNY Graduate Center.
Deadline: September 15
Entry fee: donation optional
Prizes: $1,000, publication, ten copies of the chapbook, and a feature reading

TOM HOWARD/MARGARET REID POETRY CONTEST

winningwriters.com/our-contests/tom-howard-margaret-reid-poetry-contest

Description: Sponsored by Winning Writers. Poetry in any style or genre. Published poetry accepted. Length: 250 lines maximum.
Deadline: submit between April 15 and September 30
Entry fee: $12 per poem
Prizes: Tom Howard Prize, $3,000 for poem in any style or genre; Margaret Reid Prize, $3,000 for poem that rhymes or has a traditional style; $200 each for ten honorable mentions in any style

VIOLET REED HAAS PRIZE FOR POETRY

www.snakenation.press/contests

Description: Sponsored by Snake Nation Press. Length: 50–75 pages. Previously published eligible.
Deadline: March 31
Entry fee: $25
Prizes: $1,000 plus publication

WERGLE FLOMP HUMOR POETRY CONTEST

winningwriters.com/our-contests/wergle-flomp-humor-poetry-contest-free

Description: Sponsored by Winning Writers. Submit one published or unpublished humor poem up to 250 lines.
Deadline: submit between August 15 and April 1
Entry fee: none

Prizes: first place, $2,000; second place, $500; third place, $250; ten honorable mentions, $100; plus the top 12 entries will be published online

RESOURCES FOR CONTESTS

These websites are sources for announcements about other contests.

DAILY WRITING TIPS
www.dailywritingtips.com/25-writing-competitions

FREELANCE WRITING
www.freelancewriting.com/writing-contests

FUNDS FOR WRITERS
fundsforwriters.com/contests

NEW PAGES
www.newpages.com/classifieds/big-list-of-writing-contests

POETS & WRITERS
www.pw.org/grants

THE WRITE LIFE
thewritelife.com/writing-contests

THE WRITER
writemag.com/contests

DENOMINATIONAL PUBLISHERS

Note: Not all of these houses and publications are owned by denominational publishing companies, and some publish for a broader audience than the denomination.

ANGLICAN
Anglican Journal

ASSEMBLIES OF GOD
Influence
LIVE
My Healthy Church
Take 5 Plus

BAPTIST
B&H Kids
B&H Publishing
The Baptist Bulletin
Baptist Standard
The Brink
D6 Family Ministry
HomeLife
Judson Press
Light
Mature Living
ParentLife
The Secret Place

CATHOLIC
America
American Catholic Press
The Arlington Catholic Herald
Ave Maria Press
Catholic Book Publishing Corp.
Celebrate Life Magazine
Chrism Press
Columbia
Commonweal
Franciscan Media
LEAVES
Ligouri Publications
Liturgical Press
Living Faith
Living Faith Kids
Loyola Press
Our Sunday Visitor, Inc.
Our Sunday Visitor
Paraclete Press
Parish Liturgy
Pauline Books & Media

Paulist Press
Resurrection Press
Scepter Publishers
St. Anthony Messenger
U.S. Catholic

CHARISMATIC/ PENTECOSTAL

Charisma
Charisma House
Chosen
Emanate Books
testimony/Enrich
Whitaker House

CHRISTIAN CHURCH/ CHURCH OF CHRIST

Christian Standard
College Press Publishing
Leafwood Publishers

CHURCH OF GOD

Beginner's Friend
Bible Advocate
Explorers
Gems of Truth
Now What?
Warner Christian Resources
Youth Compass

EPISCOPAL

Church Publishing Incorporated
Forward Day by Day
Forward Movement

EVANGELICAL COVENANT

The Covenant Companion

LUTHERAN

Augsburg Fortress
Beaming Books
Broadleaf Books
Café
Canada Lutheran
The Canadian Lutheran
Christ in Our Home
Fortress Press
Gather
The Lutheran Witness
Northwestern Publishing House
The Word in Season

MENNONITE

Canadian Mennonite
Ink & Quill Quarterly
The Messenger
Rejoice!

MESSIANIC

The Messianic Times

METHODIST

Abingdon Press
The Upper Room
Upper Room Books

NAZARENE

The Foundry Publishing
Holiness Today
Reflecting God
Standard

ORTHODOX

Ancient Faith Publishing
Chrism Press

PRESBYTERIAN

byFaith
Flyaway Books
Presbyterians Today
These Days: Daily Devotions for Living by Faith
Westminster John Knox Press

QUAKER/FRIENDS

Friends Journal
Fruit of the Vine

REFORMED

Celebrate Lit Publishers
Christian Courier
P&R Publishing
Tulip Publishing

THE SALVATION ARMY

Caring Magazine

Faith & Friends
Just for Kids
Peer
The War Cry

SEVENTH-DAY ADVENTIST

Guide
The Journal of Adventist Education
Ministry
Our Little Friend
Pacific Press
Primary Treasure

WESLEYAN

The Foundry Publishing
Invite Resources
Light from the Word

PUBLISHING LINGO

My first week working in a bookstore I learned a valuable lesson. I had a stack of books in my arms that I had taken from a shipment in the back room. My boss walked by; said, "Steve, please put those in the dump"; and kept walking.

I paused and thought, *Why should I throw these away? They are brand new books!* To my chagrin, I discovered that, in bookstore lingo, a dump was a cardboard display in the front of the store.

The lesson I learned is that knowing the lingo can keep you from being confused or potentially misunderstanding some instructions. Like bookstores, writing and publishing have their own lingo. The following definitions will acquaint you with some of the more important terms.

ABA: American Booksellers Association. This acronym has come to mean the general market, as opposed to CBA, the Christian market.

Advance: Money a publisher pays to an author up front, against future royalties. The amount varies greatly from publisher to publisher and is often paid in two or three installments (on signing the contract, on delivery of the manuscript, and on publication).

AE: An abbreviation for Acquisitions Editor. Not all publishing houses use this abbreviation, but they all have people who acquire in their editorial departments.

All rights: An outright sale of a manuscript. The author has no further control over any subsidiary rights or reusing the piece. You must sign a contract for this agreement to be legal.

Anecdote: A short, poignant, real-life story, usually used to illustrate a single thought. It need not be humorous.

ARC: Advance Reader Copy. An early paperback (or ebook) version of a book sent out for reviews around four to six months prior to publication.

Assignment: When an editor asks a writer to create a specific manuscript for an agreed-on price.

As-told-to story: A true story you write as a first-person account about someone else.

Audience: The people who are expected to be reading your manuscript, in terms of age, life experience, knowledge of and interest level in the story or subject. Editors want to be sure writers understand their assumed audiences well.

Audiobooks: Spoken-word books available by streaming via the Internet, on compact disc, or MP3 file.

Backlist: A publisher's previously published books that are still in print a year or more after publication.

Bible versions:
AMP–*Amplified Bible*
ASV–*American Standard Version*
CB–*Confraternity Bible* (Catholic)
CEB–*Common English Bible*
CEV–*Contemporary English Version*
CJB–*Complete Jewish Bible*
CSB–*Christian Standard Bible*
ESV–*English Standard Version*
GNB–*Good News Bible*
GW–*GOD'S WORD Translation*
HCSB–*Holman Christian Standard Bible* (replaced by CSB)
ICB–*International Children's Bible*
KJV–*King James Version*
KJV21–*21ˢᵗ Century King James Version*
MEV–*Modern English Version*
MSG–*The Message*
NAB–*New American Bible*
NABRE–*New American Bible Revised Edition*
NASB–*New American Standard Bible*
NCV–*New Century Version*
NEB–*New English Bible*
NET–*New English Translation*
NIrV–*New International Reader's Version*

NIV–*New International Version*
NJB–*New Jerusalem Bible*
NKJV–*New King James Version*
NLT–*New Living Translation*
NRSV–*New Revised Standard Version*
NRSVue–*New Revised Standard Version Updated Edition*
PHILLIPS–*J.B. Phillips New Testament*
RSV–*Revised Standard Version* (replaced by NRSV)
TEV–*Today's English Translation* (aka *Good News Bible*)
TLB–*The Living Bible*
TNIV–*Today's New International Version*
VOICE–*The Voice Bible Translation*
WEB–*World English Bible*

Bio: Brief information about the author.

BIPOC: Black, Indigenous, and People of Color.

Bluelines: The last printer's proofs used to catch errors before a book or periodical is printed. May be physical pages or digital proofs in PDF.

BOB: Back-of-Book ad for the author's previous book(s) or a similar book released by the publisher. It uses the blank pages in the back of a book or extra pages at the end of an ebook.

Book proposal: Submission of a book idea to an agent or editor. It usually includes a hook, summary and purpose of the book, target market, uniqueness of the book compared to similar ones in the marketplace, chapter-by-chapter summaries or plot synopsis, marketing and promotion information, your credentials, and delivery date, plus one to three sample chapters, including the first one.

Byline: Author's name printed below the title of a story, article, etc.

Camera-ready copy: The text and artwork that are ready for the press.

Category romance: Novels of around 50,000–60,000 words that are published in categories and according to strict guidelines. For example, Love Inspired novels, the Christian division of Harlequin.

CBA: Christian Booksellers Association. The acronym has come to describe the Christian market as opposed to ABA, the general market. As an entity, CBA folded in 2019, but the acronym still applies when referring to the Christian publishing industry.

Chapbook: A small book or pamphlet containing poetry, etc.

Circulation: The number of copies sold or distributed of a periodical.

Clips: Copies of articles you have had published in periodicals.

Colophon: The publisher's emblem or imprint used on the title page or spine of a book or a statement at the end of a book with information about its production, such as the type of font used.

Column: A regularly appearing feature, section, or department in a periodical with the same heading. It's written by the same person or a different one each time.

Comp copies: Complimentary copies given to the author by the publisher on publication.

Comps: Shorthand for "comparable." The publisher may have comps on cover designs or titles to help position the book in the marketplace.

Concept statement: A 50- to 150-word summary of your proposed book.

Contributing editor: A freelance writer who has a regular column or writes regularly for the periodical.

Contributor's copy: Copy of an issue of a periodical sent to an author whose work appears in it.

Copyedit: The editor checks grammar, punctuation, and citations to make sure the work is accurate. More detailed than a developmental edit. Some publishers refer to this as the line edit.

Copyright: Legal protection of an author's work. A manuscript is automatically copyrighted in your name when you produce it. You don't need to register it with the Copyright Office unless you are self-publishing a book or other publication since a traditional publisher registers it for you.

Cover copy: Or "copy." The text on the back cover of a book, in the online description, or in marketing materials. For a hardcover, it can also include flap copy, the text on the inside dust-jacket flaps.

Cover letter: A letter that accompanies some article submissions. Usually it's needed only if you have to tell the editor something specific, to give your credentials for writing a manuscript of a technical nature, or to remind the editor that the manuscript was requested or expected. Often used as the introduction to a book proposal.

Credits, list of: A listing of your previously published works.

Critique: An evaluation of a manuscript.

Defamation: A written (libel) or spoken (slander) injury to the reputation of a living person or organization. If what is said is true, it cannot be defamatory; but that does not prevent the injured party from bringing a lawsuit.

Derivative work: A work derived from another work, such as a condensation or abridgment. Contact the copyright owner for permission before doing the abridgment, and be prepared to pay that owner a fee or royalty.

Developmental edit: Usually the first round of editing done on a manuscript. The editor helps "develop" the book by shaping its content and structure. Also called a substantive edit or line edit.

Devotion: A short manuscript based on a Scripture verse or passage that shares a personal spiritual discovery, inspires to worship, challenges to commitment or action, or encourages. A book or periodical of devotions is called a devotional.

Ed board: Editorial board meeting. The editors meet to discuss the new proposals they received to determine which ones should go to the pub board.

Editorial guidelines: See "Writers guidelines."

Em dash (—): Used to create a break or set off nonessential material or extra information in a sentence instead of using commas. *The Chicago Manual of Style* calls this punctuation mark "the most versatile of the dashes."

En dash (–): An en dash is longer than a hyphen but shorter than an em dash. Often used between numbers and dates to show a range. It was called the "en" dash because in the early days of typesetting it was the same width as the capital letter N.

Endorsements: Flattering comments about a book, usually printed on the back cover or in promotional material.

Epub: File format used for ebooks.

Essay: A short composition expressing the author's opinion on a specific subject.

Evangelical: A person who believes that one receives God's forgiveness for sins through Jesus Christ and believes the Bible is the authoritative Word of God. This is a broad definition for a label with broad application. Often mistakenly used as a synonym for "Christian."

Exegesis: Interpretation of a Scripture passage.

Feature article: In-depth coverage of a subject, usually focusing on a person, an event, a process, an organization, a movement, a trend, or an issue. It's written to explain, encourage, help, analyze, challenge, motivate, warn, or entertain, as well as to inform.

Filler: A short item used to "fill" a page of a periodical. It could be a joke, anecdote, light verse, short humor, puzzle, game, etc.

First rights: A periodical editor buys the right to publish a manuscript that has never been published and to do so only once.

Foreign rights: Selling or giving permission to translate or reprint published material in another country.

Foreword: Opening remarks in a book to introduce the book and its author. Often misspelled as *forward*.

Freelance: Supplied by freelance writers.

Freelancer or freelance writer: A writer who is not on salary but sells his or her material to a number of different periodicals and publishers.

Galley proof: A typeset copy of a book or magazine used to detect and correct errors before printing.

General editor: Usually, the person who oversees a large work that has multiple authors writing individual chapters for a book or a series of books. This person is not an employee within a publishing house.

General market: Non-Christian market, sometimes called secular market.

Genre: Refers to a type or classification, as in fiction or poetry. For instance, westerns, romances, and mysteries are fiction genres.

Glossy: A photo with a shiny, rather than matte, finish. Also, a publication printed on such paper.

Go-ahead: When an editor tells you to write or submit your article.

Hard copy: A printed manuscript, as opposed to one sent via email.

Independent book publisher: A book publisher who charges authors to publish their books or buy a certain number of copies, as opposed to a royalty house that pays authors. Some independent publishers also pay a royalty. Sometimes called a subsidy, vanity, self, or custom publisher.

ISBN: International Standard Book Number, an identification code needed for every version of a book.

Journal: A periodical presenting information in a particular area, often for an academic or educated audience.

Kill fee: A fee paid for a completed article done on assignment that is subsequently not published. The amount is usually 25-50 percent of the original payment.

Libel: A published false statement that is damaging to another person's reputation, a written defamation.

Line edit: See "Developmental edit" and "Copyedit." Check to see how your editor defines each process.

Little/literary: Small-circulation periodicals whose focus is providing a forum for the literary writer, rather than on making money. Often they do not pay or pay in copies.

Mainstream fiction: Other than genre fiction (such as romance, mystery, or fantasy). Stories of people and their conflicts handled on a deeper level.

Mass market: Books intended for a wide, general market; produced in a smaller format, usually with smaller type; and sold at a lower price. The expectation is that their sales will be higher.

Matte finish: A nonglossy, nonreflective finish on a book cover. Has a textured feel.

Ms: Abbreviation for manuscript.

Mss: Abbreviation for more than one manuscript.

NASR: Abbreviation for North American Serial Rights. Permission for a periodical targeting readers in the US and Canada to publish a manuscript.

New-adult fiction: A developing fiction genre with protagonists ages 18–25. In the general market, these novels often explore sexual themes considered too "adult" for the YA or teen market. They tend to be marketed to older teen readers.

Novella: A short novel, usually 20,000–35,000 words. The length varies from publisher to publisher.

On acceptance: Editor pays a writer at the time the manuscript is accepted for publication.

On assignment: Writing a manuscript at the specific request of an editor.

On publication: Publisher pays a writer when his or her manuscript is published.

On speculation/spec: Writing something for a periodical editor with the agreement that the editor will buy it only if he or she likes it.

Onetime rights: Selling the right to publish a manuscript one time to more than one periodical, primarily to nonoverlapping audiences, such as different denominations.

Over the transom: Unsolicited manuscripts sent to a book editor. Comes from the old transom, which was a window above the door in office buildings. Manuscripts could be pushed "over the transom" into the locked office.

Overrun: The extra copies of a book printed during the initial print run.

Pen name/pseudonym: A name other than your legal name used on a manuscript to protect your identity or the identities of people included or when you wish to remain anonymous. Put the pen name in the byline under the title and your real name with your contact information.

Perfect binding: When pages of a paperback are glued together (bound) on the spine and the cover is then attached.

Periodical: A magazine, journal, newsletter, or newspaper.

Permissions: Asking permission to use text or art from a copyrighted source.

Personal experience: An account based on a real-life experience.

440

Personality profile: A feature article that highlights a specific person's life or accomplishments.

Plagiarism: Stealing and using the ideas or writing of someone else as your own, either as is or rewriting slightly to make it sound like your own.

POD/Print-on-demand: A printing process where books are printed one at a time or in small numbers instead of in quantity. The production cost per book is higher, but no warehousing is necessary.

POV: Point-of-view. A fiction term that describes the perspective of the one telling the story, such as first person or third person.

Press kit: A compilation of promotional materials for a book or author, used to publicize a book.

Pub board: A formal meeting where people from editorial, marketing, sales, finance, and management meet to discuss whether or not to publish a book.

Public domain: Work for which copyright protection has expired. Copyright laws vary from country to country; but in the US, works published more than 95 years ago have entered the public domain. Because the US copyright law has changed several times, check with the Copyright Office (*copyright.gov*) to determine if a work is in public domain or not. Generally, since 1978, copyright endures for the author's life plus 70 years.

Query letter: A letter sent to an editor about an article or book you propose to write and asking if he or she is interested in seeing it.

Recto: The right-hand page in printing.

Reprint rights: Selling the right to reprint an article that has already been published. You must have sold only first or onetime rights originally and wait until it has been published the first time.

Response time: The number of weeks or months it takes an editor or agent to get back to you about a query, proposal, or manuscript you sent.

Review copies: Books given to reviewers or buyers for bookstore chains and online sellers.

Royalty: The percentage an author is paid by a publisher on the sale of each copy of a book.

Running head: The text at the top of each page that can show the author's name, book title, chapter, or page number.

SASE: Self-addressed, stamped envelope. Always send it with a hard-copy manuscript or query letter.

SASP: Self-addressed, stamped postcard. May be sent with a hard-copy manuscript to be returned by the editor to indicate it arrived safely. Rarely used.

Satire: Ridicule that aims at reform.

Second serial rights: See "Reprint rights."

Secular market: An outdated term for the non-Christian publishing market.

Self-publisher: See "Independent book publisher."

Serial: Refers to publication in a periodical, such as first serial rights.

Sidebar: A short feature that accompanies an article and gives additional information about the topic, such as a recommended reading list. It is often set apart by appearing within a box or border.

Signature: All books are printed in 16-page increments or signatures (occasionally in 32-page increments for large books like Bibles). A large sheet of paper is printed, then folded multiple times. Three sides are cut (top, side, and bottom). The fourth side holds eight double-sided pages. The signatures are compiled and bound into the finished book.

Simultaneous submissions: Sending the same manuscript to more than one editor at the same time. Usually this action is done with nonoverlapping periodical markets, such as denominational publications or newspapers in different cities, or when you are writing on a timely subject. Most periodical editors don't accept simultaneous submissions, but they are the norm in the book market. Be sure to state in a cover letter or on the first page that it is a simultaneous submission.

Slander: The verbal act of defamation.

Slanting: Writing an article to meet the needs of a particular market.

Slush pile: The stack of unsolicited manuscripts that arrive at an editor's desk or email inbox.

Subsidiary rights: All the rights, other than book rights, included in a book contract, such as translations, audiobooks, book clubs, and movies.

Subsidy publisher: See "Independent book publisher."

Substantive edit: See "Developmental edit."

Synopsis: A brief summary of a work, ranging from one paragraph to several pages.

Tabloid: A newspaper-format publication about half the size of a regular newspaper.

Take-home paper: A small periodical given to Sunday-school students, children through adults. These minimagazines are published with the curriculum.

Think piece: A magazine article that has an intellectual, philosophical, or provocative approach to a subject.

Trade book: Describes a 5½" x 8½" paperback book (sometimes 6" x 9"). This is a typical trim size for a paperback. Mass-market books are smaller, around 4" x 6".

Trade magazine: A magazine whose audience is in a particular business.

Trim size: The size of a book after being trimmed in the printing process. (See "Signature" for more information.)

Unsolicited manuscript: A manuscript an editor did not specifically ask to see.

Vanity publisher: See "Independent book publisher."

Verso: The left-hand page in printing.

Vignette: A short, descriptive literary sketch of a brief scene or incident.

Vita: An outline of one's personal history and experience.

Work-for-hire: A manuscript you create for an agreed payment, and you give the publisher full ownership and control of it. You must sign a contract for this agreement to be legal.

Writers guidelines: Information provided by an editor that gives specific guidance for writing for the publication or publishing house. If the information is not offered online, email or send an SASE with your request for printed guidelines.

INDEX

NOTES